The Master Musicians

# Dufay

Series edited by Stanley Sadie

The Master Musicians

# Dufay

David Fallows

With twelve pages of photographs, eighty music examples
and three maps in text

J.M. Dent & Sons Ltd
London Toronto Melbourne

First published 1982
© Text, David Fallows 1982

Printed in Great Britain by
Biddles Ltd, Guildford, Surrey
for J.M. Dent & Sons Ltd
Aldine House 33 Welbeck Street London W1M 8LX

Music examples set by Tabitha Collingbourne

This book is photoset in 10/12 Sabon by
Inforum Ltd, Portsmouth


British Library Cataloguing in Publication Data

Fallows, David
    Dufay. – (The Master musicians series)
    1. Dufay, Guillaume
    2. Composers – France – Biography
    I. Title         II. Series
    780'.92'4                 ML410.D/

    ISBN 0-460-03180 5

# Preface

Dufay now stands unchallenged as the leading composer of the Middle Ages. Performances of his music are increasingly frequent, and most of it can be heard on commercial recordings, so it is time for a study of his life and work that attempts to show why he has found so much favour with performers and listeners today. Over the last thirty years, and particularly over the last decade, an enormous burst of scholarly endeavour has added immeasurably to our knowledge of the subject. This book is primarily an attempt to assemble the most important of that information which was hitherto available only in articles, dissertations and books produced in many parts of Europe and the United States.

With that in mind I have made a rather special use of the Master Musicians format. Many characters who appear in Dufay's life are well known in non-musical spheres, and others are known scarcely at all. A particular need for understanding his work is a fuller documentation of those people. The expanded list of 'Personalia' in Appendix C helps to fill that need. The same applies to the chronological tables in Appendix A. Because he travelled so much and because he seems to have maintained contacts in many parts of Europe, the political and cultural events of his time affected Dufay more than many other great composers. The church councils, the changing axes of power across Europe, the creations of architects, sculptors and poets of his time are often directly relevant to his life and to the changes in his music. No apology need be offered for taking up space on these topics in the following pages.

I have done very little original source research for this book. There is still much to do, but that would have resulted in a different kind of study; and the main documentary research has been well done by others. I saw the most urgent biographical task as being to collate the information that is already available – in itself no easy matter. But a few brief visits to the archives were necessary to check the documentary information I had reported from other people's research and to clear up some doubts in my mind. These brought a surprisingly rich harvest of 'adjusted' information as well as some new documentation which is incorporated here.

One consequence of re-examining and collating the work of a wide range of scholars was that many accepted 'facts' now seem based on flimsy or incorrect evidence. In this, as in many other subjects, factual history is often a network of interrelated hypotheses giving an appearance much more solid than the available documentation can support. That is why the listing of references and documents (particularly in Appendix A) is fuller than would normally be expected in a book of relatively modest pretensions.

Similarly with the works. Their manuscripts and notation are scarcely discussed here. Many of the editions have been checked against the known sources; and the musical examples nearly all differ from the complete edition as a result of such checking. But the urgent tasks seemed to be to describe the music, to place it in a context, to give some impression of how I myself hear it, and to guide the reader to further significant discussions (this last aim being the reason for much of the footnoting to the second half of the book).

Specific questions of performance practice have been given very little space. This was a decision taken sadly and reluctantly. But it seems to me that there is at the moment too little agreement on fundamental issues, too much agreement on matters that cannot be documented adequately, and evidence of growing agreement on several details whose discussion would take the story well away from the prime focus – Dufay and his music.

Research continues unabated. This book would not have been possible without the generous help of many experts who have pointed out material that I might have overlooked, helped me in unfamiliar subjects, given me the benefit of unpublished findings on specialized topics, and offered many kinds of help or encouragement.

First among these stands Alejandro Enrique Planchart who plans also to write a book on Dufay and has unfailingly treated me as a colleague rather than a competitor. Equally Edmond Dartus, canon of Cambrai Cathedral and until his retirement director of the choir which in earlier days was directed by Dufay, has been most generous with his astonishing knowledge of the archives at Lille and Cambrai. Others include: Margaret Bent, Stanley Boorman, Roger Bowers, Danilo Curti-Feininger, Gareth Curtis, Richard Davies,

Kenneth Hyde, Balduinus Janssens de Bisthoven, Lewis Jones, Roger Jones, Bonnie and Edward Lowinsky, Rosemary Morris, Jacques Nazet, Jeremy Noble, Christopher Page, Giorgio Pestelli, Anthony Pryer, Christopher Reynolds, Adalbert Roth, Annie Scottez, Ephraim Segerman, Richard Sherr, Frederick Sternfeld, Brian Trowell, Thomas Walker, Andrew Wathey, Ronald Woodley and Peter Wright. But my main debt is to my wife Polly who helped in innumerable ways and put herself to considerable inconvenience to enable me to finish the book. It is only right that the book should be dedicated to her and to our son Benjamin, born exactly a fortnight ago into a world where the performance and understanding of medieval music are among the few things likely to improve.

*Old Trafford*  D.F.
*29 May 1981*

## Abbreviations

CMM: Corpus mensurabilis musicae (American Institute of Musicology)

CSM: Corpus scriptorum de musica (American Institute of Musicology)

DTO: Denkmäler der Tonkunst in Österreich

*JAMS*: *Journal of the American Musicological Society*

*The New Grove*: Stanley Sadie (ed.), *The New Grove Dictionary of Music and Musicians*, 20 vols. (London, 1980)


Dufay's works are referred to by the volume number and piece number in the complete edition, Besseler *Dufay*. Thus v/1 is piece no. 1 in vol. 5.

Musical examples throughout are in quartered note-values. (The reduction in the complete edition varies.) Bar numbers, in the examples and in the text, follow the complete edition even if they happen to conflict with the barring in the musical examples.

Currency mentioned is usually in the so-called Parisian money: *livres* (£) of twenty *sous* (s), each of which contains twelve *deniers* (d).

Technical terms used in the text are normally defined at their first appearance. The index will guide the reader to such definitions.

# Contents

# List of illustrations

# Music in fifteenth-century society

In 1467 Piero de' Medici described Dufay as 'the greatest ornament of our age'. This was the age of such artists and architects as Botticelli, Brunelleschi, Donatello, Alberti and the brothers Van Eyck, such statesmen as Philip the Good of Burgundy, Pope Pius II and Louis XI of France, such poets as Charles of Orleans, François Villon and Alain Chartier. Certainly Piero knew that his comment would be passed on to the old composer who was fifteen years his senior, and he was expressing his gratitude for Dufay's help in improving the Florence Baptistery choir. But his remark still gives Dufay unusually high status among the men of his time; and one purpose of this book is to define that status.

With astonishing unanimity modern critics have found Dufay by far the most interesting and fulfilling medieval composer. His music embraces the best of everything that happened in the fourteenth and fifteenth centuries, and it is difficult to think of another composer with comparable scope before the very end of the sixteenth century. There is more biographical information for him than for any other early musician. And among the two hundred works that fill six large folio volumes in the modern complete edition there is an extraordinary range of styles and techniques. Moreover many of these works contain a strong personal element which seems particularly attractive today among the elaborate masks that conceal so many of the creative figures from the Middle Ages: the texts of his motets and songs often vividly evoke occasions, people, social contexts, reactions and political views. His creative development is relatively easy to trace, partly because of those references, partly because his life is so fully documented, and partly because the intensive scholarly activity of the past forty years has made it possible to fix the broad chronology of his work with considerable clarity.

But some features that make the study of Dufay attractive have little to do with his qualities as a composer, so another aim of the following chapters is to explain why we know so much about Dufay's life, why so many of his works survive, and why much of his music now seems so rich and vital. Nevertheless Dufay's position as the greatest composer of his day remains unchallenged, and it is possible to hear in Dufay – far more clearly than elsewhere in the music of his time – that change in attitudes which has been seen as representing a transition from the Middle Ages to the Renaissance.

In general it is unfashionable nowadays to view music or any other aspect of history in terms of 'great men'. That was an indulgence of the nineteenth century which we now see as somewhat falsifying the true historical picture. But to consider fifteenth-century music in terms of Dufay is to do so with the assurance that one is dealing with music of the highest quality. And the study of Dufay can still reveal many aspects of medieval music and of its context which may not otherwise be clear.

But various features of fifteenth-century society and music do indeed make the study of Dufay's work by itself potentially misleading. Certain general points therefore need stressing before Dufay's own life and work are discussed.

The word 'music' in the fifteenth century had two main meanings, neither of which includes the material found in the collected edition of Dufay's work though they are relevant to its study.

Its first meaning is the one implied in most documents, eye-witness descriptions and indeed pictures of music-making through-out the Middle Ages: monophonic music. The minstrels who were paid enormous salaries at the great courts almost certainly never played part-music as we now understand it until quite late in the fifteenth century. They played improvised or semi-improvised music that was essentially monophonic – melodic music with an accompaniment that would rarely have been more than a drone or some-thing equally independent of written traditions. Apart from a few tantalizing scraps, which are difficult to evaluate, there is no trace of this music. Most of the players concerned were probably illiterate or nearly so.

Monophony was also the main music in church. The many surviving lists of choirmen and choirboys, the payments for singing services, the pictures of choirs singing – these almost always concern plainchant. The polyphony that appears in the innumerable editions which are now available was largely for special occasions and par-ticularly for special musicians, usually soloists. Its quantity is small

2

alongside the enormous body of medieval chant.

In the later Middle Ages the Gregorian chant repertory was expanded and extended in many ways. Special feasts were constantly being added to the church year; particular churches or dioceses developed their own liturgies, needing new music; and the composition of chant continued. Unfortunately we can rarely identify the composers (nor indeed can we identify many of the pieces with certainty) because to compose chant was to add something to the sacred liturgy of the church; it was not an occasion for individual show or for wilful originality.

Most chant was seasonal, with different music for each Sunday or feast day in the church year; and the average churchman knew these pieces quite as well as the churchgoer today knows the melodies and words of many hymns and particularly of seasonal pieces such as Christmas carols. Dufay, like practically all composers of his time, was employed for most of his life as a church musician and more specifically as a singer. Monophonic chant was the mainspring of his musical experience.

The other meaning of 'music' was rather different. As a university study music belonged to the *quadrivium*, the four main disciplines of intellect – the others being arithmetic, astronomy and geometry. Broadly speaking the musical theory of the Middle Ages tells us relatively little about the surviving polyphony. Music in the universities was a matter of intervals, of the three harmonies, of the logical relationship of one note to another. To attend lectures in music was to hear reasoned disquisitions on the great theorists of the past, including Plato, Aristotle, Aristoxenus, Isidore of Seville, Boethius and, to represent modern practice, perhaps Johannes de Muris, whose writings were already a century old when Dufay was young.

The reasons why university musical study had so little to do with the polyphony we now revere are complicated. Suffice it to say that the fundamental simplicity of sound and the harmonic series, as supposedly discovered by Pythagoras, were seen as a clue to the underlying simplicity of the universe. Music provided a yardstick, even a paradigm, against which progress in the natural sciences could be measured; and even today we are only just learning – with the discovery of DNA and subatomic particles – how music revealed its true and beautiful simplicity long before the other sciences gave any hint of the same thing.

3

Thus to study the surviving polyphony is to consider only a small portion of what medieval man meant by 'music'. This portion, however, is the one it is possible to isolate and to admire in a manner that seems appropriate today.

A related matter concerns the rise of general literacy and the concomitant changes in attitudes towards art. The fifteenth century saw an immense growth in readership, in the desire to buy books, in the ability to read without the help of the clergy. Schools became more widely accessible. Large scribal shops in all parts of Europe produced books in quantity, creating the market that allowed the introduction of printing to Europe by Gutenberg in 1454 and the mass-production of books by Aldus Manutius at Venice in the 1490s.

While direct evidence about the reading abilities of musicians has yet to be fully assembled, the general picture seems to be that early in the fifteenth century the church singer, like the court minstrel, was musically all but illiterate. He knew his chants largely from memory even if he happened to have the book open in front of him as he sang: at Cambrai two copies of the chant books seem to have been sufficient for the entire choir of some twenty musicians. The reading of polyphony was an almost impossible task for most of these singers before Dufay's day.

Two features of fifteenth-century polyphonic music shed light on this growth of literacy and on the changes that were coming about. First, there are many surviving manuscript fragments containing simplified notations, apparently attempts to write down extremely unpretentious polyphony for the singer who was not privy to the complexities of the mensural notation in which nearly all medieval polyphony survives. Evidently these were for the mass of singers who were for the first time expected to take part in polyphony. Second, musical notation changed in the fifteenth century more quickly and more fundamentally than at any other time in history. That change was from complexity to simplicity; and by 1500 notation was essentially as it is today. Well into the fifteenth century it is likely that most polyphony was for performance by single voices, by special musicians who were a class apart from the majority of singers. As the century progresses there is more and more evidence that the music was composed for a larger group of singers and that choral polyphony was expected in the richest institutions. That change can be seen in Dufay's music.

Ꮒꞁꞇ ꞇꞇꞇꞇ... (inscription)

1. Dufay's funeral monument. With the exception of the
death-date at the bottom it was completed before he made his
will in July 1474.

2. Sharp-angle close-up of Dufay on his funeral monument.
Both views are discussed on p.82-3.

3. Cardinal Pierre d'Ailly with the Virgin and Child, from an early fifteenth-century collection of his works at Cambrai. His arms are in the corner, surmounted by a cardinal's hat.

Ritratto del B. LODOVICO ALEMANNI Cardinale
del Titolo di S. Cecilia, e Arcivescovo d'Arles.
Mandato da Mons.r Giacomo Fourbin Ianson Arciv.o d'Arles,
a Mons.r Federigo Alamanni Vescovo di Pistoia, e di Prato
nel Mese di Dicembre dell'Anno 1690

4. Cardinal Louis Aleman. Eighteenth-century engraving.

5. Jean de Bourgogne, Bishop of Cambrai from 1439 to 1480.
Sixteenth-century drawing.

6. King Sigismund of the Romans entering Rome with Pope Eugenius IV
on 21 May 1433. Relief made by Filarete in 1445. This is almost
certainly the meeting that was followed by the performance of
Dufay's motet *Supremum est mortalibus bonum*, see p.34.

7. Dufay and Binchois. Miniature from a copy of Martin le Franc's
*Le champion des dames* prepared at Arras in 1451. For the passage of
text below the picture, see p.20.

The social position of the composer was also changing, though more slowly, and it remained entirely different from that of other kinds of artist. A painter, sculptor or architect lived by selling his work; he was recompensed specifically for what he produced. There is no evidence that this happened to a composer. The documents of Cambrai Cathedral record a payment in 1452 in recognition of Dufay's musical contribution, but the payment was simply an advance of his emoluments for the coming year during which he proposed to be absent. This kind of patronage is perhaps the nearest we have to payment for composition. The enlightened employer might have procured for the composer a certain ecclesiastical preferment partly in recognition of his creative achievement; and the apparent ease with which Dufay travelled across Europe is perhaps some token of the esteem in which he was held (though we shall see that most of his moves were the direct result of political developments). But throughout his life full-time employment for a composer was almost entirely within establishments primarily concerned with the celebration of divine Office. Today Dufay is revered for his secular songs perhaps above everything else; and it is always important to remember that in official terms their composition was a mere by-product of his main occupation. Equally, his secular work is in a musical language that is best understood in terms of the sacred music that was fundamental to his lifestyle.

The final preliminary observation about the music of Dufay's time concerns its aesthetic effect and brings us back to Piero de' Medici. It is difficult to compare Dufay with the great painters, sculptors and architects of his day: their work survives more or less as it was conceived, whereas medieval music survives merely as notes on paper needing live performance before it can be appreciated. Even for the specialist the musical language of the fifteenth century is far less familiar than either the visual language of the time or, for instance, the musical language of the nineteenth century. This book attempts to tackle the problem, but repeated listening is of course an essential adjunct.

In many ways the increase of understanding over the past forty years has far from simplified the problems of producing a responsible performance of fifteenth-century music. In an age when more and more performances of baroque music can be described as 'authentic', the difficulties of playing medieval music with comparable fidelity to the original intentions seem all the more perplexing.

Each year there is more evidence of performers coming closer to the spirit of the music; each year there are recordings which provide increased aesthetic pleasure; but there is still some way to go before a full appreciation of medieval music on its own terms will be possible.

Indeed one of the more exciting aspects of the study of Dufay's music today is to become aware of new and better kinds of performance that bring us closer to his work. The rediscovery of medieval music is continuing and will continue for many years to come. But, on a personal note, I would add that much of my own love for Dufay's music – particularly the works that are still not recorded – derives from playing it on that most anachronistic of instruments, the modern grand piano; and it would be a pity to allow a misguided purism to disguise the possibilities that the piano offers as a means of getting to know this distant and strange repertory. The music presents a challenge, and it is worth using every possible means to gain an understanding of it. Dufay's music has many characteristics that speak immediately across the centuries; that is why a book such as this is possible. But the full meaning of Piero de' Medici's praise may not be clear for some years yet.

Lastly, before turning to consider Dufay's life, a word on names and pronunciation. Many original documents concerning him give the name as two words: 'du Fay'. This orthography appears in some modern publications, but the traditional spelling is retained here as being the current modern form. Moreover it seems to be the spelling that Dufay preferred as a mature man. There is only one surviving autograph example of the name written out in full (the two other examples use a musical rebus which confuses the issue). It is in the receipt for the salary of the late André Picard which he wrote in November 1455 (see ill. 19). The name appears in line 1 quite unambiguously as a single word.

It is now agreed[1] that his name is pronounced as three equally stressed syllables (like 'Debussy') and that the middle syllable is long (*fah*). By contrast, the city of Cambrai where he spent so much of his life has two syllables and rhymes with the French *j'ai*.

# 2

## First years: c. 1400–1414

Cambrai Cathedral received a new choirboy in August 1409. He was entered in the register as 'Willemet' – little William – but among the accounts for 1410–11 he appears as 'Willermus'; and in 1413–14, at the point when he ceased to be a choirboy and became a *clericus altaris* provided with a small chaplaincy, he is listed in full as 'Willermus du Fayt'.[1] There is no continuous documentation of the composer Guillaume Dufay in the cathedral records until nearly a quarter of a century later, but his funeral monument at Cambrai, made on his own instructions, calls him 'olim huius ecclesie chorialis' – a former choirboy of this church – and his will includes a bequest for the Cambrai Cathedral choirboys to pray for him 'who as a boy served in their order'.

To have even this much information is exceptional. For the other great medieval composers we must rely on guesswork to reconstruct their first training; and documentation of choirboys tended to be minimal, often using names that are difficult to identify with the grown man. That Dufay's early years at Cambrai Cathedral can be pinpointed is a witness not of his own importance, of course, but of the eminence of Cambrai Cathedral. It was one of the richest cathedrals in the Low Countries and therefore had an excellent accounting system; and it was rich primarily because it then had an enormous diocese reaching up to Antwerp, across to Arras, and including Brussels which was quickly becoming the political capital of the fast-rising house of Burgundy. Partly because of its influential political position Cambrai Cathedral's documents survive in enormous quantity and make possible a reconstruction of many details in Dufay's life. But even so there is an element of chance in the survival of the date on which he was received as a chorister – the week of 10 August. It is in the accounts of the choirmen, the *petits vicaires*, which happen to survive for only two years before 1450, the years 1409–10 and 1411–12.

Even these documents cannot tell us when and where Dufay was

7

born. Baptismal registers of the Middle Ages do not exist, simply because the vast majority of surviving documents record financial transactions: a baptism, being of no financial importance, merited neither the cost of materials nor the labour of copying. For an heir to an enormous fortune we usually have a birthdate (often recorded primarily in connection with casting horoscopes), but – to take an example from a few years earlier – not for King Henry IV of England, largely because he was born merely the son of a nobleman and nobody expected him to become king. Most often it is references to a man's age on a portrait or legal document which give the birthdate within a margin of about two years; but nothing of the kind exists for Dufay. Since he was a chorister from 1409 to 1414, at which point his voice had presumably broken, it seems fair to estimate that he was born around 1400. The margin of error is about two years, and it would only be honest to admit that if 1400 were a less simple number one could just as well have chosen 1398, or, perhaps most likely of all, 1399.

It has been suggested that his birthday fell on 5 August.[2] This is because there is no obvious reason why the annual Mass in his memory at Cambrai Cathedral was celebrated on that day. The suggestion is difficult to confirm or refute: obits and obit-dates often do seem incomprehensible at five hundred years' distance. For what it is worth, at St-Vincent in Soignies Dufay's obit was celebrated – equally inexplicably – on 12 June.[3]

Where he was born is a far more intractable question which will probably never be answered with certainty. But the search for a solution leads up important avenues. Two suggestions can firmly be rejected. One is that he was born at a place called Fay near Soignies, a town midway between Cambrai and Brussels.[4] The theory is based primarily on his appearance, just mentioned, in the obit-book of the collegiate church of St-Vincent; but this is fully explained in a hitherto unpublished paragraph from the executors' accounts of his probate: after everything had been paid off an enormous surplus remained, and with part of it Dufay's former *clerc* at Watiebraine, the composer Johannes Regis, established that Mass at Soignies.[5] Regis was a canon of Soignies.

Another proposal, which still appears in some reference works, is that the composer was born at Chimay as suggested a century and a half ago by Fétis who claimed to have seen a theory treatise containing material 'secundum doctrinam Wilhelmi Dufais

Cimacensis Hann.'. Most later students of Dufay (and of Fétis's sometimes impulsive scholarship) have agreed that 'Cimacensis' must have been a misreading of 'Cameracensis' and that the sentence refers to 'Dufay [a canon] of Cambrai in Hainault'[6] – thus providing no evidence of his birthplace but merely connecting him with the town where he spent most of his mature years.

Two more suggestions take as their starting point the closing line of one of his motets.[7] In the unique manuscript it reads 'Guillermus cecini, natus est ipse Fay' which, in spite of its shaky grammar, has been taken as an unequivocal statement of his birthplace. This is somewhat weakened by the emendation originally proposed by Albert Vander Linden:[8] he suggested the reading 'natus et ipse Fay' which not only tidies up the syntax but, far more important, makes the line scan correctly as an elegiac pentameter (since Dufay motet texts which use classical metres seem to follow classical precepts of scansion rigorously). If that emendation is accepted the line could still be a statement of his birthplace ('born at and called Fay'), but it could just as well be a flowery declaration of his name ('born and called Fay'). And even if it is the former this still provides relatively little information: the place-name 'du Fay' or 'du Fayt' ('of the beech grove') is common throughout northern France and the Walloon Low Countries.[9] Nevertheless the possibility gives rise to some permissible speculation.

One theory was that since Cambrai Cathedral had a far-reaching influence and reputation a chorister could well come from, for instance, as far away as Laon. Although some 85 km. from Cambrai, it was in particularly close touch because the new teacher at the Cambrai choirschool in 1408–9, the composer Nicolas Grenon, had recently been the trainer of the choristers at Laon Cathedral; and there is evidence suggesting that when Grenon changed position he took choristers with him.[10] It is just possible, then, in spite of evidence to be offered shortly, that Dufay came from Laon or more particularly from the nearby village of Nouvion-le-Vineux where there is an area still called 'du Fay'. This would explain some otherwise surprising links with Laon and Nouvion-le-Vineux later in his life.[11]

It has also been suggested that he could have been born at Troisvilles, a hamlet some 20 km. south-east of Cambrai between Caudry and Le Cateau. Troisvilles contained three *seigneuries*, one of them 'Le Fayt' where the seigneurial family 'du Fayt' or 'du Fay'

9

can be traced back to the eleventh century.[12] Two facts have been offered to support this theory. First, when Dufay's mother died in 1444 she was accorded the unusual privilege of burial within Cambrai Cathedral.[13] But this does not necessarily imply that she had seigneurial rank. Dufay was by then an immensely eminent man, having led both the papal choir and the Duke of Savoy's choir as well as having composed enough music of unprecedented quality to assure his position as the greatest composer of his day. That could just as well explain why the Cambrai chapter so readily allowed Marie Dufay to be buried in the cathedral. Moreover she is described on her tombstone[14] not in terms of her family but simply as the mother of Guillaume Dufay the canon of Cambrai. (Indeed the curious absence of her husband's name has even led to the suggestion, so far unpublished, that the composer could have been illegitimate.[15])

The second factor in favour of his having seigneurial rank is Dufay's easy assembly of benefices in later life as well as his coat of arms, mentioned several times in the inventory of his property made after his death. But these privileges too could have been acquired on the basis of his excellence as a musician. The possession of a coat of arms was – as it remains to this day – a privilege accorded to all canons of Cambrai. And we shall see that most of his benefices originated from direct papal patronage. The skills of a fine composer may have brought only certain kinds of advantage in the Middle Ages, but they did bring advantages. Moreover, it seems that Dufay was a man of considerable social ease, to judge from his apparent contacts with men such as Donatello and Brunelleschi, his series of motets composed for Pope Eugenius IV, his surviving correspondence with the Medici family, with Antonio Squarcialupi and with the ducal house of Savoy, to mention only a few examples. And if Dufay had a parentage to be proud of he would surely have declared it, for the commonest way of defining a person legally at this time was in terms of his father, particularly if the father had any social standing.

But the most recent information points to what may seem the obvious solution – that he was born in Cambrai itself. It has often been observed that the name Dufay was relatively common in Cambrai town records for some three hundred years before his birth;[16] and therefore that other speculations are unnecessary.

Two newly discovered documents show that Marie Dufay, the

*Cambrai and the surrounding areas on the present French-Belgian border*

Straits of Dover

Antwerp

Bruges

Ghent

Brussels

Lille

Tournai

Soignies

Condé

Mons

Arras

Cambrai

Troisvilles

Chimay

River Oise

Noyon

River Meuse

Laon

Nouvion-le-Vineux

- - - Boundary of the Holy Roman Empire

Rheims

composer's mother, must have been living in Cambrai continuously from at least the early 1420s until her death in 1444 even though Dufay himself was living in Italy and Savoy until 1439.

The first is the will of Johannes Huberti, a canon of Cambrai, made on 29 July 1424. In it he leaves 20 francs to 'Marie Du fayt ma cousine et servante'.[17] There is always the danger that this was another Marie Dufay, not the composer's mother, but the second document eliminates that possibility: it shows that when the composer was granted leave from the court of Savoy in 1434 'to go back to his homeland in order to visit his mother' he in fact went to Cambrai (see below p. 42).

'Homeland' (*patria*) can mean many things, particularly in a document intended to justify a payment, not meant as a biographical memoir. But if Marie Dufay was living in Cambrai all those years while her son was elsewhere it is difficult to avoid the conclusion that this was his family home and therefore that he was born there (or at least that mother and child lived there from early in his life). 'Cousine' is also a very general word, but it surely implies some kind of blood-relationship, in which case it may be relevant that Johannes Huberti was from 1407 provost of the church of St-Géry,[18] where Dufay had his earliest benefice: perhaps some kind of nepotism was involved here. Finally 'servante' seems incompatible with the idea that his mother belonged to the highest echelons of society, though at the same time Huberti's eminence in Cambrai circles was such that no 'cousine et servante' of his was likely to be particularly low down on the social ladder.

Beyond that, his training at Cambrai Cathedral would have put him in a position of privilege as a musician; and in his will Dufay mentions specifically that he had subsequently profited from his years as a choirboy there. Cambrai's musical tradition was exceptional. When Dufay joined as an *altarista* in 1409 there were six choristers with their own master. They received free tuition in music and grammar in return for singing in the daily services. (There is a payment record in the accounts for his receiving a *Doctrinale* in 1411–12.) In addition the twelve singing men, the *petits vicaires*, had their own choirmaster and were to include over the coming years several distinguished composers. How often these two groups of musicians actually sang polyphony, as opposed to chant, it is impossible to say, though evidence from later in the century shows that by then they relatively often sang polyphonically, and that each of the two groups could also form an independent polyphonic choir.[19]

Throughout the fifteenth century Cambrai Cathedral was considered one of the Western Church's elite institutions for music. Shortly after Dufay's death the new bishop, Henri de Berghes, wrote: 'in the Christian world there is scarcely any church superior to ours in the number and skill of the singers it employs'.[20] And in 1428 Philip of Luxembourg, Count of St-Pol, wrote that in spite of all the troubles with English invasions over the preceding years Cambrai Cathedral still exceeded the entire Christian world 'en beaux chants, en riche luminaire et en tres doulce sonnerie'.[21] Of the 'doulce sonnerie' we know that the cathedral had a magnificent thirty-nine-bell chime; of the 'riche luminaire' there is no more trace, since the cathedral was brutally demolished after the French Revolution, though early accounts record enormous sums paid for stained glass; of the musicians there is rather more information.

Nicolas Malin, master of the choristers from 1392 to 1412, is perhaps the least distinguished. No compositions by him survive, though the complete lack of polyphonic manuscripts of this date from the north makes it impossible to say with confidence that he was not a composer. Twenty years holding his position in so famous a choir are perhaps their own recommendation.

But Richard Loqueville, who succeeded Malin, has left more compositions than any other musician known to be associated with Dufay's early years: a dozen works by him appear in various Italian manuscripts.[22] On the face of it his musical style has little in common with Dufay's, but various details point to his influence and he is normally described as Dufay's composition teacher.

Loqueville's songs show the occasional use of voice-crossing with the discantus becoming for a moment the lowest voice, something to which Dufay became particularly partial in the 1430s. A paired Gloria and Credo use the technique of dividing the text between two upper voices but without telescoping: according to an annotation in the index of the manuscript now in Oxford, this technique was known as 'cursiva',[23] and it is otherwise extremely rare among continental composers except in a Gloria–Credo pair (iv/1) and a separate Gloria now ascribed to Dufay.[24] Loqueville's one surviving isorhythmic motet contains two unusual features later used by Dufay: it has two main sections of approximately the same length differentiated by a move from major prolation (C, transcribed as 6/8) to perfect time (O, transcribed as 3/4), used by Dufay in his motet *Rite majorem* (i/11); and it repeats its tenor in retrograde as happens in three works by Dufay, the motet *Balsamus et munda cera* (i/13), the Agnus of the Mass *L'homme armé* (iii/8) and the possibly spurious Agnus Dei 'Custos et pastor ovium' (iv/7).

From each composer we have a Sanctus setting built on a monophonic tenor known as 'Vineus' or 'Vineux'. It has been argued that Dufay's Sanctus 'Vineux' (iv/2) is among his earliest surviving pieces, written while he was a pupil of Loqueville.[25] This seems unlikely because Dufay probably left Cambrai very soon after 1414 and stylistically this work seems closer to 1426 when Loqueville had been dead for eight years. And one reason for proposing that later date (which is further discussed in chapter 13) is the similar style of Dufay's rondeau *Adieu ces bons vins de Lannoys* (vi/27) which is dated 1426 in its only source and is perhaps the only one among Dufay's songs to show Loqueville's influence in its style, having similarities with his rondeau *Puisque je suy amoureux* in its melodic ductus, its extraordinary melodic economy, and its harmonic style. Only the notation of Dufay's song suggests that it must have been composed some years after Loqueville's.

Taken together, these features in common between the twelve surviving works of Loqueville and the two hundred of Dufay are not conclusive proof that Loqueville was Dufay's teacher: Dufay's music contains such a range of ideas that almost anything could be found by the searcher who looks hard enough.[26] But they at least suggest that Dufay was aware of Loqueville's music and that Loqueville may have been an important influence on his early work.

What makes these common factors particularly striking is that the music of Nicolas Grenon has by contrast very little in common with Dufay's. Grenon has already been mentioned as choirmaster at Laon from 1403 to 1408. From then until 1409 he was at Cambrai teaching grammar to the choirboys, and his time there overlapped with Dufay's arrival by only two months: Grenon left in July, and Dufay had been present for eleven weeks receiving private instruction from Jean de Hesdin before he was admitted as a *puer altaris*. But later Grenon was to appear frequently in Dufay's life, spent many years at Cambrai and was evidently a close friend of the younger composer. He twice served as Dufay's proctor in Cambrai and the two composers were in later years neighbours in the rue de l'Ecu d'or. So it is worth noting that Grenon's songs and motets are significantly different from Dufay's. The only possible connection between the two is that a now fragmentary Gloria by Grenon also uses the rare 'cursiva' technique.[27]

Another important composer in the Cambrai choir has hitherto been overlooked. For the week of 14 December 1409, the register notes that 'Gillet was received' as a *petit vicaire*;[28] and the commons account gives his full name (twice) as Gillet Velut.[29] As with Grenon, Velut's eight surviving compositions[30] give little clue to any direct influence on the young chorister who had been admitted three months earlier; but what Velut shows in his works is an endless fascination with technical problems and their solution – a preoccupation that is often characteristic of Dufay's work and seems lacking in most other composers of the time. Perhaps Velut did not stay long: in 1411 he arrived in Cyprus as chaplain to Charlotte of Bourbon.

Two more composers can be associated with the Cambrai circle of Dufay's youth. Franchois Lebertoul was a choirman until 1410 and is now known from five compositions, all in song form though one has Latin text; they are for the most part approximately similar in style to those of Loqueville.[31] There also survives a Credo setting in three voices, probably from the earliest years of the century, ascribed with the name '[de] Cameraco' – of Cambrai.[32]

This group of surviving compositions by men who were at Cambrai during Dufay's earliest years there is impressive and cannot be matched in size by any other institution at the time except for the English Chapel Royal. It gives some clue to the nature of Dufay's privileged position as a musician. And it provides opportunities for seeing the stylistic context of his earliest works.

Perhaps it is significant in this context that of the thirty-six pieces mentioned, nineteen are secular. To interpret this information accurately is difficult, but at least it suggests that secular music was a serious occupation for the Cambrai Cathedral musicians. And this may be supported by the inventory *post mortem* of one of the canons, Ernoul de Halle, who died in 1417: his property included a harp, a lute, a gittern, a rebec, two vielles and a psaltery.[33] Moreover Richard Loqueville, before coming to Cambrai, had been a singer in the Duke of Bar's chapel where he had been paid in 1410 both for performing on the harp and for teaching the duke's son to play the instrument.[34]

A final negative detail should be added on Dufay's earliest musical education. A century later the Italian theorist Pietro Aaron published an ambiguous sentence that could be read as stating that Giovanni de Monte was Dufay's teacher. In fact he was paraphrasing Ramos de Pareia who, writing in Latin, had described Johannes de Monte as his own teacher.

One early teacher of Dufay – though there is no clear evidence that he taught him music – was Jean de Hesdin who was paid seventy-seven *sous* 'for having educated (*pro gubernacione*) the said Wilhelmus before he was received as an altar boy'. Jean taught him for eleven weeks, and the rarity of such a document leads one to suspect that Dufay was not fully prepared for life at Cambrai Cathedral, that he was therefore not necessarily a local boy bred up to being a chorister but rather one who had been discovered as having obvious talent.[35]

But the true celebrity of Cambrai Cathedral in the first years of the century was its bishop, Pierre d'Ailly, a former chancellor of the University of Paris and considered the leading French theologian of his generation. As Bishop of Cambrai he had been largely absentee until about 1409, when he remained there fairly continuously until his promotion to the rank of cardinal in the summer of 1411. On 17 November 1414 with a substantial retinue he arrived at the Council of Constance where he was to be one of the Council's intellectual leaders.[36] Indeed it has been said that 'the development of the Schism and particularly the events of the Council of Constance cannot be understood apart from the personal action of Pierre d'Ailly; one could write a history of these forty years under the title *Pierre d'Ailly and his epoch*'.[37]

It may be gathering coincidences a little too strongly to point out that d'Ailly was resident in Cambrai during the first two years that Dufay was there as a chorister. But d'Ailly was knowledgeable about music. In earlier years he had been *grand chantre* at Noyon and *chantre* at Rouen.[38] His *Jardin amoureux de l'âme dévote* includes an elaborate metaphor for the perfect prayer:[39] 'This song is extremely melodious for it is sung more by grace than by nature, without discord or excess, without *faulse ne fainte musique*, but with full agreement between heart and mouth and with perfect concord between voice and thought.'

And it seems likely that in the choice of retinue he would look favourably on a talented young man – as Dufay presumably was – who had just finished his term as a choirboy at Cambrai.

It must be stressed that the nearest thing to direct evidence for suggesting that Dufay joined d'Ailly's retinue is that the composer owned at his death twelve cushions embroidered with the cardinal's coat of arms.[40] Moreover, if Dufay went to Constance, he could equally well have done so in the 36-strong retinue of Pierre d'Ailly's successor as Bishop of Cambrai, Jean de Lens, who arrived at Constance on 11 January 1415. But it will soon be clear that later events in his life are almost impossible to understand unless Dufay was present at the Council of Constance, and they are most easily explained if he was there with Pierre d'Ailly.

In any case, it is here that the story of Dufay's life becomes more like that of most medieval composers. So far as documents are concerned he disappears from the record until 1427.

# 3

# Constance, Rimini, Laon and Bologna: 1414–1428

> With the exception of the Fourth Lateran Council in 1215, the Council of Constance was the most memorable gathering of the Latin clergy in the history of the medieval church. It was also the most successful hour of the great councils which hopefully began at Pisa in 1409 and ended in despair at Lausanne in 1449.[1]

In 1409, at about the time when Dufay had become a chorister at Cambrai, the Council of Pisa elected Peter Philarges pope as Alexander V, thus launching western Christendom on a decade with three rival popes. Over the next forty years Dufay was to be directly involved in the ensuing struggle for church unity, not as a protagonist himself but closely allied with many of the protagonists, among them two leading conciliar theologians, three popes and several other churchmen or politicians concerned with the conciliar movement. He himself composed works for some crucial occasions in conciliar history, and for a few months in 1438–9 he represented Cambrai Cathedral at the Council of Basle.

There is no documentation to say that Dufay was at the Council of Constance.[2] As already mentioned, it is merely the balance of probabilities which suggests that he could have been there in the retinue of either Cardinal Pierre d'Ailly or Bishop Jean de Lens. But somehow between 1414 and 1420 he had established contact with Italy and the Malatesta family. It has been argued that he could have met Pandolfo Malatesta da Pesaro while the latter was resident as Bishop of Coutances (1418–24) near the Norman coast;[3] but in fact Coutances is scarcely closer to Cambrai than is Constance. Dufay's presence at the Council of Constance is easily explained, and it is the hypothesis that makes the best sense of what followed.

The Council (1414–18) was perhaps one of the most important events in the history of fifteenth-century music. It was the largest of the councils, attended by over eighteen thousand clerics[4] (a staggering figure, particularly when compared with the population of Constance at the time, estimated at less than eight thousand).[5] In addition, the chronicler Ulrich von Richental mentions that seventeen hundred instrumentalists were present at one time or another.[6] All kinds of music would have been heard, and it was surely here that Dufay came into contact with English music.

On 24 September 1416 the bishops of Lichfield and Norwich arrived with their entourages. Two weeks earlier they had stopped at Cologne Cathedral where they sang for the feast of the Nativity of the Virgin Mary, and a local chronicler reported that 'here the English sang as well as had been heard in the cathedral for thirty years',[7] Having arrived at Constance they sang for the feast of St Thomas of Canterbury (29 December) drawing this report from Richental:[8] 'And in the morning the [English] celebrated the feast beautifully with a great noise, with great burning candles, and with angelically sweet singing at Vespers, with organs and *prosunen*, above which were tenor, discant and medius . . .' The word *prosunen*, as used by Richental, can mean any brass instrument. But here it probably means some kind of slide trumpet capable of performing polyphony, for elsewhere Richental describes the instrumentalists of Richard Beauchamp, Earl of Warwick, present during the first few weeks of the council:[9] 'They played with their slide trumpets together *(prusonettend überainander)* in three parts, in the way that one normally sings.' Taken together these comments – and indeed several others in Richental's chronicle – lead to two important conclusions. First, contrary to the assertions in some recent literature, slide trumpets were used already at this date in sacred polyphony, at least by English musicians.[10] Second, English musicians were heard at Constance and made a significant impression.

So if we are looking for the occasion when Dufay and other continental musicians were so strongly influenced by English music and by Dunstable in particular we need look no further.[11] Some writers have attempted to see a stylistic change in Dufay's music during the mid-1420s, the years when the English occupied Paris and much of France. These stylistic judgments are extremely subjective; and they seem unnecessary in view of the enormous gatherings at Constance.

A quarter of a century later Martin le Franc wrote in his long poem *Le champion des dames* what are perhaps the most famous lines commenting on the history of music in the fifteenth century.[12] They describe the sudden change in style since the days of Carmen, Tapissier and Cesaris – all of whom had almost certainly written most of what survives of them by 1410[13] – and attributed the change to the influence of the *contenance angloise* and particularly Dunstable.

> Tapissier, Carmen, Cesaris
> N'a pas longtemps si bien chanterrent
> Qu'ilz esbahirent tout Paris
> Et tous ceulx qui les frequenterrent.
> Mais onques jour ne deschanterrent
> En melodie de tel chois –
> Ce m'ont dit qui les hanterrent –
> Que G. du Fay et Binchois.
>
> Car ilz ont nouvelle pratique
> De faire frisque concordance
> En haulte et en basse musique,
> En fainte, en pause, et en muance,
> Et ont prins de la contenance
> Angloise et ensuy Dunstable,
> Pour quoy merveilleuse plaisance
> Rend leur chant joyeux et notable.

What the 'English countenance' may have been in this case has been extensively discussed without any clear answers. What is important here is that Martin le Franc, although probably too young to have been at Constance unless as a chorister, was later himself involved in the conciliar movement as secretary to Pope Felix V at the Council of Basle. Moreover, in the 1430s he would have had contact with Dufay at the court of Savoy (as another passage in his poem witnesses). The Council of Constance was surely the main catalyst for the extraordinary interest in English music on the continent during the first half of the century.[14]

Equally strong circumstantial evidence suggests that Dufay made his first contact with the Malatesta family at Constance. Amid so many people this may seem improbable. But at the Council of Pisa Pierre d'Ailly and Carlo Malatesta da Rimini – the head of the senior branch of the family – had negotiated closely towards arranging the abdication of Pope Gregory XII, for whom Carlo was spokesman.[15] This failed; but Carlo also acted as Gregory's spokesman at the Council of Constance, announcing his eventual abdication on 4 July 1415. Presumably Cardinal d'Ailly, as a theological leader of the council, was again involved; and if Dufay was in the cardinal's retinue he could well have met the other Malatesta who was there, Carlo's cousin Pandolfo, then Bishop of Brescia, soon to be Bishop of Coutances and later appointed Archbishop of Patras. Pandolfo was the eldest son of the cadet branch of the family, the branch based not at Rimini but a few miles further down the Adriatic coast at Pesaro.

Later on the two Malatesta families were to become bitter rivals, but in the early 1420s they were closely allied and had their centre at Rimini. Of the three works by Dufay connected with the Malatestas of Pesaro, the first two are for celebrations that took place actually in Rimini.

It was one of the more embarrassing events at the Council of Constance that indirectly gave rise to Dufay's first dateable composition. The Emperor of Constantinople had sent a deputation to discuss the matter of uniting the Eastern and Western Churches. Since the Western Church was busy attempting to cure its own schism there was little opportunity for these discussions. But the emperor also requested that his six sons be allowed to marry Italian catholic princesses as a preliminary move towards church unity. Two princesses were chosen almost immediately for his two eldest sons: for his second son, Theodore Palaiologos II, Despot of the Morea, the bride was to be Pandolfo's sister Cleofe. The wedding contract was signed on 29 May 1419.

Cleofe, though a member of the Pesaro branch of the family, had grown up at the Rimini court, and it was from Rimini that she set sail for the East on 20 August 1420.[16] Two musical works survive apparently celebrating that occasion.[17] One is Hugo de Lantins' Italian song *Tra quante regione*[18] and the other is Dufay's motet *Vasilissa ergo gaude* (i/7).

This event points to two more composers who must have had a considerable influence on Dufay's formative years. The main isorhythmic section of *Vasilissa ergo gaude* precisely follows the plan of Johannes Ciconia's motet *Ut te per omnes celitum*.[19] Ciconia, who had died in 1412, occupies a special place in musical history as the first known northern composer to make a career in Italy, thereby establishing a tradition that was to last well into the sixteenth century. The wide distribution of his works among manuscripts of the time establishes him as probably the most influential composer of that generation. Hugo de Lantins, the composer of the other piece for the occasion in 1420, is more difficult to pin down. No documents for him are known. But some of the texts he set suggest both that he

21

was active in the same area along the Adriatic coast and that he had some further connection with the Malatesta family. Moreover a Gloria by Hugo paired with a matching Credo by Dufay (iv/3, discussed below, pp. 175ff) suggests some kind of friendly rivalry between the two composers.

There is more information about Dufay's next Malatesta piece four years later, the song *Resvelliés vous* (vi/11) celebrating the wedding of Carlo Malatesta da Pesaro (brother of Cleofe and cousin of the Carlo mentioned earlier). He married Vittoria di Lorenzo Colonna at Rimini on 18 July 1423. The papal dispensation allowing him to marry Vittoria in spite of being distantly related to her describes Carlo as resident in Rimini.[20] But Vittoria first entered the family's own town, Pesaro, on 17 June before proceeding to Rimini a month later for the *sontuosissime nozze* (to use the words of the chronicler Clementini). Most sumptuous wedding it must have been: Vittoria was the pope's niece, and the marriage represented an important step for the less powerful branch of the Malatesta family.

*Resvelliés vous* could itself be described as *sontuosissima*. It is in ballade form, as was customary for such occasional pieces. The merit of the form in this context was that each stanza ended with a refrain line that could contain a reference to the patron, in this case 'Charle gentil, qu'on dit de Maleteste' – honourable Carlo, called Malatesta. That the text should be in French is a reminder that French was an important cultural and artistic language in northern Italy: most of the papal chapel were French speaking; most of the early fifteenth-century music manuscripts from northern Italy contain French songs with accurately copied texts; and very little music with Italian text survives from the years 1420–80.

What is most surprising about *Resvelliés vous* is the way in which Dufay's music contains brilliant roulades and considerable technical complexities. Evidently a special singer was intended (even if it is assumed that some of the florid sections were taken by an instrumentalist) and the voice part contains all kinds of tricks. Equally evidently the composer was demonstrating an enormous range of musical material and techniques. It is as though Dufay in his early twenties was intent on proving that he had more musical invention and resource than any other composer living. No other piece of the time contains such a plethora of musical ideas;[21] and it is all the more astonishing that the work should hold together as a musical entity.

One other important feature of *Resvelliés vous* is the way it shares musical material with Dufay's earliest known cyclic Mass (ii/1), normally called the Mass 'sine nomine' but perhaps better described as the Mass *Resvelliés vous*. The precise details of the relationship between the two works will be discussed later in their proper context (pp. 165ff); but they suggest that the two works are more or less contemporary. It might almost be suggested that this was the nuptial Mass for the bridal couple; and in any case 1423 must be agreed as an approximate date for Dufay's first surviving Mass cycle.

The third Malatesta work has a more complex history. In 1424, shortly after the wedding that tightened the bond between their families, Pope Martin V appointed Pandolfo Malatesta da Pesaro as Archbishop of Patras in the north of the Peloponnese. The political situation in the Peloponnese was delicate. Since the thirteenth century the area had been jointly occupied by Italians with catholic churches and Byzantines with orthodox churches. Gradually the Byzantines were gaining control, and the Despot Theodore Palaiologos II ruled from the southern city of Mistra. To resolve the situation it must have seemed to the pope a good idea to install Pandolfo, younger brother of the Despot Theodore's wife, Cleofe Malatesta. In the event this was not a success because the appointment was against the wishes of the Venetians who accordingly failed to provide the necessary military aid to Pandolfo when Theodore's brother Constantine invaded Patras in 1429; and Cleofe had by then turned to the Orthodox faith. Pandolfo had to flee, and in 1430 Patras again became part of the Byzantine Empire after over two hundred years of Venetian rule.[22]

During his short tenure as archbishop, however, Pandolfo restored one of the churches in Patras,[23] perhaps one of several in that town dedicated to St Andrew (who had been crucified there).[24] The rededication of that church in 1426 was almost certainly the event celebrated in Dufay's motet *Apostolo glorioso* (i/10). By strange contrast with *Resvelliés vous* this is a work that makes a maximum possible use of restricted musical material: the few actual motifs in the work are treated in imitation, in inversion, and in augmentation; when the metre changes, as it so often does in a motet, the melodic material remains almost unchanged.

That marked difference in style perhaps emphasizes that the three

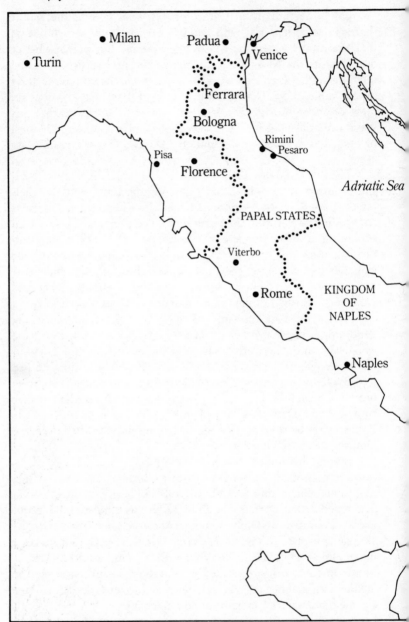

*Italy and the Peloponnese*

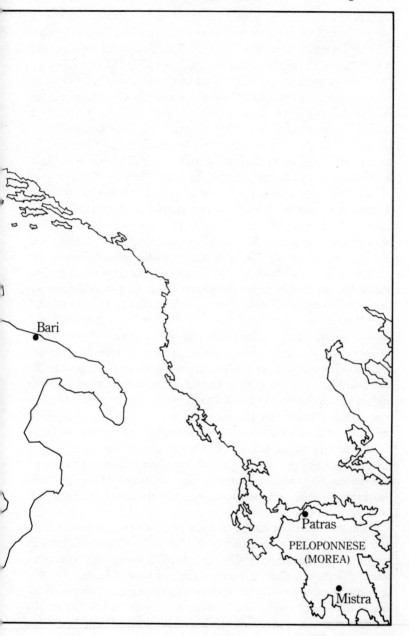

years between *Resvelliés vous* and *Apostolo glorioso* occurred at a crucial formative moment in Dufay's career and that much must have happened in the intervening time. The three pieces for members of the Malatesta family at Pesaro – dated 1420, 1423 and 1426 – offer only indirect information about his movements. Presumably he was at Rimini in August 1420, and he must surely have been there for the wedding in July 1423, if only because the ballade *Resvelliés vous* is of such complexity that the composer's presence was probably necessary for its performance. No precise documentation for the Rimini household survives (nor for that at Pesaro); but it is unlikely that Dufay was there throughout the years 1420–26.[25]

One small detail that might just be a clue to his movements is an item in an inventory of French royal chapel property made at the command of Henry V in 1422–3.[26] It notes that an altar-cloth belonging to the chapel had been stolen, stripped of its gold and silver, and then burned by a certain jeweller named Denisot de Chartres who was duly executed. Those officially responsible for the altar-cloth on that occasion were two clerks of the church of St-Germain-l'Auxerrois, one of them called 'Guillaume Fays' in the full French transcript but 'Guillelmus de Fays' in the Latin summary provided in the margin. The altar-cloth was stolen on 31 July 1420, and the official release of Fays and his colleague from any further responsibility was signed at Melun, near Paris, on 13 August 1420; so it is unlikely that the same man could have been at Rimini for the performance of the motet *Vasilissa ergo gaude* on 20 August 1420 (if indeed that is the correct date for the motet). This is characteristic of the kind of document that so often appears for other medieval figures: the name fits, but it is surely not so rare that there cannot have been two clerics in Europe with approximately the same name; and there is no other evidence that the composer was ever in Paris. Biographers of the composer have generally dismissed this document as being irrelevant.[27]

But the evidence that the composer was in France between 1423 and 1426 is much more persuasive. This is his rondeau *Adieu ces bons vins de Lannoys* (vi/27), dated 1426 in its only surviving source.[28] Its text is a sad farewell to the area around Laon, to its fair ladies and to its wines. In the final stanza a reference to 'remembering you in the wood/where there is no path or route' irresistibly recalls the dark uncharted forest of our lives with which Dante began his *Commedia*. If Dufay wrote the text or had a hand in its composition (and it seems likely that he often did) the implication of that might be that Dufay was already steeped in Italian culture — which was inevitable even though only the last of the Malatesta works actually has Italian text: some of his surviving Italian songs seem to date from the early 1420s, among them the Petrarch setting *Vergene bella* (vi/5). But more important is the poem's implication that he had been in Laon and was now leaving.

As yet the details of Dufay's residence in Laon have not been traced. Indeed it is fair to say that recent writers have been so keen to reject an earlier theory that he spent much of the 1420s in Paris that the matter of his Laon years has scarcely been mentioned. But there is another song which contains a direct reference to the Laonnais. His ballade *Ce jour le doibt* (vi/18), celebrating May Day, includes the lines:

> Je suy fermé comme a la plus joyeuse
> Qui soit jusques a Meuse ny a l'Euse.

The rivers Meuse and Oise form the boundaries of the diocese of Laon, and it is difficult to think that this song, so similar to *Adieu ces bons vins* in its harmonic movement, can have been composed anywhere but in the area of Laon.

Since the text of *Adieu ces bons vins* gives the impression that Dufay had been in Laon for some time, I would like to suggest that he had been there for at least two years, which is to say that he had left Italy shortly after the Malatesta wedding of July 1423 and taken up residence at Laon until early in 1426. That would help explain why he was granted two prebends in that area later while he was in the papal choir. The essence of such a prebend is that you must have some way of collecting the income from it, which in turn entails having a trustworthy representative nearby. Two years' residence at Laon in the 1420s would have provided the necessary contacts and made the choice of this area for two of his papal livings a logical one.

Another work can be placed in these years because of the date added in the same manuscript that dates *Adieu ces bons vins*. The ballade *Je me complains piteusement* (vi/14) is dated 12 July 1425. This information seems surprisingly precise for a piece whose text contains no apparent reference to a particular event; but only its first stanza survives, so perhaps an allusion appeared in the second or third stanzas which must surely have existed at one time. In those years the use of ballade form was normally confined to special occasions. One small detail helps to support the theory that Dufay was in Laon when he composed the song. The manuscript containing these dates, now at Oxford, was copied in the Veneto, relatively close to the area occupied by the Malatesta court. The absence of the later stanzas for this ballade could suggest that it had travelled some distance; indeed in the same manuscript it is only a later addition that gives us the subsequent stanzas of *Adieu ces bons vins*.[29] This detail is hardly conclusive proof; but Dufay's presence at Laon, rather than in Italy, would explain why it happened.

Among the many other works whose style and manuscript distribution place them firmly in the years before 1427 there are two isorhythmic motets which would also have been composed for specific occasions yet to be identified. *O sancte Sebastiane* (i/8) is a prayer for release from the plague.[30] Its canonic opening, fully isorhythmic writing, and extended 'Amen' section (very much in the style of Ciconia) mark it as an early work; and Besseler observed stylistic features in common with the ballade *Resvelliés vous*.[31] It probably dates from 1421 or 1422. As will be discussed later, Dufay's song *Resvelons nous* (vi/28) derives its musical material directly from this motet and is likely to date from about the same time. *O gemma, lux* (i/9) is an isorhythmic motet in honour of St Nicholas, Bishop of Myra, patron of Bari (at the extreme south of the Adriatic coast in Puglia); and Besseler suggested similarities with the ballade *Je me complains piteusement* (vi/14) of July 1425.[32] Firm occasions – which must surely have existed – for these two motets would help considerably in filling in the details of Dufay's life before 1427.

Beyond that it is clear that by 1426 Dufay was already a mature composer with an extensive and varied output. Apart from the works already mentioned, he had probably composed both of his two surviving 'partial' Mass cycles (iv/1 and iv/2), at least one of his Gloria–Credo pairs (iv/4), the two matched cantilenas *Alma Redemptoris mater* (first setting, v/47) and *Anima mea liquefacta est* (v/46), and much else. Together this amounts to a substantial and impressive group of works – perhaps even enough to establish him in his mid-twenties as the leading composer of his day.

From April 1427 we return at last to documentary evidence for Dufay. Two letters recorded in the chapter acts of the Cambrai parish church of St-Géry show that he was then living in Bologna. On

12 April Cardinal Louis Aleman, the papal legate to Bologna, had written to St-Géry on Dufay's behalf requesting privileges of absence from his diaconate held at the altar of St-Géry in the chapel *Salve* in that church. The letter was received on 30 May. A year later on 24 March 1428 Aleman wrote again, this time describing the composer no longer as a deacon but as a priest.[33] Presumably it was his ordination as priest that made the second letter necessary, so he was probably ordained some time early in 1428. The letter was received in Cambrai on 19 May. Nicolas Grenon acted as Dufay's proctor on this occasion (whereas previously it had been a certain Johannes Nicolai).

While in Bologna Dufay may well have had his first contact with somebody who later became a canon of Cambrai, Robert Auclou. Auclou was a curate of the parish church of St-Jacques-de-la-Boucherie in Paris, though he had almost certainly not been there since about 1422.[34] From the summer of 1426 he was in Bologna as secretary to Cardinal Aleman. Dufay's motet in honour of St James the Greater, *Rite majorem Jacobum canamus* (i/11), has an acrostic in its text: the first letters of each line combine to form the words ROBERTUS ACLOU CURATUS SANCTI JACOBI. 'Curate of St-Jacques' would be the normal way of referring to Auclou who retained that curacy until his death. The motet's style suggests a date around this time, though since Dufay and Auclou were to be contemporaries at the papal curia in Rome (1428–33) as well as at Cambrai Cathedral and elsewhere, there can be no documentary certainty about the motet's date. It is not even clear whether the acrostic should be taken to mean that the motet was composed partly in honour of Auclou or merely that Auclou had written the poem.

It is possible that Dufay's next cyclic Mass, the plenary Mass *Sancti Jacobi* (ii/2), dates from about the same time. Earlier writers, who thought that Auclou was in Paris all the time from 1424 to 1428 and suspected that Dufay was there during the same years absorbing English style for the first time, had naturally assumed that the Mass for St-Jacques and the motet for the curate of St-Jacques were closely connected and composed in Paris. That is now unacceptable in view of Auclou's absence from Paris after 1422 and in view of the surviving liturgies for that church which seem incompatible with the Alleluia text included in the cycle. With fuller information on Auclou's movements, however, a more recent view is that the Mass and the motet were both composed in Bologna. The Mass could then have been for the church of San Giacomo Maggiore,[35] and perhaps for the saint's name-day on 25 July, in either 1427 or 1428.[36] There is at least some indirect evidence that the liturgy of that church was compatible with the rhymed Proper text which Dufay used for the Alleluia: *Hispanorum clarens stella*.[37] Yet the evidence is slight and the undermining of long-accepted dates for both the Mass and the motet shakes many of the received views on the chronology of Dufay's works. The main problem here is that to associate the Mass with the church of St James in Bologna is implicitly to dissociate it from the motet and from Auclou who was curate of an entirely different church for St James, that in Paris. Nevertheless the date should perhaps remain tentatively, for the style and the source distribution of the work do seem to point to some time between 1426 and 1430.

One more tentative date can be offered here. Dufay's ballade *Mon chier amy* (vi/15) is not dated, but its style points to these years. The text is one of condolence directed to a man mourning the death of another man: its refrain line is 'Car une fois nous fault ce pas passer' – For at some time death must come to us all. Pandolfo Malastesta da Rimini died on 3 October 1427 at the age of fifty-seven after an eventful life as a *condottiere* and a generous patron of humanists.[38] (It was his natural son Sigismondo Pandolfo Malatesta who is famous in cultural history for having commissioned the church of San Francesco in Rimini, still known as the Tempio Malatestiano, from Leone Battista Alberti – to many minds the first true renaissance man.) Pandolfo was the younger brother of Carlo Malatesta da Rimini. And although the three established Malatesta works of Dufay are associated with the Pesaro branch of the family, we have already seen that two of the events celebrated took place at Rimini, under the aegis of Carlo Malatesta da Rimini. Moreover Pandolfo was at his death Archdeacon of Bologna and titular head of Bologna university. 'Death must come to us all': Carlo was two years older than his brother and indeed died in 1429 at the age of sixty-one. Every detail of Dufay's song seems appropriate for a work addressed to Carlo on his brother's death in October 1427.

If Dufay was still in touch with the Malatestas at the end of 1427 that might have helped him gain admission to the papal choir at the end of 1428, for one of the major scandals of Pope Martin V's reign was his support of that family. Not that Dufay's appointment is inexplicable otherwise, however. His past career and particularly his compositions marked him as an outstanding figure. Moreover it looks very much as though political events brought him to Rome.

Only five months after sending his second letter to Cambrai on Dufay's behalf Cardinal Aleman and all his supporters were chased out of Bologna, on 23 August 1428.[39] Clearly Auclou was among them, as the cardinal's secretary. But apparently Dufay was among them too. All three men appear in the next surviving list of papal employees, from December 1428. And a document dated 14 April of the next year states that Dufay had been a papal singer for over six months. He does not appear on the choir payment lists for October or November; but he was presumably in the papal establishment from around the beginning of October 1428, within six weeks of Aleman's leaving Bologna.

This in turn implies that when he was in Bologna Dufay was actually a member of Cardinal Aleman's retinue. It has been suggested[40] that he was studying at the University of Bologna for the degree of bachelor in canon law – *baccalaurius in decretis* – which is credited to him later and had presumably been acquired by September 1436 when he obtained a prebend *libera jurista* at Cambrai Cathedral.[41] But this degree would require several years' study whereas he can hardly have been in Bologna for more than about eighteen months if he was really at Laon in 1424–6. The only place where he demonstrably stayed in his early years long enough for such studies was Rome (1428–33), and the theory that he was in the cardinal's entourage is supported, if only slightly, by evidence of the cardinal's musical interests. When Nicolas Grenon took four choirboys from Cambrai to Rome, where they joined the papal choir for two years (1425–7), they stayed en route with Aleman in Bologna.[42] Perhaps, too, one reason why Cambrai Cathedral later (in April 1438) appointed Dufay and Auclou as its representatives at the Council of Basle was that both had previously been associated with the leader of the council, Cardinal Aleman, appointed two months earlier.

But from his arrival at the papal chapel in October 1428 Dufay's life is much more fully documented. After fifteen years with only two clear documents, the biographer returns to solid ground.

# 4

# The papal chapel and Savoy: 1428–1439

When Martin V was elected the first post-schismatic pope by the Council of Constance in 1417 he took over the chapel of John XXIII, with five chaplains and seven singers.[1] By June 1420 there were fifteen singers, including the composers Guillaume Legrant and Pierre Fontaine;[2] and although numbers fluctuated they remained healthy throughout the 1420s. From June 1425 to December 1427 the choir had even included boys (four and then six) under the direction of Nicolas Grenon, though by the time Dufay arrived they had returned to Cambrai whence they came, and Grenon with them. But it is significant that the choirboys and their master were from Cambrai; moreover, when Dufay joined the choir four of the singers were Cambrai canons and another four had smaller prebends in the diocese of Cambrai.[3] Ties between the papal chapel and Cambrai were close and were to remain so throughout the century.

At the time of Dufay's arrival in the autumn of 1428 the papal chapel had recently lost not only Grenon and the choirboys but also two further choirmen, one of them the composer Fontaine who was returning to the Burgundian court which he had left in 1419.[4] The finances saved by these departures made it possible to expand the choir slightly from nine to eleven men:[5] the total monthly salaries came to sixty-eight florins early in 1427; with Dufay's arrival and the expansion this figure fell to fifty-one florins.

Bertold Dance *tenorista*, from the diocese of Beauvais, had been there since Martin V's accession and had held the title of *capelle magister* since 1422. This is some indication of the position of chapel singers under Martin V and his successor Eugenius IV; both before and after that they were headed by an administrator, not a singer.[6] Other singers who had been there for some years included Toussaint de la Ruelle (intermittently since 1420) and Philippe Foliot (since 1425), both of whom were also soon to follow Fontaine to the Burgundian court chapel. In addition the *contratenorista* Gilles Flannel, called 'L'enfant', had been there since 1418; he was from the diocese of Cambrai and his career was now to run alongside Dufay's for many years.

Lists of the choirmen under Martin V were normally by seniority, as were their salaries. The first two received six florins per month; the next five received five florins; Dufay was initially among the next three who received four florins. Also on the same salary as Dufay were Bartholomeus Pugnare (or Poignare), who had been one of Grenon's choirboys from Cambrai and became a choirman one year before Dufay, and Gautier Libert who seems to have joined at the same time as Dufay but did not stay long. Both are known as composers. Pugnare's single surviving piece, probably from some years later, is a Gloria setting[7] significant in being bitextual with the tenor having the text and paraphrased melody of the antiphon *Ave regina celorum* which Dufay set three times and was to use as the tenor of his own (also bitextual) final Mass cycle. Gautier Libert is known by three songs, one of which was composed in 1423.[8]

The privileges of papal singers were considerable. In addition to his salary of four florins per month (paid in advance,[9] and to rise to five florins in the next year) Dufay was granted the right of all papal singers to hold three absentee livings with healthy incomes attached. In a list of such benefices dated April 1429 Dufay is recorded as being perpetual chaplain of the altar of St-Fiacre in Laon Cathedral in addition to his chaplaincy at St-Géry, Cambrai; a year later, in April 1430, a chaplaincy was added at the church of Nouvion-le-Vineux, close to Laon, giving him a total income from his livings of forty *livres tournois*.

But if Martin V was a congenial pope for Dufay because of the Malatesta connection and his evident support for music, his successor was to become one of the composer's finest patrons. In March 1431 the Venetian Gabriele Condulmer was elected pope as Eugenius IV. One of his first acts was to reinstate Martin V's chapel,[10] and within three weeks of his election he ordered that each of his nine singers should be found two new canonries with expectatives of prebends. The document recording this shows that by now Dufay already had a further chaplaincy, at the parish church of St-Pierre in Tournai; and by 22 August 1431 he had not only been found a canonry and prebend at Lausanne but also had canonries with expectatives of prebends at St-Donatien in Bruges[11] and at Tournai Cathedral. In view of that he was asked to resign his chaplaincy at St-Pierre, Tournai, which was duly passed on to another papal singer.

As already mentioned, this effort was made for all the papal singers, not just Dufay; but there is evidence that Eugenius had a particular interest in composers. The first list of his singers includes a new name, that of Johannes Brassart whose motet *Magne decus potencie* celebrates the papal coronation.[12] Later in the year the composers Arnold de Lantins and Guillaume Malbecke joined the choir.[13]

And within the next few years Dufay was to compose some of his finest motets specifically for Eugenius. First was *Ecclesie militantis* (i/12) with a fighting text which may well have represented some kind of papal manifesto: this motet is usually considered to have been composed, like Brassart's motet, for the pope's coronation on 11 March 1431, though conclusive evidence for that date is lacking.[14] Certainly from a few weeks after that is *Balsamus et munda cera* (i/13), a motet in contrasting style and for once not polytextual; it is on the traditional text for the service of the distribution of the Agnus Dei, a septennial feast which happened to fall in the next month, on 7 April 1431.[15]

Two years later Dufay composed the third and longest of these motets, *Supremum est mortalibus bonum* (i/14), praising the now peaceful relations between the pope and King Sigismund of the Romans – 'Eugenius et Rex Sigismundus', as the motet announces in held homophonic chords. This motet has normally been connected with a 'Peace of Viterbo' in April 1433. But the only peace in that month was a relatively informal treaty made at Rome by the king's representative Kaspar Schlick; although Sigismund happened to be in Viterbo at the time, the pope remained in Rome. The first meeting of the pope and the king was in fact on 21 May, when Sigismund entered Rome at the pope's invitation. He was received on the steps of St Peter's and was allowed to kiss the pope's feet, hands and face before entering the church for a grand ceremony. This is the occasion commemorated by Filarete's famous relief on the doors of St Peter's (ill. 6). Poggio Bracciolini described the event in a letter written shortly afterwards: 'It was a most memorable day, distinguished by new and extraordinary spectacle, for nobody recalled such an event having taken place.' Moreover this spectacle included music. Clearly this was the event for which Dufay composed his motet. He had ample warning of the king's impending entry; this was the first meeting of king and pope; and since Sigismund is described as 'Rex' the motet must be earlier than 31 May, only ten days later, when he was crowned emperor.[16]

Much speculation has gone into identifying the other music that Dufay composed during his five years in Rome. His Italian song *Quel fronte signorille* (vi/7) has the annotation 'Rome composuit' in its only manuscript source; but all its music appears in an evidently earlier[17] rondeau *Craindre vous vueil* (vi/61) so it is not clear whether the music was itself composed in Rome or merely adapted to the new text. On the same page as *Quel fronte signorille* is another unique Italian song, similar in style and apparently identical in form, *Dona i ardenti rai* (vi/6); perhaps this too was composed in Rome.

Of the other works previously associated with his Roman years[18] a surprisingly large number have recently been re-allocated to a slightly later date. His cycle of hymns was once thought to be for the papal chapel because it appears in a Vatican manuscript from later in the century; but it is now thought to be liturgically incompatible with papal use at this time and much more likely to have been written later for the court of Savoy.[19] If so, the cycle of sequence settings and the homogeneous group of Kyrie settings must also be slightly later, as suggested below in chapters 10 and 13.

So it looks very much as though Dufay composed very little during these five years at his life's prime.[20] There are three considerations that might be relevant here. One is that while the preservation and distribution of music from the early 1430s sometimes seem very good – certainly far better than from the early 1440s – we still know far too little about the way in which music travelled. The surviving manuscripts are all from northern Italy and it is perfectly possible that some of Dufay's works from the Roman years have been lost. Another is that all critics have agreed that there is a change in his style some time around 1431. This could be at least partly because of a chronological gap in his output. And finally, it looks increasingly as though the only time when Dufay could have obtained his degree in canon law was when he was at Rome.[21] The evidence of the motets is that he did not entirely stop composing; but his studies, his duties in the papal choir and indeed the new-found stability of having arrived in the most prestigious choir of western Christendom may well have slowed down his output.

Politically, the reign of Eugenius was turbulent from the very beginning. Eugenius shared many ideals with his predecessor; but after having worked closely with Martin V during the early years of that pope's reign, he had fallen out of favour in about 1425, for reasons yet to be explained. And his election in 1431 brought opposition from the Colonna and Malatesta families which had been so strongly favoured by Martin V. Fighting began almost immediately. As early as 23 April 1431, only six weeks after his coronation, the Colonnas launched their first attack on Rome, though they soon retreated for lack of popular support. In June an attempt to poison the pope was discovered and duly punished. By August 1433 Eugenius was in an impossible position. A former papal *condottiere*, Nicholas della Stella called 'Fortebraccio', invaded Rome on behalf of the Duke of Milan and obtained control of four of its gates, opening the way for the Colonna family. Subsequently three of the Colonna brothers were excommunicated, but this achieved little: the political climate in Rome was now extremely unstable.[22]

The lists of papal singers tell the same story. In April 1433 there were twelve of them, but the numbers fell steadily to seven in July, and from October there were only five.[23] In such circumstances it is understandable that Dufay would welcome an invitation to leave Rome: the family of two former patrons (Vittoria Colonna and Pope Martin V – Oddo Colonna) together with the entire Malatesta family were in direct confrontation with his present patron. By August 1433 Dufay had himself left the papal chapel. On his eventual return to the chapel two years later he was reinstated at his previous position of seniority, so he was presumably granted just an extended leave from his duties, perhaps partly for political reasons and partly because Eugenius was in financial straits: the Council of Basle had severely reduced his income.

In any case, Dufay's move at that stage to the relatively neutral and apparently affluent Duke of Savoy seems to have been eminently logical. It was to be important for most of the rest of his career.

It is one of the ironies of cultural history that many of the great and discriminating patrons are recorded by political commentators as weak or ineffectual. Eugenius IV has never counted as a strong pope, and any attempts to justify his reign in political terms contain more than a touch of special pleading. Similarly with the Dukes of Savoy. Amadeus VIII comes down in history as a colourful man who in 1434 irresponsibly abandoned his duties as duke to retire to a small monastic community on the edge of Lake Geneva where he later contrived to be elected one of the least successful antipopes of all

8. Duke Amadeus VIII of Savoy (Antipope Felix V) with his son Louis
and his daughter-in-law Anne de Lusignan, representing God the
Father and the Son crowning the Virgin Mary, see p.282 n24.
Miniature from the Hours of Louis of Savoy, c.1460.

9. Cosimo and Piero de' Medici representing Wise Men
(right, on horseback). Detail from Benozzo Gozzoli's fresco,
*The Journey of the Magi*, 1459.

10. Lorenzo de' Medici representing a Wise Man.
Detail from Benozzo Gozzoli's fresco.

11. Duke Philip the Good of Burgundy, wearing the pendant of the
Order of the Golden Fleece, with his son, Duke Charles the Bold.
Sixteenth-century drawing.

time. His son Louis, who was left in nominal control of Savoy as Prince of Piedmont from November 1434, appears as an exceptionally insipid man who was dominated by his frivolous but fabulously beautiful wife, Anne de Lusignan (see ill. 8),[24] and accordingly allowed his court to be riddled with petty intrigues between her Cypriot toadies and his native French courtiers.

Whatever the truth of these judgments, the Dukes of Savoy were to provide the opportunity, and perhaps the stimulus, for a large quantity of music by the greatest composer of their age; and for that they surely deserve more than passing credit.

Louis was married to the sister of the King of Cyprus in October 1433. But the ceremony took place in Cyprus by procuration: husband and wife did not meet until Anne arrived in Chambéry the following February. Shortly before her arrival Dufay joined the Savoy household, and the forthcoming celebration was clearly the reason for his employment there. It was the first major wedding in the family since Amadeus VIII had so significantly increased his fortunes and political importance. In 1416 King Sigismund had advanced him from count to duke; and in 1419 Amadeus had added Piedmont to his already considerable domains which, together with the acquisition of the Genevois in 1401, gave him complete control of the crucial area covering the main Alpine crossings between France and Italy as well as the cities of Lausanne, Geneva, Nice, Turin and Chambéry. Indeed his promotion to duke may be seen as Sigismund's attempt to acknowledge and establish a power in the south of France comparable with that of the Duke of Burgundy in the north. So the wedding of Amadeus's heir to Anne de Lusignan was an occasion at which the Duke of Burgundy would place some value on being present. Burgundy had in addition plans for an alliance with Savoy against the Duke of Bourbon.[25]

And it is likely that when Amadeus knew that Burgundy proposed to attend with an enormous retinue and his entire court chapel, some significant counter-attraction would seem necessary to minimize the danger of the visitors from the north upstaging the Savoy court. To employ the finest possible musician as leader of the Savoy choir would help this aim. And in the circumstances Dufay was surely the obvious choice. Irrespective of aesthetic considerations, his five years in the papal chapel, his now long list of prestigious commissions and his astonishing variety of compositions marked him clearly as the leading musician of his day.

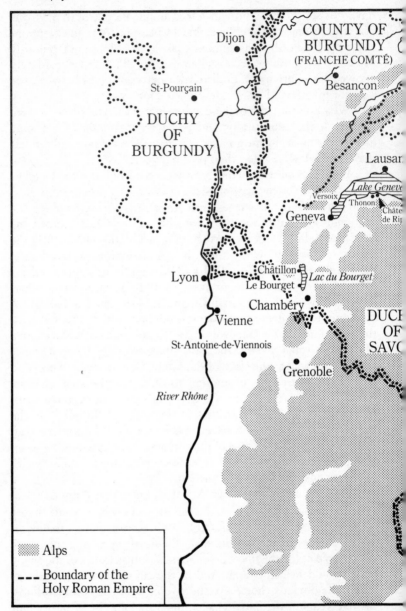

*Savoy and surrounding areas on the Alpine border
now dividing France, Switzerland and Italy*

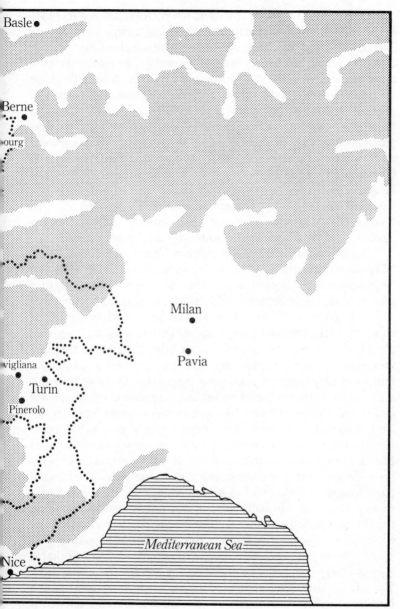

Basle

Berne

ourg

Milan

Pavia

vigliana

Turin

Pinerolo

*Mediterranean Sea*

Nice

Of the music at the Savoy court when Dufay arrived there we know enough to say that it flourished. It was a large court of over 250 people at the time. The duke and his wife were both interested in music. From the first twenty years of the century the names of eleven minstrels survive in the sadly incomplete records. Among them are 'Henrico Horoflu [or Horublos] tedesco, menestrello di corde e di organo' (1401–20), two *citariste* (1415–20) and in 1418 a certain Freminest *trompete menestreriorum* (a position recorded at the Burgundian court only five years later).[26] From the year Dufay arrived there is a list of seven court minstrels, including three trumpeters, Giovanni d'Ostenda *citarista* and the famous brothers Roleto and Peroneto des Ayes. Several chapel singers are named, including Reynaud Joly (1427–51), Godofreddo (retired by November 1434), Nycodo de Menthone *magister organorum* (1433) and Pietro Teobaldi (1435) who was also employed as a music copyist.

But the head of them was Adamo Grand (sometimes called Magister Adam) who in 1433 was *magister cantus* but in 1434 and 1435 was merely master of the four choirboys, appearing as *magister musice* again on 16 September 1438.[27] It seems quite possible that this is the composer 'Adam' known from three rondeau settings of about that date.[28] If so there can have been little question of his giving place to the eminent if young Dufay, for Adam's pieces are distinctly unimpressive. But evidently this was a court with a substantial musical establishment; it had unusually sophisticated minstrels and a chapel choir that included an organist, a music copyist and four choirboys. The grand Sainte-Chapelle in the castle at Chambéry (ill. 15) had recently been finished, with a particularly remarkable organ.

If we are to trust a somewhat ambiguous payment record from March 1434, Dufay became master of the Savoy chapel on 1 February 1434, only a week before the celebration; but since he had left the papal chapel by August 1433 it is likely that he arrived at Savoy shortly thereafter. His ballade *C'est bien raison* (vi/16) honouring the Marquis of Ferrara, Niccolò III d'Este, and praising his skill as a peacemaker is sometimes thought to date from 1433 and to refer specifically to the peace signed at Ferrara in April 1433. If that is correct Dufay could well have stopped at Ferrara on his way from Rome to Chambéry and composed the piece then; but recent opinion favours a later date for that work, associating it with a document from the Ferrara archives mentioning a payment to Dufay in 1437 (a date which would, incidentally, involve redating the completion of the

Oxford manuscript which contains the song).[29]

Whatever the truth of the Ferrarese matter, it is unlikely that Dufay arrived in Chambéry as late as 1 February 1434.[30] On Sunday 7 February Philip the Good arrived with his Burgundian retinue of some two hundred. On the same afternoon Anne de Lusignan entered Chambéry with her uncle – the Cardinal of Cyprus – and a large retinue. Here she met her husband for the first time, and they celebrated their nuptial Mass the same day in the new Sainte-Chapelle, a building which still stands today overlooking the town of Chambéry. Dancing followed after dinner, and the next four days were filled with appropriate festivities, sacred as well as secular – trumpets, minstrels, jousts, various kinds of disguisings and all the routines of medieval pageantry.

Particularly important for our purposes are two reports, one direct and the other indirect. The Burgundian court chronicler Jean le Fevre gives the fullest and most detailed description of the event, laying special emphasis on the Mass sung on the Monday by the Burgundian court chapel 'so melodiously that it was a fine thing to hear'.[31] This choir had some twenty men, including Binchois and several former members of the papal choir[32] (which in turn now numbered only five), so his comment is understandable. Equally understandably – in view of Le Fevre's own position as Burgundian court chronicler – he makes no mention of the Savoy choir.[33]

Martin le Franc's poem *Le champion des dames*, mentioned earlier, gives the other report. It tells of Dufay and Binchois – the leading composer of the Burgundian court – listening astonished and shameful to the magnificent playing of the blind minstrels of the Burgundian court:

> Tu as les avulges ouy
> Jouer a la court de Bourgogne,
> N'as pas certainement ouy
> Fust il jamais telle besongne:
> J'ay veu Binchois avoir vergongne
> Et soy taire emprez leur rebelle
> Et Dufay despite et frongne
> Qu'il n'a melodie si belle.

This is almost certainly a reference to the same occasion, for the two blind minstrels Jehan Ferrandez and Jehan de Cordoval are first recorded in the Burgundian accounts for the previous year, 1433;[34] and a special payment is recorded for their visit to the wedding.[35]

Of the music that Dufay must surely have composed for the event no information survives. It has been suggested that his Gloria 'de Quaremiaux' (iv/23) was composed for the Tuesday celebrations, since Shrove Tuesday fell on that day.[36] This is a slight work, however, and is in many ways hardly suitable for so festive an occasion, so its association with the wedding must remain an unsubstantiated guess. Moreover its musical style points towards that of the rondeau *Adieu ces bons vins de Lannoys* (vi/27) of 1426, and a date around that time would make more sense.[37]

In August of that same year Dufay was granted leave from court duties to go back to his homeland in order to visit his mother – 'eundo ad patriam ipsius e causa visitandi eius matrem' – apparently being paid ten florins by Duke Amadeus (at Thonon, 8 August, received 10 August) and another ten florins by Louis (at Geneva, 12 August).[38] In the later document Dufay is described for the first time as curate of St-Loup at Versoix, a small parish on the lakeside just a few kilometres east of Geneva.[39]

Hitherto it has always been assumed that Dufay went to Cambrai on this occasion. That can now be confirmed: the *Office du four et du vin* of the cathedral states in its accounts that on 14 October provisions were given to 'Domino Guillermo du Fayt', as was customary for distinguished visitors to the cathedral. And even though there is no further evidence of his presence there he is not recorded again at the Savoy court until 18 April 1435, when a payment was registered at Thonon for his clothing for the coming year. So he could have been away from Savoy for up to eight months.

How far this visit to Cambrai was professionally connected – apart from being purely a visit to his mother – it is difficult to say. Perhaps he then re-established his contacts in Cambrai, making it easier for him to secure the prebend he was to obtain two years later and perhaps also to prepare for his eventual return to Cambrai at the end of 1439. But that speculation seems unnecessary. Dufay already had a representative at Cambrai in the person of Nicolas Grenon. Cambrai was the obvious place for the pope to find him a major benefice since Dufay had been a chorister there, and in any case the ties between the Cambrai chapter and the papal curia were close; moreover Dufay's eventual return to Cambrai was not planned or voluntary, as we shall see.

Equally, it is hard to be sure whether he is likely to have composed music for Cambrai while he was there. If he was really there for seven months or so, it seems unlikely that he would have allowed his pen to rest. But it may be unwise to see this brief visit to the north as an important stage in his artistic development.[40]

However, the payment of April 1435 brings to an end the documentation of Dufay's first sojourn at the court of Savoy – fifteen to eighteen months of which up to eight were spent on leave. He apparently composed his cycle of hymns during that time: some of the melodies used are incompatible with the papal liturgy, and he spent the remainder of the years 1428–37 in the papal choir.[41] The evidence is that the sequences and the Kyrie settings followed shortly afterwards; and recent writers have placed many other works in those years.[42]

One more can perhaps be added. The rondeau *Je veuil chanter* (vi/37), with its still unexplained acrostic JEHAN DE DINANT, contains in its third stanza the following lines: 'Ne sauroit on jusqu'a Paymie/ trouver ne qui me pleusist mieux' – One would not know how to find a lady who pleases me better this side of Paymie. 'Paymie' has not been identified and seems to be a mistranscription of the manuscript which reads something more like 'Paine' or – more probably – 'Pavie'. (In such respects the handwriting of the time is often ambiguous.) If 'Pavie' is the correct reading it is surely relevant that Pavia was the first substantial town outside the area ruled by the Dukes of Savoy in Italy. The song would therefore need to have been composed for the court of Savoy.

But, with or without this song, the current view of his chronology suggests that Dufay's arrival at Savoy opened the floodgates, that after a relatively non-productive five years in Rome he composed an enormous quantity of music in the years immediately after 1433.

By June 1435 Dufay was again in the papal chapel, listed as the second singer in order of seniority. In August he was recorded as first singer, in the temporary absence of Gilles Flannel (and indeed Dufay appears as the first name on the payment list for July, but here Flannel's name seems to have been omitted by oversight, for above Dufay's name there is a blank space against which a normal monthly payment is entered – which is to say that somebody was paid that sum, and it can only have been Flannel). From October, however, he appears firmly as first singer and was to remain so for the rest of his time in the papal chapel. (Earlier writers seem to have misread the documents in putting his promotion to first singer eight months later.) This position may not be of enormous significance, since under Eugenius all the singers received the same salary; but over the next months Dufay is several times called 'master of the chapel' in other papal documents. And – to attempt to look beyond the documents for a moment – it seems possible that the position of first singer was necessary as an inducement to him to return from the court of Savoy. Since he had accepted advance payment for his clothing at Savoy only six weeks before reappearing among the singers of the papal chapel it is likely that his decision to leave Savoy was sudden.

Yet certainly the moment was a good one, for the papal curia had now moved to Florence. The events described earlier had culminated in the pope's having to flee from Rome in June 1434[43] and accept an invitation to take up residence in the city that is so inseparably identified with the Renaissance in fifteenth-century Italy.

Here Cosimo de' Medici had just returned from a brief exile to become the unofficial but universally recognized ruler of the city, starting the unique non-constitutional rule that was to make Florence the most powerful city-state in Christendom. The brilliant Masaccio, almost exactly Dufay's contemporary, had died seven years earlier leaving his unfinished frescoes in the church of the Carmine for artists of many later generations to emulate. Luca della Robbia was finishing his *cantoria* for the cathedral; Donatello had just started his own *cantoria* for the same building. His friend Brunelleschi, having recently all but finished his most public masterpiece, the cupola of the cathedral, had begun what was to be perhaps his most perfect work, the church of Santo Spirito. Cosimo de' Medici had commissioned from Andrea del Castagno what was to be his masterpiece, the now lost fresco cycle depicting the Pazzi conspiracy. In the next year Fra Angelico was to begin the cycle of frescoes at San Marco which assured his immortality. Ghiberti was toiling on his second pair of Baptistery Doors – the 'Doors of Paradise' as Michelangelo was to call them – in continuation of a project which was to last him fifty years. And Leone Battista Alberti, now a member of the papal curia, was writing his most famous and influential book, *De pictura*. The pope himself resided in the building for which Alberti was later to create the façade, Santa Maria Novella. Here there were two paintings of the most enormous importance: Masaccio's extraordinary Trinity, done in collaboration with

Brunelleschi, and in the Spanish Chapel Andrea di Bonaiuto's fourteenth-century painting of Florence Cathedral as it was to be – as it now was.

Although the papal curia was to remain in Florence for only ten more months after his return, Dufay composed several of his most famous works during that time. And they suggest his awareness that Florence at this moment was the very crucible of the renaissance movement.

First among them is the motet *Nuper rosarum flores* (i/16) for the dedication of the cathedral, Santa Maria del Fiore, on 25 March 1436. This is by far the most extensively and intensively discussed of his works not only because of its own fascinating qualities but also because its occasion was one of the great events of Florentine history and indeed of the Renaissance itself.

Florence Cathedral had been begun in 1294 but had long lacked the planned dome to cover its enormous crossing. By providing the technology for this and completing the dome, Filippo Brunelleschi definitively established his position as one of the greatest architects of all time. In fact he achieved that feat largely by examining one of Rome's neglected classical monuments, the Pantheon, a building with an unsupported dome slightly larger than that of Santa Maria del Fiore. But it is precisely this approach to solving the problem that marks his dome as one of the striking and characteristic achievements of the early Renaissance. And it is perhaps partly a token of Eugenius's recognition of that significance that he agreed – quite against normal papal practice – to consecrate the completed cathedral himself.

Unfortunately, the most extensive description of that event, while a glorious example of humanistic rhetoric, is so full of hyperbole and pretentious comparisons that it gives little useful information other than that the occasion was a magnificent one with a lot of music from both singers and instrumentalists.[44] The payment records show that the papal chapel had ten singers at the time,[45] and it may be supposed that it was for them that Dufay composed his motet – basically in four parts with the two lower voices giving every impression of being instrumental while the second voice, the motetus, often divides into two, adding to the magnificence of the sound.

But the work is particularly notable in that its isorhythmic proportions, 6:4:2:3, have been seen as corresponding precisely to the length of the nave, the width of the crossing, the length of the apse and the height of the crowning dome of the cathedral. Beyond that, each section of the motet contains twenty-eight bars, corresponding to the modules of twenty-eight *bracchia* from which the building is designed. And the system of a double shell which Brunelleschi used to construct his dome seems to correspond to the system of two tenors, using the same melody but rhythmically interlocked and at different pitches, on which Dufay based his motet.[46] Architectural magnificence and ingenuity found their true mirror in Dufay's carefully contrived musical structure.

A work which might well also have been for the same occasion is Dufay's Sanctus 'Papale' (iv/7): its date is difficult to fix with any certainty, but Charles Hamm suggested that it belongs to 1435–7, basing his conclusion on musical features.[47] And features of the melodic treatment and scoring put it alongside the motet *Nuper rosarum flores*. It seems to contrast and combine a men's choir with a group of choristers supported by two solo voices,[48] something quite possible in Florence which contained many richly endowed churches. And if the Agnus Dei 'Custos et pastor ovium', apparently paired with it, is really by Dufay, it too must date from the same time, perhaps even the same occasion.

Two more motets praise the city of Florence and were presumably composed during the same ten-month period. 'Presumably' because the motet *Salve flos Tusce gentis* (i/15) seems to belong to a new stylistic world and bear more similarity to the works of the 1450s than those of the 1430s; but in different ways the same could be said of *Nuper rosarum flores*, and the orthodox opinion is the logical one, that it was composed in this year. It has a text in elegiac couplets and a tenor from the liturgy for Palm Sunday (which fell on 1 April in 1436, only a week after the dedication of the cathedral). A smaller work is *Mirandas parit hec urbs florentina puellas* (i/5) which is not isorhythmic but freely composed and has a text entirely in classical hexameters.

Dufay's use of strict classical Latin verse-forms for these motets is not unique, by any means; several of his earlier works have texts in such forms, and there are even some examples in the motets of the fourteenth century. But what is impressive here is the richness of allusion to classical myths: *Mirandas parit* mentions Helen of Troy and Diana; *Salve flos Tusce gentis* mentions Nymphs and Naiads, Amazons and Venus; and from two years later his motet *Magnanime gentis* refers to Pegasus.[49] The spirit of humanism and neo-platonic study which was so strong in the Florence of these years seems to have permeated Dufay's work. Whether these motet texts are his it is impossible to tell; but his degree in canon law would have required fluency in Latin; the single letter from his hand shows an educated elegance of style; his will is a splendidly composed document in Latin whereas most of those of his contemporaries at Cambrai were in French; and the instructions for singing the *fauxbourdon* part for the Communion of his Mass *Sancti Jacobi* are written in pure classical hexameters. Some at least of his song and motet texts are likely to be by him; and the use of the first person singular with his own name at the end of *Salve flos Tusce gentis* suggests the same: 'Guillermus cecini, natus et ipse Fay'. Moreover it is difficult to think of a man in his position in fifteenth-century Florence remaining immune to the humanistic movement.

The text of *Mirandas parit* (i/5) praises the ladies of Florence and specifically their extraordinary beauty. Given that Dufay was there for only ten months it is difficult to avoid sensing a certain valedictory air in the music and suggesting that it could only have been written for the papal curia's departure from Florence on 18 April 1436. If that is accepted, and if the date of 1 April for *Salve flos Tusce gentis* is correct, he produced the three motets within a month. Three more radically different works are difficult to imagine. All three are masterpieces of the utmost perfection; and they are as clear an embodiment of the Renaissance as is Brunelleschi's dome.

After the pope moved to Bologna, Dufay stayed with him only one more year. In September the pope procured him a canonry at Cambrai Cathedral with a prebend *pro libera jurista* – one for a man with a degree in law. He was received (*in absentia*) at Cambrai on 12 November 1436; his proctor was again Nicolas Grenon who had been his proctor eight years earlier at St-Géry and whose life so often seems linked with Dufay's, so far as we can tell through the distant screen of the documents.

From a few weeks before Dufay finally left the papal choir there is an entry referring to him in the accounts of the Ferrarese court. On 6 May 1437 Michael de Benintendis requested twenty ducats to be added to his own account in order to repay the twenty ducats which he had given to 'Guielmo de Fait, cantadore in la capella del papa' on the instructions of the Marquis Niccolò III. It is not stated whether Dufay had visited Ferrara (some 50 km. from Bologna) or whether the occasion had been a visit by Niccolò III to Bologna.[50] But this could well be part of a more extended series of transactions between Dufay and the Este court. In October 1443 when Dufay was back in Cambrai he received another twenty ducats from the Marquis – now Leonello d'Este, since Niccolò had died in 1441 – via the Borromei bank in Bruges. And this second document should therefore advise caution about suggesting that his ballade *C'est bien raison* (vi/16) in honour of Niccolò d'Este was necessarily connected with the payment of May 1437. It may be reading the poem too literally (or rather, not carefully enough) to associate it[51] with the peace engineered by Niccolò and signed in April 1433; but to put the work much later than that[52] is to dissociate it too gratuitously from the neighbouring pieces in its only manuscript source: the latest dateable work in that manuscript is from 1436. In the present state of our knowledge, both of the received dates for *C'est bien raison* (1433 and 1437) must be treated as guesses, though I incline towards the earlier.

There are several possible reasons why Dufay left the papal chapel at the end of May 1437. In broad terms, Eugenius was beginning to regard his choir, and music in general, with the kind of austerity that he applied to his personal life: the magnificent music of the preceding years was losing favour in his mind and giving way to a preference for simpler chants.[53] More specifically, though, if Dufay felt any personal commitment to either Amadeus of Savoy or Cardinal Aleman, this was the moment at which continuation in the papal choir would have been difficult.

On 7 May 1437 the anti-pope party had achieved a resounding majority at the Council of Basle. Louis Aleman was the leader of that party. After six years of cautious dealing the Council had dictated – in direct opposition to Eugenius – that any discussion on uniting the Eastern and Western Churches should take place in Basle or, if that seemed unsuitable to the representatives of the Orthodox church, either at Avignon or somewhere in Savoy.[54] In this, of course, Duke Amadeus VIII of Savoy was directly implicated, even if he played his cards with the most brilliant ambiguity over the next three years.

As had happened before in Dufay's life – and was to happen again – his present and past patrons were in direct opposition. June 1437 was probably Dufay's last chance to re-establish contact with the court of Savoy. On 3 July 1437 the Council of Basle demanded that Pope Eugenius come to Basle to stand trial.[55] On 18 September Eugenius issued the bull *Doctoris gentium* transferring the council to Ferrara: the result was, inevitably in the circumstances, two concurrent councils and ultimately once again two concurrent popes.

From an unspecified date in 1437 a payment for Dufay's clothing at the court of Savoy suggests that he returned there soon after leaving the papal choir. His second stay at Savoy would therefore have lasted about two years.[56] During that time he evidently had some freedom of movement – far more, for instance, than the members of the Burgundian ducal chapel whose attendance was required every day. Dufay was present at chapter meetings of Lausanne Cathedral on 25 and 26 August 1437. And in April 1438 he was appointed one of Cambrai Cathedral's representatives at the Council of Basle.

This occasion may well have been a reunion of old friends. Another representative of the cathedral there was Robert Auclou, the 'curate of St-Jacques' whose name had appeared a decade earlier in Dufay's motet *Rite majorem Jacobum canamus*; and on 14 February 1438 Cardinal Aleman, the employer of Auclou and possibly of Dufay in Bologna, had been elected president of the council after his predecessor had obeyed the papal summons to the competing Council of Ferrara. And it is most likely that 1438 is the year in which Dufay composed his curious Latin cantilena *Juvenis qui puellam nondum septennem duxit* (vi/9). Couched in the manner of a legal argument (as might have been appropriate for a bachelor in canon law), the text seems on the surface to be a discussion of the canonical propriety of a youth marrying a girl 'not yet seven years old' and then marrying her cousin. But that girl is surely the Council of Basle, which had opened in July 1431 and was therefore not quite seven years old when Dufay joined it, when Aleman became its president, and when the Council of Ferrara was opened (8 January 1438).[57]

One motet by Dufay definitely comes from this time. *Magnanime gentis* (i/17) has a formal scheme similar to that of his motet for Florence Cathedral, *Nuper rosarum flores*,[58] though it is in only three voices. The pattern that had worked once with such success was being tried again though with modifications and with the smaller forces appropriate to the Savoy court establishment. Its occasion was the peace signed in Berne on Saturday 3 May 1438 between Louis of Savoy (still Prince of Piedmont while his father Amadeus VIII was still nominally duke) and his younger brother Philip, Count

49

of Geneva – 'pregenitum Ludovicum comitemque Philippum' as the motet text has it. The tenor is labelled 'Hec est vera fraternitas' – this is true brotherhood – though their quarrels in the preceding years had been far from fraternal. Both brothers brought extensive retinues with them, as the Berne city accounts testify; and a few days later the celebrations were continued at Fribourg. Here the city accounts record payments for Louis' singers and minstrels.[59]

This motet and the payment for clothing in 1437 are two pieces of evidence that Dufay was at the time nominally with the court of Savoy again. The third and last is a document dated 16 October 1438. In it the treasurer-general records that Dufay with four other court chaplains – the curate of Chanaz-en-Bugey, Elino Fustien, Guillot, and Girardo Bourdon – left Le Bourget for Pinerolo in the hills behind Turin where Louis and his wife Anne de Lusignan were to spend the winter. If Dufay stayed the whole winter there perhaps he was present for the Carnival celebrations early in the next year at which the morality *Tempio dell'Onore e delle Vertù* was performed with elaborate scenery and panoply.[60]

But that summer the Council of Basle took a more complicated turn putting Dufay again in a position that must have made a further move necessary. On 25 June it formally deposed Eugenius IV; and on 5 November it eventually nominated as pope none other than Amadeus VIII of Savoy, now long retired from control of his duchy and living in the monastic Order of St-Maurice which he had founded in his château of Ripaille at Thonon on the banks of Lake Geneva.

This development naturally polarized the European powers. Louis, Duke of Savoy from January 1440, supported his father who had taken the papal name of Felix V; and there was considerable support for this cause both in Eastern Europe and in the universities.[61] But very few of the major powers unequivocally supported the decisions of the small and now strictly non-constitutional Council of Basle, and after ten years of considerable chaos Felix V resigned in April 1449. Meanwhile Duke Philip the Good of Burgundy had firmly established his position as the most powerful political leader in western Europe: he was now the direct overlord of Cambrai Cathedral[62] where Dufay had his most valuable prebend, procured for him by Eugenius IV; and Philip the Good was himself the strongest supporter of Eugenius. Dufay was therefore again in an untenable position. He had received generous patronage from both the present pope and the present antipope; he was employed by the antipope's son in whose lands he had two smallish prebends; but he had in the Low Countries not only his prebend at Cambrai Cathedral but three others at Bruges, Tournai and Cambrai. Personal, political and financial considerations must have made it easy for him to decide to return to Cambrai until things sorted themselves out.

By 9 December 1439 Dufay was back at Cambrai. He was about forty years old, with a lucrative prebend and a list of compositions marking him as the greatest composer the world had yet seen. His *Wanderjahre* had ended.

# 5

# Interim assessment: 1440

Returning to Cambrai at the age of about forty may well have been an occasion for stocktaking. Though he had been there as a choirboy and knew many of his new colleagues from other contexts, Dufay had apparently been back there only once in the intervening twenty-five years; and in the event he remained in Cambrai for all but seven of the thirty-five years left to him.

This is a good point from which to look backwards and forwards because in terms of the surviving information 1440 is a kind of watershed. From 1440 we have much fuller documentation of his life, but paradoxically it is at this point that the information about his compositions begins to seem distressingly scattered. That can be explained by noting various features of the documentation, of the distribution of his music and of modern views on the chronology of his works.

Apart from items in the archives of Cambrai Cathedral and the papal curia, Dufay's life up to 1440 is extremely poorly documented. There are only ten items, one of which has normally been rejected as concerning somebody else of the same name — the one about Guillaume Fays of St-Germain-l'Auxerrois at Paris in 1420. The remainder are: the minutes of two letters requesting his absence from St-Géry at Cambrai which witness his presence in Bologna in 1427–8; four payment records chronicling his first visit to the court of Savoy in 1434–5; two documents concerning his second visit to Savoy; and an entry in the registers of Lausanne Cathedral noting his presence at two chapter meetings in 1437. There is nothing exceptional in this shortage of documents; and indeed what is perhaps more unusual is that Dufay was lucky enough to spend considerable portions of his life at two institutions whose documentation is so complete and so fully preserved. To give a few examples from composers of the time: any original document unequivocally concerned with John Dunstable has yet to be found; our knowledge of Lionel Power's life is based on seven documents, most of which have been found only in the last few years;[1] and Ockeghem's life is pieced together from a handful of documents such as we would have for Dufay if all the documents at Cambrai and Rome were lost. From the biographer's viewpoint, then, Dufay occupies a special position merely by virtue of his association with two particularly well documented institutions.

Further information of considerable value comes from references in his own motets and chansons. Here, however, there really is something exceptional about Dufay. Of other fifteenth-century composers perhaps the only one to leave such a large proportion of clues to occasions within his motets and chansons is the man who seems to be the greatest composer of the preceding generation, Johannes Ciconia. Dunstable left no direct clue anywhere in his music, even though most of his motets and possibly his Masses would have been composed for specific occasions: some have been tentatively identified. Binchois – by all accounts the ceremonial composer extraordinary of the Burgundian court – leaves clues among his extensive surviving work in just one motet (which itself survives in only fragmentary form) and in the acrostic of one of his chansons – referring to a certain 'Robin Hoquerel' who cannot now be identified. One consequence of this is that there is very little tangible information on Dunstable's life, and the same would be the case with Binchois were it not that he spent over thirty years at the court of Burgundy, an institution whose documents are as full and as carefully preserved as those of Cambrai Cathedral (and for the same reason: sheer affluence which needed careful controlling and was worth recording for future generations).

With Dufay the situation is quite different. During the years 1420–40 he composed many ceremonial pieces of various kinds, mostly containing direct evidence of a patron and often at least indirect evidence of an occasion. But what is so tantalizing about this is the information that is still missing. The occasions for the motets *O sancte Sebastiane* (i/8) and *O gemma, lux* (i/9) are still to be identified.[2] And many songs offer a rich source of material for future students of his life in their passing references to particular people. There is still no clue to the identity of 'Cateline Dufai' (or perhaps just a Cateline who was some how linked with Dufay) the acrostic in *Craindre vous vueil* (vi/61), of 'Maria' and 'Andreas' whose names are linked in the acrostic of *Mon cuer me fait* (vi/54, as 'Maria AndreasQ'),[3] of Jehan de Dinant who appears from the acrostic of *Je veuil chanter* (vi/37),[4] or of 'Franchoise' in *Franc cuer gentil* (vi/74); and all but the last of these songs must have been composed before 1440, possibly giving clues to hitherto unsuspected travels and associations in his early years. It is the same with the names included within his song texts: *Ce moys de may* (vi/39) mentions a certain 'Perinet' as co-author, probably as the poet;[5] and, most frustrating of all, *Hé, compaignons* (vi/49) includes no fewer than nine names of those addressed who are exhorted to join in the May Day merrymaking – 'Huchon, Ernoul, Humblot, Henry, Jehan, François, Hughes, Thierry et Godefrin'.[6]

Similarly there are references to occasions that may never be defined. Even among the works that happen to survive there are as many as ten songs that refer specifically to New Year's Day (vi/26, 30, 32, 33, 38, 52, 53, 58, 59, 63), of which all but the last almost certainly predate 1440; and a further five refer to May Day (vi/18, 28, 37, 39, 49), all firmly before 1440. They raise many questions that are difficult to answer. Were they necessarily composed for secular courts or were the choirmen of the papal chapel accustomed to celebrating in this way?[7] Did Dufay perhaps, though a member of the papal chapel, compose such seasonal songs to send to secular courts where they were appreciated? Could Dufay have composed several of his New Year songs for a single year, or can we search for a chronology on the basis of one song per year? If there were occasions when several songs were composed for one New Year's celebration, which songs are likely to belong together in this way? Why is it that Dufay seems to separate himself so clearly from his contemporaries in composing such a large number of these seasonal and convivial songs? How many more such songs by Dufay have been lost? How many more of the songs that do survive were in fact composed specifically for such celebrations but happen not to make any direct reference to the occasion? And is there a clear tradition of such songs discernible not only in Dufay but also among the other composers of his time?[8]

All these questions bear directly on our conception of Dufay's life and work, not only because they could carry clues to further specific evidence of his movements but also because it is precisely these pieces that have played such a large part in making Dufay as a composer seem so sympathetic to modern ears – works with occasions, works that imply a gathering, an audience and an ambience. In this respect Dufay is special. Very few of Binchois' songs, for instance, seem convivial in the same way: they are part of a courtly tradition that is far more distant from the aesthetic that appeals most readily to the modern listener.[9] But at the same time this trend in Dufay's work is characteristic of a new generation, of a certain breaking away from the courtly introspection of the previous three centuries, of a move towards more direct communication, something which will become clear not only from the songs but also from other genres in his work.

So much for documentation. The distribution of his music suffers from a similarly one-sided set of historical accidents. On the basis of the complete edition it looks very much as though fully three-quarters of his music had been composed by 1440 and that in the final thirty-five years of his life he composed rarely – albeit magnificently.

To some extent this is a misleading impression. Various documents refer to works by Dufay which have been lost. Among them there are a Requiem Mass, three laments for the Fall of Constantinople in 1453, a Mass in honour of St Anthony Abbot, a Magnificat in the 7th tone and a sequence in honour of Mary Magdalene.[10] Moreover when he left Cambrai for Savoy in April 1452 the chapter paid him a year's salary in advance 'on account of the virtues and merits of [Dufay] who has adorned this church with musical songs'.

But there is a simple reason for this loss of works from Dufay's later years. The manuscripts containing his music were almost all compiled in Italy or at least in southern Europe.[11] From the Franco-Flemish area where he spent most of his life after 1439 there are only four surviving manuscripts of any consequence: two interrelated choirbooks at Cambrai (nos. 6 and 11), each containing about a tenth of the quantity of music found in the great Italian codices of the time and containing a repertory that is unlikely to go much later than 1435;[12] one chansonnier from the late 1430s (Escorial V. III. 24) evidently compiled when he was still in Italy and therefore containing only five songs by Dufay; and one very mixed choirbook (Brussels 5557) partly compiled at about the time of his death, containing his last two surviving Mass cycles.

From Italy, on the other hand, there are several enormous manuscript collections from the 1430s. Two in Bologna are particularly important, that in the University Library (Ms.2216) and especially that in the Civico Museo Bibliografico Musicale (Q 15, known as BL) which contains some three hundred pieces and nearly all of the sacred music that Dufay is likely to have composed before about 1435. The information from these is amply supplemented by that in the equally large choirbook at Aosta and – more cautiously – by three slightly later sources, the St Emmeram choirbook at Munich (clm 14274) many of whose ascriptions seem doubtful, and the two earliest of the famous Trent codices, Trent 87 and Trent 92.

For the secular music considerable help comes from the manuscript completed in or near Venice in about 1436 which is now in the Bodleian Library at Oxford (Canonici misc. 213). It contains some two hundred pieces of which about sixty are by Dufay, mostly songs. To judge from the evidence of concordant sources, it includes practically all the surviving secular music of Dufay (as well as of Binchois) that had been composed by that date. Here two of Dufay's songs are dated and another has the rubric 'Rome composuit'. That information has been used several times in the preceding chapters, for it must be the backbone of any chronology of his works. The dates are among seven works so dated in the Oxford manuscript and they evidently represent a special effort by the compiler to add historical meaning to his enormous and magnificent collection.[13] Historical awareness of this kind is noticeable in many of the larger medieval music manuscripts. Collections such as the great Notre-Dame manuscripts of the thirteenth century, the beautiful Chantilly codex from the very end of the fourteenth century or the English 'Old Hall' manuscript from early in the fifteenth: all these, and several others, can be seen as attempts to assemble a whole repertory largely for the benefit of posterity. If the Oxford manuscript is a conscious historical document in this sense, it has perhaps contributed uniquely to our perception of Dufay and of his position within fifteenth-century music. It has done so by giving him the lion's share of the representation within what was perhaps a carefully balanced anthology; and to that extent it would seem to reflect the aesthetic and evaluative tastes of the time.

As noted earlier,[14] all these manuscripts are from the north of Italy or from the Empire and it is possible that they therefore give an incomplete account of Dufay's Roman years, 1428–33; but they still provide ample material for an understanding of his stylistic development and an estimate of his interests as a composer up to about 1440.

Moving on past 1440, however, the terrain becomes more

confusing with only one manuscript giving any clear evidence of his work. This is the large manuscript presumably for the Ferrarese court (now Modena, Biblioteca estense, alpha X.1,11, known as ModB) which contains his complete hymn cycle and all that survive of his motets after 1433 as well as a few shorter pieces. It has been dated 1448, but may well be slightly later.[15]

Apart from that and a few manuscripts compiled after his death, there is only the group of seven Trent codices, that astonishing and sometimes terrifying assembly of music from the middle of the fifteenth century, containing nearly fifteen hundred different pieces. The difficulty with the Trent codices is that the two earliest (Trent 87 and 92, perhaps from the mid-1440s for the most part) contain many ascriptions to Dufay which happen to coincide with those in the basically more trustworthy BL and Aosta sources; but the five later manuscripts have very few ascriptions indeed.

More specifically, whereas about half of all the pieces in Trent 87 and 92 have their composers named, and there are forty-one ascribed works in Trent 90, the other manuscripts have practically nothing: nine ascriptions among the 279 works in Trent 93 (with only two for Dufay), thirteen among the 308 pieces in Trent 88 (again two for Dufay, but one is for the now rejected Mass *Caput*), eleven among the 273 pieces in Trent 89 (the only appearance of Dufay's name being carefully erased) and a mere three among the 240 pieces in Trent 91 (with no reference to Dufay).

It is probably in these last three sources that one would expect to find some of the work Dufay composed during the 1440s and 1450s, if it found its way to Italy at all. There could be a hundred pieces or more by Dufay here, but their identification still presents overwhelming difficulties. Laurence Feininger attempted to attribute to Dufay a large series of Mass Proper settings in Trent 88,[16] and I shall offer some tentative support for that in chapter 14; but in general later students have had considerable difficulty in finding ways of agreeing or disagreeing with his views – largely perhaps because with so little clearly identifiable Dufay work from these years there is far less evidence about the ways in which he might have composed.

Crucial to these considerations is the chronology of the later works that happen to survive. And this is perhaps the moment to add a few words on what is probably the most incisive and influential recent book on fifteenth-century musical style, Charles Hamm's *A Chronology of the Works of Guillaume Dufay Based on a Study of*

*Mensural Practice* (1964). Hamm divides Dufay's works into nine main groups on the basis of their notation and mensural treatment; and he assigns each group approximate dates – hence the chronology. But although the grouping is done on largely objective lines, his dates for each group are approximate at best, being based on those apparently firm dates that have come down in the literature. Several of these dates are now shown to be wrong, several more are received guesses, and the ones that do hold can scarcely be used to define the times at which Dufay began or discarded a particular notational usage. That is to say that while the groupings are useful, their chronological implications should be regarded with considerable caution.

To attempt a detailed revision of Hamm's chronology would go well beyond the scope of this book. It is a task for the future. But certain suggestions are offered here: the proposal that many of his songs in fact date from the 1450s (chapter 12), the proposal that the Mass for St Anthony of Padua could have been composed in 1450 (chapter 14) and the observation that throughout his life three-voice music and four-voice music are so different in style that direct comparison is difficult. The biographical chapters question many of the accepted documentary dates for particular works, and much of the chronology needs reconsidering in view of what may be called a new-found ignorance. Moreover the new biographical findings published since 1964 have their direct effect on the chronology of his works; and there is much important work now in progress on the detailed structure of the main manuscripts containing Dufay's music. If this book has a scholarly ambition it is to clear some of the ground for that revision.

# 6

# Cambrai and the south: 1439–1458

A payment record of 9 December 1439 shows that Dufay was back in Cambrai by then, though other less specific records suggest that he had returned some time in the summer or autumn. Documentation is scattered because the chapter acts for 1439–42 are missing, and these are usually the most reliable witness to whether a canon was present. But the chapter acts do show that he was at Cambrai for the remainder of the 1440s, and the accounts indicate that he was often present – probably in permanent residence – during the years 1439–42.[1]

The chapter acts for 1442 also list the other canons who included several former colleagues.[2] Nicolas Grenon and Robert Auclou were there; so were three men who, like Dufay, had enjoyed the privilege of being master of the papal chapel – Matheus Hanelle (1418–20, 1431), Gilles Flannel (1431–3, 1435, 1437–41) and Jehan de la Croix (1433). Beyond that the dean of the chapter from 1431 to 1472 was Gilles Carlier, an eminent theologian who had been at the Council of Basle and was the author of some theoretical writings on music. Of these men only Grenon is now known as a composer, but the new ambience must have been favourable to a composer of Dufay's standing.

Duke Louis of Savoy missed his former chapelmaster. On 5 November 1441 he wrote to Duke Philip the Good of Burgundy in quite specific terms. The letter asks Philip to grant permission for Dufay to return to Savoy without losing the benefit of his prebends in the north. Louis also says of Dufay: '[He] has had the direction of my said chapel and served there in such a manner that I would gladly see him there once again   [and], according to what I understand, [he] would be content to return to my service if it were your pleasure to command him so.'[3] Given the political circumstances – Philip supporting Eugenius IV against the claims of the antipope Felix V, father of Louis – it is unlikely that Philip the Good replied. In fact one might say that it was characteristic of Louis's tactlessness to write such a letter at all. But it suggests that at first Dufay did not regard his return to Cambrai as more than a temporary measure.

If that was the case, Dufay had already changed his mind by the time Louis wrote the letter. Seven weeks earlier he had obtained papal permission from Rome to resign three of his benefices; and early in the next year he resigned the two benefices which he held in Savoyard lands, the curacy of the church of St-Loup at Versoix and the canonry at Lausanne Cathedral. Within the next few years he was to obtain replacement benefices at two churches close to Cambrai: Notre-Dame at Condé and Ste-Waudru at Mons.

This evident decision to remain at Cambrai for the foreseeable future is further confirmed by his acceptance of several administrative obligations in the cathedral. Given the loss of the chapter acts for 1439–42 some details may be missing. But in December 1442 he was asked to oversee the statutes of the chapter; at about the same time he succeeded Grenon as master of the *petits vicaires*; he was appointed to review many of the cathedral accounts; and in 1445 he moved from the Maison du Bregier (where he had presumably lived with his mother who died in the previous year) to one of the finest canonical residences, the large house in the rue de l'Ecu d'or next to the house occupied by Nicolas Grenon.[4] Illustration 13 shows a view of the magnificent cathedral almost exactly as it would have been seen from Dufay's new home.

Two motets that have always been considered to belong to the 1440s can now be placed with some confidence in 1442.

One is *Fulgens iubar* (i/18) with an acrostic in its second text, *Puerpera, pura parens*: the first letters of each line combine to form the words PETRUS DE CASTELLO CANTA. The earliest reference to Petrus in the Cambrai accounts has hitherto been overlooked and appears in the Almonry Office for 21 January 1442 as a payment to 'Domino Petro du Castel magistro puerorum altaris'.[5] Petrus remained master of the choirboys until 1447, at which point he seems to have left under a cloud. The accounts in that year include several increased payments for choirboys who came and went with considerable frequency. The final entry, dated 1 August 1447, reads: 'Item: solute fuerunt domino Petro du Castel pro expensis unius pueri de Perona qui non fuit receptus quia non habebat vocem: £12.'[6] The sum paid for this boy from Péronne who was not admitted to the choir 'because he had no voice' is enormous; and it is no surprise to see that the next reference to a master of the choirboys is to 'Goberto' – Gobert le Mannier who was later a beneficiary of Dufay's will. The first boy added by Gobert cost the chapter £2.[7]

This description of Petrus du Castel's demise is relevant because it increases the possibility that the motet *Fulgens iubar* was composed early in his career at Cambrai, when he was still in favour. In fact it would be reasonable to suppose that it was for his induction around the beginning of 1442. Since the tenor is based on a Responsory for the Virgin Mary and the triplum text refers specifically to the feast of the Purification it seems likely that the motet was composed for that day – 2 February 1442.

This in its turn makes it possible to reconsider the occasion of the other motet, *Moribus et genere* (i/19). Since it mentions the town of Dijon in its text several earlier writers associated it with the year 1446 when Dufay was sent by the Cambrai chapter on a mission to the Burgundian court. But the Burgundian court was at the time in Brussels, not Dijon;[8] and in fact after about 1420 the Burgundian dukes scarcely ever went to their nominal capital in far-away Burgundy except to be buried. So the date 1446 for the motet must be discarded. Yet in its structure and its style the work is remarkably similar to *Fulgens iubar* and a date close to it would make more sense.

In 1439 Jean de Bourgogne, the illegitimate half-brother of Duke Philip the Good, had been appointed Bishop of Cambrai. At the time he was still a student and he never developed much attachment to the ecclesiastical life or to Cambrai. His consecration as bishop was itself done at Hesdin.[9] But his first entry into Cambrai in 1442 was celebrated in considerable style. Its description appears in the records of the church of St-Aubert – understandably enough since this was the religious house at Cambrai which was open primarily to the nobility, and the one in which members of the Burgundian ducal house tended to stay on visits to the city.

His proposed entry was announced two months ahead, early in May 1442. When he arrived at Cambrai on Tuesday 10 July, he was met by various dignitaries of the city, including Robert Auclou, before going to Mass at the cathedral where it was *bien solempnellement cantée*.[10] On the last day of his visit, 3 August, there was a grand dinner in his honour at St-Aubert. The description of that event includes the following comments: 'At dinner there was great jubilation with the choirboys of Notre-Dame [Cambrai Cathedral] and St-Géry who sang several times one after the other, with trumpets, with minstrels, with the singers of our lord [the bishop] and many instruments."[11]

The motet *Moribus et genere* mentions Dijon at the end; but the reference could well be simply to the city from which Jean de Bourgogne took his name, perhaps even to the city where he was born. More important, the main dedicatee of the motet is St John the Evangelist, which could have been taken as an eminently suitable reference to Bishop John. The evidence is circumstantial, but to suggest that *Moribus et genere* was written for the occasion fits well with its style and with the available facts.

I therefore wish to propose 1442 as the possible date for both motets. They are not only similar to one another but strikingly different in style from Dufay's previous motet, *Magnanime gentis* of 1438. They are broader works, more detailed and more expansive in their efforts to supply long-range tonal design to the isorhythmic schemes that Dufay had inherited from the previous century. Their musical complexity is a reminder that Dufay was once again resident in one of Europe's premier musical establishments, comparable only with the papal choir of the early 1430s and the Burgundian court choir.

So it is all the more surprising that so little of his surviving work seems likely to date from the 1440s. It is possible that some of his antiphon settings (v/37–45) were composed during these years; and in chapter 14 I shall propose tentatively that he may have composed a systematically conceived set of Mass Proper cycles.

But the only other work normally placed in these years is the brief song *Seigneur Leon, vous soyés bienvenus* (vi/85) which Dragan Plamenac ingeniously attributed to Dufay and dated 1444.[12] About the attribution there can be little doubt: it rests primarily on the visible tail of the letter 'y' from an ascription formerly in the Pixérécourt manuscript and cut off in binding. There is just a slight possibility that the name could have been 'Joye' or 'Busnoys'; but the stylistic similarity of Dufay's *O proles Hispanie* (i/6) adds strong support to the identification, and Plamenac himself noted similarities in *Juvenis qui puellam* (vi/9).

More problematic is the date. Working from the text, Plamenac suggested that it was a welcome song for the elevation of a bishop or archbishop named 'Leon' or Leo; and he concluded that the only feasible subject of the song was Leonard of Chios who became Archbishop of Mytilene in 1444. Mytilene was a crucial province in the history of attempts at union between the Roman and Byzantine churches in the conciliar epoch; and Dufay's interest in Byzantine matters through the Malatesta connection twenty years earlier is further testified by the four laments for the Fall of Constantinople which he was to compose a decade later. Leonard of Chios is famous today for having provided the fullest western eye-witness account of the Fall. But this remains a worrying identification, not least because Dufay was at Cambrai in 1444 (information probably not known to Plamenac in 1953 when he published his article: the orthodoxy of the time was that Dufay was studying law in Turin); and there is little to suggest that he was at all interested in an Archbishop of Mytilene. Nor is it entirely clear that the 'Leon' named in the text is a bishop; he could be any eminent personage. Various suggestions have been offered;[13] but the name that springs most easily to mind is perhaps that of Leonello d'Este, Marquis of Ferrara, particularly in view of Leonello's payment to Dufay of twenty ducats received through the Borromei bank at Bruges in 1443. The poem is compatible with the theory that the work was composed for Leonello's induction as marquis early in 1442; the style of the music suggests a similar date; and the payment is evidence that Dufay was then in touch with the Ferrarese court.

Yet if there is only slim evidence that Dufay continued composing at all prolifically during the 1440s, there are many other activities which could have filled his time. His administrative duties at Cambrai Cathedral have already been mentioned; but there were more. Early in 1446 he began to supervise the methodical recopying of the cathedral music books that was to continue for many years.[14] In February the chapter acts record his contract with Jean de Namps of Amiens for the preparation of new graduals and antiphoners into which the chant would be added by Girard Sohier of Douai (apparently a member of the family which included the composer Jean Sohier, called Fedé); and very soon after that we find payments for copying done by the *petit vicaire* Simon Mellet who was to continue this activity until after Dufay's death.[15] Mellet's music copying seems to have been largely of polyphony whereas Jean de Namps and Girard Sohier almost certainly copied only chant. Many subsequent entries in the accounts record Dufay's continued involvement with this copying in a supervisory capacity; and we shall see in due course that it may well have entailed a careful rescrutiny of the chants and their musical readings.

Another preoccupation at this time may have come from his canonry at the collegiate church of Ste-Waudru in Mons: Dufay's funeral monument gave a prominent place to the figure of Ste-Waudru, suggesting that this church was of some importance to him. Binchois was born in Mons and had been organist at Ste-Waudru from a relatively early age, becoming one of its ten male canons in 1438.[16] The chapter acts of St-Donatien in Bruges show that in the mid-1440s Dufay was having some difficulty collecting his full income there,[17] and on 4 October 1446 he resigned that benefice appointing, among others, Binchois as his proctor for obtaining a new one. Three days later he was sent by the Cambrai chapter to the Burgundian court at Brussels to resolve a small legal dispute. Ten days after that, on his way back from Brussels, he was received in person as a canon of Ste-Waudru.

Two and a half years later Dufay again visited Mons. This was to consider the plans for a new church of Ste-Waudru.[18] The chapter had decided that their Romanesque church was too small for such an eminent establishment (though a surviving drawing shows that it was a beautifully decorative church in the finest thirteenth-century style). So they planned to demolish it in favour of the grand edifice which stands today. In February 1449 they summoned their absent canons; and on 3 March Dufay arrived with Binchois and Nicaise du Puis, first chaplain to the Duke of Burgundy.

Quite how Dufay felt about the demolition of that old building history does not relate. As one who had probably known Alberti and Brunelleschi, who had been in Rome and Florence through some of the most crucial years of the early Renaissance in architecture he may have felt somewhat ambivalent; but for the same reasons his advice was perhaps especially welcome. The resulting new building (ill. 16), which impressively overlooks the town of Mons and is visible from some distance, shows an uneasy compromise between the still remaining Gothic ideals of the north and the classical aspirations of the new Italian Renaissance. And in its ungainly way Ste-Waudru could be seen to symbolize a stylistic dichotomy that was still being resolved in Dufay's own music, particularly in the two large motets of 1442: the fall from favour of intricate gothicism and the increased desire for clarity on a large scale.

When Dufay attended the meeting at Mons in March 1449 he arrived from Brussels together with two members of the Burgundian court choir. How long had he been there? It has been suggested that he left Cambrai with Philip the Good's court in January.[19] The court had visited Cambrai, arriving on the evening of Sunday 19 January, and leaving on Tuesday 21 January. The duke's own chapel had sung Mass on both Sunday and Monday (in the cathedral; Grenon read the gospel). The report of their visit describes how the departure was delayed and two of the choirboys sang a chanson with one of the gentlemen: 'Après fut grant tamps attendant apres ses gens especialement M. d'Estampes et vinrent devant luy II petits des enfans d'autel et canterent une canchonette de le quelle un de ses Gentils Hommes tint le tenure.'[20]

It seems possible that Dufay indeed left Cambrai at that time and spent the next six weeks at the Burgundian court, for there is considerable evidence that he had some official connection with the court. He never appears in the exceptionally full court accounts and therefore almost certainly did not have a salaried position. But the document recording his privilege of absence from St-Donatien at Bruges in June 1440 describes him as 'familiarus et cappellanus . . . domini ducis'[21] – a member of the household and a chaplain to the Duke of Burgundy – precisely the same wording used a year earlier for Binchois[22] who was a permanent member of the ducal choir. Moreover it was to Philip the Good that Louis of Savoy wrote in 1441 requesting Dufay's return; and when he eventually did return to Savoy in 1450 he was described in the Savoy court accounts as 'cantor illustrissimus domini ducis burgundiae' – most illustrious singer of our lord the Duke of Burgundy.

Of course these comments must be treated with caution: the court of Savoy need not necessarily have been fully informed of Dufay's precise situation, and the letter of 1441 is more concerned with political matters over which Philip the Good unquestionably had control. But there is a further detail. When in 1446 Dufay was installed at Ste-Waudru he seems again to have been described as a chaplain to the Duke of Burgundy ('seems' because the actual document was destroyed by bombing in 1940 and is known only from a French summary which has sometimes been interpreted as though it were the document itself). It has been suggested that this was an error made because when he was installed Dufay happened to have come straight from a visit to the court of Burgundy, where he had been on Cambrai Cathedral business.[23] Moreover one could add that the canonry and prebend at Mons had been obtained for him by several of the Burgundian court chaplains.[24] But these details taken together

– including the previously unnoticed documents in Bruges – make it difficult to avoid the conclusion that he had official standing at the Burgundian court even though nothing appears in the court account books. Philip the Good had many pressing matters of state to attend to, but it is more than probable that he – like the canons of Cambrai – valued the return to the north of the man who was by then uncontestably Europe's leading composer.

In 1450, however, Dufay returned south. In February 1447 Pope Eugenius IV had died and was succeeded by Nicholas V who predictably saw his first job as to resolve the schism with diplomacy. Accordingly, in April 1449 the Savoyard antipope Felix V was persuaded to sign his act of abdication: the Council of Basle had been acting against Eugenius, not against the Roman papacy in general. Ten years of schism in western Europe thereby ended. Dufay was once again free to visit Savoy without risking his northern prebends; and the speed with which he made use of the new opportunity suggests a certain eagerness to leave the city where he had had considerable standing and security but perhaps little production as a composer.

Between 11 March and 15 December 1450 he is not named as being present in any Cambrai document; and Jehan de la Croix was appointed master of the *petits vicaires* as a temporary replacement. The only record of Dufay's presence elsewhere is the payment registered in the Savoy court accounts for him and nine monks to stay at the inn 'del Capello' in Turin for a week at the end of May. Duke Louis of Savoy paid these costs, perhaps as a way of re-establishing contact with his former chapelmaster.

Normally this visit to Italy is taken as being a pilgrimage to Rome for the Jubilee declared by Pope Nicholas V. Its purpose was to restore confidence in church unity after many years of schism and conciliar debate; all pilgrims received complete absolution of their sins – something perhaps specially necessary to a man who had been present at the Council of Basle. But the enormous crowds that descended on Rome brought with them disease, and by Ascension Day there was an epidemic in Rome from which many pilgrims died.

By an attractive coincidence there is another probable reason for Dufay's visit to Italy. Exactly two weeks after he and the nine monks left Turin there occurred one of the great events of fifteenth-century cultural history, the dedication of Donatello's magnificent altar in the basilica of St Anthony at Padua.[25]

Dufay's will mentions a volume containing his Mass for St Anthony of Padua, directing in particular that the Mass be sung annually at Cambrai in his memory. The evidence of the will is that he felt some special devotion to this saint, who was widely revered throughout western Europe; so it does not necessarily follow that a Mass by him for St Anthony of Padua was for this occasion. But at that stage in history it is likely that most complete Mass cycles were for particular events; and here we have an event at which Dufay could have been present with a group of nine 'religiosi' (as the document describes them) who may well have been singers.

Fortunately the will is unusually precise in specifying the performing forces needed for this Mass when it was to be sung in his memory; it calls for several of the better singers, whether they be *grands vicaires* or *petits vicaires*, as well as the master of the boys; and more particularly it leaves 30s to pay for it, specifying that each singer should receive 3s 4d – that is to say that there were nine singers, all men, precisely the forces Dufay seems to have had with him at Turin a fortnight before the dedication of Donatello's altar.

There are at least two occasions on which Dufay could have met Donatello. The sculptor was at Rome in 1433 at the time of Sigismund's coronation as Holy Roman Emperor just after the event celebrated by Dufay's motet *Supremum est mortalibus bonum* (i/14).[26] Art historians today mostly reject Vasari's story that Donatello was there to advise his brother Simone on the tombstone of Pope Martin V at Santa Maria Maggiore,[27] but there is clear documentation that he was in Rome. Whether the two met then is obviously a matter of speculation; but it is more than likely that they would have met in Florence in 1435–6 since Donatello was Brunelleschi's bosom-companion, and the form of Dufay's motet *Nuper rosarum flores* (i/16) argues strongly that the composer had consulted specifically with the architect. While there is no documentation that Dufay and Donatello met, it would perhaps be surprising if Dufay was not acquainted with the contemporary whose career and manner of artistic expression so closely matched his own.

Padua throughout the fourteenth and fifteenth centuries had a distinguished record of arts patronage – a record beginning with Giotto's paintings in the Arena Chapel (possibly celebrated in a motet by Marchetto of Padua),[28] including the state motets of Ciconia and crowned by Donatello's great altar. So even without any direct evidence that Dufay was present for the dedication or wrote his Mass for it, the coincidence of dates and of the number of singers is difficult to resist.[29]

As it happens, Dufay's Mass for St Anthony of Padua can now be identified. We shall see in chapter 14 that it is the one formerly known as the Mass for St Anthony *de Viennois* (ii/3); and that will be the place to discuss the feasibility of putting the work as late as 1450.

A recent suggestion that during this year Dufay composed his four-voice Mass *Se la face ay pale* (iii/7) for the wedding of Charlotte of Savoy to Dauphin Louis (March 1451) has now been withdrawn.[30] This was a short visit to Italy and Savoy. By December 1450 he was back at Cambrai playing an active part in running the cathedral chapter, attending meetings, installing new singers and canons, debating the matter of a new bell for the cathedral's magnificent chime, arranging – as he had done so often before – at Trinity 1451 that new robes be bought for the choirboys.

But in April 1452 the chapter paid him a year's emoluments in advance in recognition of his contribution to the cathedral music. And although he is mentioned in another Cambrai document, of June 1452, he need not necessarily have been present at the time. So far as we can tell he left Cambrai in or after April 1452, not to return until the end of 1458.

This absence from Cambrai is the one mentioned in the executors' account of his will which notes a payment to Pierre de Wez for having looked after Dufay's house during the seven years he was at Savoy. Strictly speaking it was six and a half years (seven summers if not seven winters) though this perhaps included the six months' absence in 1450.

Exactly where the fifty-year old composer spent these years is not at all clear. The function of a legal document compiled after his death twenty years later was to account for payments, not to chronicle his life. And it would be taking it too literally to assume that Dufay actually spent the whole time at the Savoy court. In fact only three documents have so far been found to witness his association with that court during the 1450s.

The first is a letter written to him evidently while he was in Cambrai on 22 October 1451: the year does not appear on the letter, but it is now bound together with other letters from that year and all writers have assumed 1451 to be the correct date. The letter thanks

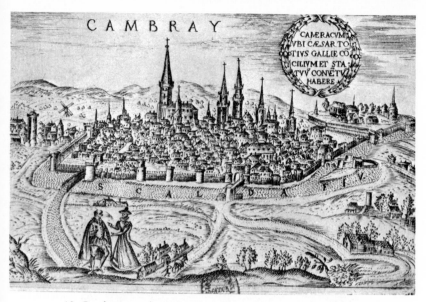

12. Cambrai seen from the West. The cathedral is left of centre.
In front is the River Scheldt (Escaut), the notional boundary line
between the Holy Roman Empire and the Kingdom of France (though at
this point the boundary went round the west of the Diocese of Cambrai).
Sixteenth-century engraving.

13. Cambrai Cathedral as it was in Dufay's day.
View from approximately where Dufay lived in the rue de l'Ecu d'or.
Eighteenth-century painting.

14. Nouvion-le-Vineux, near Laon. Parish church.

15. Chambéry, château of the Dukes of Savoy. The Sainte-Chapelle,
venue for the nuptial Mass of Louis of Savoy and Anne de Lusignan,
is on the right, with an added (seventeenth-century) façade.
Seventeenth-century engraving.

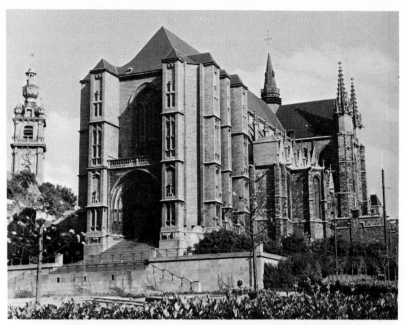

16. Mons, Ste-Waudru as rebuilt while Dufay was a canon, see p.64.

17. Florence, Santa Maria del Fiore and Brunelleschi's dome,
consecrated with Dufay's motet *Nuper rosarum flores* in 1436.
To the left is Giotto's bell-tower, and to the left of that is
the Baptistery, the home of the polyphonic choir for which
Dufay provided singers in 1467.

18. Dufay's autograph letter to Piero and Giovanni de' Medici, see p.71

19. Dufay's autograph receipt for salary due to the late André Picard.

him for sending some cloth to the court (presumably the famous cambric), begs him to return to Savoy as soon as possible, and addresses him as 'counseiller et maistre de la chapelle de Monseigneur' – councillor and chapel-master to the duke. Assuming the date to be correct, he was therefore already master of the chapel while still residing at Cambrai.

The two other documents are both from 1455. On New Year's Day he received the traditional gift from the duke and duchess. And on 8 November he signed a receipt (ill. 19) for salary due to André Picard, a recently deceased singer in the chapel for whom Dufay was executor. Both documents describe him as master of the chapel. Yet the complete payment registers for the chapel happen to survive for the 1450s, and Dufay's name appears nowhere among them. Moreover, as we shall see, a letter to the Medici brothers written early in the next year is suspiciously devoid of any reference to such a position.

Clearly he had some kind of association with the court. Equally clearly – it seems to me – his position was largely an honorary one and by no means bound him to residence in Savoy. And at this stage Dufay was such an eminent man that he could well have been able to negotiate an association with the court on his own terms, perhaps simply as a general adviser on musical matters.

Since Dufay's previous residence at Savoy in the 1430s some aspects of court life and its music had changed. With the death of Amadeus VIII in January 1451, Louis and Anne were for the first time fully in control of their personal and political fortunes. The chapel establishment now included nine to eleven singers (including two called *tenori*) as well as an organist and a *tromba* – presumably a slide trumpet player capable of performing sophisticated polyphony with the choir.[31] There is no longer any evidence of boy choristers – though the instruction and administration of choirboys was often a separate matter accounted separately or even arranged in connection with some nearby church, so this should not be taken as evidence that they were not available to perform Dufay's music. (Turin Cathedral had choirboys from 1438.)

It is probably with reference to these later years that the anonymous author of the *Chronica latina Sabaudiae* described Louis as being a particularly avid musical patron: 'His glory was in having numerous and sumptuous singers . . . and he took pride in hearing *cantus* and *cantilenas* [perhaps: polyphony and songs] each day.'[32]

Certainly surviving sources suggest that this last visit to Savoy gave rise to a new spate of song composition. Over twenty of his secular works can be dated with some confidence in the 1450s (see p. 159); and it is as though Savoy now had the same effect that it had had on him twenty years earlier when an apparently fairly thin period in Rome gave way to a new burst of creative energy.

Perhaps these years also saw the composition of his first great cantus firmus Masses, on *Se la face ay pale* (iii/7) and *L'homme armé* (iii/8). On the basis of their surviving sources they could have been composed much later; and the stylistic evidence of the four cantus firmus cycles is difficult to evaluate. But the *Se la face ay pale* cycle might reasonably be connected with the Savoy court since the ballade on which it was based (vi/19) almost certainly dates from his Savoy years in the late 1430s and could well have been associated with Duke Louis and his duchess. In fact it is even possible that the Mass could be for the consummation of the wedding of Louis' eldest son Amadeus (later Duke Amadeus IX) and Yolande de France, daughter of King Charles VII. Yolande had been resident at the Savoy court since their marriage as infants in August 1436; the consummation followed the payment of the dowry at the treaty of Le Cleppé on 27 October 1452.[33]

The treaty of Le Cleppé led to an even grander treaty at St-Pourçain in December 1455. On this occasion Duke Louis took his entire household to the king's castle: there is a payment record for the choir's new clothing specifically for the visit;[34] and it seems that Dufay was there also. Charles VII also had a large retinue at St-Pourçain. Ockeghem was probably present as head of the royal chapel; and it has even been suggested that the *L'homme armé* Masses of both composers were for that occasion (though considerations raised in chapter 15 make that seem unlikely, or at best unproven).

Another person present at St-Pourçain for the treaty was the foremost statesman and poet of the age, Duke Charles of Orleans.[35] I have elsewhere drawn attention to the fact that three of Dufay's chansons set texts by poets of Charles's circle.[36] *Malheureulx cueur* (vi/24) is by Le Rousselet, *Mon bien m'amour* (vi/71) is by Charles d'Albret, and *Les douleurs* (vi/84) is by Anthoine de Cuise. And I speculated that Dufay must therefore have had some contact with the court of Charles of Orleans during the 1450s. Surely this was the occasion? And even if Dufay could have made a special visit to the duke's court at Blois, St-Pourçain is the one place where we know for certain that the composer could have met the most renowned poet of his day.

This fits in neatly with the information in Dufay's sole surviving autograph letter (ill. 18), written from Geneva on 22 February, probably of the next year, 1456.[37] The letter is addressed to Piero and Giovanni de' Medici in Florence. In it Dufay states that he is sending 'some chansons which I made recently while I was in France with Monseigneur de Savoye at the request of several lords of the king's household' – evidence that the meeting was a musical and social as well as a political one.

Dufay also writes that he has recently composed four laments at the Fall of Constantinople (May 1453), three of which are in four parts. Only one of these survives – *O tres piteulx* (vi/10), in four parts. The other two four-part laments and the (presumably) three-part lament have been lost.[38] So the letter is the earliest unambiguous evidence of missing Dufay works. He writes that the texts had been sent to him from Naples, a city with which he is not otherwise known to have had any association. But the composition of these four laments betokens a substantial concern with the Fall of Constantinople, something which is perhaps to be expected from the composer who wrote a motet for a princess who married into the Byzantine imperial family and another for the last major celebration of Catholic rule in the Peloponnese.

The tone of the letter is surprising. Dufay gives the impression of seeking employment. Although he mentions the Duke of Savoy, it is only in passing – 'while I was in France with Monseigneur de Savoye'. He omits to describe himself as the duke's chapelmaster, but rather signs the letter 'your humble chaplain and insignificant servant, Guillaume Dufay, canon of Cambrai'. To interpret this formula precisely may be impossible: an isolated fifteenth-century document is far too easily misconstrued. But it would be no surprise if subsequent discoveries were to show that between 1456 and his return to Cambrai at the end of 1458 Dufay was somewhere far from Savoy and possibly even in Florence.

One possibility is that he visited the art-loving Duke René of Anjou – known as 'Good King René' though his throne of Sicily was effectively lost to Alfonso of Aragon in 1441. In his will Dufay mentions among his property a knife sent to him by the King of Sicily; and by a strange coincidence René gave a similarly described knife to Charles of Orleans when on a visit to Charles's court at Blois in 1457.[39] The knife that apparently matches one given to so important a political and artistic figure as Charles of Orleans implies a more than casual association between René and the composer.

The final document of Dufay's years away from Cambrai tells of a visit to St-Etienne, Besançon, on 14 September 1458; since he was back in Cambrai by 6 November the visit was probably a stage on his route from the south. One reason for the visit may have been that a canon there, Pierre Grosseteste, was a former colleague at the papal chapel in the 1430s.[40] Grosseteste was one of the two witnesses of the document recording Dufay's presence at Besançon. The fascination of the document, however, is that it relates how the canons asked Dufay to judge the mode of the antiphon *O quanta est exultatio angelicis turmis*.[41] His opinion was that it was in the second mode, not the fourth, and that if it seemed otherwise this was because of scribal corruption.

That a former papal singer was among those seeking his opinion on this suggests a considerable respect for what today would be called Dufay's musicological insight and knowledge. And his response is one that seems truly musicological in its nature. He had of course been in Florence and Rome during the 1430s at precisely the time when the great text-critical scholars were first coming to grips with such problems in the Greek and Latin classical texts. But other evidence of Dufay's musicological interests can be seen in the marginal references to his statements on mensuration in an early Gafori manuscript (now at Parma) as well as from Fétis's statement that he had seen a theory treatise ascribed to Dufay.[42] Further to this it is worth pointing to the series of manuscripts copied at Cambrai under Dufay's supervision: some were of new polyphony, but the Graduals, Alleluias and antiphons copied in the late 1440s sound from their descriptions (including later references to correction) very much as though they represent a new redaction by Dufay of the Cambrai chants. His works point to the same conclusion; again and again they show a careful reconsideration of notational principles, an absorption of different styles and a preoccupation with new technical problems.

# 7

# Last years and aftermath

Dufay was now about sixty years old, and perhaps no further explanation is needed for his return to Cambrai even though he was to live for another sixteen years.[1] Yet his activities show that he was scarcely decrepit. Not only did he again take control of the *petits vicaires* until 1464 but he served the cathedral in many other administrative positions. There are even documents that show him going out to survey canal damage (3 March 1461) and directing a tree-cutting expedition (9 June 1461) – both events followed by apparently lavish entertainment in his own house.[2] Also in 1461 he helped prepare an inventory of cathedral property: among the items recorded was a magnificent reliquary of gilded silver which had been donated to the cathedral by Dufay himself.[3]

Similarly, in 1460 he joined Nicolle Boidin and Jehan de la Croix in recommending the dismissal of the master of the choristers, Robert le Canonne, who seems to have followed the pattern of Petrus du Castel a decade earlier in becoming increasingly unsuitable. In this case Dufay may have shown his age for he was entrusted with the appointment of a successor, but after two years' unsatisfactory negotiations with the composer Johannes Regis he only managed to give a permanent appointment to the temporary master, Jean du Sart.[4]

On the other hand there is plenty of evidence that in these years he was a considerable adornment to Cambrai's musical life. It was presumably partly on account of Dufay that Charles, Count of Charolais, visited Cambrai in October 1460. The future Duke of Burgundy had composed a motet which was sung for him, as casually recorded on a leaf at the back of one of the cathedral's chant books: 'Charles Count of Charoloys, son of Philip Duke of Burgundy etc, made a motet and all its music, which was sung in his presence after Mass had been said in the venerable church of Cambray by the master and the boys, on 23 October 1460, which was the day of St Severin.'[5] The motet is lost, but two songs apparently by Charles survive.[6] In many ways Charles was an even greater patron of music than his father Philip the Good. It was Charles who cultivated Busnoys and Hayne van Ghizeghem as well as several other important composers, and there is copious evidence of his love for music – whereas the available information about Philip the Good suggests that he regarded music simply as a magnificent ornament to his glory.

It may have been on this occasion or one of Charles's later visits to Cambrai (in December 1462 and with King Louis XI in October 1468) that Dufay gave six music books to him. The executors' account of Dufay's will mentions them: 'Item: six books of various music (*divers chanteries*) which the said deceased had given to . . . the Duke of Burgundy: because the gift was made during his lifetime and he merely retained the use of them they have not been valued and no sum is received for them.'[7] The books were duly sent to the duke at Doullens.

Another visitor to Cambrai was Ockeghem who was there in June 1462 and again in March 1464.[8] On the latter occasion the documents record that he actually stayed at Dufay's house, and it seems likely that he did so also in 1462. Ockeghem had by then been first chaplain to the King of France for over ten years and was the most distinguished living musician apart from Dufay. In the year 1463–4 Dufay's Mass *Ecce ancilla Domini* (iii/9) was copied twice into the cathedral music books. Since it shows certain similarities to Ockeghem's Mass of the same name (though based on a different chant) there is every likelihood that the Mass was newly composed when it was copied and had some direct connection with one of Ockeghem's two visits.

Certainly the copying accounts show that Dufay was almost as active as ever. From 1459–60 Simon Mellet appears in the accounts as having copied music on the instructions of Dufay: over the next fifteen years the works Mellet copied make an impressive list in several ways.[9]

First, there is simply the quantity of copying – this time mostly polyphony whereas much of the copying from the 1440s was of monophonic chants. In the first year 120 folios of large paper were filled, though there is no information about precisely what they contained. The payments in subsequent years show that the quantity continued.

Second, most of the works are by younger composers; and

Dufay's music right up to the end shows an inexhaustible curiosity in the work of his juniors. Some of these pieces can be related to compositions by Dufay: in 1462–3 there is the Mass *L'homme armé* by Regis, who had recently declined the invitation to become master of the boys at Cambrai; and an anonymous Mass based on Dufay's rondeau *Le serviteur* – perhaps the four-voice one by Guillaume Faugues. Other works copied in the same year include a Sanctus and a new sequence for St Anne, both by Petit Jehan. In the next year there is a Mass by Rasse de Lavanne and the Kyrie of the anonymous English *Caput* Mass as well as two Masses brought from Antwerp; in 1464–5 follow Regis's Mass *Crucis* and an unascribed Mass *Da pacem*. In later years we find works by Caron, Fremiet and Ockeghem.

But third, there was a considerable body of compositions by Dufay himself. Some writers have tended to conclude that many items mentioned without the name of a composer are in fact by Dufay. But even apart from such dubious works he is specified as the composer of several large pieces. In 1462–3 his newly composed Magnificat in the 7th tone was added; in 1463–4 as well as the Mass *Ecce ancilla Domini* (iii/9) there was the newly composed hymn *O quam glorifica*; and in 1464–5 his sequence for Mary Magdalene. Apart from the Mass, none of these works can be identified today.[10]

Age was perhaps telling, however. In September 1460 his contemporary Binchois had died at Soignies; and it seems most likely that Dufay's song *En triumphant de Cruel Dueil* (vi/72) was composed in his memory[11] – a magnificent and elaborate rondeau that makes a worthy companion to the work more clearly composed for the same occasion, Ockeghem's ballade *Mort tu as navré de ton dart*. In 1464–5 Mellet was paid for copying Dufay's antiphon *Ave regina celorum* which filled two openings and is therefore almost certainly the late four-voice setting (v/51) with interspersed tropes in which the composer names himself and begs forgiveness for his sins. These tropes effectively exclude the antiphon from general liturgical performance. And in fact it was surely intended to be sung at Dufay's own deathbed, precisely as later requested in his last will.

Some documents from a few years later show Dufay maintaining contact with the court of Savoy and with Italy. In 1468–9 the Savoy court accounts record a payment of four ducats to 'Messire Gile Crepin,'[12] who had come from Picardy and was on his way to Rome bringing from 'Messire Guillaume Du Fays' some Masses newly composed (probably his Mass *Ecce ancilla Domini* but presumably at least one other about which we otherwise know nothing).

From about the same time is a letter of 1 May 1467 from Antonio Squarcialupi to Dufay. The great Florentine organist was writing on behalf of the Medici family, and the obsessive flattery pervading his letter is perhaps a clue to the success of Medici patronage. At the time of Dufay's stay at Florence thirty years earlier in 1435–6 the young Squarcialupi had been organist of Santa Maria del Fiore for three years;[13] and it is again characteristic of the Medici style that Squarcialupi should have been chosen to write the letter. He acknowledges a letter from Dufay[14] and discusses some singers who had recently arrived at Florence for the Baptistery choir. According to Squarcialupi's letter they had been trained and recommended by Dufay; and documents survive recording the journey three months earlier of a Medici emissary to find new singers in the Low Countries and particularly at 'Cambrai and Douai where there are many singers and . . . friends'.[15] Squarcialupi tells how much the success of these new singers had pleased Piero de' Medici (who was effective controller of the choir). Piero 'asserts . . . that you are the greatest ornament of our age'.

Squarcialupi then passes on to talk of Piero's son Lorenzo – then eighteen years old – who, he says, 'delights exceedingly in the greater refinement of your music, and for that reason admires your art and respects you as a father'. The letter continues:

> He too wishes to have something of his own from your extraordinary achievement. So I enclose a poem which he desires to have set to music and adorned with song by you. I earnestly beg you to do this and send it to him. Because of his nobility and generosity he is worthy of your offering.
>
> This would also give me great pleasure; and I tender deep thanks to you. Would that I could see and hear you, as you also seem to wish, according to your letter. I would certainly value no other pleasure more highly. I am entirely your servant. I recommend myself to you.
>
> From Florence, on the first day of May 1467: Antonio Squarcialupi of Florence, called Master Antonio the organist of Florence.

That Dufay was seriously contemplating another visit to Italy seems unlikely. Squarcialupi's eager welcome is merely a further aspect of Medici flattery. So, perhaps, is the date: May Day. Dufay had excelled in the composition of May Day songs, and the date could well acknowledge the fact: a musician concerned with secular musical activity (as Squarcialupi apparently was) would surely have had little time for letter-writing on that day. It is as though everything in the letter was carefully calculated to charm Dufay and persuade him to set Lorenzo's poem.

The complete poem follows, *Amore ch'ai visto ciascun mio pensiero*.[16] It is in ballata form, with twelve hendecasyllabic lines rhyming abb/cde/cde/ebb, needing only a reprise of the first three lines to match the form that appears several times in Dufay's later French songs. But there is no trace of his setting; and even though much of his later work is obviously lost it seems most unlikely that a setting by Dufay of a poem by Lorenzo would have been allowed to perish. Florence is still particularly rich in chansonniers from the last quarter of the fifteenth century, most of them containing some works by Dufay.

As it happens, however, it is quite possible that a breakdown of relations caused the poem either not to be set or not to be sent to Florence. By November 1467 one of the musicians provided by Dufay was sent to prison for a fortnight; and feeling seems to have run high in the choir during the following months, for by next summer there was a complete walkout of the singers.[17]

But Squarcialupi's tribute from one musician to another is matched by a motet that may have been composed shortly afterwards. Loyset Compere's *Omnium bonorum plena* begins as a standard prayer to the Virgin Mary but in its second part becomes a plea for intercession on behalf of fourteen musicians. First of these is named Dufay 'luna totius musice atque cantorum lumine' – moon of all music and light of singers.

The cantus firmus is from Hayne van Ghizeghem's rondeau setting *De tous biens plaine* which is hardly likely to have been composed before about 1465 since Hayne was a choirboy in 1457. The text of the motet implies that all the musicians named are still alive; and it may even be taken to imply that all were present on the occasion for which it was composed. If so there is one event which invites connection with the motet. For many of the composers named there is no biographical information during these years: Caron, Corbet, Faugues and Compere himself (though he was in Milan by August 1474). The same goes for a man called Despres who has sometimes been identified as Pasquier Despres,[18] a minor singer in the Burgundian court, but could well be Josquin. Of the others more can be said. Dussart (du Sart), Georget de Brelles and Hemart were all masters of the boys at Cambrai Cathedral during the 1460s; Tinctoris was a singer at Cambrai for a short time in the 1460s but cannot be traced between then and about 1472, when he went to the Aragonese court at Naples. Ockeghem was master of the French royal chapel. Busnoys, Molinet and possibly Caron were at the Burgundian court, as was Hayne van Ghizeghem (who is not named but is included by implication since the cantus firmus is his). A meeting of the Burgundian court, the French royal court and the Cambrai Cathedral singers took place on 16–17 October 1468 when Charles the Bold and Louis XI came to Cambrai to venerate the famous picture of Notre-Dame de Grace – believed to have been painted by St Luke the Evangelist. The only musician named in the motet who was definitely not in one of these three groups is Johannes Regis who was a resident canon of Soignies; but his connections with Cambrai and particularly with Dufay were close: it is perfectly possible that he would have been able to come to Cambrai for what was evidently a most auspicious occasion.

In suggesting that *Omnium bonorum plena* was composed in 1468 I am pushing it slightly earlier than the received date 1470–4. The later date derives largely from our ignorance of chronology for the early works of both Hayne and Compere: a 'comfortable' reconstruction of their lives makes it tempting to push both the chanson and the motet as near to 1474 as possible; but on the other hand none of the received opinions about either composer is severely shaken by an earlier dating, and the event when the three groups of musicians would have met and venerated a portrait of the Virgin Mary is too appropriate and attractive to be overlooked.

For the remainder of Dufay's life just two musical events are important. In the year 1470–1 Mellet copied the Requiem Mass 'newly composed by Dufay'. The work is lost but was presumably a setting of the Propers for the Requiem;[19] his will implies that it ends with the words of the standard Postcommunion, 'Requiescant in pace', and directs it to be sung by twelve good adult singers on the day after his death. Again it seems likely that he composed the Mass primarily for his own obsequy, and its loss is a serious impediment to the full understanding of his development during the last years. Particularly so because the last Mass, on *Ave regina celorum*, is significantly different in style and vastly more elaborate than the two known works of the 1460s, the four-voice antiphon *Ave regina celorum* (v/51) and the Mass *Ecce ancilla Domini* (iii/9).

In 1473–4 Mellet copied the Mass *Ave regina celorum*; and although the account omits to name a composer this must surely be Dufay's (iii/10). Moreover there is every likelihood[20] that Dufay composed his Mass for the dedication of Cambrai Cathedral which took place on 5 July 1472. Since the Bishop of Cambrai was unavailable, the chapter invited Pierre de Ranchicourt, Bishop of Arras, to dedicate the church. Ranchicourt had himself been a canon of Cambrai and was evidently a close friend of Dufay: the accounts record several occasions when he stayed in Dufay's house during the preceding decade,[21] and he stayed with the composer again on this occasion.[22]

The dedication lasted from 3 a.m. until midday and was attended by all the clergy of Cambrai.[23] Surely this was the final event of Dufay's musical career; and a more fitting climax can hardly be imagined.

Almost exactly two years later Dufay made his last will; and on the evening of 27 November 1474 he died after six or seven weeks during which he had been visited twice a day by a surgeon-cum-barber who had bled him 'on account of the sickness in his legs and elsewhere'.[24] His last moments came quickly. In his will he made a special request for music at his bedside after he had received his last sacrament: the hymn *Magno salutis gaudio* sung in falsetto ('submissa voce' in the will, translated in the executors' account as 'en fausset') followed by the antiphon *Ave regina celorum* sung by the choirboys with three men 'if time permits'; the executors' account reports that time did not permit and the items were sung along with the Requiem Mass on the next day.[25]

Repeatedly in the preceding pages the last will and the executors' distribution account have been useful for establishing facts. These are unusually full documents. The will runs to some 1800 words and is so far as I know the only surviving will for any medieval composer. The executors' account (still published only in excerpts), filling sixty-five manuscript pages, is over three times as long as that for Binchois which happens also to survive; and it includes an extensive inventory of books, household effects and spare cash found in his house as well as of all the details of his funeral and how the executors disposed of his property.

Comparison with Binchois's account[26] can give some idea of

Dufay's wealth, bearing in mind that Binchois spent most of his career in the Burgundian court choir on a steady salary from the most expensive such ensemble in Christendom. Binchois was highly successful: his cash in hand and his income from prebends were on a comparable level. A comparative table appears on p. 216.

Binchois was only about sixty when he died, so he still possessed a horse whereas Dufay had none at his advanced age. The largest excess of Dufay's property over that of Binchois is in the furniture and household fittings, themselves equal in value to all of Binchois' possessions. But the nature of the goods valued is significant. That Dufay's additional wealth was largely in silver, jewellery and furniture is perhaps characteristic of a successful musician who travelled extensively.

The expenses are less easily compared since Binchois seems not to have made a will: any legacies were at the discretion of his executors, and the accounts are therefore differently organized. But the total outgoings for Binchois were £1503 7s (leaving a slight deficit which was made up later) and those for Dufay were comparable, £1368 1s 3d, leaving an enormous credit of nearly £2000.

Binchois' accounts name six relatives living in the area and refer several times to apparently large numbers of 'oncles, parens et proismes'. Dufay's on the other hand name only two: Jacobus des Priers[27] living in Tournai, who had at one stage lived with Dufay for eighteen months; and Jennin du Chemin living in Bruges. Both are a considerable distance away and somewhat weaken the theory that Dufay's family was from Cambrai. By contrast Binchois was born in Mons of a well-documented bourgeois family, died in Soignies, 17 km. north of Mons, and spent much of his working life in Brussels and Lille, both within a day's ride. Thus both the nature of the finances and the listing of relatives help define the lifestyle of the much-travelled Dufay who had contact with prominent political and artistic figures all over Europe as against the more stable and sedentary existence of the equally successful Binchois.

Moreover, Dufay remembered only one of his two relatives in the will. Jennin du Chemin complained to the executors that he had been left out in spite of having sent the composer delicacies from Bruges annually for seventeen to twenty years. He was made a substantial gift of £100 from the enormous surplus after the legacies had been paid. Nor was he the only one. Two of Dufay's servants also complained at having been overlooked and were similarly paid off. So was Pierre de Wez, himself one of the executors and already a substantial beneficiary of the will itself. As though to protect the composer's reputation, modern writers have printed only the first half of the relevant entry. It begins:[28]

> Item: to Messire Pierre de Wez in payment for having looked after the house of the said deceased for seven years while he was living in Savoy, received his prebends owed each year and accounted for them, and for several other services to the said deceased

but it continues:

> without having been recompensed for it: given to him for those reasons and others when he showed this to the said executors: £30.

Such items need to be interpreted with care: there may be a perfectly honourable explanation for Dufay's not having paid a debt outstanding for some sixteen years. But it looks from this and the other entries as though the great composer was in his later years a difficult and mean man.

Not that friends and relatives were entirely overlooked. He left his godson Antoine Hardi two books worth £4; and to the wife of Jacobus Hardi (perhaps the mother of Antoine) an Agnus Dei of pure gold, worth 6s 8d. To Martin Courtois he left two pictures worth £1; and Gobert le Mannier received a picture worth 1s 6d. To others he was more generous, leaving £100 to his servant Alexandre Bouillart (who in the event predeceased him) – a matter which makes the omission of his other servants all the more surprising. Pierre de Wez received £30 from the will apart from his later claim; and Dufay had bequeathed £10 'to the table of the Abbot of St-Aubert where I have frequently and excellently eaten'. But this last is in some ways a special and characteristic case. St-Aubert was the religious house for the nobility. The gift is comparable with the legacy of a precious knife to the Bishop of Arras and of various musical manuscripts to Duke Charles the Bold. Apart from these, most of the legacies were to religious foundations: to many of those in Cambrai, the churches at Condé, Valenciennes, Lille and Mons, as well as the one church significantly outside the immediate vicinity, the Grande Chartreuse in Savoy near Grenoble.[29]

Among the books he left, several are of musical interest. The inventory lists a copy of the greatest of all medieval music treatises, Guido of Arezzo's *Micrologus*. Several books of poetry include a 'book of Virgil' and *eglogas* of Martin le Franc, which if it survived might well show that some of Dufay's songs were set to words by that poet who was a colleague at the court of Savoy.[30] There is a book of 'old songs' – *vieses canteries* – which had formerly belonged to Simon le Breton. The books sent to Charles the Bold are itemized as follows:

1 small book bound in red with copper clasps
4 large books containing various kinds of music (*diverse chanterie*)
1 small book of songs
1 book of *loenges de musique* and the Mass *Ave regina celorum*.[31]

Finally two books of music were left to the chapel of St Stephen where he was buried: the parchment book containing the Mass for St Anthony of Padua 'with several other antiphons in black notation'; and the large paper manuscript containing the Mass for St Anthony Abbot and the Requiem Mass. The Mass for St Anthony of Padua and the Requiem were to be sung annually in his memory.

He was buried in the chapel of St Stephen within the cathedral, as had been his close colleague Simon le Breton, a former Burgundian ducal singer. His funeral monument (ill. 1) had been made before his death to his own specifications, leaving only the death-date to be added – as was customary.

It is a remarkable and fascinating monument. Dufay kneels on the left. Behind him is St Waudru with (presumably) her daughters, Adeltrude and Madelberte, and her son Dentelin. To the right is a representation of Christ rising from the tomb, with the soldier lying at the edge emphasizing a certain resemblance to the resurrection scene in one of Donatello's last works, the south pulpit in the church of San Lorenzo in Florence. Nevertheless the total design is very much of the north, particularly in its somewhat cluttered structure and its use of the architectural surround. At each corner is a rebus, a condensed form of the one which Dufay used to sign his two surviving autograph documents (ills. 18–19): within a capital 'G' are the letters 'Du', the musical note 'fa' and the letter 'y'.

His death-date was added not in relief like the rest of the monument but engraved, even though the area for the date was left raised so that a relief would be possible. This use of the cheapest and quickest method despite an artistic incongruity may further support the idea that Dufay in his old age failed to attract the devotion that one might expect from those around him.

But perhaps the most tantalizing feature of the monument is the figure of Dufay himself. Given that it was made before his death, the figure is presumably an attempt at a true representation of the composer – the most secure that we have, since the miniature of him and Binchois (ill. 7) is surely more general in its iconography. Unfortunately the figure was broken at some stage: the monument is made of the particularly brittle stone of Tournai and spent many years underground. But the face has apparently been reconstructed from the original pieces, clumsily but clearly enough for a close-up photograph (taken at a very sharp angle from the extreme right of the monument) to stand as a reasonable likeness of Dufay as an old man (ill. 2).

To some extent Dufay's later reputation is puzzling. In 1475–6 Simon Mellet received payment for copying *lamentations* by Ockeghem, Busnoys and Hemart;[32] they are lost but were perhaps composed in Dufay's memory. Yet there is very little further evidence of musical tributes to the composer. Few of his works formed the basis for later cantus firmus Masses, for instance. Copies of the music of his later years are relatively rare and practically none of them can be dated later than 1500 – a mere twenty-five years after his death. It is as though the mature years of Ockeghem, Busnoys and Hayne van Ghizeghem brought about a move towards a more aggressively Franco-Flemish style that eschewed some of Dufay's Italianate characteristics. Even Josquin shows no direct debt to Dufay although the seeds of his mature works may perhaps be seen in Dufay's purest Mass cycle, that on *Ecce ancilla Domini*.

But this may be a misleading interpretation of ambiguous and incomplete documents. Dufay appears repeatedly in the theoretical and literary writings of later years.[33] Some merely mention him in a list of important past composers, often in the same breath as Binchois and Dunstable (Tinctoris (several times), the anonymous Escorial theorist, Hothby, Cretin, Molinet, Eloi d'Amerval, Moulu, Heyden, Coclico, Finck, etc). Some fairly early writers began crediting him quite unjustifiably with an expansion downwards of the musical range (Adam von Fulda, Petrus Gregorius) – a notion which naturally appealed to several writers in the eighteenth century. But several up to about 1535 quote specific works, particularly in discussions of intricate mensuration practice or the use of conflicting metres (Tinctoris *Proportionale*, Gafori, Spataro – all giving in particular extraordinarily detailed descriptions of passages in the Mass for St Anthony of Padua).

Between then and the 1820s Dufay's name appears in two kinds of book: first, the institutional histories which name him as a churchman without having any awareness of his musical importance (Le Carpentier 1664, Foppens 1731, Le Glay 1825); and second, musical histories which had merely gathered information from previous writers. Among these the most fastidious and complete is Forkel (1801) whose collection of early references is remarkably full; and the most evocative is Gerber, who describes Dufay as 'einer der ältesten Graubärte unter den Kontrapunktisten' – one of the oldest greybeards among contrapuntists. None of these writers knew a note of Dufay's music.

Modern research began with Baini's book on Palestrina (1828) and the competition essays of Kiesewetter and Fétis (published in 1829). All three recognized Dufay's importance, though in shadowy terms. Shortly afterwards, in 1834, Kiesewetter followed up the trail by publishing some of the music for the first time, two years before the first extended article devoted to Dufay, nearly five columns of chaotic but stimulating detail in Fétis's *Biographie universelle des musiciens*.

Misleading information in Baini and Fétis led to considerable confusion until the publication of two studies which remain to this day the basis of any biographical work on Dufay: Jules Houdoy's *Histoire artistique de la cathédrale de Cambrai* (1880) and Franz Xaver Haberl's 'Wilhelm du Fay' (1885 = *Bausteine* i). These outlined the documentation at Cambrai and Rome. Two important Italian articles of the 1920s (Cordero 'Dufay' and Borghezio 'Fondazione') furnished information on the Savoy years which was incorporated into the major monograph by Charles van den Borren (1926). Since then some details were added by the mercurial André Pirro in his *Histoire* (1940) – information which was unfortunately overlooked by Besseler in his influential article for *MGG* (1954), as a result of which many important facts remained incorrect in the majority of studies until Craig Wright's complete overhaul of Cambrai documents published in 1975.

Purely musical assessment really began with van den Borren's book of 1926 which devoted over 250 pages to an appreciation of the works available to him (mainly in Stainer's *Dufay* and in early volumes of DTO). Since then many writers have given detailed consideration to the music: work of particular value is in Pirro's *Histoire* and Heinrich Besseler's systematic but brilliant *Bourdon und Fauxbourdon* (1951).

Not until 1966 did Besseler finish the complete edition of Dufay's works, but since 1950 the rapidly increasing number of performances and recordings as well as the immense growth of musicological research has inevitably resulted in a body of writing on Dufay's music which probably far exceeds the quantity of reading he himself would have encompassed in his entire lifetime.

So the general picture is relatively simple: his name was never entirely forgotten and his music was revived as interest in medieval music grew. More problematic and confusing is his reputation in the years immediately after his death. There is room for more research on why his music was so soon forgotten except by the theorists.

Yet in Cambrai his music was evidently sung and appreciated forty years later. An entry in the cathedral chapter acts for 8 January 1515 shows a continued interest unparalleled in any other medieval composer: 'The lords [of the chapter] ordain that in future the motet sung for Epiphany should be removed and replaced by another for the same season from the works of the late Dufay.'[34] Part of the interest of this is that practically no trace survives of music by Dufay for the Epiphany season. We have only the Epiphany antiphon *Magi videntes stellam* (v/38) and the lost Mass for St Anthony Abbot (17 January). Clearly even more music is now lost from the man who in any case counts as by far the most prolific composer of his time.

Nor is this evidence of continued interest at Cambrai isolated. Two years after that Dufay's Requiem Mass was again added to the regular round of annual services, this time for the foundation set up by Jean de la Pierre: 'And the Requiem Mass of Dufay is to be sung by the master of the choirboys with four or five companions chosen at his discretion.'[35] This too is a lost work, of course. For all the information that makes Dufay the most fully documented composer of the Middle Ages, the works that seem to have survived him longest can no longer be traced; and it is therefore something of a relief that chapter 14 will be able to report the retrieval of the work which stayed longest in the minds of theorists, the Mass for St Anthony of Padua. But it is also comforting to know that this particular prophet – in spite of the feelings which apparently surrounded him at the time of his death – was so long acknowledged in his home town.

# 8
# The early songs

Of all Dufay's music the songs have long been the favourites. This is partly because they were the first of his works to be published in any quantity.[1] It is also because a few compact works can easily show the range of style he encompassed within a relatively short time-span: the Oxford manuscript that formed the basis of the first collection to be published was finished in about 1436, so the forty-five songs by him which it contains, with their amazing stylistic variety, must have been composed in the first fifteen years or so of his career. In fact about two thirds of the eighty-odd surviving songs securely ascribed to him[2] seem to have been composed before 1440.

But perhaps the main reason for the success of the early songs is that they speak directly in a relatively familiar idiom – something which is far less true of his other works. The rondeau *Adieu ces bons vins de Lannoys* (vi/27), his nostalgia-filled farewell to the people and places around Laon, is dated 1426.[3] To refer to its nostalgia may beg questions about the kind of expression to be found in any medieval song, but that seems the best description of its top voice line which is relatively unusual for French songs of its time in having so many gently falling phrases (Ex. 1).

**Ex. 1**

(Further text follows)

Several characteristic features can be mentioned at once. The untexted introduction and coda may possibly be for instrumental performance, as may be the small codetta passage in bars 23–5. They are more florid than the rest of the line. Quite often in other songs of the time the untexted passages are so much more florid that it is tempting to see them as specifically instrumental rather than vocal: a classic case of this is the ballade *Resvelliés vous* (vi/11) of 1423. But equally often florid material seems to be written inseparably into the texted passages, and it becomes impossible to make any logically watertight distinction between vocal and instrumental style in fifteenth-century music.[4] Rigid conclusions cannot be drawn. There are many different kinds of song in Dufay's output; the very lack of specific instructions as to instrumentation in medieval music may well indicate a certain flexibility in performance practice; and several details even suggest that some of these lines were intended for a free interchange between a singer and an instrumentalist.

What is clear, however, is that the shape of the melodic line here needs no help from varied orchestration. It is not merely that the untexted sections are more florid: each line of the poem is matched by an equally clearly defined melodic shape. The first texted line falls from the high B flat down to a cadence on D, the final or 'tonic' of the piece; this four-bar phrase is balanced by another a fourth lower, leading to a cadence on A, the lowest note in the melody. A third phrase, this time of five bars, bridges the two areas, cadencing on E.

The sign over that note, called *signum congruentiae* (sign of congruence), shows that this is the mid-point cadence of the stanza, the main internal structural division and the note from which the music must return to the beginning at several points within the rondeau scheme. If we use the letters 'A' and 'B' to denote the sections before and after this sign respectively, the musical form of the rondeau becomes AB AA AB AB. What this means is that the 'B' section is stated once in the first stanza but then has to wait until near the end of the song before it reappears. This in its turn means that one formal technique in rondeau composition is to give the 'B' section a distinctive character, particularly at its opening.

So it is no accident that the 'B' section of *Adieu ces bons vins* begins with a line that is unique within the song both in moving upwards and in rising to the only high C in the melody; nor that the final line returns to the material of the first line but puts it into an equally distinctive syncopated form.

Each texted line has its own range and its own cadential pitch (repeated only when the last line paraphrases the first). Each line ends with the dipping cadence figure that is so typical of its generation: the figure can fall only one note before returning to the cadence note (as in bars 8–9, 22–3 and 28–9) or employ a variety of cadential embellishments falling two steps below the final pitch (as in bars 4–5, 14–15, 17–18, 24–5 and 32–3).

With these details in mind it is possible to see a precursor for the song within Dufay's own work. His Gloria setting called 'de Quaremiaux' (iv/23) has a strikingly similar melodic and harmonic style, and although it has sometimes been dated 1434[5] it seems stylistically far more likely to precede *Adieu ces bons vins*. This Gloria is based on a simple melodic tenor line which repeats several times and therefore controls what happens above it. The top line carries the Gloria text with many repeated notes and a more declamatory style than the song; but its shape is remarkably similar (Ex. 2).

Ex. 2

Et in terra (etc)

The important difference here is that the line in the Gloria never reaches above the note B (which is flattened by *musica ficta*, accidentals not written but assumed by performers of the time and restored in modern editions by being written above the note rather than before it). It is as though Dufay noted the effect of the expected climax on the high C, which never actually arrives in the Gloria, and reworked the material to create a song in which he built on that experience to produce a work of extraordinary perfection.

Listening to these two works will demonstrate that point more clearly than is possible with a brief description; the point is endorsed by the movement of the lower voices. But lest the parallel should seem unnecessarily far-fetched it is worth noting another case where Dufay more demonstrably reworked material that arose as a result of structural techniques. His motet *O sancte Sebastiane* (i/8) includes in its third isorhythmic section the following passage in which the rhythms exactly repeat those of the two preceding sections and the pitches of the tenor also belong to a predetermined pattern which is exactly repeated in a later section. That is to say that many details in the passage arise largely as a result of what one might call precompositional considerations (Ex. 3). The resulting canon between the contratenor and the tenor forms the basis of Dufay's song *Resvelons nous* (vi/28)[6] where it is repeated four times beneath a florid top line which opens with a shape closely resembling that in the motet (Ex. 4).

Ex. 3

Ex. 4

This song may well belong to the same period in his life as *Adieu ces bons vins*: the broad shape of its melodic line is remarkably similar though its cadence notes are less carefully placed, partly because *Resvelons nous* is to some extent predetermined by the repeating pattern of the canon in the lower voices.

But both pairs of examples point to the important conclusion that in much of Dufay's early work the techniques and compositional inspiration often remain the same irrespective of genre. Songs, motets and Mass movements have significant common material; and the genres influenced each other. Several more examples of this will be seen in due course. And in this respect Dufay contrasts significantly with his contemporary Binchois, in whose work the different genres show entirely different styles.

So the upper voice of *Adieu ces bons vins* is characteristic of much that Dufay was doing at the time. Its lower voices show in some ways an equally characteristic pattern. As nearly always happens in this repertory, the lower voices are labelled 'tenor' and 'contratenor'. In medieval music these names never refer to the voice-range of the parts; rather they define their function. The tenor is the main structural voice throughout the repertory. In the motet the tenor usually carries a borrowed chant melody: this seems to have been the origin of the word in the thirteenth century and remains its function for most of Dufay's motets. But in the chansons the word 'tenor' merely denotes that this is the main structural voice which controls the harmonic movement. Almost invariably the tenor and the upper voice make perfect two-part counterpoint between them, a counterpoint that corresponds precisely to the fundamental principles of more modern counterpoint: the main vertical intervals are thirds, fifths, sixths and octaves; fourths are treated as dissonances, as are seconds and sevenths; and the voice-writing is in contrary motion whenever possible (Ex. 5).

Ex. 5

Equally characteristically, each cadential figure in the upper voice is matched by a stepwise falling line in the tenor: between them the two voices provide the entire contrapuntal structure of the work. The principles of counterpoint are fully described in many theoretical treatises of the Middle Ages under the heading 'discant';[7] and the importance of the relationship between these two voices is so fundamental throughout the repertory that the upper voice here will be called 'discantus'. (It is more commonly called 'superius', a word that is equally well documented in the writings of a slightly later generation but fails to emphasize the importance of its relationship with the tenor and also perhaps too strongly implies that this is the highest voice, which is often the case, but not always.)

Alongside the clear contrapuntal structure of the discantus and tenor comes the contratenor. Again, this name is a description not of range or of voice quality but of contrapuntal function – that of a part which in some respects matches the tenor. In *Adieu ces bons vins* the contratenor has the same range as the tenor and often moves homophonically with it. As in many other pieces of the time its prime functions here are twofold: to add colour to the texture and to add rhythmic impetus particularly at cadential points when, for the reasons outlined above, tenor and discantus are likely to be holding long notes or resting.

In any three-voice piece of the fifteenth century the contratenor can be omitted and the resulting piece will make perfect sense. Omit the tenor and at this stage in the century the result will have many irrational dissonances of a fourth; later in the century fourths may not appear but the piece will still be felt to lack the binding part. Omit the discantus and the piece will in most cases be consonant but will lack the essential shape provided by the discantus–tenor duet.

For the opening bars of *Adieu ces bons vins* the contratenor moves homophonically with the tenor (Ex. 6). From bar 5 other functions can be seen: the leap of an octave is characteristic of contratenor movement; the hint of imitation at bars 6–7 is an equally

Ex. 6

common feature of the style, just a hint to keep the texture alive, but nothing too rigorous; the 6/8 figure in bar 11 again enlivens the rhythmic movement, but it also summarizes the entire shape of the discantus for that second text line, and by moving for a moment above the discantus it allows that figure to appear even more tellingly. At the mid-point cadence the contratenor has continuous movement in preparation for the next section while the discantus-tenor pair are still.

Sometimes the tenor and contratenor can move more slowly than the discantus, as though to emphasize their function as primarily harmonic voices. This is not particularly common in Dufay because in general his aim appears to be to integrate the style of the three voices while retaining their contrapuntal function. But a good example is in the ballade *Ce jour le doibt* (vi/18).[8] Its melodic and harmonic style recall *Adieu ces bons vins*; and we have already seen (p. 27) that its text suggests composition in the Laon years. Again, the tenor and contratenor begin homophonically, but relatively soon the contratenor begins to move more independently, later introducing small details of rhythmic movement and hints of imitation (Ex. 7).

Ex. 7

It may be a less polished song than *Adieu ces bons vins* but it must belong to the same stage in his development: musical style endorses what the texts have already suggested. And to some extent these two songs can be seen as representing the classic northern style in his music, the style of many songs by Binchois, with a discantus which is quite clearly the main interest-bearing part and two lower parts whose function is primarily to provide harmonic background.

Dufay's other dated piece in the Oxford manuscript represents an entirely different tradition in his work. *Je me complains piteusement* (vi/14) is dated 12 July 1425 and is therefore only a few months earlier than *Adieu ces bons vins*. Here he seems to discard the hierarchy of discantus, tenor and contratenor and writes for three equal voices all in the same range. The voices overlap constantly; and their musical equality is stressed by the three different rhythmic settings of the opening words 'Je me complains' (Ex. 8). But the change here is more apparent than real. The two upper voices form a perfect and complete counterpoint; the bottom voice on the other hand forms a dissonant interval of a fourth with the top voice (bar 4) and does so later with the second voice. This is characteristic of contratenor parts in fifteenth-century music; another characteristic is the use of angular lines and particularly the octave leap in bars 9–10. That is to say that although the three voices have more apparent equality than in *Adieu ces bons vins* they still retain their functional relationship. Although the manuscript – exceptionally – fails to name the parts, we compromise nothing by referring to them as discantus, tenor and contratenor in that order.

Ex. 8

It seems likely that in this ballade Dufay was approaching a particular compositional problem: the use of three voices with equal ranges and of equal importance. If so, he achieved his end more successfully in another song that is outwardly very similar in style, *Ma belle dame souveraine* (vi/44). Here the three voices again occupy the same range, but although they happen to be labelled 'triplum', 'tenor' and 'cantus' in the only source, there is far less trace of any consistent structural relation between them.[9] To make that possible there is a fourth voice in a lower range. Presumably this is not intended to carry text, to judge from its long notes, irregular rhythms and extensive use of ligatures (that is, several notes written in the manuscript as a single symbol, denoted in modern editions by a square bracket joining the notes so grouped). The voice is called 'contratenor' in the manuscript; and its movement includes many leaps of an octave and a fifth (Ex. 9).

Ex. 9

This is the kind of contratenor which Besseler termed *Harmonieträger* (harmony-bearer) and regarded as evidence that Dufay was strongly influenced by the *caccia* of the Italian trecento composers as well as by the motets of Ciconia in his development of a fully tonal harmonic scheme: practically every vertical sonority in the song can be construed as a tonic, dominant or subdominant triad in D minor.[10]

*Ma belle dame souveraine* shares with *Adieu ces bons vins* the quality of being one of the most consummately perfect pieces from Dufay's earlier years. Each of the three upper voices rises to its peak note, D, just once in each half of the song (which is to say that although the first and third voices reach that note twice in the second half, they amount in each case to just one melodic peak); and these peaks are interlocked so that each voice takes its turn rising to a climax above the others. Similarly each voice reaches the lowest pitch, A, just twice in the course of the piece. But if that description makes the song seem dry and formalistic, it is misleading. The texture of the voices is itself richly sensuous. In the opening bars the falling line of the first voice works so that the dissonances on the G and the E make their full effect, leading to the rising figure in the third voice; and although these non-harmonic pitches are in textbook terms perfectly normal passing notes, they are spaced so that they bring out the individual qualities of the voices.

As in *Je me complains piteusement*, the opening words of the poem appear in three different rhythmic configurations; but it is as though the idea pleased Dufay, for in this song the same happens for the second and third lines of the poem as well. On the other hand, the overlapping unison canon that occurs later in *Je me complains* is discarded: imitation appears only for the concluding fourth line at the words 'Nuit et jour' where the close imitation (and therefore the identical declamation of the text) comes as a surprise – if perhaps in retrospect an inevitable one – and at the same time provides a contrast in the 'B' section of the music for the same reasons that such a contrast was needed in the 'B' section of *Adieu ces bons vins*, though using entirely different means.

Dufay's use of rhythm is one of the most consistently fascinating features of his work. Again the simplest place to begin is *Adieu ces bons vins*, where there are almost always two 'chords' in each bar. That is to say that the tenor usually changes pitch on the third beat and the song works as a continuous trochaic flow of regularly undulating harmonies. That regularity is relatively unusual in his work as well as in that of his contemporaries (and this is another feature that supports the suggestion that the composition of *Adieu ces bons vins* grew out of work on the Gloria 'de Quaremiaux' where that regularity is predetermined by the structure of the evidently borrowed tenor).

More characteristic in this respect is the rondeau *Je requier a tous amoureux* (vi/32). Here trochee and iamb are equal partners in the rhythmic flow. Although practically every beat in the song contains some kind of action, the essential activity is on either the first and third (trochaic) or first and second (iambic) beats in each bar; and it seems that a successful performance will be one that allows a gentle undulation centred on just two stresses per bar. At least, experience shows that any attempt to 'bounce' off the first beat in an iambic pattern destroys the music's flow (Ex. 10).

Ex. 10

As so often, the phrase lengths are balanced but basically irregular. The four lines of the poem are matched by phrases of $4 + 5 + 5 + 5$ bars. It is a style that is most easily understood within the context of Gregorian chant, where regular phrase-balancing is rigorously avoided but the musical lines balance one another in a far less literal sense. A certain irregularity of phrase lengths gives the musical flow a wayward unpredictability in spite of an overall balancing of phrases which seems to have been the ideal of the time; and it is just possible that the extraordinary memorability of *Adieu ces bons vins* is at least partly a function of our more recent listening habits, for its first, second and fifth text lines have four-bar phrases, as does the coda, so that the five-bar and seven-bar phrases elsewhere are still heard as soothing irregularities within a fundamental four-bar pattern. Something similar happens in another popular early piece, the first of his *Ave regina celorum* settings (v/49), a work whose melodic and harmonic style, phrase-structure and part-ranges also suggest composition at about the same time as *Adieu ces bons vins*.

It is difficult to speak with much confidence about attitudes to simple rhythmic patterns in the fifteenth century because the dance music and improvised music are lost. There is a general feeling that they would have included the regular pattern of four-bar phrases which characterizes nearly all dance music since the earliest clear records in the sixteenth century. But it is possible to say that regular four-bar balancing is extremely rare in the written polyphonic music of the fifteenth century. Most of the surviving polyphony is courtly; and the ideal seems to have been that in this style such strict regularity was carefully avoided in favour of a more elegant balance.

But that is not to say that Dufay entirely avoided dance-like rhythms in his music. In complete contrast with the music just discussed is his rondeau *Ce jour de l'an* (vi/38). In looking at the opening with its triadic figure repeated in all three voices it is worth remembering that the standard hierarchy of the parts described above retains its force: discantus and tenor remain the basis of the contrapuntal structure and the contratenor is, syntactically speaking, a subordinate voice moving in the same range as the tenor. As in so many of Dufay's works, part of its success lies in the way the melodic style of these three functionally dissimilar voices is unified, though within the structural scheme of the time.

Ex. 11

Here, as elsewhere, the original note-values have been quartered. Thus the 3/4 metre of *Adieu ces bons vins* and similar pieces reflects an original notation moving primarily in *brevis* and *semibrevis* values, or 'perfect time with minor prolation', denoted by the mensuration sign ○; equally the 6/8 of *Je me complains* and other pieces reflects movement primarily in *semibrevis* and *minima* values, or 'imperfect time with major prolation', denoted by the sign ℂ. In neither case is anything in the original notation compromised by this reduction of note-values which is now customary for transcriptions of fifteenth-century music, though occasionally matters can be clarified by consulting the few modern editions which retain the original notation.[11] Nor is anything essential compromised by the use of barlines for music which originally had none. To describe the notation of Dufay's time would go far beyond the scope of this book; but it should be said here that anything in triple time required that the musician reading it was aware of those regular triple groupings, for otherwise he would probably misread the notation. In theory the quaver (in modern transcription) of 6/8 was the same length as the quaver in 3/4; and there are many examples of the two mensurations used simultaneously which demonstrate this.

Very few people today believe that all comparable pieces of a particular date should go at the same tempo (though that was once a surprisingly popular assumption), but it is still worth bearing in mind the possibility that the quaver of *Adieu ces bons vins* could be the same length as the quaver in *Ce jour de l'an*. My own instinct was once to perform *Ce jour de l'an* considerably faster than that, allowing the high spirits of the text and particularly of the bouncy opening lines to suggest the liveliest tempo that is compatible with clarity in the intricate counterpoint. This is all a matter of degree and is to some extent determined by several factors that may be unique to the performance in question. But I now think that my instinct may have been wrong and that an important feature of this song, and many others like it, is the alternation of trochaic and iambic patterns which becomes predominant from about bar 5. It is far too easy to make Dufay's early 6/8 songs sound merely jolly and ebullient; and while the ebullience is an important factor in these works, there is much more than that happening.

In this context it seems particularly important to note the difference in style between *Ce jour de l'an* and the two 6/8 pieces discussed earlier, *Je me complains* and *Ma belle dame souveraine*. The latter must surely be slow sensuous pieces whereas *Ce jour de l'an* needs to retain the dancing manner implied by its text and faithfully reflected in the leaping intervallic structure of its first half. Judgment, not rule-of-thumb, must determine tempi in this music. And remarkably often the spirit of the poem leads to the same conclusion as the nature of the music. In this respect Dufay's songs often seem significantly different from those of his predecessors and contemporaries, and that is one clue to the success of his songs today.

For reasons not yet fully explained, composers throughout Europe seem to have avoided the 'major prolation' (6/8) style about 1430. For the first thirty years of the century it had been the most common mensuration pattern, and many more examples of its use in Dufay's earlier work will appear in the coming chapters. But one further example must be added here as being characteristic of the style Dufay inherited. *Ce moys de may* (vi/39)[12] makes extensive use of the contrast between 6/8 and the hemiola pattern of 3/4 within the bar (which was achieved notationally by means of *color*, most often writing the notes in black within a context of void notes; this is normally denoted in modern transcriptions by means of half brackets above the notes in *color*) (Ex. 12).

Ex. 12

Its effect here is strongly rhythmic with the juxtaposition of the various rhythmic elements – the hemiola, the trochaic 6/8 and the iambic 6/8. But by Dufay's time this style had become something of a cliché. The style seems to have emerged initially as a reaction against the extraordinary complexity of late fourteenth-century music: something robust and clear was needed after the more precious and rhythmically extravagant music of the previous generation. *Ce moys de may* is often produced as being characteristic of Dufay's songs. In fact part of the fascination of his songs is how rarely he duplicates himself, how practically every song is an attempt to solve a different compositional problem. But even with that in mind, *Ce moys de may* is distinctive in being rhythmically by far the most aggressive song in his output.

Among Dufay's early songs several general features can be noted. First, while the rondeau form is by far the most common (usually

99

with a four-line or five-line stanza), he occasionally used the ballade form for songs to commemorate particular events: the chapters on his biography have mentioned several of these; but he seems to have stopped using the ballade by the mid-1430s. Second, throughout his career Dufay, more than any of his contemporaries, had a special predilection for passages of contrasted texture in which the three voices overlap in the same range. An example of this is the opening of the rondeau *Navré je sui* (vi/34) (Ex. 13).

Ex. 13

This song shows a third characteristic that seems to have fascinated Dufay particularly from about 1430: the alternation of major and minor triads, particularly when based on C. This matter has been discussed by Besseler who called it *Terzfreiheit* – mobility of the third.[13] In *Navré je sui* the interlocking of the voices at the outset asserts the C major triad as strongly as possible so that the appearance of the E flat in bar 3 and particularly in bar 7 makes its point almost too clearly. This mobility of the third in the triad on C will continue to appear in Dufay's works, to find its apotheosis in his last Mass, the *Ave regina celorum* (iii/10).

The next chapter will show evidence that in the 1430s Dufay was losing interest in the intense complexity of some of his earlier motets and striving for a simpler kind of musical expression, using the most economic means possible. This can be heard in some of the songs of the time, particularly in the ballade *Se la face ay pale* (vi/19) which will be discussed later in the context of the Mass cycle based on it. Another fine example is *Bon jour, bon mois* (vi/59), a rondeau for New Year's Day which unfortunately survives with only its first stanza – a matter that has not stopped it being one of Dufay's most widely performed songs today.[14] Each line but the third begins with the same declamation pattern of three crotchets plus a minim; the third line begins in the discantus with a melodic pattern which will be inverted for the fourth line at the beginning of the 'B' section; the melodic writing throughout makes special use of the leap of a fourth; and there is considerable imitation, particularly in the 'B' section, leading to an extraordinary economy of musical and melodic material. In just one detail Dufay allows himself considerable freedom. At the end of both 'A' and 'B' sections there is an enormous melisma, rhapsodically composed as though to clear the ears of the intense concentration elsewhere in the song. That kind of melismatic writing is something with which Dufay was constantly experimenting at this stage of his career and can be found in many of his most successful works.

As a final example of Dufay's early song style becoming more focussed in its aims, the rondeau *Hé, compaignons, resvelons nous* (vi/49) shows a certain complexity at one level. It is in four voices; and we shall see that whereas the three-voice texture has consistent rules that nearly always apply, the four-voice texture for Dufay was something far more irregular, syntactically speaking. Two texted upper voices seem to be in the relationship of discantus–tenor to one another. Certainly they overlap, but then that happens often in even the most stereotyped songs of the time; and to a certain extent the voices seem to interchange roles, but that too is not uncommon. Below them are two untexted voices, described in the manuscript as 'contratenor' and 'concordans cum omnibus' (concording with all the other voices), but confining their movement primarily to the

Ex. 14

notes of the minor common chord on G. This means that for a large proportion of the song the bass note is either G or D. That is to some extent alleviated by the fluidity of the two texted voices, and by a quantity of melismatic writing between the lines, as at bars 5–6 (Ex. 14).

But the self-imposed limitations of the piece go further than that: at bar 3 and bar 7 there is a momentary augmented triad formed by one of the voices falling on B flat before resolving to A; and this progression occurs a further three times at crucial points within the song.[15] It is as though the song is to some extent an exercise in using these two devices.

Once again, however, these are ideas that seem to derive from another work, his extended sequence setting *Gaude virgo, mater Christi* (v/1). Here the total range of the four voices is wider, but their contrapuntal and rhythmic movement is markedly similar. The lowest voice has the curious wide leaps based – as in *Hé, compaignons* – on a minor version of the harmonic series on G (trumpet-like in manner though probably unperformable on a trumpet of the time); and the same cadential pattern with augmented triads appears, though not so often as in the song. Among the enormous variety of Dufay's works the similarity of these two pieces is particularly striking; and both are quite dissimilar from anything else in his work.

Many composers, both before and since Dufay, have found that they needed to create artificial compositional problems to focus their creative energy and channel it into directions that might not otherwise have occurred to them. It is an idea most cogently expressed by Stravinsky, but perhaps best exemplified in the composers of the second Viennese school. In *Hé, compaignons* Dufay was inspired, presumably by these self-imposed limitations, to produce a song quite unlike anything else by him or his contemporaries; and even if he was not entirely successful in transcending those limitations, the work has a special position of its own in the gallery of his finest creations. And it serves well as a transition to the motet, perhaps the most significant example of a form with externally imposed compositional problems in any music before the rise of serialism.

# 9

# The isorhythmic motets

Details in the story of his life show two important characteristics in Dufay: that he was an intellectual and that he was in his early years quick to make use of any opportunity to display his technical skill and inventive resource. These characteristics appear most clearly in his motets, works built on a form reaching back some two hundred years.[1]

Some time late in the fourteenth century the isorhythmic motet had become pre-eminently the form for celebrating great occasions of state. All the motets by Dufay's great predecessor Johannes Ciconia contain allusions to political events and personalities connected with the cities of Venice and Padua; and although the motets of John Dunstable are less obvious in their references it seems likely that his were also for special occasions. Of Dufay's thirteen isorhythmic motets,[2] all but two can be connected with specific occasions, people and places. To study them is to study Dufay's public voice.[3]

But they represent only the first half of his career. By the middle of the century the isorhythmic motet had fallen from favour. It is as though musicians and their patrons now realized that it was an empty form based on aesthetic criteria of an age long gone, principles scarcely relevant to the age of humanism, of sensuality in the arts, of the individual. The two main features of the motet were entirely contrary to those modern beliefs. Normally the motet had at least two different texts sounding simultaneously; and while the texts were usually related in some way, perhaps even sharing rhyme-words, their simultaneous singing inevitably resulted in a richness born partly of aural confusion which may have pleased the Gothic mind but must have seemed hopelessly unrealistic in fifteenth-century Italy. And the isorhythmic structure – a form based on the idea that at least one voice should contain a rhythmic pattern which was repeated with different pitches – was a neat and ingenious scheme that appealed to the thirteenth-century desire for numerical system and entelechy but had relatively little to say to the contemporaries of Donatello and Brunelleschi who felt that their art should actually be perceived as perfect.

When Dufay used the form of the isorhythmic motet he was, by his very historical position, playing several roles. First, he was displaying and developing his technical skill by using the most difficult of styles. That perhaps helps to explain why he seems to have continued writing in this form after most other composers had discarded it. Second, he was building on a highly respectable historical tradition of which he must have been strongly aware. His motets may show little evidence of the thirteenth-century schemes, but they show the strong influence of the two great fourteenth-century masters of the form, Philippe de Vitry and Guillaume de Machaut (whose works still appear in fifteenth-century manuscripts); and there is even more direct evidence of his building on the work of his immediate predecessors Ciconia and Dunstable. But third – and this will be the main theme of the present chapter – he was continually adapting the form to his own purposes, finding ways of reconciling the motet with fifteenth-century cultural values. Dufay's motets contain an unsurpassed range of techniques, expanding some features of the old style, rejecting others, experimenting and re-experimenting with various musical figures, constantly reconsidering the form. And it is really only in the last motets that we see all the features reassembled to produce works of classical purity combined with personal vision.

*Vasilissa ergo gaude* (i/7), probably of 1420, may be his earliest surviving work.[4] Its form is relatively simple. Leaving aside the two-voice canonic introduction which is not part of the isorhythmic scheme, the motet is characteristically built on a tenor cantus firmus taken from a Gregorian chant Gradual. He gives this melody a rhythmic pattern which is quite independent of the chant's own shape and phrasing; and that very independence of the rhythmic scheme from the original texting argues strongly that this tenor was intended to be taken by an instrument or perhaps sung to neutral vowels. Example 15 shows the original Gradual (or at least the version of it in the *Liber usualis*) against the entire tenor of Dufay's motet. A glance at the two versions shows that there are melodic differences: while it is perfectly possible that Dufay altered certain chants to suit his own purposes it seems in this case far more likely that the precise version he used has not yet been identified.[5]

The tenor is cast in two rhythmically identical parts. That the

Ex. 15

rhythmic scheme (technically called *talea*) fits twice into the melody (*color*)[6] with two notes left over for the closing cadence is characteristic of Dufay's motets, though in two cases the *talea* fits three times into the *color* and in three cases the *color* and *talea* are of the same length.[7] What is significant about *Vasilissa ergo gaude* is the strictness of the form beyond that point. The two isorhythmic halves of the motet have the same rhythmic pattern not just in the tenor but in all four voices. This 'total isorhythm' or 'panisorhythm' is an expansion of the isorhythmic technique which appears spasmodically in the fourteenth century, becoming established as a principle around 1400 in the work of Ciconia. But whereas Ciconia, like

Dunstable, used total isorhythm somewhat loosely, altering certain rhythmic patterns in the upper voices to fit the text more easily, Dufay was invariably literal in his use of the technique. Example 16 shows the openings of the two isorhythmic sections of *Vasilissa ergo gaude*.

Ex. 16

What is interesting here is not so much that the rhythms should be repeated with different notes but the way in which the notes are changed. The opening imitative pattern of the notes A and D in the two upper voices appears again in the second *talea* but this time using the lower pitches D and A. Moreover the cadence on E in bar 26 is mirrored by one on A in bar 65. Contrasted tonal areas a fifth apart are remarkably often important in Dufay's early work and have their precursors in some of Ciconia's motets.

As though to make the relationship of the two sections clearer, the rhythmic scheme becomes more complicated towards the end of the *talea* (see the tenor in Ex. 15) so that the transition to the second isorhythmic section at bar 62 is underlined by a sudden reversion to the longer note-values of the opening. The move to the second *talea* is therefore quite clearly audible in a way that it sometimes was not in earlier motets; and the same technique appears particularly clearly in other Dufay motets from the 1420s, especially *O gemma, lux* (i/9) and *Apostolo glorioso* (i/10).

There is a further important aspect of the motet's effect in broad formal terms. Various passages which in the second *talea* give rise to unison imitation between the upper voices have in the first *talea* something much looser – imitation at an interval or in some cases no imitation at all. That is to say that the final section of the motet has considerable unison imitation.[8] If this is taken alongside the non-isorhythmic canon which opens the motet it becomes easy to hear the work in three sections: the opening section of 22 bars all in unison imitation; the second section, comprising the first *talea* of 39 bars, with loose imitation; and the final section, the second *talea* of 39 bars, with more unison imitation. So while in isorhythmic terms the motet has the form X + A + A, in terms of imitation between the two upper voices it has something closer to A + B + A.

As concerns the contrapuntal syntax, it should be clear even from Ex. 16 that *Vasilissa ergo gaude* is more complex than the three-voice songs. In general Dufay's four-voice works are less easy to describe contrapuntally: simple rules cannot be generally applied. Moreover the syntax of the motet is throughout its history difficult to define. Strictly the tenor is of course the foundation; the upper texted parts in the earlier motets were called 'motetus' (or 'duplum') and 'triplum' – terms whose hierarchical implications are obvious, though it is usually difficult in Dufay's motets to decide which is which (in general the manuscripts of the time gave no title to texted voices). Names given to those voices in the musical examples should therefore be treated as tentative.

*Vasilissa ergo gaude* contains many parallel octaves and fifths between the parts (though they do not appear in the section quoted above). Among Dufay's predecessors parallel movement was relatively common: Machaut, Dunstable and even Ciconia allowed such movement throughout their four-voice writing. With Dufay such parallels were becoming rarer. In *Vasilissa ergo gaude* practically all the parallel movement is between the contratenor and another voice – something which may suggest a certain lack of technical control and support the idea of 'consecutive composition' with one part being written after another and the contratenor composed last to fit in as best it could.[9] Probably the truth is more a matter of changing values, an increasing belief that each part should be self-sufficient and independent: particularly in Dufay's motets and Mass cycles it is possible to trace his career as a composer in terms of a growing independence and equality of the voices. The quantity of parallel writing in *Vasilissa ergo gaude* would in that context strongly support the evidence that this really is one of his earliest compositions. Until the very end of the fifteenth century certain kinds of movement in parallel fifths are quite common, but it is possible to see in Dufay's later motets how he went to special lengths to avoid the kinds of parallel movement found in *Vasilissa ergo gaude*.

In its isorhythmic scheme this motet follows Ciconia's motet *Ut te per omnes celitum*, a work that shows evidently intentional traces of the sorts of thematic and tonal relationship between the two halves which appear more clearly in Dufay's motet. Yet an important difference is that Dufay used the same text in both upper voices, a departure from tradition which seems to have been new at the time. This principle of using a single text – with correspondingly increased directness of communication – does not appear again in Dufay's surviving isorhythmic motets until the works of the 1430s; but among the four remaining motets of the 1420s it is possible to see him striving in other ways to master the various isorhythmic techniques inherited from the fourteenth century and to adapt them to the needs of his own day. Three of these as well as *Ecclesie militantis* (i/12) of 1431 include an opening canonic or pseudo-canonic passage outside the isorhythmic scheme. Several earlier motets had had non-isorhythmic introductions: there are five, for example, in the works of Machaut; but these differ from Dufay's in being much simpler. *Vasilissa ergo gaude* may be the earliest example of a motet in which the opening duo is canonic, though the style is anticipated in earlier motets and strict canon is a characteristic of the fourteenth-century *caccia*. Dufay's introductory duets show a curious similarity to one another, as though he was repeatedly trying out a single idea which had been successful but was worth remodelling and perfecting. In each case in Ex. 17 the second voice enters at the *signum congruentiae* ( $\mathcal{S}$ ), 17a–c in pure canon, 17d (the latest example) in canon only as far as the present example stretches.[10]

Yet the most fascinating of the motets from the 1420s is *Rite majorem Jacobum canamus* (i/11), the only one without an introductory non-isorhythmic passage and the only one to share with

Ex. 17

*Vasilissa ergo gaude* the characteristic of having its main sections the same length. At least, to be more precise, the second half of *Rite majorem* is just slightly shorter – 62 bars to the 66 of the first half – as a result of a move from *prolatio* to *tempus* (6/8 to 3/4) notation. The other motets of the 1420s follow a well-established tradition in speeding up the tenor for later sections so that the work moves to an impressive climax. *Rite majorem* is in every way a gentler and more subtle work. Each half is in two fully isorhythmic sections over a single *color*, so each half contains within itself the formal structure of the entire isorhythmic part of *Vasilissa ergo gaude*.

But the additional detail here is its isomelic structure. Isomelism is a word that has been applied to various manifestations in the motet. In general it amounts to the use of the same melodic outline in two or more sections, and its most famous appearance is in Dufay's *Nuper rosarum flores* (i/16) of 1436 where the four isorhythmic sections can be seen as a set of variations on the melodic outline of the first.[11] What happens in *Rite majorem* is rather different. The two upper voices, the triplum and the motetus, exchange their melodic outlines for the entire second half of the motet.[12] The openings of the two halves appear in parallel in Ex. 18.

In itself that is not a particularly inspired idea. To some extent it perhaps derives from a technique found in English motets of the fourteenth century and earlier, though there the sections exchanged are much briefer and are exchanged literally. Since the actual pitches of the lower voices remain the same in the two halves of *Rite*

Ex. 18

*majorem* it might be argued that to retain the same melodic outline for the two upper voices is almost the simplest way of composing the second half of the motet and that to exchange them is merely a way of disguising this to the eye. But Dufay apparently used this technique as another self-imposed limitation, as a test of his inventive skills: the differences between the two halves seem very carefully calculated. One difference comes from a device reminiscent of the scheme already noted in *Vasilissa ergo gaude*: the first half of the motet contains not the least trace of imitation between the two upper voices, whereas in the second half he introduces imitation at every possible juncture, as can be seen even in the brief passage in Ex. 18; and the closing passage of the motet reaches its gentle climax with prominent triadic imitation.

But that is not all. As already mentioned, each half is in two *taleae*, isorhythmic in all voices, giving a total structure of four approximately equal sections. The first of these sections, while containing no imitation, has the two upper voices taking over from one another to explore the melodic region between G and the high C (Ex. 19), an area all but ignored in the matching third section. The second section equally explores the lower region below the A (which remains throughout the motet a kind of foundation note), whereas the concluding fourth section produces a balance between the two areas. In short, *Rite majorem* shows a careful attempt to impose on the received number-based form various elements of melodic coherence and a more contemporary approach to long-range shape.

One further feature taken from the earlier motet tradition appears in both *Rite majorem* and *Apostolo glorioso* (i/10): they

Ex. 19

[Triplum]

[Motetus]

(Lower voices and text omitted)

have an extra voice, labelled 'solus tenor', which is a reduction of the lower voices. The purposes of the 'solus tenor' have been much discussed,[13] though without clear conclusions. To suggest that it represented an alternative performance style for smaller forces seems unsatisfactory if only because these works were normally composed with but a single performance in mind: they are occasional pieces, not works to be performed many times in different parts of Europe. Perhaps the 'solus tenor' was merely a simplified bass part intended for use when rehearsing the complex upper voices.

The two texts for the upper voices of *Rite majorem* in fact form a single poem with a continuous narrative describing the life and miracles of St James the Greater:[14] the triplum contains quatrains 1–4 and the motetus contains quatrains 5–8; and as though to confirm this the acrostic ROBERTUS ACLOU CURATUS SANCTI JACOBI runs through the quatrains in that order. Since the triplum and the motetus occupy the same range it is just possible that the work was intended to be sung twice through: the first time the triplum could be texted, with the motetus performed instrumentally or vocalized, and the second time the roles could be reversed so that the total added up to a continuous narrative easily heard throughout. That may seem a wild idea totally at variance with the whole world of the isorhythmic motet; but the broader picture of Dufay's motets may help to put the suggestion into perspective.

The same pattern can be seen in other motets: the two texts of *Apostolo glorioso* (i/10) form between them a single Italian sonnet;[15] those of *O sancte Sebastiane* (i/8) appear together as a single poem in

*111*

five poetic sources of the time;[16] and in another motet of the 1420s, *O gemma, lux et speculum* (i/9), the two texts have the same poetic form and again an apparently continuous thread of meaning. That accounts for all the motets of the 1420s except the first, *Vasilissa ergo gaude*, which we have seen was novel in having only a single text anyway. Three of the motets from the 1430s have a single text: *Balsamus et munda cera* (i/13), *Supremum est mortalibus bonum* (i/14) and *Nuper rosarum flores* (i/16). Beyond that, *Magnanime gentis* (i/17) and *Salve flos Tusce gentis* (i/15) both have their two texts in the same poetic metre (elegiac couplets) with a continuous logical thread; and *Moribus et genere* (i/19) has, according to its one surviving manuscript source, a single poem for both voices although the motetus begins at the third quatrain.[17] This leaves only two motets which follow the traditional form in having simultaneous texts which are unrelated except in treating of a similar subject.

Quite what this means it is hard to say; and that perhaps hints at the difficulty of studying music from five centuries' distance. My own present feeling is that the voices in these works are so perfectly matched and the grand formal scheme is so perfectly conceived that it would be the height of musical insensitivity to perform them twice on end with different voices texted. Others may feel differently. But it is clear that in this, as in so many other features of the motets, Dufay is adopting an approach to form different from that of his predecessors: there is a kind of simplification here which fits in with the mood of his time.

And it is in this context that *Ecclesie militantis* (i/12), probably of 1431, shows the first aspect of its exceptional nature: apart from its two tenors based on different chants it has three different texts in different metres for its three upper voices. It also merits special attention because its magnificent structure is so audacious and at the same time risks not being classed as isorhythmic at all.[18] Its two tenors are both based on chants associated with the Archangel Gabriel and therefore particularly appropriate for the papal coronation of Gabriele Condulmer. They are simple to the point of absur-

Ex. 20

(These are performed in augmented values, so one bar of ex. 20 fits to three of ex. 21)

112

dity, indeed probably the shortest in the entire later history of the motet. The higher tenor has only two pitches, G and D, each repeated; and the lower is not much longer. They combine as in Ex. 20 and appear six times with the proportional lengths 6:3: 4:2: 6:3.

With them appears a third cantus firmus (labelled 'contratenor') underlaid with a text built of two elegiac couplets:

> Bella canunt gentes: querimur, Pater optime, tempus.
>    Expediet multos, si cupis, una dies.
> Nummus et hora fluunt magnumque iter orbis agendum
>    Nec suus in toto noscitur orbe Deus.

This cantus firmus is stated three times, each taking up exactly two statements of the lower tenors, giving the proportional lengths 9:6:9. It moves quickly enough for its opening, at least, to be relatively easily recognized when it reappears, in spite of the rich five-voice texture (Ex. 21).

Ex. 21

Bel - la    ca - nunt    gen - tes:    que-ri-mur,    Pa - ter    op - ti-me, tem - pus.

Above this framework the two upper voices have complete rhythmic freedom – something which was normal in the motets of Philippe de Vitry and Machaut but extremely uncommon in the fifteenth century. Dufay was to use that freedom in three more motets of the 1430s. But in this case he resorted again to the isomelic techniques of *Rite majorem*.[19] After a free introductory duo that begins canonically (see Ex. 17d) he lays out the upper voices in three sections corresponding to the three statements of the 'Bella canunt gentes' melody. In these three main sections the voices exchange their melodic outlines as follows:

|   |   |   |
|---|---|---|
| a | b | a |
| b | a | b |

And again he follows a technique similar to that of *Rite majorem* but perhaps closer to that of *Vasilissa ergo gaude* in his use of imitation. The free introduction and the first main section have some imitation, but not much; the second section carefully avoids it; and the third section includes enough to provide a striking contrast with all that went before, culminating in the jubilant triadic imitations at the final 'Amen'.

Although in this case Dufay makes a gesture to standard practice by giving the upper voices independent texts with different metrical structures, the overwhelming impression is of his struggling once again to adapt the techniques of the isorhythmic motet to produce a larger canvas that is not only bafflingly complex – with two chants, one repeated 'tune' and two melodically active but largely independent upper voices – but assembled in a shape that is easily perceived as a result of its formal simplicity.

*Ecclesie militantis* is in many ways the most thrilling of all Dufay's motets: its richness of ideas, its crowded texture and the triadic resolution of the final 'Amen' all give it a truly Gothic splendour. Yet at the same time its magnificence is tempered by a certain severity, and none of the motets so far shows the freedom of lyrical line so often found in the songs of those years. The intellectual, the virtuoso and the public orator in Dufay almost exclude the poetic and sometimes intensely personal musician.

And it is therefore no surprise that this *tour de force* should have been followed only a month later by a work of softer melodic contours, *Balsamus et munda cera* (i/13). In some ways this panisorhythmic motet has formal severities beyond those of the earlier works: the tenor and contratenor appear in forward and then in retrograde motion before doing the same again in shorter note-values (an unusual scheme which is, however, found in the only surviving motet of Dufay's presumed teacher, Loqueville); and the tenor reverts to a popular fourteenth-century practice in being divided up by rests which add up to precisely one third of its length[20] (the same happens in the lower tenor of *Ecclesie militantis*). But the two upper voices luxuriate in a freely imitative melodic style that has all the surge of the most passionate of his chansons. Perhaps for the first time among his motets, Dufay produced a work with a melodic power that justifies itself and can be enjoyed quite independently of any admiration one may have for his technical or formal skill. And the mood of the music amply reflects that of the text which is the same in both upper voices, a fourteenth-century poem in Leonine hexameters (that is to say the classical hexameter with the added detail that each line contains an internal rhyme at the caesura): the mystic sanctity of the aromatic wax figures distributed by the pope is credited with giving comfort and salvation.

With *Supremum est mortalibus bonum* (i/14) of May 1433 several important changes come to Dufay's motet style. The first concerns texture. Whereas all his previous essays in the genre had their two main texted voices in the same range, the texture from now on has only a single voice in the upper register, and the second texted part is lower, usually in the same range as the tenor and contratenor. This motet texture is new only for Dufay: there are plenty of fourteenth-century motets with this layout. But the same change seems to happen at about the same time in Dufay's Mass music.

It is just possible that the change results from a change in the performing ensembles available to him, but there is no apparent evidence of a significant alteration in the papal singing establishment between 1428 and 1437; moreover, the style with two equal high voices reappears in a non-isorhythmic work from 1435–6, *Mirandas parit* (i/5). So a more reasonable conclusion is that the change reflects a new kind of solution to the continuing problem of reconciling motet form with the aesthetic ideals of the fifteenth century. It is also possible that Dufay now became more interested in the works of Dunstable: Dufay's 'new' texture appears in all but one of Dunstable's surviving motets; and later Dufay motets show further traces of apparent influence from Dunstable. But here, as always, Dunstable's influence on Dufay is difficult to pin down. The textural change in Dufay's motets awaits full explanation.

The second change is formal. From now on his motets show a move away from the isorhythmic practices of previous generations. The nature of the isorhythmic motet with its diminutions in the tenor was such that the pace normally increased towards the end of the work. Dufay never entirely discarded this idea, because he used it in two of his late cantus firmus Mass cycles and in a modified form in his last motets; but for the motets of the 1430s he tried various other schemes to move towards alternative designs.

*Supremum est mortalibus bonum* occupies a special place among his works because it appears in six surviving manuscripts, something equalled among his earlier works only by certain pieces for the Mass and the Office – pieces that were appropriate for all kinds of occasions and were therefore often recopied. This motet is in only three voices, though several sections have an additional *fauxbourdon* voice;[21] and only the tenor is isorhythmic, so the musical flow of the piece is almost unfettered by schematic considerations.[22] Moreover it is also unusual in containing extended free sections not only at the beginning but at the end as well – a coda that is itself as long as any of the isorhythmic sections. Beyond that, the tenor is unique among his isorhythmic pieces in not following a chant except for a brief passage in the non-isorhythmic coda.[23]

Formally, then, Dufay was free to adopt various other devices. The motet begins in a startling fashion: the free opening section is in *fauxbourdon*, a style of writing that allows for optimum communication of the text; and comparison of the lowest voice in that section with the first *talea* of the tenor shows that the two are melodically related (Ex. 22).

Ex. 22

Ex. 23

But more important and significant is the way the *fauxbourdon* texture of the opening is integrated into the rest of the piece. Since each *talea* of the tenor ends with three bars' rest, the composer is free to do as he wishes at those points, and twice (out of the six *taleae*) he returns to the *fauxbourdon* texture of the opening. He also uses

116

*fauxbourdon* in the non-isorhythmic coda. And as though to loosen the scheme as much as possible, he incorporates *fauxbourdon*-like writing into the beginning of the fourth *talea* (Ex. 23). Here and in other passages that use parallel sixths the writing recalls the opening, as though the *fauxbourdon* or a reference to it acts as a kind of refrain for the entire length of the work (it can last up to eight minutes). In addition there is a hint of isomelism between the third and sixth *taleae*, alerting the listener to the approaching end of the isorhythmically structured part of the work but here using that technique in a far subtler and gentler manner than in some of the other works.

The next motet, *Nuper rosarum flores* (i/16) of 1436, has been discussed elsewhere in this book; and indeed it has elicited more discussion than any other single piece between *Sumer is icumen in* and Monteverdi's *Orfeo* with the possible exception of the *Caput* Mass.[24] In the present context it must suffice to make a few quick points: to recall that the structure of the tenors and the proportional scheme seem to match the structure of the cathedral for whose dedication it was composed, Santa Maria del Fiore in Florence; to note that it shares with *Supremum est mortalibus bonum* and *Ecclesie militantis* its freely composed texted voices; that it is unique among the motet repertory in having two tenors which use the same melody (*Terribilis est locus iste*) a fifth apart but with different rhythmic configurations; and that its isomelic design is more elaborate than elsewhere in Dufay.

Concerning the two-tenor structure, *Nuper rosarum flores* shows another feature of the stylistic change in Dufay's motets of the 1430s. Although the 'tenor secundus' can be associated with plainchant only in *Ecclesie militantis* and *Nuper rosarum flores*, it appears in all the later motets. In practical terms this means that the 'tenor secundus' is in long notes, like the tenor, and is subjected to precisely the same isorhythmic procedures as the tenor whereas the contratenor voices in Dufay's earlier motets had more angular, faster-moving lines and were much more independent of the tenor. With the two-tenor structure (which curiously harks back to the structure of Machaut's three surviving four-voice motets) Dufay has a more solid framework which in its turn contributes to the increasing formal complexity of his later motets.

*Nuper rosarum flores* is structurally unusual in that the proportional scheme 6:4:2:3 has the last section longer than the one before it, thereby affording a more imposing balance to the sections; and something similar happens in *Magnanime gentis* (i/17) of 1438 with its proportional scheme 12:4:2:3. The one is to some extent a reworking of the other, and many pages could profitably be filled comparing the two in detail. But at the same time both pieces retain the formal feature that is normally a direct consequence of the more usual sequentially reduced tenor mensurations: the final isorhythmic section is still, to the ear, the fastest-moving of all because the upper voices have the shortest note values thus driving the motet to an accelerated conclusion. One part of the inherited tradition is therefore rejected, but a closely related part of it is retained and developed. Structure alters, the resulting formal design remains almost as it was. (And hints at the evolution of this idea are apparent in *Ecclesie militantis*.)

In the last five motets there are several features that again point to a concentrated reworking and reconsideration of similar materials. Four of them, for example, are remarkably similar in their opening duos (Ex. 24).[25]

In function these duos differ: that in *Magnanime gentis* is a free non-isorhythmic introduction, that in *Nuper rosarum flores* is within the isorhythmic scheme of the tenors but is again freely composed, and those in *Fulgens iubar* (i/18) and *Moribus et genere* (i/19) are part of a fully isorhythmic scheme. Another slightly surprising detail is that *Nuper rosarum flores* and *Fulgens iubar* have the same music for the closing 'Amen', though the structural function differs slightly in that the motetus of the one takes over the second tenor line of the other.[26]

In their scoring the late motets have two significant features. In all of them one or other voice divides into two, even if only for a single note. This seems clear enough evidence that they were composed for a choral ensemble, not for soloists. (And the same could well be the case with his early motets, though here firm evidence is lacking: for what it is worth there seems every probability that solo performance was intended for the motets of the thirteenth century and of Machaut's generation.) Second, their structure gives a further hint to scoring. If the tenors are to be performed instrumentally then the two texted voices will also need to be doubled by an instrument: this is because their long unaccompanied duos will otherwise almost certainly result in a change of pitch level, which will lead to an extremely ugly sound when the tenors re-enter. Whatever the intri-

Ex. 24

cacy of the lines, then, the music is for a largish ensemble, perhaps indeed for the eight to ten singers in the papal chapel during those years, possibly augmented by instrumentalists employed for the occasion.

*Fulgens iubar* (i/18) is one of the two motets which I have earlier attempted to show were composed at Cambrai in 1442; and it is perhaps the most perfect combination of the various received features of motet technique. For this motet (as for its twin, *Moribus et genere*, i/19) Dufay employed the three-stage double-*talea* structure that Dunstable had used in five of his eleven surviving motets. There is room for dispute as to whether it really has the proportional lengths 3:3: 2:2: 1:1 which are implied in the two modern editions,[27] but certainly the motet belongs in that category: it could be said to belong there in theory even if not in practice. And that may explain why *Fulgens iubar* appears within an otherwise exclusively English motet fascicle in the Modena manuscript. (It appears there immedi-

*119*

ately after the Dunstable motet *Salve scema sanctitatis* which follows the same broad structure and is the only Dunstable motet to have the two-tenor structure that characterizes Dufay's later motets.) Dunstable's motets with this mensural scheme probably date back to the 1420s or earlier[28] and they are in a sound-world entirely different from Dufay's. To explore that difference fairly would entail an extended appreciation of Dunstable's harmonic and contrapuntal style. But part of the difference is that Dufay's lines and progressions are clearer, more familiar to the ear that is accustomed to expecting logical harmonic patterns and formal designs. To return from *Fulgens iubar* to Dunstable's motets is to enter a world of apparent shapelessness, of poorly-controlled textures, of unregulated dissonance and of relatively graceless lines. To see Dunstable in that light is not to denigrate him but to note how the musical priorities in Dufay's work are entirely different. By contrast with the comments made earlier about the middle-period motets and the early ones in Dufay's work, here the structure remains the same but the form is developed in an entirely different manner. Of the three formal features in *Fulgens iubar* to be discussed, two are dimly present in Dunstable's works and indeed in Dufay's early motets, but they are exploited here with an added thoroughness and an added clarity.

The first of these features is the use of transposed material in complementary positions within the motet. Between any two *taleae* in the same mensuration there are implied key-relations and key-tensions. Thus the opening sections of *taleae* III and IV are as in Ex. 25; and those of *taleae* V and VI are even more clearly related as in Ex. 26.

Ex. 25

**Ex. 26**

This in its turn supports a clearly audible key-scheme for the whole motet.[29] Since each pair of *taleae* has the same set of pitches in the two lower voices, each pair correspondingly has the same broad tonal progression: beginning on D, the first *talea* moves towards a final cadence on F, and the second *talea* moves from here to the final on G. G is therefore the tonal focus of the motet, though in the opening section the first two cadences on G are gentle passing ones (bars 11 and 26), so the tonality is not firmly established until bar 37 shortly before the important F cadence at the end of the first *talea* (bar 48). G is established more clearly in the second *talea*, but although this and the fourth *talea* end on G that key is relatively soft in its impact, with cadences on D often appearing at stronger positions. The middle section of the fifth *talea* again re-establishes G (bars 160–65), but its final cadence on F leads to a fairly extended section based around F (bars 167–79). The concluding sixth *talea* very carefully avoids G cadences until the very end at bars 192–4; but the progression towards that G is made inevitable by what has gone before. The final section serves as a climax – a climax made clearer by the top voice which rises to its highest pitch (E) just once in the entire motet, at bar 180. Again, the aural form transcends the underlying isorhythmic structure.

Finally, the isomelism in *Fulgens iubar* is clearer and richer than in any other Dufay motet. Example 27 shows the point where the tenors enter in the first, third and fifth *taleae*.[30]

This offers a hint of how the motet could have been composed. As early as 1336 the theorist Petrus dictus de Palma Ociosa had given precise instructions for motet composition.[31] He said that one should

## Dufay

**Ex. 27**

(Texts omitted)

122

begin with the tenor and build a simple note-against-note counter-point above it; the upper-voice notes so formed could then be connected by embellishing patterns, what he called 'flores'. It is easy to reconstruct such a groundwork pattern for *Fulgens iubar* (Ex. 28).

Ex. 28

Hints of isomelism are present in several English motets of the fourteenth century and in some works of Dunstable; but if earlier motet composers actually followed the instructions offered by Petrus, they must have made a special effort to avoid any parallelisms between the sections: complexity of invention and variety were their ideals. In *Fulgens iubar*, and to some extent in his earlier motets, Dufay moved towards something simpler and more lucid, something stricter in certain ways but correspondingly richer in formal coherence and musical communication.

For composers of the early fifteenth century the position of the motet was in many ways similar to that of the fugue for nineteenth-century composers. It was a style based on aesthetic criteria that had obtained two hundred years earlier but had little to do with the ideas that were now current; and it was increasingly a style associated with seriousness of tone and scholasticism, a style used to suggest formality, to be chosen for auspicious occasions. Yet another feature shared by the motet and the fugue in the later stages of their history was that while their difficulties and formality often drove a lesser composer to produce his most pompous and turgid efforts, they equally spurred a certain kind of resourceful mind to sublime heights of musical invention. The evidence suggests that Dufay's was such a mind.

# 10

# Cantilenas and related works

If the isorhythmic motets represented Dufay working within a long-established tradition, the pieces to be considered next show him exploring a new and exciting style that belongs very much to the fifteenth century. These works follow no particular formal scheme – neither the strictness of rigid isorhythm nor the repeating patterns of the secular songs nor the liturgical confines that to some extent predetermine the shape and context of his Mass and Office music. It is in these free-form works that Dufay's lyric gift comes through most clearly; and here more than elsewhere in his work a more modern-seeming expressive style comes through.

The tradition to which they belong cannot reach back much earlier than 1400. Both Dunstable and Lionel Power composed cantilenas of this kind with a freely developing form: most were Marian, and many of the works discussed in this chapter are similarly on texts to the Virgin Mary. But perhaps the stylistic context for Dufay's pieces is in works written in northern Italy by Feragut, particularly his two occasional works *Excelsa civitas* (probably of

Ex. 29

1409) and *Francorum nobilitati*,[1] and in Johannes de Lymburgia's *Pulchra es amica mea*; further traces are in works composed in the Veneto by Ciconia, Antonio Romano and Nicolas Zacharia.

Nowhere is this style more attractive and luxurious than in Dufay's florid three-voice cantilenas. *Flos florum* (i/2)[2] and *O beate Sebastiane* (i/4) have much in common, in their melodic style, their voice ranges, their length and their use of fermata passages. They also open in remarkably similar fashion (obscured in the complete edition by the use of different note-reduction for the two transcriptions). See Ex. 29.

But at the same time in their musical effect they seem to belong to two different worlds, with the chord-structure and tonal movement of *O beate Sebastiane*[3] giving it a more detailed and perhaps hesitant colour. One reason for this is that the contratenor here runs slightly lower to make possible wide textures like that in the cadence with which it closes.

Ex. 30

That texture is further expanded in *Ave virgo* (i/3)[4] where the tenor and the contratenor lie a fifth lower than in *O beate Sebastiane*. In fact this relatively unpretentious-looking piece has the widest total range of any Dufay work, three octaves: elsewhere a span of two octaves is far more common. Moreover there is plenty of evidence that *Ave virgo* is something of an experiment. It contains many progressions in parallel fifths, something scarcely found in Dufay's three-voice writing at any stage of his career. It also shows a kind of dissonance treatment that is most unusual in Dufay and more characteristic of Binchois:[5] the fluid lines of the discantus often include dissonant passing notes; and all three voices include suspensions that are resolved either by a leap or by a step upwards (Ex. 31).

In spite of their differences, however, these three cantilenas share a single language. Their similar discantus figuration is perhaps what strikes the ear first, and even though their total of seven sources

**Ex. 31**

Tenor
Contra

(Text omitted)

contains only one mensuration sign in one voice (for the discantus of *O beate Sebastiane*) they clearly all have the same mensuration, *tempus perfectum diminutum* ($\emptyset$) – which happens to be the mensuration of the Feragut and Lymburgia pieces already mentioned. One Dufay rondeau, incidentally, has the same kind of discantus figuration and much else besides: this is *Pour l'amour de ma doulce amye* (vi/48)[6], which must also be in the same mensuration.

A further feature that particularly characterizes *Flos florum* and *Ave virgo* is the apparently careful exploitation of rhythms.[7] The opening of the discantus of *Ave virgo* gives an example of this variety (Ex. 32): not until bar 25 is the rhythm of one bar repeated in another bar; and only from bar 32 does such repetition become at all frequent. This elasticity of rhythm seems again witness of a composer endlessly absorbed by technical questions; but its result is a fascinating and continuous unravelling of musical ideas within a unified style.

Along with the formal freedom of these works comes an increased use of fermata chords to underline particularly solemn

**Ex. 32**

A -      ve vir -    go que de ce -
- lis Dul - ce per os Ga - bri - e -
- lis Su - sce - pi - sti gau -

Ex. 33

words (Ex. 33). Many other Dufay works contain such writing. Most of his early Gloria settings have fermata chords at the words 'Jesu Christe', and several early Credo settings have them at 'ex Maria virgine'. Elsewhere it occurs at particular moments for a special sentiment or a dedication: it comes for the statement of the name 'Charle gentil' in *Resvelliés vous* (vi/11) and the names 'Eugenius et Rex Sigismundus' in *Supremum est mortalibus bonum* (i/14). Normally performers interpret these simply as unmeasured held chords. But occasionally the chords show signs of distinguishing between the *longa* and the *brevis*, therefore remaining to some extent measured – as in the two *Alma Redemptoris mater* settings (v/47 and v/48).[8] Strictly such a fermata should perhaps be described as *signum congruentiae*, a sign mentioned already in chapter 8 in one particular context, but used in the sources in so many different ways that its meaning is perhaps best described as simply: 'something happens here'. Among the suggestions about what happens, one that deserves serious attention is the *punctus organi*, an organ point on which at least one of the voices should introduce embellishments.[9] Such a

Ex. 34

127

solution would work extremely well in the stylistic context of Dufay's cantilena compositions.

In several ways the two *Alma Redemptoris mater* settings belong with the cantilenas.[10] The second of them (v/48), and by far the more famous, is closer to the style of the cantilenas: its discantus figuration is similar and it too must have $\phi$ mensuration, even though one of its sources states otherwise. Its famous opening unaccompanied discantus line very closely follows its chant (marked by crosses in Ex. 34) and leads to a passage in which the three voices overlap before separating out into their distinctive ranges.

If this and the other pieces already mentioned are from the years around 1430, the other *Alma Redemptoris mater* (v/47) is considerably earlier and aligns itself stylistically more with the Mass *Resvelliés vous* (ii/1) of around 1423. Again it is essentially a lyrical piece, through-composed and clearly structured. But whereas v/48 has the original chant much decorated in the discantus, v/47 has the chant in the tenor leaving the discantus free to rhapsodize without restraint. It is in four sections: opening in 6/8 ($\complement$), it moves to 3/4 ($O$) and then back to the original mensuration before its closing section in fermata chords.

*Anima mea liquefacta est* (v/46)[11] shares characteristics of both *Alma Redemptoris* settings. Like v/47 it carries its chant primarily in the tenor though, as the complete edition shows, all three voices have some degree of chant paraphrase (resulting in a most extraordinary pattern of imitations and pseudo-imitations as each voice takes the same chant phrase). And like v/48 it opens with a solo passage for the discantus, closely following the outline of the chant. It is a strange work with many surprising contrapuntal turns. Sometimes its dissonance treatment is reminiscent of that already mentioned in *Ave virgo*, but in general there is no other work of the time that seems quite like it either in contrapuntal treatment or in the mysterious limpidity of its overlapping imitations and rubbing dissonances.

The changes of mensuration that define the form of the first *Alma Redemptoris* setting also appear in other free pieces, works that in many ways seem and sound like isorhythmic motets but contain no hint of isorhythmic structure. One of these is the glorious and joyful *Mirandas parit hec urbs florentina puellas* (i/5) probably of 1436. Its quasi-canonic opening instantly recalls the motets of the 1420s,[12] and its tenor is in many ways similar to that of *Supremum est mortalibus bonum* (i/14) of 1433. Another is the four-voice O *proles Hispanie* (i/6) which is bi-textual (so far as the sources permit us to tell) but is again not isorhythmic. Its harmonic style with three equal-ranged voices in the lower register marks it as a relatively late work, probably the latest of all the works considered so far; but its mensural form $\phi \quad O \quad \phi$ precisely matches that of what must be a relatively early work, the Petrarch setting *Vergene bella* (vi/5).

*Vergene bella*[13] may have Italian words, but it is in every sense a sacred piece, setting the first stanza of the prayer to the Virgin Mary with which Petrarch concluded his *Canzoniere*. Curiously, the poet who was set to music more than any other in the sixteenth century was scarcely set at all in the fourteenth and fifteenth centuries; and the only Petrarch setting that was certainly composed before Dufay's is Jacopo da Bologna's *Non al suo amante* of half a century earlier. Part of the reason may well be that Petrarch – like Shakespeare in a later age – frightened composers by the very richness of his poetic imagery until the dawn of the madrigalian era when a new musical style brought with it a search for texts that demanded settings full of imagery and affect. The *formes fixes* of medieval song made such evocative setting almost impossible. So it is perhaps no surprise that Dufay should have chosen a prayer and chosen to set it as a prayer, precisely in the manner of the Marian cantilenas just described. Nor is it any surprise that Dufay should have risen to the challenge which so many other composers seem to have shunned.

But if Dufay joined many of his contemporaries in adopting a totally free formal design for his most expressive early works he also found other ways of mixing genres to produce works that stand entirely alone in the century. One such work is *Juvenis qui puellam* (vi/9)[14] which adopts the style of *fauxbourdon* psalm settings to expound the mock-legal argument which has been construed earlier as reflecting the mood of the Council of Basle in 1438 after it had officially been replaced by that of Ferrara. The work unfortunately survives only in incomplete form, but its tone splendidly captures the sense of high political seriousness coupled with the mocking style of the court jester or licensed fool.

A similar mixing of genres appears in two songs which employ the techniques of isorhythm. *Je ne puis plus* (vi/29)[15] has a free discantus over a long-note tenor which repeats the words 'Unde veniet auxilium mihi?' three times at different speeds (in the proportions 3:2:1); the same idea was used later by Loyset Compere, perhaps with Dufay's piece in mind. And Dufay's one surviving lament for Constantinople, *O tres piteulx* (vi/10),[16] hints at various motet techniques: the tenor carries a chant – 'Omnes amici spreverunt eam . . .' – which appears once in each half of the piece; and before the entry of the tenor each half begins with a passage in which the discantus paraphrases the first line of the tenor, somewhat as Dunstable had done in his four-voice motet *Veni Creator/Veni sancte*.

A tenor cantus firmus also controls one of his most charming songs, *La belle se siet* (vi/12). Here the tenor has a melody in what seems like a folksong style, repeating in the form A A'B B B C A A'. Above this two equal high voices[17] tell the sad story of the maid whose lover is to be hanged in the morning: their lines include a rapid parlando with much imitation and their overall form is A B A'. The lines are propelled by gentle dissonances similar to those noted in the rondeau *Ma belle dame souveraine* (vi/44); and the melismatic passages directly recall those of the three-voice cantilenas.

Another piece with cantus firmus treatment is that surviving with the text *Qui latuit in virgine* (i/20) and considered a doubtful work by most authorities. Its tenor later became famous as the basse danse *Je sui povere de leesse*; and above it are two intricately structured voices. Certainly the piece is in many ways unlike anything else in Dufay's work. But three factors might argue in favour of his authorship. First, its immediate stylistic context is clear and easily established. It appears in one source (Trent 87) copied by the same hand as two more works in similar style (on the tenors *Aux ce bon joure de le bonestren* and *T'Andernaken*)[18] and in a further source (Munich 14274) alongside yet another (on the English melody *Love woll I without eny variaunce*): there is a firm tradition here to which Dufay could have contributed. Second, the earlier history of that tradition is one that looks straight back to the motets of around 1300 and seems to come via certain English works in the Old Hall manuscript; that they happen also to look forward to many tenor settings of the years around 1500 is less relevant in this context. Third, taking these four pieces as a group, if one were asked to name the one most likely to be by Dufay one would unhesitatingly choose this one with its more carefully controlled textures (particularly at bars 14–15) and more sophisticated motivic development: as in *Ave virgo* the rhythms of the discantus show a careful effort at variety until the closing section which refers back to the opening. If it is his it is yet another example of his fascination with reworking various aspects of the motet tradition.

Not surprisingly the technique of canon was one that also fascinated the composer who so often sought problems to solve. The Marian piece *Inclita stella maris* (i/1) is cast as a two-voice mensural canon at the unison over two free contratenors. 'Mensural canon' in this case means that the two voices begin at the same time but each reads the notation with a different mensuration so that one voice gets further ahead as the work progresses: at the end the two voices are seven bars apart. In spite of its considerable length and apparently restricted style this piece works extremely well with its gentle undulations which give it a mood of comfort received from the very act of praying for intercession. Like most canons it is somewhat restricted in its tonal movement – though the passage in F at bars 4–8 is one of several changes of tonality which add colour to the work (Ex. 35) – but part of its success is in the way it uses those limitations to achieve its expressive ends.

Ex. 35

The work contains what may be significant information on performance. The second contratenor has the instruction 'Non potest cantari nisi pueri dicant fugam' – this cannot be sung unless the boys say the canon. Taken together with the instruction on the first contratenor, this suggests that Dufay envisaged several different possible groupings for performance: voices I and II, voices I, II and III, voices I and III, voices I, II and IV or all four voices together (and perhaps even voices II and III). But it also implies that the two canonic voices are for boys: the range is a twelfth from low G. And presumably it is for two groups of boys, not soloists, for one of the voices divides on the last chord. That the boys should be 'saying' the texted upper-voice canon whereas the contratenor voice is 'sung' may be merely one of those vagaries of medieval Latin usage which are so easily overinterpreted. But certainly the contratenors are fragmented in such a way that it would be difficult to sing them with text: is it perhaps possible that 'dicere' is to sing with text whereas 'canere' in this context is to vocalize without text? If so, and if such vocalization was common, it may be possible to reconcile the style of these works with the opinion that instruments other than the organ were not allowed in church.

And if that is the case, the same may well apply to some of Dufay's songs. There is little essential difference in structure between *Inclita stella maris* and two of Dufay's canonic rondeau settings. *Par droit je puis* (vi/43)[19] from the 1420s has two upper voices in straight canon, not mensural canon; but otherwise it closely matches the style of *Inclita stella maris*. Its voice-ranges, its repeated notes, its approach to cadences are all similar. So also is its lower-voice structure: in both works the two lower voices are labelled 'contratenor', underlining the point that in both cases the two canonic voices form a complete counterpoint in themselves. The same happens in *Les douleurs* (vi/84), probably from the 1450s. Here the two upper voices are again in mensural canon[20] (Ex. 36); and although the musical style is as different as one might expect from a piece written some thirty years later in an age of fast stylistic change, the relative voice-ranges are remarkably similar to those in *Inclita stella maris*.

Other kinds of canon add spice to several of Dufay's three-voice songs. In *Bien veignés vous* (vi/50) the canon is at the octave with the lower voice in doubled note-values. *Entre vous, gentils amoureux* (vi/26) has the canonic voices a fifth apart; and *Puisque vous estez campieur* (vi/81)[21] uses canon at the octave: both do so at least

**Ex. 36**

partly to communicate a spirit of excited playfulness. In all these works a scholarly respect for age-old traditions of musical construction goes hand in hand with a need to communicate in new kinds of ways. And in all there is a certain community of expressive and technical means that unites the Latin cantilena with the secular song.

But if the historical position of these pieces is sought, it appears perhaps most clearly in Dufay's three settings of the Marian antiphon *Ave regina celorum*. It was suggested earlier that his first setting (v/49) was composed in about 1426 when Dufay composed several other pieces with the same kind of discantus structure and similar rhythmic patterning. This one is largely chordal in nature and has simple balanced phrases with a very small range of note-values. It derives its musical identity from its opening chromaticism, from its clear declamation and particularly from its carefully controlled variety of texture. Much of the time it is in the simplest *fauxbourdon* style, so that departures from strict parallelism make their musical points with special force. In style it belongs with several other works of the early fifteenth century, particularly settings of *lauda* texts, strophic devotional songs which need to be set in a way that brings out the declamation as clearly as possible. These works are among the simplest surviving examples of three-voice polyphony from the Middle Ages, and they perhaps show at its purest the mixing of sacred and secular styles for the optimum communication.

The second setting (v/50) is one of those works that are so difficult to place chronologically. It is closer to the cantilena style, but the voices are more equal in importance than in most of the pieces mentioned so far. The free way in which the rhythmic shapes cross the barlines makes them a classic case of the elasticity which Besseler termed *der neue Stromrhythmus*[22] – the new style of flowing rhythm. In many ways the freedom of the writing here recalls that of the three-voice sections in his later cyclic Masses. It would be difficult to date this setting before 1440 and it could be much later. Its formal fluidity has no apparent boundaries except the meaning of the text.

His third setting of *Ave regina celorum* (v/51)[23] is the only surviving work apart from Mass cycles that can be confidently dated after 1460. It was copied at Cambrai in 1464–5, and while that information gives only a *terminus ante quem* for its composition its stylistic similarity to the Mass *Ecce ancilla Domini* (iii/9) copied in the previous year makes that a plausible composition date.

This is by far the most expansive of the Marian pieces: it runs to 170 bars in four voices, with the chant paraphrased in the tenor. Its main success lies in its pacing – the way a comparatively simple passage will lead to one of considerable complexity with a relatively dense harmonic rhythm. Here in fully grown form is the style of Ockeghem's and Josquin's motets; and here too is the final perfection of the expressive style in Dufay.

# 11

# Hymns and other chant settings

Dufay's gift as a melodist has already been mentioned several times in passing. But perhaps the real test of that gift is in his elaborations of liturgical chants to create the discantus lines of polyphonic works. Of his many such pieces several can be compared directly with settings of the same chant by his contemporaries; and the comparison suggests that his reputation as a melodist needs some qualification.

As stated earlier, the original version of Dufay's hymn cycle seems to have been composed during his time at the court of Savoy in 1434–5. Dufay was by then a mature man established at the top of his profession. In the previous fifteen years he had composed in an astonishing variety of styles with many works showing a considerable technical complexity. We have seen that his motets in the 1430s begin to show a retreat from outward brilliance. The cycles of hymns, sequences and Kyrie settings that seem to date from the years immediately after 1433 correspondingly show an attempt to refine his technique, almost to return to first essentials with the most economical means.

The nineteen hymn settings that appear together as a group in their earliest manuscript source are stylistically consistent:[1] they are in triple time and in three voices with the upper voice a lightly elaborated version of the plainchant on which the setting is based. These are evidently among his most influential works: several of them have eight or nine surviving sources; and the entire cycle reappears with changes and additions in two later manuscripts.

According to the admittedly patchy evidence, the only precursor for Dufay's cycle is a group of ten hymn settings in the late fourteenth-century Apt manuscript.[2] All are settings of texts and melodies that appear in Dufay's cycle; all but one have their chant paraphrase in the discantus, as in Dufay's hymns; and all have a directness and simplicity of style that separates them from most of the polyphony of the time. But otherwise Dufay's hymns of the

1430s are the earliest surviving coherent cycle and the only one until quite late in the fifteenth century.

The use of chant paraphrase in the discantus was relatively new at the time.[3] The earliest examples seem again to be those in the Apt cycle, and other examples appear in English music from the first years of the century. But the systematic exploitation of that structure is an essentially fifteenth-century phenomenon which began in the 1420s or later and fell out of use shortly after Dufay's death.

If Dufay's motets showed him adapting and refining an older formal structure, his hymns show rather the attempt to 'translate' old chants into the language of the fifteenth century. In this Dufay was by no means alone, and various features of the translation are inevitable. Whereas many chants fall to their cadences, practically all phrases of fifteenth-century music rise to theirs in the discantus voice, as should be clear from the discussion of counterpoint in chapter 8. That is to say that while chant is of its nature fairly well suited to use as a tenor, in the place it had traditionally held since the very beginnings of polyphony, it tended to require some adaptation to become a suitable discantus line.[4] Equally, chant was largely non-mensural, and the first duty of the composer using it for the discantus of a polyphonic piece was to adapt it to a metrical framework.

Nevertheless the main consideration in studying these works is that the translations were of melodies well known to performer and listener alike. Moreover most polyphonic hymns of the fifteenth century were for alternatim performance: stanzas of the original chant alternated with stanzas of the polyphonic adaptation or elaboration.

Example 37 shows three versions of the hymn melody *Ut queant laxis*. First is the chant – not the famous melody which Guido of Arezzo had used to coin the mnemonic Ut Re Mi Fa Sol La for the six steps of the scale but another melody which was far more commonly used in the fifteenth century. The version given here is in fact the one that appears for the odd-numbered verses of the hymn in the sources of Dufay's setting, so we can be fairly confident that this was the precise version he used. Below it is the discantus of Dufay's three-voice polyphonic setting, underlaid, as in the source, with the second stanza of the hymn text. Below that is the discantus of the setting by Binchois which appears with the first stanza of the hymn text. This setting keeps close enough to Dufay's chant for a compari-

**Ex. 37**

son of the two versions to be feasible.

Dufay's setting (v/26) is obviously the more elaborate of the two; and in fact most of the service music by Binchois has a kind of simplicity that arises from having been composed with a very particular liturgical purpose in mind. But the important differences between these two melodies are not concerned with simplicity and complexity – there are several Dufay hymn melodies which are as simple as the Binchois one shown here – so much as with phrase structure.

Binchois runs the seven lines of the text together to form four musical phrases; and the first and sixth poetic lines end at points where it would actually be impossible for him to put a cadence. Dufay's seven cleanly-cut phrases each end with a cadence, and they are purposefully graded to fall on the pitches E, F, G, C, F, D, D (moreover we shall see in due course that the penultimate cadence on D is all but obliterated for the ear by the movement of the lower voices). Binchois, by running the lines together, misses the opportunity of making a Phrygian cadence on E at the end of the first line – an opportunity which Dufay predictably grasps – and gives a total cadence scheme of F, C, F, D. One conclusion from this might be that Dufay had a stronger sense of duty to his musical inheritance whereas Binchois felt the need to adapt it further and to put the declamation of the text first.

Certain features of Dufay's line show an ear curious for structural detail. That the first two lines of the chant begin with the same four pitches may be considered a significant melodic feature within a style that often baffles the analyst. Evidently this seemed significant to Dufay, who not only separated off the four-note figure from the rest of the line in both cases, giving it identical rhythmic settings, but also put the two lines into what may be described as a ten-beat pattern so that the second repeats the melodic material of the first displaced by one beat within the bar structure.[5] And beyond that, Dufay characteristically makes his phrases much more irregular than does Binchois. For Binchois each double line has a five-bar melody, and the single fifth line acts as a two-bar gusset to join the lines either side of it. For Dufay, after two irregular lines at the beginning (perhaps of $3\frac{1}{3} + 3\frac{2}{3}$ bars), the phrase lengths are 4, 3, 3, 3 and 4 bars, and the phrases are given an extra fluidity by melodic emphases on soft beats as well as a lightening of first beats (as in bars 6, 10, 13, 18 and 23).

But the other structural detail of Dufay's melody is in the placement of notes outside the melodic framework. The first line peaks on F, as in the plainchant and the Binchois setting. But the second line departs from these in rising one note to the G. This prepares the ear for the first note of the third line which leads quickly to A. The chant and the Binchois setting differ from this approach in making the transition from the lower opening pair of lines to the higher third line somewhat sudden: they contrast two disparate tonal blocks whereas Dufay's approach is gentler. But here in the third line Dufay adds yet another note above the received melody: the B (flattened by *musica ficta*) acts as a melodic peak, carefully prepared over the preceding bars. This note is taken up again in bar 18, allowed to fall to the A and the G in bars 18 and 19, and taken up with the G in bar 23 which comes prominently after a rest before leading the line down to its resting point.[6]

In general Binchois is far less inclined to elaborate his melody, but time and again his liturgical works show the most careful control of declamation, the use of irregular phrase-lengths and irregular bar-lengths to give the maximum declamatory potential to the words. A sample of this is in Ex. 38 from the last line of his *Veni Creator Spiritus* setting as compared with that of Dufay (v/19).[7] Here the two settings have an approximately equal amount of embellishment to the chant line. Binchois lends weight to the opening of the line by expanding it and following it with relatively irregular declamation patterns, whereas Dufay's version seems more concerned with the flow of the line, the rhythmic parallelism of bars 18–19 with bars 20–21 and the return to the high C in bar 21 to underline that parallelism with a kind of symmetry.

Ex. 38

Similar conclusions arise from comparing Dufay's *Ave maris stella* (v/23)[8] discantus with that in Dunstable's sole surviving hymn setting (Ex. 39). Dunstable's melody is forthright and, partly as a result of its lower voices, strongly rhythmical whereas Dufay's moves gently and elegantly up the opening leap of a fifth in the chant. Dunstable's seems the more memorable and individual version: he exploits the rising fifth at the opening and makes that a significant motif in his setting by giving the two falling fifths (bars 6–7 and 11–12) a parallelism which is accentuated by his most irregularly

Ex. 39

introducing a rest after the last of these. There is something muscular about Dunstable's piece that contrasts with the more contrived elegance of Dufay's. Characteristically these examples again show Dufay carefully dividing up each text line with a rest at the end whereas Dunstable, although he has a full cadence at the end of each line, twice continues without pausing.[9]

But it seems that comparing his chant paraphrase melodies with those of his contemporaries does little to explain why his cycle of hymns should have achieved such popularity. Their quality becomes more obvious when the full polyphonic context is viewed.

Like several of his hymns, Dufay's *Ave maris stella* is set in *fauxbourdon*. This is the simplest possible harmonization scheme: a tenor is composed and the middle voice either follows the discantus a fourth below or follows the tenor in fifths and thirds above. (The procedure varies and is sometimes ambiguous: modern editions vary in their interpretations although the results are usually more or less the same.) How and why this style originated are still matters of considerable dispute.[10] More *fauxbourdon* works survive from Dufay than from any other composer, but that detail looks less impressive when it is remembered that we have more works from him than from his contemporaries:[11] in fact a rather larger proportion of the surviving music by Binchois is in *fauxbourdon* style. It is possible to say, however, that Dufay exploited the potential of the system far more fully than any of his contemporaries, and its incorporation into the motet *Supremum est mortalibus bonum* is just one example of that. Most of Binchois' *fauxbourdon* pieces are so simple that even the tenor scarcely needs writing down: it moves largely in parallel sixths with the discantus, resolving to an open octave for cadences. Both the Binchois hymns already discussed are good examples of this. Example 40 is the opening of his *Veni Creator Spiritus*.

Ex. 40

By contrast, the opening and closing bars of Dufay's *Ave maris stella* show considerable compositional invention within extraordinarily limited means (Ex. 41).

Ex. 41

141

If for the first bar Dufay follows the expected pattern, his second bar shows a detail of rhythmic movement in the tenor which implies, as so often in his work, a short 6/8 pattern moving across the barline. But the true interest of that opening is in the way it is repeated a step lower and across a cadence leading to the last line of the piece. Throughout this setting the tenor moves in such a way as to soften the triple-time framework of the discantus whereas – surprisingly, perhaps – the discantus itself contains very little of the kind. And possibly the greatest difference between the Dunstable and Dufay settings of this hymn is that Dunstable's lower voices tend to support or emphasize what is happening in the discantus: Dufay's lower voices are more independent and they seem to be the ones that produce the rhythmic life of the work.

All the sources for Dufay's *Ave maris stella* also contain a composed contratenor that can be used with the same discantus and tenor as a substitute for the *fauxbourdon* texture. This voice adds even more to the rhythmic liveliness of the piece, introducing gentle off-beat emphases or hints of imitation and giving the texture more variety by being sometimes above the tenor (several times following the line of the *fauxbourdon* voice which it replaces) and sometimes below it. But perhaps a better and more characteristic example is from the end of Dufay's *Ut queant laxis* which survives only as a fully-composed three-voice setting (Ex. 42). Here the penultimate line is worked with a device of which Dufay was particularly fond from his earliest years: each of the voices has a series of 3/8 groups which start on consecutive quavers (and if the music example has inserted emphasis marks to clarify the point, it should be clear that an emphatic performance would be inappropriate for they are mere passing gestures within the polyphonic web). Here the rhythmic effect is perhaps more important to Dufay than the part-writing, and

Ex. 42

in bar 19 he actually needs to introduce a rest into the contratenor apparently to avoid parallel fifths with the discantus.

A further detail of the polyphony here is the use of a falling three-note tag which appears twice in the discantus at bars 19–20 to be repeated an octave below by the tenor and then a fourth below in the contratenor. Presumably the evolution of this tag goes back to the discantus in bar 18, but it is the rhythmic pattern established by the 3/8 figures that makes its appearance in the discantus on the second note of bar 19 particularly clear.

Finally there is the matter of the cadence at bar 20. As we noted earlier, the hymn melody closes on D and shows a particularly careful distribution of tonal areas so a cadence on the concluding pitch so near to the end would be worth avoiding. And in fact here Dufay hardly cadences at all: none of the voices has what could be called cadential movement, and the lowest note below the D in bar 20 is G. Every other line-end in the hymn has a proper cadence.

Here, as so often elsewhere in his hymns, there are many details showing Dufay's special control of a contrapuntal idiom within the simplest means. Perhaps it is worth noting just two more: the way bar 18 opens with what we would describe as a momentary 6–4 chord which immediately resolves onto a 5–3 and thereby lightens the beginning of the bar; and the way the single dissonance in the entire passage is the F in the contratenor in that same bar, propelling the music on through the closing melisma. These are all part of the style and they all contribute to the richness of the setting.

So these examples help to show why at the age of thirty-five Dufay should have turned to a simpler style. The composer who until then had shown the most extraordinary range of techniques and styles in his music was now limiting himself, carefully exploring the simplest counterpoint.

But a more general conclusion is that the true life of these pieces is not in the melody but in the full three-voice texture, in the counterpoint. Melodic grace was a continuing ideal in much of his work; but it would be difficult to assert that his melodies were more memorable or even more inspired than those of Dunstable and Binchois. In his edition of these hymns, Rudolf Gerber described Dufay as 'one of the greatest melodic geniuses known to music history' and as the Mozart of the fifteenth century. His view has occasionally been quoted with approbation, but it is difficult to sustain. I would suggest, rather, that it makes no more sense to ascribe melodic genius to Dufay than to

Bach, Beethoven or Brahms – all of them composers who wrote fine and distinctive melodies but whose main compositional genius lay elsewhere. Very few of Dufay's melodies are particularly memorable when separated from their contrapuntal context. That is a statement that could not be made with equal force about any of his contemporaries or associates, even Ockeghem. And it may in its turn begin to explain why Dufay's melodies were so rarely borrowed by other composers in that generation during the last quarter of the century when the use of borrowed material was so widespread.

In short, then, the vitality of Dufay's hymns is in the contrapuntal treatment. That is what distinguishes them from the hymns of his contemporaries, and presumably it is what made them so influential. Relatively few polyphonic hymn settings survive from the years when Dufay composed his cycle, but the evidence from innumerable hymns in the Trent codices and later sources is that Dufay started a new spate of hymn composition throughout Europe.

Before leaving the hymns, a word on those in later sources. As already explained the cycle of nineteen hymns in the earliest manuscript (BL) is in O mensuration with the chant paraphrase in the discantus and with the lower voices in either *fauxbourdon* or fully composed three-voice texture. (In two of them a composed contratenor can replace the *fauxbourdon* voice.) In two cases a melody is duplicated with different texts; and in one case the setting appears both with a tenor for *fauxbourdon* performance and as a stylistically separate setting in three voices with a tenor and a triplex – another voice in the discantus range. All but one of these hymns set the even-numbered verses of the hymn, giving the others in chant notation. Just one piece, *Aurea luce* (v/27), stands somewhat apart in having a different mensuration, $\phi$, and a tenor that moves in slightly longer notes.

When the same cycle appears in the manuscript ModB (from around 1450), it is expanded. There is another composed contratenor to replace a *fauxbourdon* voice, and another contrafactum – that is to say that the text of *Ad solis ortus cardine* is added to the music for a different hymn, *Hostis Herodes impie* (v/13). But there are also new hymns. Two of them, *Ad cenam Agni* (v/17) and *Vexilla Regis* (v/16), are in the style of the rest, though the latter has a brief 'Amen' in a slightly different manner. All the hymn settings in ModB are ascribed to Dufay except for the two which happen not to appear in any other source and one which is ascribed to Benoit (and is also unique to this manuscript). This seems to suggest that Dufay continued expanding and adapting his cycle after its original composition.

In the much later Vatican manuscript CS15 (from the last decade of the century) the same hymns are all unascribed and the cycle is further expanded to include seventy pieces. Full three-voice settings appear for Dufay's chant-paraphrase discantus voices; *fauxbourdon* settings appear for hymns that did not have them in the earlier sources; and there are many other settings which can have nothing at all to do with Dufay. But there are some works here that are remarkably reminiscent of Dufay's style: in particular it would be difficult to say that *Deus tuorum militum* (v/59) and *Jesu corona virginum* (v/62) as well as the 'new' *fauxbourdon* settings were not his work. Commentators have in general treated their authorship with the utmost caution.

But clearly Dufay did not lose interest in the hymn after completing his first cycle. ModB also ascribes to him three hymns that are stylistically quite different from the earlier ones. *Audi benigne Conditor* (v/14)[12] has the chant in the contratenor voice, mostly in equal notes with only six added notes in the entire melody; *Aures ad nostras* (v/15) is in duple metre with the chant again far less embellished than in the main cycle; and *Proles de celo* (v/32) is also in duple time with metrical changes that suggest an interest in a different kind of formal control within the hymn medium. Moreover, from 1463–4 there is the document recording payment for the copying of Dufay's hymn O *quam glorifica* 'newly made' (*nouvellement faite*) some thirty years after the completion of the first cycle.[13]

This evident continued interest in hymn setting suggests that it is logically wrong to state, as some writers have done, that Dufay set each hymn only once. That is more or less the case with the original cycle, though even there a single chant paraphrase can have different harmonizations apparently from Dufay's hand, and it should now be clear that the melodic paraphrase was far from being the most important feature of his settings. But his composing career was exceptionally long, and he of all medieval composers was never short of ideas. Two relatively early hymns ascribed to him in sources other than BL are relegated to the appendix of the complete edition largely because they conflict with settings in the main cycle: these are *Festum nunc celebre* (v/55) and *Pange lingua* (v/56). Certainly their style is different from that of the main cycle, but they could easily be earlier settings for an entirely different purpose. We may not yet be ready to dismiss them so confidently.

Dufay's range of contrapuntal ideas in setting a chant appears perhaps most decisively in his sequence settings. Eight sequences appear in the complete edition, and Charles Hamm has suggested another two as being Dufay's on the basis of their manuscript context and mensural technique.[14] Among all these, *Gaude virgo* (v/1) stands out as being quite different in style, through-composed, in four voices throughout and not – so far as anybody can tell – based on chant. It was discussed briefly in chapter 8.

The remainder have the same kind of stylistic unity as the hymns, though two of them show slight differences (particularly in mensural treatment) and one of them, *Isti sunt due olive* (v/8), is considerably more elaborate, with several changes of mensuration and sections in two voices as well as others in *fauxbourdon*. The sequences, unlike the hymns, are scattered around various sources, but they could originally have been part of a larger cycle.

It has been suggested that the sequence settings were originally designed to go with the hymn cycle and that there was a sequence to match each hymn.[15] This can hardly be the case, because although there are similarities between Dufay's hymns and his sequences there is one vital difference. In the hymns the tenor and contratenor voices occupy a range an octave lower than the discantus: all three voices stand in the same mode and there are very few occasions where either of the lower voices rises above the discantus. In the sequences, however, the lower voices have a range only a fifth lower than the discantus, so the texture is much more concentrated and the voices quite often overlap.

There are two possible explanations of this change in texture between cycles that are otherwise similar. One is simply that the hymns are for Vespers whereas the sequences are for the Mass; but Dufay's group of matched Kyrie settings (iv/9–18) comes closer to the texture of the hymns. The other explanation would be that Dufay was composing for the needs of different institutions with different vocal resources. We do know that the Savoy chapel in 1434–5 had boy choristers whereas the papal chapel in 1435–7 did not;[16] so it is possible that the texture of the hymns reflects composition for a choir of boys and men (at Savoy) and that of the sequences was designed for the all-adult papal choir. My tentative suggestion would therefore be that the sequences were composed after the hymns and intended for the papal choir at Florence in 1435–6.

The sequence settings are, like the hymns, alternatim – chant alternating with polyphony. But the sequence is a different kind of melody, normally having the form A B B C C D D etc. Each stanza in the setting will therefore be based on a different section of the chant. But a further detail of the sequence is that quite often the different stanzas are melodically related: in two of those set by Dufay the final phrase of each stanza is the same, and in most of them it is close enough to allow the comparison of several different ways in which Dufay treated the same phrase of chant.

His setting of the Christmas sequence *Letabundus* (v/2) is a case in point. For all stanzas but the last the melody ends as in Ex. 43a. Its first treatment (Ex. 43b) is almost entirely homophonic except for the final cadence which, after a series of quickly-changing chords, closes with a dissonance of which Dufay often made a special use – perhaps more so than his contemporaries.

**Ex. 43**

Its next treatment (Ex. 43c) has the now familiar style of strad-dled 3/8 patterns in the lower voices but has no dissonances except for three implied second-inversion chords. The next (Ex. 43d) evolves out of a relatively daring cadence on B (something which occurs quite often in Dufay's sequence settings but rarely elsewhere) and has a much tighter texture with all the voices close together. Again the clashing cadential figure in the contratenor is used, and the *échappée* figuration in the discantus produces a momentary but important dissonance.

Following that (Ex. 44a) he adds considerably more freedom to the various voices, including a surprisingly long note in the con-tratenor (bars 45–6). And at its last appearance (Ex. 44b) the melodic fragment comes at the end of a stanza which is largely in the higher range and would rise well above the highest note of the discantus, so Dufay puts the chant paraphrase in the tenor line. Here the harmonic style is again extremely smooth. There is no dissonance at all; and although the chords might be said to change on every quaver but one, every chord is in either a root-position formation (often without the third) or a first inversion. Throughout these stanzas the range of rhythmic, harmonic and melodic treatment speaks for itself.

Ex. 44

It is worth concluding this description of sections of his *Letabundus* setting by quoting the entire final stanza (Ex. 45). The chant returns to the discantus, almost unembellished: indeed the preceding chant as it appears in both manuscript sources is itself rhythmicized in the same way. Below this simplest possible chant paraphrase the tenor and contratenor are more elaborate than in the previous stanzas. Rests divide up the rhythmic figures to give them more prominence; dissonances and second-inversion chords appear, partly as a result of the increasingly risky part-writing; the textures change more quickly than in the previous stanzas; and the nature of these lines brings the setting to a dramatic and optimistic climax.

Ex. 45

Even if the suggested dates should eventually require correction by one or two years in the light of further evidence, the main body of Dufay's hymns and sequence settings represents a relatively short period in his career at a time when the already experienced composer was refining and expanding his technique. They show a move away from what Besseler called the *dominantische Tonalität* – dominant-based tonal structure – of his earlier works. And they may show the beginnings of a more long-term project in which the now mature composer planned to provide a comprehensive cycle of music for the Mass and the Office. This will be discussed again later (in chapter 14).

But, whatever the details of the matter, these are the most easily placed and categorized of his chant settings. Most of the rest present a scattered picture from which it can be concluded only that much of the contextual material is lost or still unknown.

His Magnificat settings are just one example of this.[17] Four appear in the complete edition, but they are so varied in their style and so confusing in their manuscript survival that it becomes extremely difficult to draw conclusions as to their date or original purpose. In addition to these there is the puzzling Magnificat that appears in the manuscript ModB with two ascriptions: Dufay's name appears at the head of the page but Binchois' name appears further down, after the first stanza. Opinions are constantly changing as to the meaning of this double ascription, made more complicated by the work's appearance in an earlier manuscript ascribed just to Binchois. But it seems possible that this could be regarded as a case of dual-authorship: might it have been composed when the two composers met at the Chambéry wedding celebrations of 1434? It is a relatively simple work achieving its ends primarily by means of its declamation, a consideration which might ultimately favour Binchois as its composer. On the other hand, this was precisely the time when Dufay is thought to have been re-examining simplicity in his hymn cycle, and several details of this Magnificat bear comparison with his hymns. The question is better left open.

Of the four more secure Magnificat settings two in particular should be mentioned briefly. That in the fifth tone (v/35) builds all its stanzas from the same harmonic and contrapuntal framework, thus giving insight into Dufay's ways of handling different texts and different mensurations in what is essentially the same music. (Like the Magnificat in the eighth tone (v/34) it may well date from the mysterious 1440s phase in his life.) And the Magnificat in the 'third and fourth tones' (v/36) seems to be one of the few surviving works that might reasonably be ascribed to the last fifteen years of Dufay's life. It shows a bolder use of open textures and a more relaxed mastery of the supple line. But again its manuscript survival leaves some confusion about its correct form, and its only ascription is in a manuscript which is far from reliable in its Dufay ascriptions.[18]

A similar confusion covers the few surviving antiphon settings (v/37–45).[19] Their style is varied, their sources widely spread, and their music only rarely seems to rise above a modest mediocrity. Perhaps they are evidence of what Dufay was composing in the 1440s, but if so they are mostly perplexing examples of the simplest possible music being composed for the most glamorous cathedral foundation in the Low Countries. This too will be discussed further in chapter 14. But to seek the changes in Dufay's style between 1440 and the end of his life it is better to turn to the repertory which includes a relatively large number of works that can be dated in these years, the songs.

# 12

# The late songs

Some time around the middle of the fifteenth century an older song form came back into favour. Following later theorists we call it the bergerette, though in its outward shape it corresponds to the virelai which had enjoyed a particular vogue among French composers during the last years of the fourteenth century. Fashions changed, and examples of the virelai among the composers of Dufay's earlier years are not only extremely rare but nearly all demonstrably from the first two decades of the century. In Italy the earlier form had a slightly fuller history: known in Italian as the ballata, it was the favoured form for Italian song during the last quarter of the fourteenth century and continued to hold sway during Dufay's youth. Four early Italian songs by Dufay are in ballata form, or something resembling it, taking their style from the Italian composers of the previous generation.

The standard view is that the new revived form of the 1450s is called 'bergerette' rather than 'virelai' because the earlier form had three full stanzas whereas the bergerette differed significantly in having only one. But in fact long before the end of the fourteenth century composers had all but discarded the second and third stanzas, allowing the musical structure to expand so that the single remaining stanza with its internal repeating patterns created a sufficient musical unit. As it happens, one of the very few surviving examples of the full three-stanza form after about 1380 is the early four-voice *Invidia nimica* (vi/2) of which at least one voice is by Dufay; but that is a rare exception and is unique in its musical form.[1] In terms of poetic form, the bergerette was no different from the ballata and the virelai which had disappeared from the musical scene around 1420. Musically the most important difference in the bergerette was that the 'secunda pars' normally included a change of metre and a slight lightening of texture, features that never appear in the earlier virelai and ballata; and we shall see that this could have been one of the main reasons both for the reappearance of the form and for its having a new name.

The only bergerette ascribed to Dufay that is likely to have been composed before 1450 is *S'il est plaisir* (vi/21), which is almost certainly spurious.[2] For the rest, they appear only in late sources (1460 and after); and a stylistic hiatus in his songs suggests that he composed little surviving secular music during his decade at Cambrai, 1439–50, but that the return to Savoy in the 1450s brought about a new lease of life in him as a song composer, with new stylistic ideals.

His bergerette *Malheureulx cueur* (vi/24) is a superb example of this later style.[3] The poem is by Le Rousselet, a poet about whom little can be said except that he was associated with the poetic circles around the French royal court of Charles VII and the Blois court of Charles of Orleans. There is a chance, then, that this was one of the songs that Dufay told the Medici brothers in his letter of 1456 that he had recently set 'at the request of several lords of the king's household' in the preceding year.

It is a classic example of the search for a clearer texture, for a more economical style in which every note counts. The opening of the discantus is startling enough, boldly rising an octave, only to fall by a more indirect route to the low B. To begin the next line an octave higher is the kind of gesture that seems to contradict the accepted modes of the fifteenth-century chanson style; but it mirrors the mood of the poem: constant changes of attitude as the lover both sympathizes with his personified heart and upbraids it for causing him so much pain. The way the line continues with a roulade after the cadence in bars 8–9 and the delayed entry in bar 12 both similarly portray changing moods (Ex. 46).

In the lower voices the writing is at first much sparser than before: it gives the same alternation of trochaic and iambic patterns that is familiar from earlier works but is here managed with fewer gestures. When the contratenor introduces the now familiar 6/8 pattern it does so for only a moment before retreating to still simplicity and giving the cadence just a touch of extra colour by rising above the discantus in bar 5. As the song proceeds, the writing becomes more complex, particularly in the contratenor; the harmonic rhythm becomes faster, and the section ends with a Phrygian cadence approached by an animated progression of 6–3 chords recalling the old *fauxbourdon*.

Now the mood changes again for the contrasting 'secunda pars' in a different mensuration that implies a faster beat, though initially the suddenly reduced harmonic rhythm adds to the mood of excitable changing attitudes expressed in the text. This section also changes spirit remarkably quickly and includes a further surprising

Ex. 46

passage in *fauxbourdon*-like harmony. Comparisons with more recent music are always dangerous, but it might be worth saying that in its fragmentary melodic treatment, its occasional minimal textures, its close argument and its evanescent changes of mood *Malheureulx cueur* is in many ways similar to a late work of Debussy such as the Cello Sonata.

But to return to its form. The bergerette is normally described as being in the form AbbaA with the last section precisely repeating the first and the 'b' section in a contrasting mensuration. But to see the true nature of the bergerette requires noting that the 'A' section here has five poetic lines (whereas the 'b' section has only three), that its strongest internal cadence is after the third line – at bar 16 – and that in fact its form and balance are like that of an entire rondeau stanza. If we think of the 'A' section as 'A' + 'B' (by analogy with the rondeau) and redub the other section 'C', we arrive at form AB cc ab AB with the following number of lines: 3 + 2, 3 + 3, 3 + 2, 3 + 2.

Now the discussions of the rondeau form in chapter 8 concentrated on the musical shape of a single stanza. A fuller discussion would take into account the various text repetitions by using (as in the previous paragraph) capital letters only for refrain sections, that is to say sections in which musical repetition is matched by repetition of the original text: using that scheme the rondeau has the form AB aA ab AB – the final stanza repeating both words and music of the first, the second stanza including a repetition of the words and music for the first half of the first stanza.

If we now put the scheme of a bergerette such as *Malheureulx cueur* alongside that of a standard rondeau of the time with a five-line stanza – I have taken *Adieu m'amour* (vi/76) – we get the following pattern:

| **Rondeau** | A | B | a | A | a | b | A | B |
|---|---|---|---|---|---|---|---|---|
| Number of poetic lines: | 3 | 2 | 3 | 3 | 3 | 2 | 3 | 2 |
| Number of bars: | 15 | 13 | 15 | 15 | 15 | 13 | 15 | 13 |

| **Bergerette** | A | B | c | c | a | b | A | B |
|---|---|---|---|---|---|---|---|---|
| Number of poetic lines: | 3 | 2 | 3 | 3 | 3 | 2 | 3 | 2 |
| Number of bars: | 16 | 11 | 13 | 17* | 16 | 11 | 16 | 11 |

(*: the second 'c' in *Malheureulx cueur* includes a second-time ending.)

The bergerette, then, can be seen as a rondeau in which the second 'panel' is changed and made to contrast instead of adding to the internal complexity of the repeating form.[4] One consequence of this is simply that the bergerette gives more scope for expressive writing which matches the mood of the particular words being set whereas the rondeau is often limited to a more general characterization of the mood of the entire poem.

And indeed Dufay chose bergerette form for what is perhaps the most expressive of all his songs, *Helas mon dueil* (vi/23), with its opening chromaticism that makes a simple gesture with the minimum of means (Ex. 47).[5]

As in the previous song the main internal cadence is after the

Ex. 47

third line of the first section, at bar 12. And although the 'secunda pars' in this case happens not to be in a different mensuration it does have many textural and rhythmic details that contrast with the first section.

One important and characteristic feature of *Helas mon dueil* is its melodic economy: the discantus for the second line at bars 4–5 is taken over by the tenor at the next line, bars 8–9; and the discantus at that point is taken by the tenor a fifth lower for the wonderful moment at bars 13–14 where the discantus falls below the tenor. The same process is continued in the 'secunda pars', giving the song a mood of unrelieved melancholy that is perfectly calculated to the text.

The contratenor has many leaps which might at first sight suggest that this is an early work; but the function of those leaps has changed. One could perhaps hear the opening octave leap as being a disguised version of the old 'octave-leap' cadence and possibly hear the same again at its reappearance just after the end of Ex. 47, in bars 16–17; but the continued rise to peak on F on both occasions is enough to show that the entirely successful purpose of these lines is to add direction to the textural movement, to give changing colour to the music.

It would be idle to continue listing features of motivic economy and the countless affective details in the song, though there is a temptation to do so: it is one of those works that sound so much more impressive in a good performance than they perhaps look on paper.

But a new and significant feature here is the very high proportion of syllabic texting. In Dufay's earlier works there is often a strong feeling that declamation is a subsidiary consideration, and to some extent this continues in certain later works; here, however, there is a matching of words and music that seems to speak of new musical ideals.

A similar kind of declamation and motivic economy appear in *Adieu m'amour* (vi/76), a rondeau that is in many ways the twin of *Helas mon dueil*. That it is one of Dufay's most frequently performed pieces today is not merely because it is printed in the *Historical Anthology of Music*. The gradation of its discantus has a kind of perfection in itself that shows an extraordinary control of melodic line. By the gentlest possible steps it grows to the high C over the first three lines of the poem, falling equally gently after the mid-point cadence with lines that seem to be derived from inversions of those in the first half of the song.[6]

My own belief is that these two songs are rather later than *Malheureulx cueur* and that they represent a further refinement of the extraordinarily open style found in that song. They appear in a manuscript of probably Ferrarese origin now at Oporto: it has normally been dated well before 1450, but I have attempted to show that it must in fact date from some time after 1460 and contains some of Dufay's latest songs.[7] Among them are two gems showing equal perfection in the same ways, though their fragmentary texts make them basically unperformable (largely because to perform but a single stanza results in an absurdly brief piece, and to perform a full form without the rondeau text to propel it would be to lose the point of all the repetitions). These are the rondeau settings *Qu'est devenue leaulté* (vi/67), with extraordinary melodic and harmonic economy, and *Entre les plus plaines d'anoy* (vi/66) which opens with a curious rhythmic device whereby the 'bar' seems to begin on the second beat for most of the first section (Ex. 48).[8] This song has much in common with *Malheureulx cueur* in the way each line, each subphrase, seems to present a new idea and a new mood. It also contains specific recollections of that song; but the fall of the discantus down to a

Ex. 48

much lower register in bars 19–21 followed by a leap of an octave across the other voices – that is entirely its own.

A further piece in the same manuscript represents the other facet of Dufay's song style in those years. *En triumphant de Cruel Dueil* (vi/72 but see work list) seems to be written in memory of Binchois who died in September 1460.[9] Its closing line is as in Ex. 49.

Ex. 49

Particularly significant here is not so much the floridity of the discantus (though this is exceptional in Dufay's late work and that of his contemporaries) but the much thicker texture. There is a substantial group of such luxuriously scored songs from these years, perhaps the most impressive being *Les douleurs* (vi/84 but see work list). Here two voices are in canon – see Ex. 36 – and below them are two richly written *concordans* parts: one goes down to F which is as low as anything else securely ascribed to Dufay; but the other goes down another fourth to low C. Whether the notated pitches actually represent performance so much lower than anything else in his output may be doubted, especially since the upper voices are also the lowest upper voices we have from him (though they are only just lower than those in the equally surprising and in some ways comparable *Hé, compaignons*, see p. 101 above); but irrespective of actual pitch the work is a maverick among Dufay's songs as well as among those of his time.

The ascription to Dufay is to some extent endorsed by the authorship of the poem. Anthoine de Cuise is given as its author in three poetry manuscripts, and he belongs to the same circle of poets as Le Rousselet, the author of the poem *Malheureulx cueur*. If the two songs were both composed on the same occasion when Dufay visited the royal court at St-Pourçain in 1455, he would have been demonstrating a remarkable range of stylistic resource.

This 'richer' style of songwriting – which seems to have continued alongside the more open and economic style discussed earlier – is the style of many of Dufay's most successful late works. Among them is the rondeau *Le serviteur hault guerdonné* (vi/92) which was once dismissed from the body of Dufay's work as being so different from anything else by him:[10] comparison with other late works such as *Dona gentile* (vi/8) and *Par le regard* (vi/73) is sufficient to give the piece its true context and to restore it to the canon of Dufay's authentic works.

If these are indeed from after 1450, perhaps the same is the case with the rondeau *Donnés l'assault* (vi/70), which uses the idea of a military siege as a metaphor for the approach the god of love is asked to make on the singer's lady.[11] Trumpet-like lines permeate all the voices with a startling variety of figurations, while the familiar alternation of major and minor triads on C seems to betoken a shift from demanding to pleading in the lover's attitude. In harmonic terms the song is unusual: the first half comprises long sections confined to tonic (13 bars) and dominant (6 bars) chords; the second half begins with a regular alternation of the two, eventually settling down so that the concluding six and a half bars are practically all on the tonic chord. This is perhaps not the piece from which to begin discussions of an emergent tonal sense, but its tonal design shows a confidence born of earlier and wilder experiments.[12]

Perhaps the most fundamental change this book offers to our view of Dufay's work is the assertion that about twenty-five of his surviving songs must date from after 1450; and this is the moment to show why that change has become necessary.

Two pieces of wrong information in particular led to the former view that most of his songs must be much earlier than that. The first was the belief – current until six years ago – that Dufay remained in Savoy from 1439 until about 1444 and then returned to Cambrai where he spent most of his remaining days. Recent research[13] has definitively established that he left Savoy in 1439, remained in Cambrai until 1450, and then spent another seven years in the south loosely connected with the Savoy court. The significance of this is partly that there would have been little call for secular songs in Cambrai where there was no secular court (though that must be modified by the observation that there are at least two descriptions of songs being sung in fifteenth-century Cambrai, one in particular on the occasion of Duke Philip the Good's visit in 1449).[14] But more important, the earlier view of his residence in the Savoy court and of university study during the years 1439–44 led inevitably to the conclusion that there was no reason for him to have stopped composing secular songs.[15]

The second piece of incorrect information was the view that the Oporto manuscript, mentioned above, was compiled in the 1440s. From that it followed naturally that the songs in Oporto were the ones he composed during the years 1439–44 when he was supposed to be in Savoy; and the stylistic similarity of many other late songs further led to the conclusion that most of these also dated from the 1440s. Now that the manuscript can be dated much later,[16] and probably after 1460, the picture alters considerably.

A glance at the sources of Dufay's songs in the light of these new findings shows an apparently clear pattern. The Oxford manuscript seems to contain practically all of his surviving songs up to 1436. About ten more songs that appear to be relatively early are found in other manuscripts, but these are few against the forty-five in Oxford and several of them probably belong to the years 1436–9.

Against this body of songs, the twenty-five that seem to date from after 1450 offer a different picture of source distribution. Their earliest surviving sources are as follows: eight in Oporto from the 1460s; one in the Schedelsches Liederbuch also from the 1460s; one in Trent 90 probably from the 1460s; and the remainder in sources from later still. In addition this group separates itself from the earlier group by having a large proportion of songs (twelve out of twenty-five) whose texts also appear in poetic sources of the time (there is no poetic source containing any of Dufay's Oxford songs).

Nobody would wish to state unequivocally that a song in a manuscript from the 1460s cannot have been composed twenty or thirty years earlier; and indeed there is the case of the ballade *Se la face ay pale* (vi/19) which appears in the Oxford manuscript as well as in several sources from the 1460s and 1470s. But apart from that case the two groups of sources are strictly separated in both repertory and date. Nor would it be prudent to state that Dufay composed no songs during his decade in Cambrai 1439–50, but the lie of the manuscripts that happen to survive suggests that very few of the songs in the complete edition came from those years. Further to that, between the late 1430s and the 1460s there is no clearly dated song manuscript of any substance or authority, and it could be argued that the manuscripts of the 1460s are predominantly retrospective collections covering the previous twenty-five years. But probability favours the view that Dufay composed few songs during his years at Cambrai and that the return to a courtly ambience after 1450 gave rise to a new burst of song composition. Corroborative evidence lies in the authorship of three of his poems, in his letter to the Medici brothers stating that he was composing songs in the months just before February 1456, and in the coherent source spread of his late songs.

There are several important differences in the style of the later songs. First, with the exception of the rondeau *Puisque vous estez campieur* (vi/81)[17] and the combinative chanson *Je vous pri* (vi/25)[18] the songs carefully avoid the convivial atmosphere so fully portrayed in the earlier songs. The mood of the poems shows a return to the solemn courtly style of Machaut and Eustache Deschamps, with 'Love-longing' as their main theme; and the contrast emphasizes the point that Dufay's earlier songs are, for their time, surprisingly lacking in sentimentality. Whimsy, gregarious ebullience and graceful compliment are the predominating moods of his songs before 1440, and the musical texture is often crowded with incident. Apparently the young man shunned the depths of feeling that his contemporaries affected; and it is precisely this unsentimental joviality that has appealed to modern audiences: only very recently has there been much appreciation of his later songs. Equally, it seems that the older Dufay consciously moved closer to the mainstream of his time in his song composition: the rebellion of his earlier years now perhaps seemed to have given rise to a certain emotional superficiality, but with the experience gained from that he was in a position to bring something new to the full courtly 'high style'.

Second, there is far less obvious evidence of show and technical experiment. Part of the excitement of the early songs is that almost every one of them can be seen as an attempt to solve a particular technical problem, to demonstrate a brilliant resourcefulness, to explore a new idea. The later songs, on the whole, yield their secrets less easily. They move within a closely circumscribed courtly mode: above all else they are 'tasteful' whereas the earlier songs throw caution to the winds.

If these two characteristics seem largely negative, they perhaps focus on the central problem in appreciating Dufay's later works and indeed those of his contemporaries in the 1450s and 1460s. This is a music of far greater refinement, a style in which each note plays a role more important than heretofore.

The most widely distributed of all his firmly ascribed songs can serve as an example of this even though its counterpoint is denser than in most of his other works. *Par le regard de vos beaux yeux* (vi/73) appears in fourteen manuscripts of its own time but seems to have attracted no attention from modern critics until it was published in the complete edition in 1964.[19] There are two reasons for this neglect. The first is simply that the early Oxford manuscript was the first to receive the benefit of extensive publication. But the second is that the song's identity is less easy to define. Among the hundreds of songs in the manuscripts of the 1460s to the 1480s it scarcely jumps to the eye as having distinctive qualities. In general it may be said that the earlier anthologists tended to focus on the unusual rather than the characteristic. Their reasons for doing so were valid, but in this case their results were perhaps misleading for the student of fifteenth-century style at its purest.

At this point the reader may expect to receive a demonstration that *Par le regard* is a perfect masterpiece. That cannot be done, because no analysis can prove a work to be a masterpiece: the reader must experience the piece, and I can do no more than to record my opinion that its qualities repay deep knowledge. But some features can be noted (Ex. 50).

The discantus line seems at first sight to have no clear shape or parallelisms: each line begins with a different rhythmic figure, each has a different melodic direction. To the ear it is a line that has a perfection of balance: upper range and lower range complement one another; the cadences are well distributed and the continuing flow is witness to the invention so often noted in the descriptions of Dufay's other works.

But unifying details are present. The first line divides into two halves, each beginning with a long held A but moving from it in different directions. The interval of a fifth that joins them does likewise for the fourth line at bar 17, joins the two halves of the song at bars 11–12 and bridges the gap in the second line at bars 9–10 as well as in the fourth line at bar 19 (albeit with a downward leap).

Similarly falling melodic figures outlined by the fifth A–D permeate the line, as does its inversion rising from F to C. Many further melodic germs can be perceived by the enquiring eye or ear: the most important is the fall through a tenth in bars 7–9 paralleled by the rising figure in bars 20–21 bringing the piece to a close.

**Ex. 50**

1.4.7. Par le re - gard de vos beaux yeux
3. De vo - stre a - mour sui de - si - reux
5. Donc vous plai - se, cuer gra - ci - eux,

Tenor

Contra

Et de vo main - tien bel et gent.
Et tout mon vou - loir si con - sent.
Moy re - te - nir or a pre - sent

2.8. A vous bel - le vien hum - ble - ment Moy pre - sen - ter vo -
6. Por vo - stre a - my en - tie - re - ment, Et je se - ray vo -

- stre a - mou - reux.
- stre en tous lieux.

*163*

Harmonically the song shows Dufay at his most controlled, with the slow opening – rocking between D chords – paralleled by something similar at bars 12–14 though with more action. Moments of faster harmonic change appear at bars 7–9 but otherwise not until the end where Dufay considerably increases the complexity in his drive to the final cadence. Immediately before that there is one of those areas of stillness so characteristic of Dufay: bars 15–17 revolve almost entirely around the A chord which has been avoided elsewhere in the song, and the three voices intertwine on that triad in close position.

That triad of course has an additional function: with D the predominating chord-formation of the piece, and G the tonality on which the first and last lines come to a close, the A has a clearly heard position as a more distant chord, one that provides the springboard for the final leaping line. It is those notes too that set the words *moy presenter (vostre amoureux)* – to offer myself as your lover – and in the third stanza *Et je seray (vostre en tous lieux)* – and I shall remain yours wherever I am.[20]

It is a sentimental song. Its poem is as central to the courtly love style as one can get: praise of the lady's eyes and bearing which compel complete devotion. But the sentiment is wonderfully controlled, from the hesitant opening of the stanza to the optimism of the closing melisma. Only the fullest immersion in the repertory can explain why this song is musically unique. On a superficial level it is like dozens of others from the same years. But that is ultimately one definition of classicism in art: a style which is so clearly defined that the truest perfection appears in the work that keeps closest to the centre of the tradition, achieves the ultimate in good taste. After an earlier career in which he struck out in so many iconoclastic directions, Dufay as an older man returned to a classicism which makes his later works correspondingly more difficult to appreciate.

# 13

# The early Mass music

Whatever his predilections and obligations at the secular courts, Dufay was first and foremost a church musician. His music for the Mass fills three of the six volumes that make up his complete works; and two more volumes could be filled with further Mass music that has been attributed to him by modern writers. The present chapter concerns the two early cycles and the large body of independent and paired Mass movements which between them probably take us up to 1440.[1]

His earliest cycle is the Mass *Resvelliés vous* (ii/1) which has hitherto been known as the Mass 'sine nomine'. It can now take its new title[2] because much of its material is shared with the ballade *Resvelliés vous* (vi/11) composed for the Rimini wedding of July 1423.

Ex. 51

Tenor

Contra

The ballade opens with a startling gesture by leading straight to a most unusual chord which one might describe as C sharp minor within a G major framework (Ex. 51). Its logic is relatively simple: it is merely a triad built around the tenor note E which is part of a perfectly normal downward progression. It has precedents in the late fourteenth-century music of the Ars Subtilior, and something very similar appears in Ciconia's madrigal *Una panthera,* a work composed some twenty years earlier and possibly well known to Dufay. But, logical or otherwise, the opening of *Resvelliés vous* is so distinctive that it is instantly recognizable when it appears in the Gloria of the Mass at the words 'Qui sedes', beginning a new section (Ex. 52a). Here the second bar is just slightly changed.

**Ex. 52**

The same structure appears rather less literally in the Kyrie movement at the second 'Christe' (Ex. 52b); a similar 'C sharp minor' triad occurs in the second bar of the Gloria (Ex. 52c); and a comparably eccentric chord is used in the Sanctus at the word 'Sabaoth' (Ex. 52d) – this last unusual cadence reappearing at the end of the second 'Agnus Dei'.

A related idea, this time without the arresting chord, acts as a kind of motto opening that links the Kyrie and the Sanctus, further developed in the Agnus (Ex. 53).

The second texted line of the ballade *Resvelliés vous* (bars 12–15) is similarly reflected in the second sentence of the Kyrie (bars 8–14) and reappears several more times in the course of the cycle.

A further detail of the relationship between ballade and Mass cycle comes from the moment when the ballade changes mensuration to 3/4 for the opening of its 'secunda pars' (Ex. 54). Four movements of the cycle similarly change mensuration for their concluding sections, recalling the ballade at those points in a way that is admittedly much looser but instantly strikes the ear (Ex. 55).

Ex. 53

Ex. 54

Ex. 55

The recollection is there, but it is more difficult to pin down. There can be no dispute that the Mass and the ballade are related, but it may well be wrong to conclude that the Mass is a 'parody' of the ballade. The history of parody and borrowed material in the early fifteenth-century Mass is complicated, but in broad terms it amounts

*167*

to two assertions: among the few surviving examples of Mass music that share material with other works there are scarcely any two cases of similar or even comparable treatment; and the earliest example of a cycle which consistently paraphrases another piece is John Bedyngham's Mass *Dueil angoisseux* of around 1450.

Within that context it seems far more likely that the Dufay cycle is not a parody at all. Rather the reverse. As with several songs discussed in chapter 8, the ballade *Resvelliés vous* probably grew from ideas that arose in the course of composing the cycle. In the song we see the distillation of various ideas that had worked well and had evidently pleased Dufay. Using them, he created one of his richest early songs, with ideas bursting from it at every point, with florid passages and syncopations that demonstrate an extraordinary virtuosity in the composer. The Mass cycle has none of the florid passages and relatively few of the syncopations that made the ballade so unusual. It probably precedes the song.

That may explain why the Credo of the Mass contains no material in common with the ballade. Several writers have suggested that the Credo is not part of the cycle, largely because it is in duple time throughout whereas the other movements are characterized by a change from 6/8 to 3/4, with the Gloria – the most extended movement – including an opening section in duple time.[3] If the Mass was in fact based on *Resvelliés vous*, the case for the Credo seems even more dubious. But if the Mass came first the question can be reopened. Among the surviving continental Mass cycles of the early fifteenth century only one, that by Reson, has complete agreement between its movements:[4] the others display a similarly loose unity. Within the context of its time Dufay's Mass *Resvelliés vous* is relatively well unified: the voice-ranges of the movements match, and the use of duple time in the Credo is precisely like that in the duple-time section of the Gloria. Moreover there are musical details which the Credo shares with the Gloria, some of which can be seen in Ex. 56. The imitated triadic figures are structurally important to both movements, as are the falling quaver passages. The unity within the Mass *Resvelliés vous* is characteristic for its time.

That consideration is important to a discussion of the unity in his next cycle, the Mass *Sancti Jacobi* (ii/2). This is a plenary cycle, which is to say that besides the five movements of the Ordinary it includes four movements setting the Proper chants for the feast of St James the Greater. Of these, the Introit, Offertory and Communion

Ex. 56

a (Gloria)

Qui tol - lis pec-ca - ta mun-di, mi - se - re - re no - bis.

Contra

Tenor

b (Credo)

Ex Ma - ri - a vir - gi - ne, et ho - mo fa - ctus est.

Contra

Tenor

c (Gloria)

- tis Lau-da-mus te, Benedicimus te, A-do- -pter magnam glo-ri-am tu -

Tenor

Contra

d (Credo)

- tum Et ex Pa - tre na - tum ante om - ni-a secula, De-um de De - o,

Tenor

Contra

are based on the standard chants for that feast as listed in the modern Roman Gradual: each of these chants also happens to appear in the Masses for the feasts of several other apostles and is therefore not strictly confined to St James. The Alleluia, on the other hand, is based on a rhymed chant specifically mentioning St James. It has an easily reconstructed second-mode melody which has yet to be identified in any early chant book: such identification could well tell us something about the origins of the cycle (see above pp. 29f).

Leaving aside the scattered sources for various individual movements (particularly the Kyrie), the Mass appears in two main manuscripts.[5] That in Aosta contains only the five movements of the Ordinary with the title 'De apostolis' – that is, for any apostle – whereas that in Bologna (BL) gives the full nine movements, thus including the Propers for St James, and it has the title 'Missa Sancti Jacobi'. This source distribution helps focus the attention on various stylistic layers among the movements.

First, the Kyrie, Gloria and Credo. These are in three voices with contrasting sections marked 'Duo', where the two (presumably solo) voices each have the same range as the discantus in the full sections. The movements are built in panels of three sections each: 6/8 'Chorus', then 3/4 'Duo' followed by a duple-time full section, also marked 'Chorus'. The Kyrie runs through this sequence three times, the Gloria twice, and the Credo three times with a concluding section that seems to act as a summary of the same three-section panel.[6] Several details of the musical material, especially in the 'Duo' sections, seem to suggest composition at about the same time as the motet *Rite majorem* (i/11) of around 1427; and the style in general is not unlike that of the Mass *Resvelliés vous*.

The Sanctus and Agnus make up the second layer. They include duos contrasting with the 'Chorus' sections exactly as in the first layer, but here the 'Duo' sections are not in 3/4 time; and in fact the entire mensural scheme of the first layer is discarded in these two movements. They have chant paraphrase in the tenor, whereas in the first layer the only trace of chant is in the duple-time sections of the Kyrie where the outline of the Kyrie 'Cunctipotens' is clearly audible in the discantus.[7] But the most obvious difference in the Sanctus and Agnus is that the full sections are in four voices: the ranges of the two lower voices are precisely as in the first layer; and the two upper voices have the same range as the discantus in the first layer, which is to say that their range is also the same as that of the 'Duo' voices.

Finally, the Proper movements, which can be divided into two categories: those which follow the Sanctus and Agnus in having their chant paraphrase in the tenor of a four-voice texture[8] (though they are otherwise very different from those movements in their style); and those that follow the final section of each Kyrie in having the chant paraphrased in the discantus of a three-voice texture. This last category comprises only the closing 'repetitio' of the Introit and the Communion – the movement which has gone down in history as probably the very first composition in *fauxbourdon*.[9]

Applying the criteria of cyclic unification that are appropriate for a later generation, the only truly connected movements here are the Kyrie, Gloria and Credo. But we have seen that cyclic composition was not a clear concept in the 1420s; and the fact that all nine movements use the same voices in the same ranges is an indication that their presentation as a unit in the Bologna manuscript was not mere scribal whim but the composer's intention. Moreover the title

'De apostolis' given to the five Ordinary movements in the Aosta manuscript is not in itself evidence that these movements existed earlier than the others. Rather the contrary. It is only the addition of the Proper movements that defines the cycle as for an apostle; without the prior existence of those movements the title in Aosta makes little sense. Indeed a century later Giovanni Spataro quoted a passage from the Introit, describing it as Dufay's Introit 'De apostolis',[10] rather than for St James the Greater. From that point of view, if any movement is superfluous, it is the Alleluia, the only one to define the apostle as being St James.

But even here it is possible to identify musical material that recurs throughout the nine movements and tends to confirm the cyclic unity implied by the Bologna manuscript. The material appears clearly for the first time in the Kyrie (Ex. 57). Once seen in that form, it is easily recognized in the Introit (bars 6–7), Kyrie (39–40, 91–4, 117–20), Gloria (12–14, 35–9, possibly 65–6 and 73–5), Alleluia (1–3, 7, 15–16, 54–5, 72–4), Credo (1–3, 55–6, 76–8, 104–5, 119–21, possibly 173–5), Offertory (45–8, possibly 70–2), Sanctus (2–3, 13–15, 15–17, 20–2, 59–60, 67–9) Agnus (30–2) and Communion (8–10, 19–20). These recollections become more frequent and clearer towards the end of the cycle: increasingly they appear at the beginnings and ends of sections, and there are in addition several broader recollections of the shape which are less literal and so not recorded here. Some may seem mere musical small-change of the time – and indeed several other Dufay works of the late 1420s contain the same outline – but anybody who follows the outline through the cycle is likely to conclude that there is some

Ex. 57

unity here despite the range of compositional styles employed.

At the same time, this is a puzzling work. It has some extremely strange part-writing (especially in the opening Introit)[11] and seems surprisingly often lacking in the charm and elegance that distinguish the Mass *Resvelliés vous*. Perhaps its most successful movement is the Offertory where the part-writing seems clearer, the four voices seem more confidently handled, and there is a well-controlled variety of harmonic rhythm, often demonstrated by careful exploitation of a single chordal figure over several bars.

It has already been noted that some of the Ordinary movements contain reminiscences of the motet *Rite majorem* (i/11), probably from around 1427. The Offertory similarly contains recollections of the two motets dated 1431: *Balsamus et munda cera* (i/13) at bars 38–42 and *Ecclesie militantis* (i/12) in its closing section. These last two recollections are probably similar to those noted in the songs, which is to say that the Mass cycle is likely to be earlier than the motets of 1431. Some date in the late 1420s is probably appropriate, though the stylistic disparity between the movements and the often clumsy counterpoint make dating difficult. The Mass *Sancti Jacobi* bears many marks of an experiment which was not entirely successful.

If it really was intended as a cycle, it might be possible to see a dramatic organization. The Introit is elaborate, magnificent and confusing, with complicated cross-rhythms. The Kyrie and Gloria that follow are simpler in style, melodic and jaunty, with the Kyrie the only movement in the cycle that closes on A rather than on D; and this seems correct since, liturgically, the Kyrie leads directly into the Gloria. Four-voice complexity for the Alleluia leads to simplicity again in the Credo. Then follow three four-voice movements: the suave Offertory, the Sanctus, and finally the more solemn and complicated Agnus which ends with a section reminiscent of the opening Introit. And to close this whole variegated anthology of music Dufay chose the simplest possible style, apparently devised specifically for the end of this cycle, *fauxbourdon*.

To hear the Mass *Sancti Jacobi* like that is to endorse the theory that cyclic writing in the later sense was not part of early fifteenth-century musical thought. It has been suggested that Dufay's Mass *Resvelliés vous* was the first attempt at a unified cycle since Machaut's Mass of nearly a century earlier.[12] As a suggestion this merely reminds us that it is almost impossible to establish a chronology of early fifteenth-century Mass music.

Yet the broader historical picture is relatively clear. Although the idea of the unified Mass Ordinary cycle existed in chant from about the thirteenth century, the only polyphonic cycle before about 1420 that was clearly conceived as such was that of Guillaume de Machaut, composed some time around the middle of the fourteenth century. It often happens in the history of ideas that an innovation appears before its time and leads to nothing, only to turn up again in several different places simultaneously many years later. This seems to have been the case with the Machaut cycle.

Some time in the 1420s there were two, or perhaps three, groups of attempts to revive the idea. To judge from the surviving sources, the English tradition was the most successful. Evidently it was either Dunstable of Lionel Power who hit on the idea of using motto openings and a more or less uniform cantus firmus throughout a cycle. A steady stream of such works can be identified from the years 1420–50, all apparently by English composers. The second attempt at this time, if it really is part of a separate phenomenon, is represented by just one work, the cycle that appears in the manuscript originating from Cyprus, now in Turin: since there is no other surviving evidence of the so-called French-Cypriot tradition it is impossible to tell what influence that work had.

The other attempt was that of the continental composers. They could well have known the English works (if these were at all earlier). But if so they evidently favoured something less obviously schematic, something that retained the stylistic individuality of each movement. Thus systematic unification techniques are scarce in the Ordinary cycles of Arnold de Lantins, Grossin, Johannes de Lymburgia, Reson and Dufay, just as they are in the plenary cycles of Reginaldus Libert and Dufay. Yet the important historical point is that all of these works must have been composed between about 1420 and 1433; and after that the idea of the cyclic Mass – if it was an idea in that sense – was dropped on the continent until perhaps around 1450. The experiments of the 1420s apparently led nowhere.

But it may just be possible to identify traces of one further cyclic Mass by Dufay from the 1420s. A Sanctus (iv/2b) and Agnus (v/supp.) in 3/4 throughout and based on a mensural chant that appears separately with the title 'Vineux' have attracted considerable attention, not least because there is a Sanctus setting on the same

Ex. 58

tenor by Richard Loqueville, Dufay's presumed teacher. There is some evidence of common material here, though rather less than several writers have suggested. The closest correspondences are at the very opening and at the beginning of the 'Osanna' (Ex. 58). But even these similarities are scarcely overwhelming when one considers that the two works are based on the same mensural tenor. (In Ex. 58 a fourth voice of the Loqueville setting is omitted, partly to clarify what similarities there are and partly because it is probably merely an alternative to the middle voice.)

It is almost certainly wrong to see Dufay's Sanctus 'Vineux' as having been composed when he was a pupil of Loqueville who died in 1418. Far more probable is that the piece dates from the years when Dufay himself was at Laon and may have had some association with the nearby church of Nouvion-le-Vineux where he subsequently obtained a prebend. His Sanctus and Agnus match the melodic and harmonic style of other pieces which I have already suggested he wrote in those years around 1426 – particularly the rondeau *Adieu ces bons vins de Lannoys* (vi/27), dated 1426, and the Gloria 'de Quaremiaux' (iv/23).

In their only source Dufay's two 'Vineux' movements are grouped with settings of the three other Ordinary movements: the Gloria and Credo are by Antonio Zachara de Teramo,[13] are in four voices and share absolutely nothing with the style of Dufay's movements; but the opening Kyrie is by Dufay and shares the style of the two 'Vineux' movements, so Besseler has placed these three together in the complete edition (iv/2). I have already argued that the Gloria 'de Quaremiaux' is similar in style to the song *Adieu ces bons vins*; I now offer, albeit tentatively, the suggestion that this Gloria belongs as a fourth movement of the cycle formed by the two 'Vineux' movements and their preceding Kyrie.[14] The Gloria differs from them in its two changes of mensuration, but that is a characteristic of Gloria settings throughout Dufay's career; it also has a more limited range for the tenor, but that is a result of its cantus firmus which simply happens to have a smaller range than the 'Vineux' tenor. If these form a cycle and if, as I have suggested, the song *Adieu ces bons vins* grew out of the experience of writing that Gloria, the cycle must surely date from 1425 or 1426.

Among all the Mass polyphony of the early fifteenth century the clearest groupings are between the pairs of Gloria and Credo or Sanctus and Agnus. Even later in the century, when the unified cycle was standard, these pairs of movements tended to be more closely related to one another than to the rest of the cycle; and in the three cycles already discussed that pairing comes across particularly strongly. In the manuscripts of sacred polyphony from the first half of the century there are many examples of isolated pairs, and several of them are by Dufay.

One particularly tantalizing example of pairing (iv/3) hints at some kind of cooperation or rivalry between Dufay and Hugo de Lantins. The Gloria is ascribed to Hugo in two manuscripts, and it has recently been shown on palaeographical grounds that an ascription of it to Dufay in another manuscript is an error;[15] the Credo is ascribed to Dufay in three manuscripts. These movements appear together as a pair in two sources.

Although the two movements are similar in style, treat broadly similar melodic and harmonic material and have similar voice ranges, it seems clear enough that they are indeed by two different composers. Both are in duple time with hints of imitation, but Hugo's movement treats the metre more irregularly. Hugo's harmonic style tends to be more open, with far fewer dissonances (Dufay is often quite bold in his piece) and occasionally the winding round of a single chord that Dufay was to favour – though in a vastly more controlled way – in his slightly later works. The two movements open with the same material and have many similar points of imitation throughout; but perhaps the clearest moment of comparison is where the two composers use similar triple-time passages moving towards important cadences (Ex. 59). Here both composers contrast iambic movement in the discantus with trochaic in the tenor, the two voices remaining entirely consonant with one another. Both insert this rhythm into a framework of duple time. The difference is in their treatment of the contratenor: compared with the directness and simplicity of Dufay's, Hugo's seems fussy and pedestrian. Here as elsewhere in Hugo's Gloria the harmonic effect is

Ex. 59

Hugo de Lantins

Tenor

Contra

Dufay

Tenor

Contra

176

somewhat bland compared with that of Dufay's Credo. Dufay's contratenor begins with a dotted figure which adds a delicate forward drive to his rhythmic movement and then rises above the discantus only to fall below it with a gently dissonant line that prepares for the cadence.

It goes almost without saying that Dufay elsewhere in the movement tries out some of his favourite tricks: the scheme of overlapping 3/8 patterns which we have seen so often, an elaborate passage in imitation at the fifth which continues for five bars, and many similar details. This is not to say, however, that an exhaustive comparison would be entirely in Dufay's favour: Hugo begins with a striking chromaticism, uses his harmonic movement with more care, manages to make his climaxes without recourse to the high C in the discantus which Dufay uses four times, and is often more persuasive in moving from the end of one phrase to the beginning of the next. But in its aural effect Dufay's Credo has an energy that Hugo's Gloria lacks. Neither movement stands out as a masterpiece, but Hugo's more assured and perhaps more staid Gloria catches the imagination less than Dufay's more volatile Credo with its risky part-writing. Perhaps Hugo was the older and more experienced composer.

The evidence that the Gloria of this pair was wrongly ascribed to Dufay in one manuscript also suggests that the Gloria next to it is the work that should bear his name rather than that of Hugo de Lantins.[16] This movement is extremely brief, largely because of its 'cursiva' structure — each of the three voices taking turns with the quickly declaimed text. While the palaeographical arguments for its attribution to Dufay are almost conclusive, the stylistic evidence is also persuasive. In its declamation the work has much in common with Dufay's other 'cursiva' Gloria (iv/1b). The only other 'cursiva' work that is stylistically comparable is the fragmentary Gloria of Grenon where however the declamation is less fluid than in the Dufay works. To judge particularly from cadential treatment, Dufay's Gloria–Credo pair of 'cursiva' movements (iv/1b & c) would be slightly earlier than this isolated Gloria which represents an additional stage of complication in that the text is shared by three voices, not just two.

Two other Gloria–Credo pairs rank among Dufay's most successful early works, to judge from the number of manuscripts containing them. Both are predominantly in major prolation (6/8), and both are in four voices with the two lower voices occupying the same range. The earlier pair (iv/4) has raised considerable discussion[17] on account of its extended 'Amen' sections which include quotations evidently from popular songs of the time: 'Tu m'as monté sur la pance et riens n'a fait, Otre te reface Dieu que ce m'a fait' and 'La vilanella non è bella, Se non la dominica'. In the single manuscript which actually contains these words the passages also have Latin sacred words which were presumably sung in liturgical performances of these movements; but this combination of French and Italian folksongs (if that is what they are) suggests a place of composition where both languages were current. Malatesta origin therefore seems a possibility: their style matches that of the Malatesta motet *Apostolo glorioso* (i/10) of 1426; and the evidence of *Resvelliés vous* (vi/11) is that French was at least accepted in Rimini as a courtly language. This Gloria–Credo pair may therefore date from 1426–7, between Dufay's departure from Laon and his arrival at Bologna.

A somewhat later date is likely for the second pair (iv/5), even though it is mensurally very similar to the first.[18] Its melodic lines are gentler, somewhat recalling those of the motet *Balsamus et munda cera* (i/13); and the second discantus moves in a range a fifth lower than the first, thus giving a texture closer to that of some of the motets from the 1430s.

There are two more independent Gloria settings which begin in 6/8 time. One of these (iv/20) is probably not by Dufay: Bockholdt has shown that its dissonance treatment is different from that of the other early works;[19] perhaps its superficial similarity to movements of the Mass *Sancti Jacobi* caused the scribe of Trent 92 to add Dufay's name to it. The other (iv/21) is scored for three low voices with extensive unison imitation and a contratenor that has several large leaps from the bottom G, suggesting some connection with the rondeau *Hé, compaignons* (vi/49) and the sequence *Gaude virgo* (v/1) – which is to say that although its mensuration might suggest it to be a work of the 1420s its musical style (and its manuscript transmission) suggest something slightly later.

Certainly a date in the mid-1430s seems appropriate for a large group of alternatim compositions: ten Kyrie settings (iv/9–18) and three Gloria settings (iv/24–6).[20] In mensuration, voice-range and musical style these approximately match the cycle of hymns; and there are among the Kyrie settings two which have the chant in the second voice moving in the same range as the first, just as in the hymn cycle. As a group these Kyries and Glorias suggest the same preoccupation with simplicity, economy of style and the systematic exploration of a consciously limited medium which has been seen in the hymns and sequences.

A final Kyrie setting (iv/19) must be considerably later if it is his at all. It has recently been argued persuasively that the setting cannot be by Dufay and must be English.[21] If that is so, presumably the matching Gloria (iv/28) paired with it in the manuscript Trent 92 is also spurious.

Apart from the Gloria 'ad modum tube' (iv/22)[22] – a tiresome work that could be by almost any composer and betrays no hints of its origin or date – the list of Dufay's Mass Ordinary music before his return to the cycle is concluded by three Sanctus–Agnus pairs. All three would probably date from the late 1430s (though iv/8 could well be somewhat later); but by far the most elaborate of these pairs is the Sanctus 'Papale' with its related Agnus (iv/7). The Agnus is anonymous and appears in only one source, where it is described as belonging to the Sanctus. Its authorship has often been doubted, but that may well be at least partly because of some severe transcription errors in the complete edition (as well as in the edition that preceded it).[23]

The Sanctus 'Papale' is more complicated in its structure and scoring than any other Dufay Mass movement.[24] Trope sections are interpolated: lines of the poem *Ave verum corpus natum* appear in five units of two lines each. These have a scoring quite different from that of the Sanctus text itself. First a 'Duo' for high voices (but not solo voices, since the upper line splits into two at one point), then two high voices with a tenor for the second, third and fourth interpolations; and finally the two high voices come together for the last interpolation when they have a tenor and a contratenor below them.

The Sanctus text itself is set basically in three voices, with discantus, tenor and contratenor all lying in a range substantially lower than those in the tropes. For two sections, however, a second contratenor is added (though not in all sources) in a range slightly higher than that of the first contratenor. This happens in the third statement of the word 'Sanctus' and at the first 'Osanna in excelsis' – in which there is the additional luxury of the discantus splitting into three parts to produce a colouristic effect quite unparalleled in the music of the time (Ex. 60).

Ex. 60

Although these sections are written continuously in all the surviving manuscripts, it is difficult to avoid the conclusion that the Sanctus 'Papale' is for antiphonal performance on the most magnificent scale. While the three-voice writing for the trope sections has much in common with Dufay's hymns and Kyrie settings of the mid-1430s, especially those few with two equal discanting voices, the Sanctus text itself is set with a stately sense of progression that emphasizes richness of sound, becoming more intricate only in the final section where the voices suddenly burst into Dufay's favourite cross-rhythm patterns leading to a simple cadence.

Documents at Cambrai nearer the time of Dufay's death contain considerable evidence for various kinds of performing medium: the choirboys could produce a polyphonic choir of their own, perhaps supported by their master and one other singer; and the *petits vicaires* – the cathedral choirmen – could provide another that probably included falsetto voices.[25] The layout of the Sanctus 'Papale' strongly suggests that it exploits antiphonal effects between two such groups. Support for that theory appears in the sequence setting *Gaude virgo* by H. Battre.[26] Here the opening three-voice section has the upper voice marked 'mutate voces' and the next section, in a higher range with a different texture, has all three voices marked 'pueri'. Later in the work the two groups combine. Yet another work of the same kind is a Binchois Gloria–Credo pair which is in many ways similar to the style of the Dufay work, though with different voice-ranges.[27] With these parallels in mind, the following diagram can be offered representing the scheme of Dufay's Sanctus 'Papale':

| Bars | Mensu-ration | Boys with master and a contratenor | Men |
|---|---|---|---|
| – | | | 'Sanctus' (chant) |
| 1–20 | O | trope, lines 1–2: 2 equal vv (one dividing) | |
| 21–36 | O | | 'Sanctus': 3vv |
| 37–51 | O | trope, lines 3–4: 2 equal vv (one dividing) with tenor | |
| 52–63 | O | | 'Sanctus': 3vv |
| 64–74 | O | trope, lines 5–6: 2 equal vv with tenor | |
| 75–93 | ₵ | | 'Dominus . . . gloria Tua': 3vv |
| 94–105 | ₵ | trope, lines 7–8: 2 equal vv with tenor | |
| 106–20 | O | trope, lines 9–10: high voice with tenor and contratenor | |
| 121–9 | O | (perhaps joining men) | 'Osanna in excelsis': 4(6)vv |
| – | | | 'Benedictus' (chant) |
| 130–45 | ₵ | | 'qui venit': 3vv |
| 146–60 | ₵ | | 'in nomine Domini': 2vv |
| 161–88 | O | (perhaps joining men) | 'Osanna in excelsis': 3vv |

Particularly in its contrasts of texture and of movement between the sections, this work shows Dufay trying new kinds of large-scale form. The same may be said of the Agnus paired with it, a work that is in an almost uniform three-voice texture but attempts its own solution to long-range form by variety of pace. There is little in the details of syntax or figuration to suggest that this Agnus is Dufay's work; but the bold attempt at erecting an enormous form, with tenors retrograded and diminished, hints at a mind which was returning to the idea of cyclic design.

## 14

# The St Anthony Masses and other doubtful Mass music

In his will Dufay mentions manuscripts containing two Masses: that for St Anthony of Padua and that for St Anthony Abbot (*Sancti Antonii Viennensis*, named after the church of that saint in the Viennois).[1] This chapter has two main purposes: to show that the work generally known as his Mass for St Anthony Abbot (published as ii/3) is actually a part of his Mass for St Anthony of Padua; and to explore briefly how this reidentification affects the broader picture of his Mass music during the years 1440–55.

Neither of the St Anthony Masses is explicitly named in any surviving manuscript. But in his treatise *Proportionale musices* (1473) Johannes Tinctoris quotes two passages which he describes as being from Dufay's Mass 'of St Anthony';[2] and one of these passages is mentioned again twenty years later in Gafori's *Practica musice* (1496 and later editions), together with a discussion of a further passage from the same Mass.[3] Besseler identified these passages as occurring in a curious Mass cycle which appears in one of the Trent codices with an ascription to Dufay.[4] The cycle had until then been considered a doubtful work, partly because of its extremely casual-seeming cyclic structure and partly because it contains several passages most unlike anything else known by Dufay.[5] Since Tinctoris seems to have been a *petit vicaire* at Cambrai in 1460 his word on the authorship of the Mass should be taken seriously in support of the manuscript ascription; moreover he was generally punctilious in naming the composers from whom he quoted.

Besseler also pointed to a letter of the later theorist Giovanni Spataro replying to a letter from Pietro Aaron dated 22 November 1532. In this letter Spataro quotes seven ligatures from Dufay's 'Missa de Sancto Antonio da Padoa'. Since Besseler and several subsequent writers failed to locate those ligatures in the Mass quoted by Tinctoris it was concluded that the Trent Mass was that for St Anthony Abbot.

But two matters had been overlooked. First, it often happens that different sources for the same piece have different ligaturing, and a passage which could be differently expressed with Spataro's ligatures should be considered seriously.[6] Second, the ligatures which Spataro presents as being on conjunct notes are not necessarily conjunct in the sources from which he quotes. In fact all the ligatures which he quotes are written as though they were on conjunct pitches, yet three ligatures he gives as being from the Gloria of the Mass by Johannes Pulloys do actually appear in that Mass across larger intervals.[7]

Identification now becomes easy and almost conclusive because Spataro very conveniently quotes five of his Dufay ligatures (nos. 2–6) from the 'tenor of the second part' of the Gloria, which in the case of the Trent Mass is a mere thirty-nine bars long; and the ligatures he gives add up to sixteen bars. All his ligatures can be fitted into that brief section of the Trent Mass, requiring no alteration of note-values, only a regrouping of the notes in ligatures (Ex. 61). Such variants are relatively common even among excellent sources of fifteenth-century music. Moreover Spataro begins his discussion of the passage in the logical place with the ligature at bars 67–9 and ends it with the one at bars 100–102 which he describes as being at

Ex. 61

the end of that section ('circa el fine del predicto tenore'). The ten bars omitted in Ex. 61 to save space contain no passage that could conceivably be expressed with an unusual ligature. Spataro's discussion is an attempt to demonstrate to Aaron that certain rare ligature forms actually exist and have good authority; and it would be the most extraordinary coincidence if the same ligatures could be reconciled with the same section of another St Anthony Mass by Dufay.

Spataro's first ligature of all, which he quotes as being 'in the first section of the Gloria', appears close to the beginning and requires the tying together of three notes on the same pitch which are separated in the sole surviving manuscript (Ex. 62). Again this is far from being an unusual variant between sources of a single piece, though it would perhaps be risky to suggest this identification were it not for the close juxtaposition later in the movement of the ligatures already discussed.

**Ex. 62**

Trent version
(Tenor only)

Et in terra

Reconstruction of
Spataro's possible source

Spataro's ligature

1.

His last ligature is more difficult to reconcile with the opening of the 'Qui sedes', which is where Spataro says he finds it (Ex. 63). In view of the closeness of the ligature in Trent to that in Spataro the simplest explanation is that the second note of Spataro's ligature is a copying error in the sole surviving source of his letter. But at the same time the cycle as it survives in its unique source contains several

**Ex. 63**

Trent version
(Tenor only)

Qui sedes

Notated as:

Spataro's ligature: 7.

passages that are patently musical nonsense by any criteria,[8] and so the error might possibly be there.

That identification is confirmed by a further reference in the writings of Spataro which seems to have been overlooked by modern scholars since 1926. In his *Tractato* of 1531 Spataro has more to say about Dufay's Mass for St Anthony of Padua.[9] Here he gives no musical examples, but he describes in detail an extraordinary passage which had been discussed earlier by Tinctoris. At least, he discusses the section 'Et in Spiritum Sanctum' from the Mass for St Anthony of Padua and describes how it moves into the mensuration O3 half way through the section with a resulting cross-rhythm nine-against-four. Again it is unlikely that there should be two St Anthony Masses by Dufay that contain the same highly unusual mensuration sign with the same meaning in the same section; and it is equally unlikely that Spataro – whose treatise is repeatedly invoking Tinctoris and Gafori in order to rebut them – should choose a different St Anthony Mass in his discussion of a matter that had been twice discussed by Tinctoris. It is difficult to avoid the conclusion, then, that Spataro was citing the same Dufay Mass as Tinctoris and Gafori and that he considered it to be the Mass for St Anthony of Padua.

This detailed argument is necessary not only because the cycle's authenticity has been questioned but also because there is strong circumstantial evidence for believing that the Mass was performed at the dedication of Donatello's altar at Padua in June 1450 – some fifteen years later than the normally accepted date for the cycle. That evidence is laid out in chapter 6. The most important matter that needs repeating here is simply that Dufay brought with him nine 'monks' from Cambrai and that in his will Dufay was to stipulate that the Mass should be sung in his memory by nine 'of the better singers' of the cathedral.

Better singers they would need to have been. The discantus of this three-voice cycle has a range of just one note under two octaves, with the range gradually expanding as the cycle progresses: the lower G appears for the first time in the Gloria; the high D not until near the beginning of the Credo, shortly followed by the high E, and the peak note, F, which makes its first entrance splendidly at the words 'Et ascendit in celum'; moreover, as the Mass proceeds the tessitura of the discantus gradually rises, but the second 'Agnus Dei' includes within its twenty-six bars the entire fourteen-note range. This is most unusual for any fifteenth-century work and would seem to make exceptional demands on the singers.

The work needs 'better singers' also because of the bafflingly complex use of cross-rhythms particularly in the Gloria and Credo[10] – paralleled in his other work only in one short section from the Mass *L'homme armé* (Ex. 74) – passages which not surprisingly attracted the attention of theorists.

On the face of it, it may seem unlikely that a three-voice Mass with no cantus firmus and no motto – indeed none of the accepted unifying devices – could have been composed as late as 1450. But throughout his career Dufay composed four-voice works alongside three-voice works: there is no question of his having progressed, like the beginning counterpoint student, from three to four voices. Nor were 'motto' techniques and cantus firmus unification inventions of the 1450s which then supplanted all else; motto unification can be found in Dufay's earliest paired Mass movements (though not in his early cycles); and cantus firmus techniques were used in the Mass in England from at least the 1430s. And neither technique, to take just one later example, appears in Ockeghem's Requiem. There is therefore no logical bar to his having composed this Mass at any time right up to the 1460s; and in fact the cycle contains some curious reminiscences of his last Mass, the *Ave regina celorum* (iii/10).[11]

The Padua Mass opens with a concentrated and imitative style (Ex. 64) that is already reminiscent of some of the songs which in chapter 12 were dated in the 1450s, especially *Adieu m'amour*. Not until the Gloria do we find contrasting duo sections, and it is on the whole here that the greatest mensural complexity appears. But

Ex. 64

equally the Gloria includes a wonderful passage showing the kind of ascetic economy and irregularly evolving melodic freedom which were also noted in some of the later songs (Ex. 65).

Ex. 65

In some ways the cycle may arouse suspicion because the Credo and following movements have their tenor and contratenor in a range a fourth higher than the Kyrie and Gloria. But on closer inspection this merely matches the gradually rising tessitura already noted in the discantus; the lower notes are left out more and more as the cycle progresses. There is a kind of formal daring here crowned by the glorious arc that rises and subsides with perfect control in the Agnus. In all, this seems a work of astonishing beauty and complexity. It has less of the public grandeur found in the big four-voice cantus firmus cycles, but it yields nothing to them in its wayward perfection. I have no difficulty in accepting 1450 as its date of composition. It is strikingly different from the Mass music discussed already and it has much in common with the songs of the 1450s. Moreover it seems unlikely that in 1474 Dufay should have demanded a performance of a work that was by then forty years old.

There is more evidence that the differences between the Trent versions and Dufay's original were substantial. According to Spataro the section 'Et in Spiritum Sanctum' begins in C2 mensuration whereas Trent has it in ₵ . According to Dufay's executors' account the manuscript of the Mass which he left to Cambrai Cathedral (which was presumably definitive) had it in black notation[12] – something which was rare by 1450 and even rarer at the time of his death though several of Dufay's songs from the 1450s do in fact survive in black notation. The account also describes the manuscript as containing 'several other antiphons', with the possible implication that the Mass was a plenary one with Proper movements alongside the Ordinary (as in the Mass *Sancti Jacobi*).

This conclusion receives support from one further reference in Spataro's *Tractato* (chapter 24) which mentions a mensuration change from O2 to 3 in the verse ('nel verso') of Dufay's Mass for St Anthony of Padua. 'Nel verso' cannot reasonably refer to anything in a Mass Ordinary cycle and seems to suggest the inclusion of Proper movements. I can find only three examples of this mensuration pattern, and one of them happens to be in the two-voice verse of the Gradual *Os iusti* in the anonymous Proper cycle for the feast of that saint in the manuscript Trent 88.[13] (In the manuscript the cycle has no title, but the Propers are appropriate for that feast and a later folio in the manuscript (f.192) refers back specifically to this Gradual as being in the cycle for 'Missa Sancti Antonii de Padua'.)

That in its turn raises a question that has long troubled Dufay scholarship. The cycle in Trent 88 is one of a group of sixteen anonymous cycles of Mass Proper which were published in 1947 by Laurence Feininger with what seemed at the time an extraordinary suggestion that eleven of the cycles – among them that for St Anthony of Padua – were by Dufay. Feininger never published the promised demonstration of these attributions, merely saying that he had done all the work and would publish it in due course. But as he outlined it in the preface to the edition the argument included the following considerations: that those eleven cycles shared much material (which he itemized in the preface); that their style and particularly their chant paraphrase technique when put alongside all comparable work by Dufay and his contemporaries showed them to be strongly aligned with Dufay's work; and that one of the movements (the *Alleluia: Veni Sancte Spiritus*, printed in the complete edition as ii/4) appears in a further source with an ascription to Dufay.

Inevitably this last proposition was received with some distrust. To attribute sixty-five movements to Dufay on the basis of a single ascription seems more than wilful. Yet recent research has begun to offer endorsement for at least four more of the movements: Alejandro Planchart convincingly identified the Offertory *Confirma hoc Deus* and the Introit *Os iusti* on the basis of ligatures quoted by Spataro as being by Dufay;[14] Craig Wright more tentatively identified the Tract *Desiderium* as being by Dufay since a work of this title was copied at Cambrai along with the Mass *Ave regina celorum*;[15] and I have now offered the Gradual *Os iusti* as being the one quoted by Spataro. In the circumstances, these new identifications add some weight to Feininger's unpublished stylistic findings.

And there is more. It seemed originally that musical duplication between different settings could argue against authorship by any substantial composer,[16] yet Frohmut Dangel-Hofmann has pointed out that precisely the same happens among a slightly earlier group of Introits by Brassart.[17] Another argument against Feininger was that the pieces included the mensuration signs C2 and O2 not otherwise found in Dufay's work;[18] but one of the pieces of information that had been mislaid through ignoring the *Tractato* is that Spataro gives specific examples of Dufay using both mensuration signs (and indeed their absence from works more firmly ascribed to Dufay could even strengthen the arguments for attributing some of the anonymous cycles to him).

This is not to say that it is yet time to give unqualified endorsement to Feininger's attributions. The entire topic is frighteningly large and liable to the kinds of subjective judgment that always arouse suspicion. Moreover there are plenty of anomalies within the individual cycles which must be explained before the pieces are admitted, even tentatively, to a Dufay edition. The matter is a solemn reminder of how little we still know about the nature and styles of music in the fifteenth century and how little we understand about the range of style and techniques within Dufay's work.

On the other hand, however, it is surprising how much independent evidence unknown to Feininger happens to support his theory. Moreover certain patterns begin to become clearer in the light of the new evidence. If Dufay wrote this set of Mass Proper cycles he would probably have done so during the 1440s in that mysterious decade at Cambrai from which so many documents survive but about which so little is known with certainty. That would have been a logical development from his systematic projects of the 1430s – the cycle of hymns, the cycle of Kyrie settings and finally the cycle (if it was a cycle) of sequence settings. Part of the fascination of the anonymous Mass Proper cycles in Trent 88 is that they represent the first hint of an attempt at system which later reached fulfilment in the *Choralis constantinus* of Heinrich Isaac. The only known precedent for the anonymous cycles – apart from the cycles of Notre-Dame Gradual and Alleluia settings nearly three hundred years earlier – is the cycle of eight Introit settings by Dufay's one-time colleague in the papal choir, Johannes Brassart. The very conception of such a coherent series of Mass Proper cycles is one that suggests a single hand of considerable boldness. Whatever the stylistic problems, Dufay would stand high on the list of possible composers. The Proper cycles are difficult to compare with his other music precisely because this was a new venture and because the only firmly ascribed Dufay works that can be dated in the 1440s with any confidence are the two large isorhythmic motets of 1442, works whose style is unlikely to have any possible bearing on that of his liturgical music.[19] Despite the lack of clear evidence there is a considerable body of circumstantial information pointing to Dufay's authorship of the cycles.[20]

And in any case the evidence appears to show that Spataro considered the Gradual *Os justi* to be a part of Dufay's cycle for St Anthony of Padua. In retrospect that is no surprise. For a Mass cycle to be associated with a particular saint it needs some texts proper to that saint. (In fact, from the references in Dufay's will one would have assumed that this was a cycle containing only Propers had not Tinctoris and others quoted so confidently from its Gloria and Credo.)

There is similarly a more than superficial case for thinking that the other Proper movements in the anonymous Trent cycle belonged with the formally ascribed Ordinary cycle (ii/3). One further detail in its support can be added here. The late fifteenth-century source Perugia, Biblioteca comunale, Ms. 1013, contains three short passages quoted from Dufay's Ordinary cycle for St Anthony of Padua.[21] Only seven folios away from them is a two-voice passage which happens to come from the second half of the Alleluia verse in the Trent 88 Proper cycle for the same saint. This is surely circumstantial evidence; but in the context of everything else it suggests that we may not be far wrong in suggesting that the Ordinary cycle and the Proper cycle belonged together as a single plenary cycle by Dufay.

But if these were all part of Dufay's Mass the 'several other antiphons' mentioned by the executors' account as being in Dufay's manuscript must have been something else. They could have been the other Proper cycles attributed to Dufay by Feininger, but they could also have been Office music for St Anthony of Padua. This turns out to be the more likely answer. His will directs other pieces to be sung for the Office of the feast of St Anthony of Padua. After Compline on the eve of the feast six boys are directed to sing Dufay's own Respond *Si queris miracula* 'with its verse and doxology' – which is precisely how his three-voice setting of that text has come down to us (v/45) – after which they should sing the motet O *sydus Hispanie*. Dufay's non-isorhythmic motet *O proles Hispanie/O sidus Hispanie* (i/6) happens to survive next to *Si queris miracula* in what is probably the earliest of its three sources, so these must surely be the pieces intended even though the motet is in four voices and has two texts.[22] In his will Dufay also specified other Office music for the feast, but the rest seems all to be chant except perhaps for the motet *O lumen ecclesie* which is lost.

Now the texts and chant melodies of *Si queris miracula* and *O proles Hispanie* both happen to come from the rhymed Office for St Anthony of Padua by the thirteenth-century divine Julian of Speyer.[23] Two further settings of Julian's Office appear among Dufay's works, both for Vespers: the antiphon *Sapiente filio* (v/44), also for St Anthony of Padua, and the Magnificat antiphon *Salve, sancte pater* (v/43) for St Francis of Assisi – whose first great disciple was St Anthony of Padua. These pieces must surely lay claim to having been in Dufay's manuscript. Whether they were also composed for the dedication of Donatello's altar seems more doubtful. I would suggest that the anonymous Proper cycles could well be by Dufay and would have been composed during the early 1440s for use at Cambrai (where St Anthony of Padua was one of the revered saints); that the few surviving Office pieces for St Anthony of Padua were composed slightly later; and that the three-voice Ordinary cycle for that saint (ii/3) was perhaps composed specifically for the dedication of Donatello's altar in 1450.

A further consequence of reconsidering Spataro's evidence and reidentifying the surviving St Anthony Mass is that whereas scholars have been looking for traces of the Mass for St Anthony of Padua, it is now clear that they were looking for the wrong thing. They should have been looking for the Mass for St Anthony Abbot (St-Anthoine-de-Viennois).

The surviving evidence on this Mass is now simply that Dufay's will mentions it as being in a large paper manuscript along with his Requiem Mass, and that the executors valued the manuscript at 15 *sous*, whereas they valued the parchment manuscript discussed earlier at 40 *sous*.[24] He gave both volumes to the chapel of St Stephen in Cambrai Cathedral – the chapel in which he was to be buried. Since the Requiem Mass – which certainly cannot be traced – was described as new when it was copied into the cathedral choirbooks in 1470–1 the Mass for St Anthony Abbot may equally date from around 1470, which makes it unlikely that the cycle of Propers for that saint in Trent 88 belongs to the Mass in question. (For what it is worth, that is one of the cycles which Feininger does not attribute to Dufay.)

But from its title the Mass probably included Propers – just like that for St Anthony of Padua and for the same reasons. As it happens there is one plenary cycle that could just be Dufay's. It appears in the Trent manuscript 89 (ff. 59v-71) with the heading 'Introitus misse beati Anthonii' and contains the Propers for St Anthony Abbot as well as an Ordinary cycle (without the Kyrie) with loose motto openings.[25] It would be too soon to come to a firm decision on this while the Mass is still unpublished and most of the other music mentioned so far in this chapter remains unperformed. It is entirely different from the four-voice cantus firmus Masses which Dufay composed during these years, but then three-voice and four-voice music remained separate and independent in their style throughout Dufay's career. Its claim to be Dufay's lost Mass for St Anthony Abbot must eventually be examined closely.

By way of an epilogue, a few words on other doubtful cycles. First among these is the Mass *Caput* (ii/5), once considered to be the very quintessence of Dufay's style and to be his first cycle unified by mottos and a tenor.[26] Suspicion concerning its authenticity first arose when two fragments of it turned up in English sources; no other music of Dufay is found in England. With this information in mind scholars returned to Manfred Bukofzer's famous demonstration that there must originally have been an English *Caput* Mass, partly because the chant basis of all three *Caput* Masses – that ascribed to Dufay and those of Ockeghem and Obrecht – comes from the English Sarum rite, and partly because its use of a troped Kyrie is characteristically English.[27] It was then noticed that the ascription to Dufay depended on just one isolated copy of the Kyrie in a source which was anyway of dubious authenticity and that in the sole source for the entire cycle an ascription to Dufay had been erased. Finally, with an increasing understanding of Dufay's style and that of the English composers in the mid-fifteenth century it became clear that the Mass thought to be Dufay's was almost certainly itself the 'lost' English *Caput* to which Bukofzer had referred.[28] In its form *Caput* exactly follows the other English Masses of its time, with its cantus firmus layout predetermining the form of all the movements alike whereas Dufay's cycles appear to base their form more on the words.[29] Moreover, masterpiece though it is, the *Caput* Mass contains no trace of Dufay's style. That there is a payment for copying the Kyrie at Cambrai in 1463–4 merely puts it alongside the works of many other greater and lesser composers whose compositions were included among the Cambrai choirbooks. Authorities now seem to agree that the *Caput* Mass is the work of an unnamed English composer working in the 1440s.

In his edition Besseler also included the Mass *La mort de Saint Gothard* (ii/6). This appears anonymously in a later manuscript which happens also to contain Dufay's Mass *Ave regina celorum* (but with an ascription to him). Apparently Laurence Feininger first suggested that the work might be by Dufay, and Besseler stated that he found many of Dufay's fingerprints in the music, though he specified none of them and nobody else seems to have found any. When Feininger eventually published it in 1963, three years after Besseler's edition, he firmly withdrew his proposal that the work was Dufay's and suggested the much younger Johannes Martini as composer – an attribution supported a few years later by Nitschke.[30]

Feininger attributed three more anonymous cycles to Dufay on the basis of their style alone. One of these, the Mass *Veterem hominem,* he included largely because its form and tenor usage so closely matched those of *Caput*.[31] This argument has now been turned on its head, particularly in view of additional evidence that *Veterem hominem* is English in origin.[32] Feininger gave the same reasons for attributing to Dufay the Mass *Christus surrexit*;[33] and his reasons now look similarly slim, although the tenor this time is not English but the German Leise *Christ ist erstanden*. His final attribution to Dufay was the Mass *Puisque je vis,*[34] an attribution which has subsequently been discussed only in the most cautious terms.[35]

Yet another cycle was tentatively attributed to Dufay by Charles Hamm[36] largely on the basis of its mensural usage, it motto technique and its appearance in a source where one might expect to find late Dufay works. It is the three-voice cycle in the Vatican manuscript San Pietro B 80 (ff.113v–121v). Simple and relatively brief though the cycle is, its attribution seems promising.

But of all these cycles, the Mass *Puisque je vis* is the most likely contender for Dufay's authorship, having in its structure much in common with the Masses *Ecce ancilla Domini* and *Se la face ay pale*. Yet this merely emphasizes the dangers of attributing anonymous works to Dufay – or indeed any other composer.

# 15

# The cantus firmus Masses

There can be no finer summary of Dufay's work than the four great Mass cycles of his later years. They have much in common. All are in four voices, all are on a cantus firmus which is in the middle of the texture and confined to a single voice, all employ further means of unifying the five movements, and they have similar formal design based broadly on the contrast between triple and duple metre. Like the late songs, they yield their musical secrets less easily than the earlier works.

At the same time each cycle has its individual characteristics. The two based on secular chansons are normally associated with Dufay's stay in Savoy during the 1450s, though that on *L'homme armé* could well be later. Of these the Mass *Se la face ay pale* (iii/7) is perhaps the most joyful and the most elegant whereas the Mass *L'homme armé* (iii/8) is the longest of his cycles and includes several ambitious technical feats. The two on sacred chants almost certainly come from his last years in Cambrai. According to the cathedral accounts the Mass *Ecce ancilla* (iii/9) was copied there in 1463–4 and there is no reason for believing that it had been composed long before that. This is the shortest of the cycles and also the most economical, almost an object-lesson in using the minimum means. Perhaps it was a preliminary exercise for the last and most magnificent cycle, the Mass *Ave regina celorum* (iii/10), probably composed for the dedication of Cambrai Cathedral in 1472.

In the Mass *Se la face ay pale*[1] Dufay took his cantus firmus from a chanson which he had composed in the 1430s but which was in several ways atypical of his work at the time.[2] Its text is in unusually short lines of five syllables with the rhyme-scheme described by theorists as *équivoquée* – punning rhyme:

| | |
|---|---|
| Se la fa*ce ay pale* | If my face is pale |
| La cause *est amer.* | the reason is love. |
| C'est la prin*cipale,* | That is the main cause, |
| Et tant m'*est amer* | and love is so bitter |

> *Amer,* qu'en *la mer*
> Me voudroye *voir.*
> Or scet bien *de voir*
> La belle a qui suis
> Que nul bien *avoir*
> Sans elle ne puis.

> for me that I wish to
> drown myself in the sea.
> So my fair one can know
> from seeing
> that I cannot have any joy
> without her.

The poem is in ballade form (AAB for each of three stanzas), but for once the musical form does not correspond to the poetic form. Whereas every other ballade setting of the century has that same AAB form in its music, this one has a through-composed stanza. A further feature of the song's individuality is that its musical style is unusually compact: statement and counter-statement, mostly in syllabic style until the final roulade with its more characteristic triadic patterns and overlapping textures (Ex. 66).

Ex. 66

What is perhaps surprising is that the cycle contains practically no reference to anything in the chanson except its tenor. The discantus melody is ignored. Moreover, whereas the chanson scarcely ever deviates from C tonality, cadencing brilliantly on the high C at the end, the Mass is firmly in F with every structural cadence but one having a strong F chord. The C on which the tenor concludes each section appears as the middle note at these cadences.

The choice of this cantus firmus is less surprising than it may initially seem. Certainly the later tradition was normally to borrow a cantus firmus or a parody model from another composer, but the earliest history of such borrowing was often self-borrowing. Antonio Zachara da Teramo based Mass movements on his own secular songs, and Dufay's last cycle was to be based on his own antiphon setting *Ave regina celorum* (v/51). There may be some significance in the use of his own chanson for the *Se la face ay pale* cycle in view of the chanson's unusual position within his own work. It has been suggested that the reason for the choice goes back to a particular occasion and that the song itself had a special place in the history of the Savoy court.[3] If the song was for the beautiful Anne de Lusignan, Duchess of Savoy, the Mass could well have been for some family celebration during the 1450s.

The full texture of the Mass is precisely that of the other three later cycles and can be seen from the opening of the Kyrie (Ex. 67).

Ex. 67

Tenor and contratenor occupy the same range. In this opening passage the contratenor remains above the tenor, as though to keep the opening statement of the cantus firmus unambiguous; but for the most part the two voices intertwine, favouring textural fullness and perhaps mindful that a constant emphasis on the independence of the tenor would be oppressive.

The discantus is in a range approximately a fifth higher; and in all four cycles it is firmly melodic. In this Mass the opening motif in bars 1–3 reappears constantly in differing guises, always exploring and re-exploring the falling figure. Another feature of melodic control can be heard in this first Kyrie, where the discantus ascends only gradually to its peak note, E, which appears just once shortly before the end of the section.

The lowest voice has a range a fifth below the tenor and contratenor; and in the full sections it regularly functions as a bass line bearing the harmonic structure. The clear emphasis on C and G in Ex. 67 shows that function working strongly. In the complete edition each Mass has a different title for this lowest voice; but those titles are based simply on the main source used, and the range of titles in the remaining sources is entirely lacking in either consistency or apparent logic.[4] The function of this voice remains the same in all four cycles; we shall call it 'bassus'.

With the ranges overlapping as they do, Dufay could introduce what was evidently still one of his favourite devices, the intertwining of three voices around a triadic figure as in bars 25–7 of the chanson. In the Mass he uses it towards the end of each movement, both as a signpost and as a unifying element. Usually the bassus holds the low C to stabilize these passages, as here in the Kyrie (Ex. 68). At the corresponding point in the Gloria and Credo (bars 192–4) the upper voices in fact quote exactly from all three voices of the chanson, again over a held C in the bassus. And the device reaches its culmination in the more subtle texture of the final 'Agnus Dei' (Ex. 69).

Ex. 68

This cycle is unique among the four in that the cantus firmus remains unchanged in all five movements (though brief cadential figures are added in three sections). Throughout the Kyrie, Sanctus and Agnus the song tenor also retains the same mensural relationship to the other voices: it is read in double note-values so that a single bar

Ex. 69

of triple time in the tenor matches two bars of triple time in the other voices (as in Exx. 67–9). This clearly audible and consistent relationship of the mensurations has two important consequences: it gives a regularity of two-bar groupings which is rare in Dufay's work; and it adds an element of softening to the triple metre of the other voices, making the flow of the lines more gentle.

For the two longer movements, the Gloria and the Credo, Dufay runs the tenor through three times in motet fashion:[5] first each note is augmented three times, then twice as in the other movements, and finally it is performed at the written speed, which is to say that for the last section the four voices have the same metre and tempo, the excitement is increased, and the texture is furthermore arranged so that the tenor melody is now more clearly audible. (It is with this in mind that writers have seen the cantus firmus Masses as taking over the role earlier filled by the isorhythmic motets: occasional works for particular celebrations.)

These two movements are of equal length, thus emphasizing their difference in pattern from the other movements. But all five movements intersperse the sections of tenor statement with other material, usually in the form of duos: some two-fifths of the length of this Mass are in duo texture. The identical length of the Gloria and Credo is unusual and shows a kind of schematic design that appears to be absent from Dufay's other late cycles. Another difference is that although all the movements in all four cycles contain contrasting sections in duple time, those duple sections in the Mass *Se la face ay pale* provide rather less contrast since the bars move in groups of three with a resulting metrical structure which precisely matches that of the tenor when it is in its normal form (as in Exx. 67–9), i.e. a long bar of 3/2 time. Here, also from the Kyrie, is the end of the duo section showing that metre and giving the return of the contratenor to bring in the cadence (Ex. 70). The passage of imitation at the octave is relatively unusual in this cycle but becomes more common in the other three cycles.

Ex. 70

Motto openings were still by no means an invariable feature of Mass cycles. In the anonymous English Masses *Caput* and *Veteruem hominem* each movement begins with an identical passage of several bars, but among over fifty cyclic Masses in the Trent codices fewer than ten have a motto literally repeated in all five movements. Among the four Dufay cantus firmus cycles only the Mass *Ave regina celorum* has a strict motto. In the Mass *Se la face ay pale* the Kyrie has an opening (Ex. 67) different from the other movements which begin as in Ex. 71. The similarity is easily perceived, but the separate treatment of the Kyrie suggests that literal treatment seemed simplistic. In the Masses *L'homme armé* and *Ecce ancilla* there is a two-

**Ex. 71**

voice motto which is relatively loosely treated and in each case appears once with an extra voice added: in the Sanctus of *Ecce ancilla* and in the Kyrie of *L'homme armé* (Ex. 72), where the contratenor is the added voice.

**Ex. 72**

There may be some significance in the way the opening here inverts the motto in the discantus of the Mass *Se la face ay pale*. We have several times noted how Dufay liked to rework similar material in comparable pieces, and the same happens in these four cycles, as we shall see.

The opening of the Mass *L'homme armé*[6] points to a particularly characteristic feature of the cycle. Here the entry of the cantus firmus is concealed within the texture: the opening note of the tenor is immediately preceded by the same pitch in the bassus, the line's movement is matched by that of the other voices, and the voice constantly interlocks with those around it. The early part of the cycle seems deliberately designed to disguise both the presence and the identity of the cantus firmus. If the work is performed by voices without instruments the *L'homme armé* tune does not really become recognizable until near the end of the Gloria; and although it sometimes comes through the texture thereafter, the predominating impression is that every attempt has been made to hide it. The tenor is laid out in varying note-values which conceal its identity, the bassus overlaps with it far more than in the Mass *Se la face ay pale*, and embellishments often hide its contours.

200

If that purely musical observation is valid it casts some doubt on the theory that the work was composed for performance at the Savoy court where the choir included an organist and a trombonist who could play that line.[7] The way the tenor is enmeshed into the texture and emerges from notes in the other voices seems difficult to explain except as the kind of disguise that would be spoilt by the use of a contrasting tone colour for that line.

There is therefore no particular reason for associating the work with Dufay's Savoy years. At least two recent writers have seen it as being rather later: Wolfgang Nitschke's intensive stylistic study placed it as a very late work, particularly in view of its considerable complexity; and Charles Hamm's mensural study placed it alongside the Masses *Ecce ancilla* and *Ave regina celorum* somewhat later than the Mass *Se la face ay pale*.[8]

Several objective tests lead to the same conclusion.[9] They remind us that while there is a satisfying symmetry in placing the two cycles with secular cantus firmus in Savoy and the two with sacred ones in Cambrai this is a pattern that is perhaps too easily imposed on the works that happen to survive. If Dufay composed other Mass cycles during his later years the pattern looks less compelling. Several such cycles have been suggested (as noted in chapter 14) and the Cambrai documents tell us that he composed a Requiem Mass around 1470.

There is a further consideration here. The *L'homme armé* melody may be secular, but it is not comparable with the tenor of the Mass *Se la face ay pale* which is extracted from a courtly chanson. *L'homme armé* is a monophonic melody in popular vein with a text whose overtones are political and possibly satirical.[10] The earliest polyphonic settings of it are difficult to date. They include Dufay's cycle and one by Ockeghem – which is significantly different in that the tenor is usually easy to hear, employs a different version of the melody, and never disguises it by embellishment or by changing the relative lengths of the notes. Beyond these two works, the tune appears in a combinative chanson by Robert Morton which has sometimes been dated before 1450 but which I have recently attempted to show was probably composed in 1463;[11] and there is a cycle of six anonymous *L'homme armé* Masses in four and five voices which survive with a dedication stating that they had brought pleasure to Duke Charles the Bold of Burgundy who became duke only in 1467. If there is any personality of the fifteenth century who could be identified with the 'armed man' of the melody it was surely Charles, the irascible duke who spent most of his short reign on military campaigns. There is therefore at least a possibility that the early history of *L'homme armé* in polyphony belongs largely with Charles, the duke to whom Dufay donated six manuscripts; and that in its turn would support the musical evidence suggesting that Dufay's cycle was written after his final return to Cambrai in 1458.

But the main contrast between this and the *Se la face ay pale* cycle is that this is the more showy, outgoing piece. Whereas the earlier cycle was one of elegance, balance and beautifully modulated textures, this is rich in surprising melodic turns, in cross-relations between B natural in the discantus and B flat in the lower voices (somewhat reduced by unnecessary *musica ficta* in the complete edition), various ambitious uses of multiple proportions, and lastly the use of the cantus firmus sung backwards for the final 'Agnus Dei'.

Perhaps some idea of the outgoing nature and the elements of technical show in the Mass *L'homme armé* can be seen from the Credo, which happens to be the longest movement in any of Dufay's four cantus firmus cycles. This begins with an enormous introductory

Ex. 73

duo between discantus and contratenor, a full thirty bars long. When the lower voices enter (Ex. 73) the cantus firmus is in very long note-values, divided by rests as though to conceal its features; and once more it not only emerges out of the last note of the duo but passes its first note on to the bassus, as it were. So four bars are filled with nothing but the triad on G. The line in the contratenor at bars 31–3 is one that recurs so often in the cycle that it can be considered a fundamental motivic element.[12] When the bassus reaches the low C in bar 36 the listener will experience a sound not heard previously in the work. In fact this is the first time the voice has gone lower than D; that low C appears only six times in the course of the Credo and after that returns just once in the Sanctus and once in the last 'Agnus Dei', on a magically scored low C minor chord.

Quite apart from the stillness of the harmonic rhythm in Ex. 73, the first four-voice section of the Credo moves generally in note-values longer than in the opening duo; and the pace does not return until a shorter duo at the words 'verum de Deo vero' (bars 73–80). This leads directly to a passage of startling complexity, with three voices in entirely different metres (Ex. 74).[13] Here the declamatory repeated notes of the bassus provide the central reference point, held in place by the longer notes of the tenor; above those the con-

Ex. 74

tratenor and discantus dance in their respective independent rhythms. The outline of the contratenor at bars 83–4 follows the thematic motif already mentioned.

Shortly afterwards comes the main internal cadence of the movement and a change to duple time introduced by a duo in which the voices overlap and imitate freely (Ex. 75).

Ex. 75

Now begins the second performance of the cantus firmus which culminates in a passage with the tenor imitated by the bassus (Ex. 76). This imitation is a precise repetition of one at the same point in the Gloria (a matter which helps to unite the Gloria and Credo as a pair, something achieved in all of Dufay's cantus firmus cycles). The discantus and contratenor here do not refer back directly to the Gloria, however, though there are brief and perhaps significant moments of similarity. What the passage does do in both the Gloria and Credo is to emphasize the cantus firmus more strongly than elsewhere in the cycle; and the spacing of the texture here in the Credo emphasizes the cantus firmus even more strongly in that towards the end of the imitative passage the tenor is exposed as the highest voice with the discantus well below it.

Once again the thematic contratenor motif appears in bars 172–4. But there is more to the motivic structure of this section. The metrical shape of the cantus firmus in bars 170–1 with its 3 + 3 + 2 is not made into a feature of the counterpoint here; but in the Gloria the counterpoint is simple and tends to emphasize that structure which appears even more strongly towards the end of the movement at the 'Amen'. That is just one of many details in the Mass

Ex. 76

where motivic material is carried from one section to the next; melodic recurrences permeate the whole structure and the cycle can be heard as perhaps Dufay's most extended exercise in motivic development.

Its culmination is perhaps apparent in the use of a 'tail-motif': the last five bars of the Agnus precisely repeat the end of the Kyrie. Structurally this detail may seem puzzling, for although the section in the final movement corresponds to the last phrase of the cantus firmus in its final 'original tempo' statement, in the Kyrie it behaves as a kind of afterthought: after a complete statement of the cantus firmus in longer note-values, the last phrase (or it could be the first, for the two are identical) appears alone at the end. There is only one reasonable explanation for this irrational aspect of cantus firmus usage in the Kyrie: that Dufay was consciously planning a symmetry with the Agnus and that the brief passage was added to the Kyrie after the Agnus had been conceived. As so often in these works, the number-based framework is merely a starting point: beyond that, considerations of musical form and of text setting can take priority.

This could be used as evidence to support the theory that Dufay's Mass cycles were not necessarily composed in their playing order.[14] A logical view might be that the paired Gloria and Credo were composed (or at least planned) first, then the Sanctus and Agnus, and that the Kyrie was fashioned last – a theory that would explain why the opening motto of the Kyrie in both chanson Masses is more complex than that of the other movements. It is as though Dufay waited until the end before composing his Kyrie movements, keen to include within them traces of everything that was to follow.

Needless to say, however, the careful planning of the cycles was not geared towards a continuous performance of the five movements. Particularly in the Masses *L'homme armé* and *Ave regina celorum* the extraordinary density of the writing makes it important to follow liturgical form by running the Kyrie and Gloria together but hearing the other movements as independent units within a larger liturgical canvas. This could explain why it is so often the Kyrie that seems to be different in these cycles. The details of Dufay's liturgies have yet to be discovered; but given the often irrational relationships between movements of his cyclic Masses (something rarely found in the Masses of his contemporaries) it is likely that examination of their liturgical context would explain much that is still not clear. In recent years art historians have used comparable techniques towards understanding the great renaissance cycles of paintings.[15]

In some ways the Mass *Ecce ancilla Domini/Beata es Maria*[16] (to give it the full title from the two chants it borrows) seems different from the other late cycles because its voice-ranges are lower. But they retain precisely the same relationship to one another. The difference here may well be a matter of clef combinations and of modality: it seems sensible to transpose this Mass up to the range of the others (or vice versa: there is no evidence of a standard pitch-level in the fifteenth century, that any written pitch corresponded to a particular sounding pitch). There is plenty of evidence from a later generation that music at an apparently lower pitch was transposed upwards by a system known as *chiavette*. The difference in pitch-level here can be seen as an inessential one, whereas the difference already noted in the actual relationship between voices in Dufay's hymns and sequence settings is surely essential.

On the other hand the lower written pitch of this cycle points to an important comparison with Ockeghem's Mass *Ecce ancilla*, a work which has sometimes been considered quite unrelated to Dufay's because it uses an entirely different chant that merely happens to have the same opening words. A comparison of Dufay's opening motto with the opening of the Ockeghem Mass shows that the two have at least something in common (Ex. 77). Here as elsewhere the interchange between the two composers is a slippery subject difficult to define, but Ockeghem's presence in Cambrai only a few months before Dufay's *Ecce ancilla* Mass was copied into the cathedral choirbooks hints strongly that the two cycles may have a more than casual connection.[17]

Ex. 77

a; Dufay

Discantus
Contratenor

[Bassus: in
Sanctus only]

b; Ockeghem

Discantus
Contratenor

## Dufay

### Ex. 78

a: Kyrie

b: Sanctus

c: Gloria

d: Credo

(Note: ligature signs are omitted throughout )

Dufay's *Ecce ancilla* is the most lightly scored of his cycles, a work showing in addition an economy that contrasts particularly with the *L'homme armé* and *Ave regina celorum* Masses. Fully one half of its length is devoted to duo texture showing an extraordinary wealth of invention, exploiting to the full a texture that may seem too lacking in resource for true variety. In this and the Mass *Ave regina celorum* Dufay displays an increasing preference for pure canon in the duos and does so with a range of skill that was never to be challenged except by Josquin (who in this respect seems to have learned much from Dufay).

In this cycle passages in three voices are relatively rare; normally the two lower voices enter together. The contrast between long duos and richly scored full sections is thus an important structural element. But even here there is a surprising economy. Example 78 shows the four different ways in which he sets the opening of the second chant, *Beata es Maria*. (The music of the second 'Osanna' in the Sanctus is repeated exactly for the final 'Agnus Dei',[18] so only four settings of the chant appear in this cycle.) Of these the Kyrie and the Sanctus are extremely close apart from their rhythmic changes. In all four settings the contratenor has a falling figure from C to G against the second and third notes of the tenor. The setting in the Gloria stands slightly apart in being in only three voices with the tenor clearly exposed as the highest and slowest-moving voice. But elsewhere the similar movement in the bassus as well as the opening pitches on E in the discantus show a remarkable similarity of treatment – possibly even a reflection of the isomelic techniques in his motets.

This economy is further emphasized by Dufay's choice of the two chants. Each movement has the antiphon *Ecce ancilla Domini* in the first half and *Beata es Maria* in the second (though the Credo has a third section based on the *Ecce ancilla* chant).[19] In Dufay's versions both chants begin with an upward leap of a fourth; and beyond that their opening and closing sections are strikingly similar. This choice of such musically related chants was surely another conscious compositional decision. While the Mass *Ecce ancilla* has none of the showy splendour of the other late cycles, it is by its very economy one of Dufay's most perfect creations.

For the last and most complex of his cycles, the Mass *Ave regina celorum*,[20] Dufay used three methods of unification. Each movement

Ex. 79

begins with a motto which lasts a full eight bars (Ex. 79) and is not
varied except in one repeated note to accommodate the more verbose
texts of the Gloria and the Credo. The motto is longer and more
consistent than his others and is unusually long in the tradition of the
motto Mass. It is also a motto of an extraordinary musical richness:
bassus and tenor have imitation at the fifth; and the discantus begins
with a figure that is audibly related to them but in its turn serves to
generate much melodic material later in the cycle. The very complexity of the motto as compared with the openings of his other cycles is a
harbinger of what is to follow. No work of Dufay's is more full of
astonishing musical detail.

Second, the Mass is built on a chant that is performed just once
in each movement. This chant always begins in the same rhythmic
form (since it begins during the statement of the motto) but is
otherwise presented in a wide variety of embellished and rhythmicized forms, varied more freely than in his other cycles. That freedom
of presentation allows the cantus firmus to be more fully integrated
into the musical texture; and the other voices in their turn make
considerable use of its thematic material. Indeed it should be clear
even from Ex. 79 that the voices here are contrapuntally more
integrated than in the other cyles.

Third, it contains elements of parody. This concept, which has
been mentioned several times in passing, is perhaps more characteristic of the sixteenth-century Mass cycle, though there are several
fifteenth-century examples. It involves borrowing not merely a single
voice but harmonic progressions and contrapuntal features from
another work. In Dufay's Mass the second 'Agnus Dei' contains a
section taken straight from his big four-voice setting of the antiphon
*Ave regina celorum* (v/51); and traces of the antiphon setting appear
elsewhere in the cycle: the cadence in bars 118–20 of the Gloria

(from antiphon bars 130, 132–3), the chant entry at bars 23–6 of the Sanctus and bars 23–7 of the Agnus (antiphon bars 30–2, literally followed in the lower voices, outlined in the upper voices), the imitative material at the climax of the first 'Osanna' (Sanctus bars 86–9, following antiphon bars 61–5) which is repeated in a more condensed form for the second 'Osanna' (bars 140–4). Beyond that it might be possible to see in the tripla section of the antiphon (bars 150–4) the germ of the tripla section which heralds the end of the Gloria and the Credo of the Mass – a passage which, as no reader should by now be surprised to learn, is almost identical in the two movements (Gloria bars 139–49, Credo bars 196–205). But these amount to relatively little among the enormous range and variety of this massive cycle, and the most distinctive is certainly that in the Agnus with its passionate chromaticisms instantly recalling the trope words inserted into the motet: 'Miserere supplicanti Dufay' – Have mercy on the beseeching Dufay (Ex. 80).[21]

Ex. 80

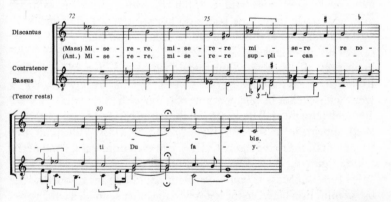

The antiphon includes several such personal tropes within the text, two of them including Dufay's name. (It is the work intended to be sung at his deathbed.) In the same way the Mass is an intensely personal statement; but it is also a public statement, for it makes no direct allusion to Dufay's own name and it is perhaps significantly not mentioned in his will.

The circumstantial case for suggesting that the cycle was composed for the dedication of Cambrai Cathedral in 1472 has already been outlined. Another point in evidence of that date is its style compared with that of the antiphon *Ave regina celorum*. The antiphon was copied into the Cambrai choirbooks in 1464–5, the year after the Mass *Ecce ancilla*. Its style is far closer to the open and economic style of that cycle. Two duos fill the first twenty bars, leading to the entry of the full four-voice texture with an astonishing minor chord at the words 'Miserere tui labentis Dufay'; the second section at the words 'Salve radix' is more densely scored and imitative; a change from triple to duple time introduces the third section, 'Gaude gloriosa', which includes the passage quoted above in Ex. 80; the last section begins with thin textures at 'Vale valde decora', moves towards the third surprising moment, the low cadence at 'miserere nobis' (bars 130–3, quoted in the Gloria of the Mass), and then introduces writing of more complexity leading to the close via a brief tripla section. Like the Mass *Ecce ancilla* it is a work of open clarity, reserving its truly affective writing for just a few special moments.

Yet the Mass *Ave regina celorum* has incident throughout. Its main peaks are carefully placed, but the entire context is so much more elaborate that those peaks do not strike the ear so strongly.

In several ways this cycle can be seen as a summary and extension of his other late works. Many of the ideas that had worked well in his previous cycles are found again here, expanded and enriched. Its motto recalls the opening of the Mass *Se la face ay pale* (Ex. 67), a work whose tenor has elements in common with that of the last Mass and which might well have offered the germination of two ideas that keep appearing in the *Ave regina celorum* Mass – the imitative treatment of the rising figure C, D, E, F in even note-values and of the falling figure C, B, A, G in dotted note-values.

From the Mass *L'homme armé* it could be said to borrow the use of imitation between the tenor and the bassus (an idea which goes back to the motet *Nuper rosarum flores* (i/16) of 1436 or even further to the little song *Resvelons nous* (vi/28) a decade earlier than that); it perhaps also borrows from here its use of complicated mensural proportions, though in the Mass *Ave regina celorum* they are more extended and more persuasively integrated. But the two cycles particularly share the use of complicated cross-relations: the Mass *L'homme armé* makes considerable play of the B natural in the upper voice against the B flat in the lower voices; the Mass *Ave regina celorum* seems to expand on this by adding the play of E natural against E flat.[22] I say 'seems' advisedly: the surviving manuscripts disagree considerably and modern scholarship is still not entirely clear on the details of how this works; but Ex. 79 gives some clue to the nature of the mixed tonality.

Finally, from the Mass *Ecce ancilla* it borrows at least one musical detail and almost certainly a feature of scoring. The detail is that the second 'Christe' in the Mass *Ave regina celorum* takes its opening straight from the second 'Agnus Dei' of the Mass *Ecce ancilla*. The feature of scoring is one that emerges from a closer study of that other still confusing fundamental area in our understanding of fifteenth-century music – texting. Recent study suggests that both cycles are bitextual: the discantus and contratenor take the text of the Mass Ordinary, as expected; but the tenor and the bassus appear both to take the antiphon text throughout.[23] The other cantus firmus Masses therefore all play their part in the germination of Dufay's final masterpiece.

But there is something else. The last Mass also shows evidence of new ideas, of iconoclastic formal experiments, indeed of the same extraordinarily youthful energy noticed in the earliest works of some fifty years before. Again, just two details, both from the Kyrie. It is a large nine-section movement, but section III is a precise repeat of section I and section VI is a repeat of section IV. That scheme is common enough in the fifteenth-century Kyrie, but the difference here is that it is associated with the borrowed cantus firmus and destroys the sequence of events in that chant. Here as elsewhere in the cycle the architectonic form is for Dufay far more important than the sequence and layout of the cantus firmus; what began as a structural framework in the earlier cycles is now simply another tool to be used as seemed suitable. The second detail in the Kyrie is the inclusion of an optional third voice for three of the two-voice sections. Here, as with the texting and the chromaticism, the manuscripts disagree; but it seems clear enough that Dufay offered several different performance means for these sections – something which would seem to conflict with the theory that the work was composed for one particular occasion but which fits in well with the bursting cornucopia of musical invention elsewhere in the work. One might almost say that just as certain works of the 1420s appeared to show Dufay in an insecure mood, intent on demonstrating that he was more technically gifted than any of his contemporaries, so this late work shows a similar insecurity, shows the slight bitterness that we noticed in his will, perhaps even shows an awareness that the styles he represented were passing away ahead of him. As earlier in the ballade *Resvelliés vous* (vi/11) and the motet *Ecclesie militantis* (i/12), he seems here almost to be trying too hard.

But equally, like those two pieces, it is a glorious and endlessly fascinating work. More than anything else this cycle shows the most inexhaustible invention as well as sovereign control of musical pace and texture. Given the many doubts that remain concerning its texting and chromaticism, given the irregular treatment of the cantus firmus, given above all the sheer profligacy of musical and especially metrical material – given those things it would be absurd to claim for the Mass the perfection of either the *Se la face ay pale* or the *Ecce ancilla* cycle. Nor is the Mass easy for performer or listener. In fact it sometimes seems as though the old man no longer felt any need to compromise.

The Mass *Ave regina celorum* is the work which more than any other of Dufay's leaves the listener, like the critic or the analyst, feeling that he has scarcely touched the surface, that each new listening will reveal more.

## Sums recorded in executors' accounts of Dufay and Binchois (see page 80)

Both accounts include a section at the end recording income from prebends received later and additional expenditures. But they are not essential to the comparisons made here.

### *Valuation of property*

|  | **Dufay** | **Binchois** |
|---|---|---|
| Cash in the home | £265  4s  9d | £342 |
| Silver | £565  2s  6d | £280 |
| Jewels | £47  18s  2d | none |
| Books | £104  4s | £12 (one book only) |
| Furniture etc | £840  1s | £82  2s |
| Horse | none | £33  12s |
| *Total:* | £1822  10s  5d | £749  14s |

### *Income from prebends received in first account*

| **Dufay** | | **Binchois** | |
|---|---|---|---|
| Cambrai Cathedral | £248  3s  1½d | Ste-Waudru, Mons | £100 (1459) |
| Ste-Waudru, Mons | £115  7s  9d | St-Pierre, Cassel | £61 7s (1459) |
|  | (1473) | St-Donatien, Bruges | £78 4s (1459) |
|  | £100 (1474) | St-Vincent, Soignies | £147 (1461) |
| Peruwez | £19  5s  10d |  | £60 (1462) |
|  |  | Pension from Duke of Burgundy | £218 |
| *Total:* | £518  16s  8½d |  | £664  11s |
| *Sum total:* | £2341  7s  1½d |  | £1414  5s |

# Appendix A

## Calendar

Some of the Cambrai documents are in account books running from the summer of one year to the summer of the next. They are listed under the earlier year and followed by a qualifying date.

| Year | Age | Life | Contemporary Musicians and Events |
|------|-----|------|------------------------------------|
| 1398–1400 | | Guillaume Dufay born, son of Marie Dufay; father unknown, place unknown. | Binchois born in Mons at about the same date; Ciconia (c.27) motets O felix templum and Venetie mundi splendor; Dunstable (c.10); Lionel Power (c.20); Richard II of England (33) dies, Feb. 14, succeeded by Henry IV. |
| 1404 | 4 | | Philip the Bold, Duke of Burgundy, dies April 27, succeeded by John the Fearless; Leone Battista Alberti born, Feb. 18. |
| 1405 | 5 | | Eustache Deschamps dies; Aeneas Silvius Piccolomini (later Pope Pius II) born, Oct. 18. |
| 1406 | 6 | | Ciconia motet Albane misse celitus. |
| 1409 | 9 | After 11 weeks of instruction from Jean de Hesdin,[1] received as puer altaris at Cambrai Cathedral in week of Aug. 10.[2] | Ciconia motet Petrum Marcello venetum; Prosdocimus de Beldemandis treatise Brevis summula; Feragut motet Excelsa civitas Vincentia; Council of Pisa opens. |
| 1411 | 11 | Receives a Doctrinale (1411–12).[3] | Pierre d'Ailly made cardinal, June 6. |
| 1412 | 12 | | Ciconia dies at Padua, ? July. |
| 1413 | 13 | Described as clericus altaris and provided with a chaplaincy (1413–14).[4] | Henry IV of England dies, March 20; coronation of Henry V, April 9. |

217

| | | | |
|---|---|---|---|
| 1414 | 14 | | Council of Constance opens, Nov. 1; Cardinal d'Ailly arrives with his retinue, Nov. 17; Antonio Romano motet *Ducalis sedes*, Jan. |
| 1415 | 15 | | Battle of Agincourt, Oct. 25. |
| 1416 | 16 | | Performance of Dunstable motet *Preco preheminencie*, Aug.; Domenico da Piacenza treatise *De arte saltandi et choreas ducendi*. |
| 1417 | 17 | | Martin V elected pope at Constance, Nov. 11; Hubert de Salinis, Gloria *Jubilacio*, to celebrate end of schism; anon. motet *Clarus ortus* perhaps for coronation of Martin V. |
| 1418 | 18 | | End of Council of Constance, April 19; Loqueville dies. |
| 1419 | 19 | | John the Fearless, Duke of Burgundy murdered, Sept. 10, succeeded by Philip the Good. |
| 1420 | 20 | 'Guillelmus de Fays', *clerc* of St-Germain-l'Auxerrois, Paris, accused of stealing but acquitted, Aug. 13 (probably not the composer).[5] | Henry V enters Paris, Dec. 1. |
| | | August: probable date of motet *Vasilissa ergo gaude*, celebrating forthcoming wedding of Cleofe Malatesta. | Cleofe Malatesta leaves Rimini for Constantinople, Aug. 20; Hugo de Lantins *Tra quante regione* probably for same occasion. |
| 1421 | 21 | | Wedding of Cleofe and Theodore Palaiologos, Jan. 19; Brunelleschi begins cupola of Santa Maria del Fiore, Florence, Aug. |
| 1422 | 22 | | Antonio da Cividale motet *Inclita persplendens*; Henry V of England dies, Aug. 31, succeeded by Henry VI; Charles VI of France dies, Oct. 21, succeeded by Charles VII. |
| 1423 | 23 | Wedding of Carlo Malatesta da Pesaro and Vittoria Colonna, July 18, occasion for ballade | Antonio Romano motet *Carminibus festos*, April; Antonio da Cividale motet |

*Resvelliés vous* (and perhaps Mass of same name).

*Strenua quem duxit*, June 8; Christoforo da Monte motet *Plaude decus mundi*; Hugo de Lantins *Christus vincit*.

1424 24 Perhaps moves to Laon until 1426.

Binchois rondeau *Ainsi que a la foiz* (lost).

1425 25 Ballade *Je me complains piteusement*, July 12.

John VIII Palaiologos, brother of Theodore, becomes Byzantine emperor.

1426 26 Rondeau *Adieu ces bons vins de Lannoys*, perhaps on leaving Laon; motet *Apostolo glorioso* for rededication of church of St Andrew, Patras, by Archbishop Pandolfo Malatesta da Pesaro.

Nicolaus de Radom motet *Hystorigraphi aciem*; possible date for Dunstable motet *Albanus roseo rutilat*, June 17.

1427 27 In Bologna, from where Cardinal Aleman writes to St-Géry, Cambrai, requesting privileges of absence from his diaconate there, April 12.[6] Suggested date for performance of Mass *Sancti Jacobi*, July 25.

Pandolfo Malatesta da Rimini dies, Oct. 3, possibly occasion for Dufay's ballade *Mon chier amy*.

1428 28 Described as priest and still living in Bologna, March 24.[7] Cardinal Aleman and his supporters, probably Dufay among them, chased from Bologna, Aug. 23. In Rome by October as member of papal choir.[9] First recorded payment (4 florins), Dec. 20.[8]

Prosdocimus de Beldemandis dies (*c*.50); Masaccio dies (*c*.27); Gentile da Fabriano dies.

1429 29 As member of papal choir, listed having living at Laon Cathedral (altar of St-Fiacre) in addition to that at St-Géry, Cambrai, April 14.[9] By December receiving 5 florins per month.[10]

Joan of Arc raises siege of Orleans, May; Charles VII crowned at Rheims, July; Duke Amadeus VIII of Savoy founds a church of St Sebastian near the château of Ripaille, May 13.

1430 30 Listed in addition as having a living at Nouvion-le-Vineux (altar of St John the Baptist), near Laon, April 20.[11]

Donatello bronze *David*.

1431 31 Motet *Ecclesie militantis* perhaps for coronation of Eugenius IV, March 11. Motet *Balsamus et munda cera* for distribution of Agnus Dei, April 7.

Pope Martin V dies, Feb. 20; Pope Eugenius IV elected, March 3; Brassart motet *Magne decus potencie* also for papal coronation; Joan of Arc burned, May 30; Council of Basle opens,

Pope reviews livings for his choir, April 24: Dufay listed as having one at St-Pierre, Tournai, in addition to those already granted.[12] Pope procures him another living, at Lausanne Cathedral; this document also describes him as expectative canon of St-Donatien, Bruges, and Tournai Cathedral; resigns that at St-Pierre, Aug. 22.[13]

July 23, after which pope attempts to transfer it to Bologna with bull *Quoniam alto*, Dec. 18; Henry VI of England crowned in Paris, perhaps occasion for Dunstable motet *Veni Sancte Spiritus*, Dec. 16; Binchois motet *Nove cantum melodie*, Jan. 19.

| 1432 | 32 | | Antonio Romano motet *Aurea flamigeri*; Jan van Eyck completes Ghent altarpiece, May 6; Leone Battista Alberti enters papal service; Antonio Squarcialupi (16) becomes organist of Santa Maria del Fiore, Florence. |

1433   33   Motet *Supremum est mortalibus bonum* for King Sigismund's entry into Rome, May 21. Dufay leaves papal chapel by August.[14] Date suggested by Besseler for ballade *C'est bien raison* (see also 1437).

King Sigismund crowned emperor by the pope at Rome, May 31.

1434   34   Choirmaster to court of Savoy by Feb. 1;[15] wedding celebrations for Louis of Savoy and Anne de Lusignan at Chambéry, Feb. 7–11.
Dufay granted leave to visit his mother and described as curate of Versoix, Aug. 8–12.[16]
Receives bread at Cambrai, Oct. 14.[17]

Burgundian court arrives at Chambéry, Feb. 7; Duke Amadeus VIII founds Augustinian Order of St Maurice, Oct. 8, and officially retires, Nov. 11, making his son Louis Prince of Piedmont and Lieutenant-General of Savoy. Pope flees from Rome, June 4, taking up residence in Florence, June 23.

1435   35   Receives clothing at Savoy court, April 18.[18]
Returns to papal chapel (now in Florence) as second singer, June; temporarily first singer, August; permanently first singer, October.[19]

Luca della Robbia finishes *cantoria* for Santa Maria del Fiore, Florence; Leone Battista Alberti *De pictura*.

1436   36   Motet *Nuper rosarum flores* for dedication of Santa Maria del

Probable completion date of manuscript Oxford, Canonici

| | | | |
|---|---|---|---|
| | | Fiore, Florence, March 25. During this year he must have composed *Mirandas parit* (perhaps April 18) and possibly the motet *Salve flos Tusce gentis* (perhaps April 1). Granted canonry and prebend at Cambrai Cathedral, Sept. 3,[20] replacing Jean Vivien, promoted to Bishop of Nevers. Confirmed with Grenon as proctor, Nov. 12.[21] | misc. 213. Pope and entourage leave Florence, April 18, taking up residence in Bologna, April 22. Niccolò III d'Este visits pope in Bologna, June. |
| 437 | 37 | Papal *littera de fructibus* grants absenteeism from Cambrai, March 21.[22] Payment of 20 ducats ratified in Este court records at Ferrara, May 6.[23] Date suggested by Lockwood for *C'est bien raison* (see also 1433). Leaves papal choir at end of May.[24] At Lausanne Cathedral for chapter meetings, Aug. 25–6.[25] Receives clothing as member of Savoy court.[26] | Pope attempts for the second time to dissolve the Council of Basle, ordering a transfer to Bologna, with bull *Doctoris gentium*, Sept. 18; Emperor Sigismund dies, Dec. 9, succeeded by Albert III. |
| 438 | 38 | Appointed a delegate of Cambrai Cathedral to Council of Basle, April 7.[27] Perhaps composes *Juvenis qui puellam*. Succeeds Guillaume de Meyere in 24th prebend at St-Donatien, Bruges, April 28.[28] Motet *Magnanime gentis* for signing of peace between Louis, Prince of Piedmont, and his brother Philip, Count of Geneva, at Berne, Saturday May 3; subsequent celebrations at Fribourg, Tuesday–Thursday, May 6–8. Leaves Le Bourget to spend winter at Pinerolo with Louis and Anne of Savoy, Oct. 16.[29] | Opening of Council of Ferrara, Jan. 8; Cardinal Aleman named president of Council of Basle, Feb. 14; Pope anathematizes any decision by Council of Basle, Feb. 15. |
| 439 | | *Tempio dell'Onore e delle Vertù* performed at Pinerolo during Carnival time, perhaps with | Council of Basle deposes Pope Eugenius IV, June 25; Council elects Duke Amadeus VIII of |

| | | | |
|---|---|---|---|
| | | Dufay contributing.<br>Dufay is back in Cambrai by<br>Dec. 9, though perhaps from the<br>summer.[30] | Savoy as Pope Felix V, Nov.<br>At Cambrai, Jean de Bourgogr<br>installed (*in absentia*) as<br>bishop, Monday Aug. 10.<br>Motet *Romanorum rex* perhaj<br>by Brassart. |
| 1440 | 40 | Dufay fully resident at Cambrai<br>until 1450.[31] | Duke Amadeus VIII abdicate<br>from duchy, leaving his son<br>Louis as Duke of Savoy, Jan.<br>Pope Eugenius excommunicat<br>Amadeus, his successors and l<br>supporters, March 3. |
| 1441 | 41 | Obtains permission to resign<br>three benefices, Sept. 14.[32]<br>Louis of Savoy writes to Philip<br>the Good asking permission for<br>Dufay to return to Savoy, Nov.<br>5.[33] | Jan van Eyck dies; King's<br>College, Cambridge, and Eto<br>College founded by Henry V<br>Niccolò III, Marquis of Ferrar<br>dies, Dec. 26, succeeded by<br>Leonello d'Este. |
| 1442 | 42 | Possible date of song<br>*Seigneur Leon*.<br>Possible date for motet *Fulgens<br>iubar*, Feb. 2.<br>Possible date for motet *Moribus<br>et genere*, Aug. 3.<br>Resigns rectorate of Versoix and<br>canonry at Lausanne, Feb. 6.[34]<br>Succeeds Grenon as master of<br>*petits vicaires* at Cambrai.[35] | Martin le Franc *Le champion<br>des dames*.<br>Bishop Jean de Bourgogne vis<br>Cambrai, June 10 to Aug. 4.<br>Brassart motet *O rex Fridric*<br>probably for coronation of<br>Frederick III at Aix-la-Chape<br>June 17. |
| 1443 | 43 | Sends Jacobus de Clibano to<br>Bruges to receive on his behalf<br>20 ducats from Marquis of<br>Ferrara, Oct. 23.[36] | Pope Eugenius IV returns to<br>Rome, Sept. 28. |
| 1444 | 44 | Dufay's mother dies, April 23,<br>buried in Cambrai Cathedral.[37] | Leonard of Chios becomes<br>Archbishop of Mitylene, July<br>perhaps occasion for Dufay's<br>song *Seigneur Leon*. |
| 1445 | 45 | Has moved into house formerly<br>occupied by canon Pierre Beye,<br>Aug. 14.[38] | Lionel Power dies (*c*.65), Ju |
| 1446 | 46 | Contracts with Jean de Namps<br>to copy service books, Feb. 9,[39]<br>Resigns prebend at St-Donatien,<br>Bruges, Oct. 4.[40] Mission to<br>court of Burgundy at Brussels,<br>Oct. 7.[41] Installed as canon of<br>Ste-Waudru, Mons, Oct. 17.[42] | Brunelleschi dies, April 15. |

| 1447 | 47 | Assigned the accounts of the wine cellar of Cambrai Cathedral, Sept. 6.[43] | Pope Eugenius IV dies, Feb. 23, succeeded by Nicholas V; Filippo Maria Visconti dies at Milan without heir, Aug. 13. |
| 1448 | 48 | Visits Mons on Cambrai Cathedral business, Feb. 5–8.[44] Visits Laon and Rheims to buy wine for Cambrai Cathedral, April 10–May 8.[45] | Emperor John VIII Palaiologos dies, Oct. 31, succeeded by his son Constantine XI. |
| 1449 | 49 | Philip the Good and his court visit Cambrai, Sunday–Tuesday, Jan. 19–21. Dufay perhaps follows court to Brussels, arriving Feb. 5. Goes to Mons with Binchois for meeting of Ste-Waudru chapter, March 3.[46] | Antipope Felix V (Amadeus VIII of Savoy) signs act of abdication from papacy, April 7; Council of Basle formally elects Nicholas V pope, April 19, and dissolves itself, April 25. |
| 1450 | 50 | Dufay's presence at Cambrai recorded for the last time until December, March 11.[47] Dufay and 9 'monks' stay at inn 'del Capello' in Turin, paid for by Duke of Savoy, Wednesday–Tuesday, May 26–June 1.[48] Dufay back in Cambrai by Dec. 15.[49] | Death of Leonello d'Este, Oct. 1; Francesco Sforza enters Milan assuming title of duke, Feb. 26. Donatello's altar for the basilica of Sant' Antonio, Padua, dedicated, June 13, perhaps occasion for Dufay's Mass for St Anthony of Padua. |
| 1451 | 51 | Resident at Cambrai. Letter from Savoy Court, thanking him for cloth and addressing him as *conseiller et maistre de la chapelle*, Oct. 22 (year not quite certain).[50] | Amadeus VIII dies at Geneva, Jan. 7; contract of marriage between Dauphin Louis and Charlotte of Savoy, Feb. 14; wedding at Chambéry, March 10. Anon. motet *In ultimo lucente*, June; Paolo Uccello dies. |
| 1452 | 52 | Paid a year's salary in advance by Cambrai Cathedral chapter in view of his fine musical services to the cathedral, April 21.[51] Thereafter not recorded as present in Cambrai until end of 1458. | Portrait of Notre-Dame de Grace, 'piously believed' to have been painted by St Luke, given to Cambrai Cathedral, Aug. 14. Savoy court goes to Le Cleppé to meet Charles VII, Sept.; treaty, Oct. 27. |
| 1453 | 53 | | Fall of Constantinople, May 29; end of Hundred Years' War; Dunstable dies (*c*.63), Dec. 24. |
| 1454 | 54 | (Possible date of letter from Geneva, see under 1456.) | *Banquet du voeu* at Lille, Feb. 17; Ockeghem first described as *premier chappelain* to Charles VII. |

| 1455 | 55 | Receives present from Duke and Duchess of Savoy, as master of Savoy chapel, Jan. 1.[52] Not named in list of Savoy chapel, May 1.[53] Describing himself as *magister capelle* of the Duke of Savoy, acts as executor of will of André Picard, a singer in the Savoy chapel, at Geneva, Nov. 8.[54] Savoy court, with all its singers,[55] goes to St-Pourçain for treaty in December. Possible occasion for Mass *L'homme armé* (Planchart) as well as for chansons *Malheureulx cueur* and *Les douleurs* (Fallows). | Battle of St Albans marks beginning of Wars of the Rose May 22. Antonio Pisanello, Lorenzo Ghiberti and Fra Angelico die. |
| 1456 | 56 | Letter from Geneva to Piero and Giovanni de'Medici, Feb 22 (year not given but almost certainly 1456).[56] | Grenon dies (*c*.76), Oct.; Leon Battista Alberti extends façade of Santa Maria Novella, Florence. |
| 1457 | 57 | | Andrea del Castagno dies. |
| 1458 | 58 | Visits St-Etienne, Besançon, where he is consulted on the mode of the antiphon *O quanta est exultatio angelicis turmis*, Sept. 14.[57] Checks wine accounts at Cambrai and has therefore returned, Nov. 6.[58] | Aeneas Silvius Piccolomini becomes Pope Pius II. |
| 1459 | 59 | Reappointed master of the *petits vicaires* at Cambrai (1459–60).[59] Arranges more copying with Simon Mellet (1459–60).[60] | Louis, son of Duke Louis of Savoy, crowned King of Cyprus Oct. 7; Josquin Desprez first documented at Milan Cathedral, July. |
| 1460 | 60 | Rondeau *En triumphant* possibly composed at death of Binchois, Sept. 20. Charles, Count of Charolais (future Duke of Burgundy), hears his own motet performed at Cambrai, Oct. 23. Dufay instructed by chapter to appoint a new master of the choirboys, Nov. 10.[61] | Binchois (*c*.60) dies at Soignies Sept. 20, leading to Ockeghem' lament *Mort tu as navré*; Bedyngham dies at Westminste (*c*.38); Johannes Tinctoris pai for having sung among *petits vicaires* at Cambrai for 4 months, July 11. |
| 1461 | 61 | As treasurer of the *petit coffre* | Edward IV crowned King of |

|  |  | directs an inventory of cathedral property, March 18–May 6.[62] | England, June 28; Charles VII of France dies, July 22, succeeded by Louis XI; Martin le Franc dies, Nov. 8; Domenico Veneziano dies. |
| 1462 | 62 | Magnificat in 7th mode copied at Cambrai (1462–3).[63] | Ockeghem visits Cambrai, June 2; Charles, Count of Charolais, again visits Cambrai, Dec. 21; Duchess Anne of Savoy dies, Nov. 11. |
| 1463 | 63 | The hymn O *quam glorifica* 'nouvellement fait' (lost) and the Mass *Ecce ancilla Domini* copied at Cambrai (1463–4).[64] | François Villon dies. |
| 1464 | 64 | Ockeghem stays at Dufay's house for two weeks, Feb.– March.[65] Antiphon *Ave regina celorum* (4vv) and sequence for Mary Magdalene copied at Cambrai (1464–5).[66] Resigns as master of *petits vicaires* (1464–5),[67] succeeded by Simon le Breton. | Rogier van der Weyden dies, June 16; Cosimo de' Medici dies, Aug. 1; Pope Pius II dies, Aug. 15. |
| 1465 | 65 |  | Charles of Orleans dies, Jan. 4; Duke Louis of Savoy dies, Jan. 29; possible date for Busnoys motet *In hydraulis*. |
| 1466 | 66 | Resigns canonry at Notre-Dame, Condé, for chaplaincy at altar of Virgin Mary at Ohain, July 16.[68] Simon Greban *Complainte sur la mort de Jacques Milet* mentions Dufay. | Donatello dies, Dec. 13; Gilles Flannel dies at Cambrai, Dufay an executor of his will. |
| 1467 | 67 | Antonio Squarcialupi writes from Florence to Dufay, May 1.[69] | Philip the Good, Duke of Burgundy, dies, June 15, succeeded by Charles the Bold. |
| 1468 | 68 | Compere's motet *Omnium bonorum plena*, praising Dufay, perhaps composed for visit to Cambrai of Louis XI to venerate the portrait of Notre-Dame de Grace, Oct. 16–17. Music brought from Dufay to Savoy court by Gile Crepin (Crispini) (1468–9).[70] | Johannes Gutenberg dies, Feb. 3. |

| | | | |
|---|---|---|---|
| 1469 | 69 | | Accession of Lorenzo de' Medici. |
| 1470 | 70 | Mass *da Requiem* 'de novo compilata' copied at Cambrai (1470–1).[71] | Fra Filippo Lippi dies, Oct. 9; Alberti completes façade of Santa Maria Novella. |
| 1471 | 71 | | |
| 1472 | 72 | Cambrai Cathedral dedicated by Pierre de Ranchicourt, Bishop of Arras, who stays at Dufay's house, July 5 – probably occasion for Mass *Ave regina celorum*. | Leone Battista Alberti dies, April 25. |
| 1473 | 73 | Mass *Ave regina celorum* (not specified as Dufay's) copied at Cambrai (1473–4).[72] | Cardinal Bessarion dies, Nov. 18. |
| 1474 | 74 | Dufay makes his will, July 8.[73] His chaplain, Alexandre Bouillart, dies, Aug. 20. Dufay dies, evening of Sunday Nov. 27.[74] | Caxton's first publication in English; Conrad von Zabern treatise *De modo bene cantandi*. |

# Appendix B

## Classified list of works

### Note on editions

Although many Dufay works were published in earlier editions, particularly Stainer *Dufay* (1898) and various volumes of DTO, the main reference is now to the two editions called Corpus Mensurabilis Musicae, series I. The first of these was by Guillaume de Van, planned in twenty volumes of which only the first four were completed (1947–9). After his death Heinrich Besseler undertook to continue the series,[1] renumbering the volumes that had already appeared. But later he produced entirely new editions also of the material already edited by de Van, so the present CMM, I (1951–66) is entirely by Besseler.[2]

All references in the left-hand column are therefore to the six volumes of Besseler's edition, giving the volume number and the number of the work within that volume;[3] this edition also contains an extensive listing of the manuscript sources. But the de Van volumes include considerable material of the first importance, so they are mentioned where appropriate (as Van *Dufay*). Equally important are two further editions which are always mentioned: Father Laurence Feininger's *Monumenta polyphoniae liturgicae* (cited as Feininger *L'homme armé*, Feininger *Dufay* and Feininger *Propria*, see bibliography); and Rudolf Bockholdt's doctoral thesis (Bockholdt *Dufay*). Both these editions use original clefs and original note-values; and they are in many ways rather better than those of Besseler. Further editions are noted only when they represent some significant improvement on Besseler.

Works are in three voices unless otherwise stated.

Fb: *fauxbourdon*.

# Classified list of works: summary of contents

# 1 Music for the Mass

*(A) Mass Ordinary cycles (in approximate chronological order)*

ii/1 Mass *Resvelliés vous*, related to own ballade, vi/11, of 1423. In one
source the Kyrie is troped 'Salvator noster'. Van *Dufay* iii.

ii/2 Mass *Sancti Jacobi*, 4vv. Includes four movements of the Proper, see
section (E) below. Van *Dufay* iv.

ii/3 Mass for St Anthony of Padua (previously identified as for St Anthony
Abbot, see p. 182); perhaps for dedication of Donatello's altar at Padua,
13 June 1450. Bockholdt *Dufay* ii, 68–86. This may well have been a
plenary cycle, perhaps including Proper movements mentioned in section (E) below.

— Mass for St Anthony Abbot (Sancti Antonii Viennensis), mentioned in
will but lost; perhaps including Propers.

iii/7 Mass *Se la face ay pale*, 4vv, based on tenor of own ballade, vi/19.
Feininger *Dufay* ii.

iii/8 Mass *L'homme armé*, 4vv. Feininger *L'homme armé* i.

iii/9 Mass *Ecce ancilla Domini/Beata es Maria*, 4vv; copied at Cambrai
1463–4. Feininger *Dufay* iv.

— Mass *da Requiem*, copied at Cambrai 1470–71 as a newly composed work;
lost. Probably including Propers.

iii/10 Mass *Ave regina celorum*, 4vv, related to own antiphon, v/51; perhaps
for dedication of Cambrai Cathedral, 5 July 1472; copied at Cambrai
1473–4. Feininger *Dufay* iii.

Spurious, doubtful and attributed cycles

ii/5 Mass *Caput*, 4vv. Ascribed to Dufay but now considered the work of an
English composer. Feininger *Dufay* i.

— Mass *Christus surrexit*, 4vv (without Kyrie of Agnus). Attributed (surely
wrongly) by Feininger. Feininger *Dufay* i.

ii/6 Mass *La mort de Saint Gothard*, 4vv. Attributed by Besseler and (briefly)
Feininger; now normally attributed to Johannes Martini. Feininger
*Dufay* iii.

— Mass *Puisque je vis*, 4vv. Attributed by Feininger. Feininger *Dufay* iv.

— Mass for St Anthony Abbot in manuscript Trent 89; plenary cycle though
without Kyrie or Communion. Tentatively attributed above, p. 192.

— Mass *Veterem hominem*, 4vv. Attributed by Feininger, but almost certainly by an English composer. Feininger *Dufay* i.

— Mass 'sine nomine' in manuscript San Pietro B 80, f. 113v–121v. Attributed in Hamm *Chronology*, 137. Unpublished.

*(B) Grouped Mass Ordinary movements*

iv/1 Kyrie, Gloria [*cursiva*], Credo [*cursiva*]. Bockholdt *Dufay* ii, 24–9.

iv/2 Kyrie, Sanctus [on tenor *Vineux*] troped 'Qui januas mortis', Agnus
[on tenor *Vineux*] (improved edition in v/supp.); cycle perhaps

including Gloria 'de Quaremiaux' iv/23. All four edited as a group Bockholdt *Dufay* ii, 30–34.

iv/19 and iv/28 Kyrie, Gloria. Kyrie claimed to be spurious in Monson 'Stylistic Inconsistencies'. Bockholdt *Dufay* ii, 58–64.

iv/3 Gloria [almost certainly by Hugo de Lantins], Credo.

iv/4 Gloria troped 'Tu m'as monté', Credo troped 'La vilanella', 4vv. Bockholdt *Dufay* ii, 38–47.

iv/5 Gloria, Credo, 4vv. Bockholdt *Dufay* ii, 48–56.

iv/6 Sanctus, Agnus. Bockholdt *Dufay* ii, 64–7.

iv/7 Sanctus 'Papale' troped 'Ave verum corpus', 2/3/4/6vv, paired with unascribed Agnus troped 'Custos et pastor'.

iv/8 Sanctus, Agnus. Bockholdt *Dufay* ii, 21ff.

## (C) Independent Kyrie settings

iv/9 Kyrie 'Pater cuncta', with Kyrie XII in discantus.[4] Bockholdt *Dufay* ii, 12.

iv/10 Kyrie 'Cunctipotens' or 'Solempne', Fb/3vv, with Kyrie IV in discantus. Bockholdt *Dufay* ii, 13.

iv/11 Kyrie 'Orbis factor' or 'De martiribus' or 'In diebus dominicis', Fb/3vv, with Kyrie XI in discantus. Bockholdt *Dufay* ii, 5f.

iv/13 Kyrie 'Jesu redemptor' or 'De apostolis', Fb, with Kyrie XIV in discantus.

iv/14 Kyrie 'Cum jubilo', with Kyrie IX in discantus. Bockholdt *Dufay* ii, 9f.

iv/15 Kyrie 'Lux et origo' or 'Pascale', with Kyrie I in discantus. Bockholdt *Dufay* ii, 8.

iv/16 Kyrie 'Fons bonitatis' or 'Sollemne', with Kyrie II in discantus. Bockholdt *Dufay* ii, 1f.

iv/18 Kyrie 'Rex genitor' or 'In semiduplicibus maioribus', with Kyrie VI in discantus. Bockholdt *Dufay* ii, 11f.

— Kyrie 'Lux et origo', Fb, with Kyrie I in discantus. Anonymous: related to iv/15 and attributed to Dufay by Dèzes, but see Bockholdt *Dufay* i, 67f. Bockholdt *Dufay* ii, 9.

iv/12 Kyrie 'Orbis factor' or 'In dominicis diebus', with Kyrie XI in second discantus. Bockholdt *Dufay* ii, 7.

iv/17 Kyrie 'Fons bonitatis' or 'In summis festivitatibus', with Kyrie II in second discantus. Bockholdt *Dufay* ii, 3f.

## (D) Independent Gloria settings

— Gloria [*cursiva*], convincingly attributed to Dufay in Schoop *Entstehung*, 48f. Borren *Polyphonia*, no.16 (with source attribution to Hugo de Lantins).

iv/20 Gloria, adjudged doubtful in Bockholdt *Dufay* i, 121ff and 148f.

iv/21 Gloria [for low voices]. Bockholdt *Dufay* ii, 35ff.

iv/22 Gloria 'ad modum tube', 4vv, with upper voices canonic.

iv/23 Gloria 'de Quaremiaux': see section (B) above.

iv/24 Gloria troped 'Spiritus et alme'; alternatim with Gloria IX in discantus.

iv/25 Gloria, beginning with the word 'hominibus'; alternatim with Gloria
XI in discantus. Bockholdt *Dufay* ii, 16ff.

iv/26 Gloria 'In gallicantu', beginning with the word 'laudamus'; alternatim
with Gloria XIV in discantus almost unembellished. Bockholdt *Dufay*
ii, 18ff.

iv/27 Gloria, beginning with the word 'bone', with Gloria XV in discantus.
Bockholdt *Dufay* ii, 14f.

iv/28 Gloria: see section (B) above.

iv/29 Gloria. Perhaps originally for some other text. Authorities agree in
classing this as an *opus dubium* but differ or fail to commit themselves
on whether any of it could be Dufay's work. Bockholdt *Dufay* ii, 57.

iv/30 Contratenor ascribed 'Dufay' added to Gloria, presumably by another
hand. Considered a very early work.

— Gloria, ascribed 'Susay' in the fourteenth-century Apt manuscript, considered by Gastoué and others to be by 'G. [D ]ufay', but firmly rejected
by all modern commentators. CMM, XXIX, no.35.

*(E) Mass Proper settings*

ii/2 Mass *Sancti Jacobi* (see section (A) above): Introit *Mihi autem nimis*,
4vv; *Alleluia: Hispanorum clarens stella*, 4vv; Offertory *In omnem
terram*, 4vv; Communion *Vos qui secuti*, Fb.

ii/4 Mass for the Holy Ghost: *Alleluia: Veni Sancte Spiritus*. Feininger
*Propria*, 8ff and 198f.

— Mass for the Holy Ghost: Offertory *Confirma hoc Deus* (ascription from
Spataro letter of 1532, see Planchart 'Notes', 15f). Feininger *Propria*,
10ff.

— Mass for a confessor: Introit *Os iusti meditabitur* (ascription from
Spataro letter of 1532, see Planchart 'Notes', 16f). Feininger *Propria*,
151ff (as part of cycle for St Francis).

— Mass for St Anthony of Padua: Gradual *Os iusti meditabitur* (ascription
from Spataro *Tractato* of 1531, see above p. 188). Feininger *Propria*,
135–8.

— Mass for St Anthony of Padua: *Alleluia: Anthoni compar inclite* (attributed above, p.190). Feininger *Propria*, 139–43.

— Mass for St George: Tract *Desiderium anime eius* (possibly the one copied
at Cambrai in 1473–4 together with the Mass *Ave regina celorum*;
attribution in Wright 'Dufay', 198f, based on assumption that both
works are Dufay's). Feininger *Propria*, 90–93.

Feininger *Propria*, I–VIII, attempts to attribute eleven Proper cycles to
Dufay, outlining the reasons but promising a further publication (which
never materialized) justifying them in detail. In view of the new ascriptions
above, the following now seem particularly promising (at least from a
documentary viewpoint):

### Dufay

— Mass for the Holy Ghost: Introit *Spiritus Domini* with doxology, 4vv; Gradual *Beata gens*; (*Alleluia: Emitte spiritum*); *Alleluia: Veni Sancte Spiritus* (Dufay); Offertory *Confirma hoc Deus* (Dufay); Communion *Factus est repente*. Feininger *Propria*, 1–13.

— Mass for St Anthony of Padua: Introit *In medio ecclesie;* Gradual *Os iusti meditabitur* (Dufay); *Alleluia: Anthoni compar inclite* (Dufay); Offertory *Veritas mea*, 4vv; Communion *Domine quinque talenta*. (This cycle could belong with the Ordinary cycle for St Anthony of Padua, ii/3, see section (A) above). Feininger *Propria*, 134–47.

— Mass for St Francis: (Introit *Gaudeamus omnes*); Introit *Os iusti meditabitur* (Dufay); Gradual *Os iusti meditabitur* (Dufay; taken from Mass for St Anthony of Padua, according to manuscript rubric); *Alleluia: O patriarcha pauperum*; Communion *Fidelis servus*. Feininger *Propria*, 148–57.

The other cycles which Feininger attributes to Dufay are: Mass for the Holy Trinity (16–30); Mass for St Andrew (31–46); Mass for the Holy Cross (46–57); Mass for St John the Baptist (58–68); Mass de Angelis (69–83); Mass for St George; (84–99); Mass for St Maurice and his companions (108–22); Mass for St Sebastian (166–76).

### (F) Sequence settings

Complete through-composed setting

v/1 Gaude virgo, mater Christi (Assumption), 4vv. No discernible chant.

Alternatim settings.

v/3 Epiphaniam Domino (Ephiphany). Chant in discantus.

v/8 Isti sunt due olive (Sts Peter and Paul). Chant in discantus, tenor and contratenor.

v/7 Lauda Sion Salvatorem (Corpus Christi). Chant in discantus and tenor.

v/2 Letabundus (Christmas). Chant in discantus and tenor, starting on G.

v/5 Rex omnipotens (Ascension). Chant in discantus and contratenor.

v/6 Veni Sancte Spiritus (Pentecost). Chant in second discantus.

v/4 Victime paschali laudes (Easter). Chant in discantus.

Lost setting

— Sequence for Mary Magdalene, occupying 3½ leaves, copied at Cambrai 1464–5. (Perhaps on text Laus tibi Christe.)

Doubtful and attributed settings (all unpublished)

— Letabundus (Christmas); anon., attributed in Hamm *Chronology*, 77, as setting verses not set in v/2, though here chant starts on F.

— Mittit ad virginem (Annunciation); anon., attributed in Hamm *Chronology*, 78, and Hamm 'Dating a Group', 71, on source context.

— Sancti Spiritus assit (Pentecost); attributed as Mittit ad virginem.

— Veni Sancte Spiritus (Pentecost). De Van erroneously recorded an ascription to Dufay in the manuscript BL; but the chant paraphrase in the discantus closely matches that in Dufay's v/6, and this sets the stanzas not set in v/6.

232

# 2 Music for the Office

## (A) Hymn settings

In the complete edition these are organized by liturgical use – as they are, on the whole, in the manuscripts. An alphabetical listing appears in the index to that edition as well as in *The New Grove* and Hamm *Chronology*. The present list follows the stylistic groupings and is alphabetical within those groups. Unless otherwise stated the hymns are settings of the even-numbered stanzas of the chant. Most of them are published in Gerber *Hymnen*: G5 means that the setting appears on p. 5 of that volume.

Hymns surviving only as *fauxbourdon* settings (in O mensuration)
v/11 Conditor alme siderum (Advent). G5
v/25 Tibi, Christe, splendor Patris (St Michael).

Hymns surviving only as three-voice settings in O mensuration
v/13 Hostis Herodes impie (Epiphany) [same music also survives with text
    Ad solis ortus cardine (Christmas)]. G6f
v/18 Jesu nostra redemptio (Ascension). G11f
v/20 O lux beata Trinitas (Trinity); sets odd-numbered stanzas in all but one
    source. G13f
v/21 Pange lingua gloriosi (Corpus Christi). G14f
v/30 Sanctorum meritis inclyta gaudia (Several martyrs). G23f
v/26 Ut queant laxis (St John the Baptist). G16
v/19 Veni Creator Spiritus (Pentecost). G12f

Hymns in O mensuration surviving in several versions
v/17 Ad cenam Agni providi (Easter), setting odd-numbered stanzas. G10
    v/17b: anon., Fb on a slightly different version of the melody and with
    related tenor. G11
    v, p.XXIII(a): anon., Fb on slightly different version of the melody and
    with related tenor (Merseburg fragment).
    v, p.XXIII (b): anon., Fb closely related to Merseburg version (Trent no.
    744).
v/23 Ave maris stella (BVM), Fb with alternative composed contratenor.
    G18
    v/58: 'Dufay sine fauxbourdon', 3vv on same discantus. G28
v/24a Christe, redemptor omnium, Conserva (All Saints), Fb. (Setting identi-
    cal with Christe, redemptor omnium, Ex Patre, v/12.)
    v/24b: 3vv with chant in second discantus. G20
v/12 Christe, redemptor omnium, Ex Patre (Christmas), Fb with alternative
    composed contratenor. G5f
v/29 Deus tuorum militum (One martyr), Fb. G22
    v/59: anon., 3vv on same discantus. G29(b)
    v/60: anon., 3vv on same discantus. G29(a)
v/28 Exultet celum laudibus (An apostle), Fb and 3vv. G20ff
v/31 Iste confessor Domini sacratus (A confessor), Fb. G24

v/61: anon., 3vv on same discantus. G30

v/31a Jesu corona virginum (One virgin), Fb (same music as Deus tuorum militum, v/29).

    v/62: anon., 3vv on same discantus. G30f

    v/63: anon., 4vv on same discantus and tenor. G31

v/22 Urbs beata Jerusalem (Dedication of a church). G15

    v/57: anon., Fb on same discantus.

    v/57a: anon., 4vv on same discantus and tenor as v/57. G27

v/16 Vexilla Regis prodeunt (Passiontide). G8f

    v/54: anon., Fb on same discantus. G9

Hymn in O mensuration but chant in contratenor
v/14 Audi benigne Conditor (Weekdays in Lent). G8

Hymn in Ø mensuration
v/27 Aurea luce et decore roseo (Sts Peter and Paul), setting odd-numbered verses. G17

Hymns in duple time
v/15 Aures ad nostras deitatis preces (Sundays in Lent). G7f
v/32 Proles de celo prodiit (St Francis). G19

Doubtful ascriptions and attributions
v/53 Aures ad nostras deitatis preces (Sundays in Lent). G25; improved edition in Pope *Montecassino*, no.39.
v/55 Festum nunc celebre (Ascension). G32
v/56 Pange lingua gloriosi (Corpus Christi). G26
(These three are rejected by most authorities largely on the principle that Dufay made only one setting for each feast and because their ascriptions appear in unreliable sources.)
— Iam ter quaternis (Vespers in Lent), anon. Bockholdt 'Hymnen', 85.
— O quam glorifica (BVM), anon. Bockholdt 'Hymnen', 86.
(These two attributed in Bockholdt 'Hymnen', probably wrongly, see p. 288 n10.)

Lost hymn setting
— O quam glorifica (BVM), copied at Cambrai 1463–4 as a newly composed work.

*(B) Magnificat settings*
— Magnificat 'primi toni'. Perhaps by Binchois, but one source has a dual ascription to Binchois and Dufay. Marix *Musiciens*, 131–7.
v/36 Magnificat 'tertii et quarti toni', 4/3/2vv. Form ABCDEBCDEBCD. Better edition in Pope *Montecassino*, no.74; alternative setting of seventh stanza in Pope *Montecassino*, 536f.
v/35 Magnificat 'quinti toni'. Sets only even-numbered stanzas after the first; even-numbered stanzas all have essentially the same music.
v/33 Magnificat 'sexti toni'. Also ascribed to Binchois (erased) and to

Dunstable, but agreed to be by Dufay. Form ABCDEBCDEBCD.
— Magnificat 'septimi toni'. Lost. Copied at Cambrai 1462–3. Tentative
identification in Hamm 'San Pietro', 44f, apparently withdrawn, see
Besseler *Dufay* v, III.

v/34 Magnificat 'octavi toni'. Form ABCDBCDBCDBC.

*(C) Benedicamus settings*[5]

v/9 Benedicamus Domino (1). Chant paraphrased in tenor.
v/10 Benedicamus Domino (2).

*(D) Antiphon settings*

v/47 Alma Redemptoris mater (1)(BVM). Chant in tenor.
v/48 Alma Redemptoris mater (2)(BVM). Chant paraphrased in discantus.
v/46 Anima mea liquefacta est (BVM). Chant paraphrased in all three
voices.
v/49 Ave regina celorum (1)(BVM).
v/50 Ave regina celorum (2)(BVM). Chant paraphrased in discantus.
v/51 Ave regina celorum (3), 4vv (BVM); copied at Cambrai 1464–5. Chant
paraphrased in tenor. Feininger *Dufay* iii, 81–7.
v/40 Hic vir despiciens mundum (for Magnificat in second Vespers for a
Confessor not bishop), Fb. Chant in discantus.
v/38 Magi videntes stellam (for Magnificat in first Vespers for Epiphany).
Chant in discantus.
v/42 O gemma martyrum (St George).
v/41 Petrus apostolus et Paulus (for Magnificat in Vespers within the octave
of Sts Peter and Paul), Fb. Chant in discantus.
v/37 Propter nimiam caritatem (for Magnificat in first Vespers for the Cir-
cumcision), Fb. Chant in discantus.
v/39 Salva nos, Domine (Compline at Eastertide). Chant in discantus.
— Salve regina, 4vv (BVM). Authorship rejected in Dèzes 'Salve regina' but
tentatively reconsidered herein. DTO, XIV-XV, Jg. vii (Vienna, 1900),
178–83.
v/43 Salve, sancte pater patrie (for Magnificat for St Francis). Text and chant
by Julian of Speyer. Chant in discantus.
v/44 Sapiente filio (for St Anthony of Padua), Fb. Text and chant by Julian of
Speyer. Chant in discantus.
v/45 Si queris miracula (for St Anthony of Padua). Text and chant by Julian
of Speyer. Chant in discantus.

# 3 Motets

*(A) Isorhythmic motets (in approximate chronological order)*

i/7 Vasilissa ergo gaude/T: Concupivit rex, 4vv. Probably for departure of Cleofe Malatesta from Rimini, 20 August 1420. Text nine octosyllabic rhyming couplets. Van *Dufay* ii, no. 1.

i/8 O sancte Sebastiane/O martyr Sebastiane/O quam mira refulsit gratia/T: Gloria et honore, 4vv. Texts O sancte and O martyr make up a single poem in praise of St Sebastian, found in many sources, in octosyllabic rhyming couplets. Text O quam mira also found elsewhere, in decasyllabic lines rhyming ABABAB. Van *Dufay* ii, no. 4 (with listing of other text sources and identification of tenor).

i/9 O gemma, lux et speculum/Sacer pastor barensium/T: [Beatus Nicolaus adhuc], 4vv. Texts make up a single poem in six-line stanzas narrating miracles of St Nicholas. Van *Dufay* ii, no. 7.

i/10 Apostolo glorioso, da Dio electo/Cum tua doctrina/T: Andreas Christi famulus, 5vv (with solus tenor for 3vv). Probably for rededication of a church of St Andrew at Patras, 1426. Texts form a single Italian sonnet in hendecasyllabic lines praising St Andrew. Van *Dufay* ii, no. 3.

i/11 Rite majorem Jacobum canamus/Artibus summis miseri reclusi/T: Ora pro nobis Dominum, 4vv (with solus tenor). Texts form a single Sapphic ode praising St James the Greater, with acrostic ROBERTUS ACLOU CURATUS SANCTI JACOBI. Tenor chant unidentified. Van *Dufay* ii, no. 6.

i/12 Ecclesie militantis/Sanctorum arbitrio/Bella canunt gentes/ T1: Gabriel/T2: Ecce nomen Domini, 5vv. Possibly for coronation of Pope Eugenius IV, 11 March 1431. Texts Ecclesie and Sanctorum each of six six-line stanzas, but in different metres. Text Bella canunt in elegiac couplets. Isorhythm in lower voices only. Van *Dufay* ii, no. 13.

i/13 Balsamus et munda cera/T: Isti sunt agni novelli, 4vv. For papal distrubution of *Agnus Dei*, 7 April 1431. Text in Leonine hexameters, found in many other sources. Tenor reverses for second and fourth statements. Van *Dufay* ii, no. 2 (with listing of other text sources).

i/14 Supremum est mortalibus bonum/T: [free but ending with chant Isti sunt due olive ], 3vv. For King Sigismund's entry into Rome, 21 May 1433. Text in decasyllabic rhyming couplets. Isorhythm in tenor only. Van *Dufay* ii, no. 5.

i/16 Nuper rosarum flores/T1 & T2: Terribilis est locus iste, 4vv. For dedication of Florence Cathedral, 25 March 1436. Form of text unclear. Isorhythm in tenors only. Van *Dufay* ii, no. 11 (with listing of one other text source).

i/15 Salve flos Tusce gentis/Vos nunc Etruscorum/T: Viri mendaces, 4vv. Both texts in elegiac couplets. Isorhythm in tenor only. For peace signed on 3 May 1438. Van *Dufay* ii, no. 12.

much later. Van *Dufay* ii, no. 10.

i/17 Magnanime gentis/Nexus amicitie/T: Hec est vera fraternitas, 3vv.

Both texts in elegiac couplets. Isorhythm in tenor only. For peace signed on 3 May 1438. Van *Dufay* ii, no. 12.

i/18 Fulgens iubar ecclesie Dei/Puerpera, pura parens/T: Virgo post partum, 4vv. Perhaps for Petrus du Castel at Cambrai, 2 February 1442. Text Fulgens iubar four eight-line stanzas of decasyllables with refrain lines; text Puerpera four eight-line stanzas of octosyllables with refrain lines and acrostic PETRUS DE CASTELLO CANTA (or PETRUS DE CASTEL LOCANTA). Van *Dufay* ii, no. 9.

i/19 Moribus et genere/Virgo, virga virens/T: Virgo est electus, 4vv. Perhaps for Bishop Jean de Bourgogne at Cambrai, 3 August 1442. Text twenty-four hexameters, all sung by triplum, last sixteen sung also by motetus. Van *Dufay* ii, no. 8.

Doubtful and attributed isorhythmic motets

— Elizabet Zacharie/Lingua, pectus concordes/T: Elizabet, 4vv. Text form unclear. Tenor unidentified. Attributed in Hamm *Chronology*, 70–73. Edited in DTO, LXXVI, Jg. xl (Vienna, 1933), 16ff.

i/22 O gloriose tiro, martyr Christi/Divine pastus, demum igni datus/T: Iste sanctus, 4vv. Each text has two rhyming quatrains of hendecasyllables, praising St Theodore and conceivably related to Theodore Palaiologos (*d*. 1448). Rejected by all authorities, though Besseler's writings show considerable vacillation; frequent parallel fifths between the upper voices argue most strongly against it. Van *Dufay* ii, no. 14.

*(B) Non-isorhythmic cantilena motets*

i/3 Ave virgo, que de celis (BVM). Van *Dufay* i, no. 5.

i/2 Flos florum, Fons hortorum (BVM). Text in Leonine hexameters. Van *Dufay* i, no. 3 (with listing of other text sources).

i/1 Inclita stella maris (BVM), 4 or 3 or 2vv. Text in equivocated heptasyllabic couplets. Rubriç specifies several different methods of performance. Van *Dufay* i, no. 2.

i/5 Mirandas parit hec urbs florentina puellas. Text in hexameters praising the ladies of Florence, perhaps for 18 April 1436. Also appears with contrafact text Imperatrix angelorum. Van *Dufay* i, no. 1.

i/4 O beate Sebastiane (St Sebastian). Van *Dufay* i, no. 6.

i/6 O proles Hispanie/O sidus Hispanie (St Anthony of Padua), 4vv. Text by Julian of Speyer. Van *Dufay* i, no. 4 (with listing of other sources for both texts).

Doubtful and attributed works

— O sidus Yspanie (St Anthony of Padua), 5vv. Anon., suggested by Ficker as the motet 'O sydus Hispanie' mentioned in Dufay's will; firmly rejected by most scholars as being quite unlike Dufay's style. Edited in DTO, LXXVI, Jg. xl (Vienna, 1933), 75f.

i/20 Qui latuit in virgine. See 'Je sui povere de leesse' under Songs (D).

i/21 Veni, dilecte mi. Also ascribed to Johannes de Lymburgia and probably by him. Van *Dufay* i, no. 8.

# 4 Songs

Note: works probably composed after 1450 are marked 'Late'; see chapter 12.

## (A) *French ballade settings*

vi/20 Bien doy servir de volenté entiere. Only two (very corrupt) lines of text.

vi/18 Ce jour le doibt, aussi fait la saison. Composed in Laonnais; published earlier with the incorrect title 'Le jour s'endort'.

vi/16 C'est bien raison de devoir essaucier. In honour of Niccolò III d'Este, perhaps 1433 or 1437.

vi/13 J'ay mis mon cuer et ma pensee. Only one stanza of text.

vi/17 Je languis en piteux martire. Probably not by Dufay, see Bent 'Songs'.

vi/14 Je me complains piteusement. Dated 12 July 1425 in only source; only one stanza of text.

Le jour s'endort. See 'Ce jour le doibt'.

vi/15 Mon chier amy, qu'avés vous empensé. Perhaps for death of Pandolfo Malatesta da Rimini, 3 October 1427.

vi/88 Or me veult bien Esperance mentir. Almost certainly not by Dufay; published in complete edition with text 'Ave tota casta virgo'. Perkins *Mellon*, no. 49 (only one stanza of text).

Portugaler. See 'Or me veult.'

vi/11 Resvelliés vous et faites chiere lye. For wedding of Carlo Malatesta and Vittoria Colonna, 18 July 1423; only two stanzas of text.

vi/19 Se la face ay pale. Version vi/87, 4vv, is surely a later arrangement by another hand.

## (B) *French bergerette settings*

vi/22 De ma haulte et bonne aventure. Late.

vi/23 Helas mon dueil, a ce cop sui je mort. Late; five lines of text missing.

— Helas, n'aray je jamais mieulx? Late; anon., but attributed in Fallows 'Robertus', 123.

vi/24 Malheureulx cueur, que vieulx tu faire? Late; text by Le Rousselet.

vi/21 S'il est plaisir que je vous puisse faire, 4vv. Incomplete, probably not by Dufay.

## (C) *French rondeau settings*

vi/27 Adieu ces bons vins de Lannoys. Dated 1426 in only source.

vi/76 Adieu m'amour, adieu ma joye. Late.

vi/75 Adieu, quitte le demeurant. Late; only 1½ lines of text.

vi/40 Belle, plaissant et gracieuse. Third stanza of text missing.

vi/46 Belle, que vous ay je mesfait. Only one stanza of text.

vi/30 Belle, veulliés moy retenir.

vi/78 Belle, vueillés moy vangier. Late.

vi/47 Belle, vueilliés vostre mercy donner.

vi/50 Bien veignés vous, amoureuse liesse. Only one stanza of text; mensuration canon.

vi/59 Bon jour, bon mois, bon an et bonne estraine. Only one stanza of text.

vi/38 Ce jour de l'an voudray joye mener.

vi/39 Ce moys de may soyons lies et joyeux. Text perhaps by 'Perinet'.

vi/61 Craindre vous vueil, doulce dame de pris. Acrostic: CATELINE DUFAI. Shares its music with Italian song 'Quel fronte signorille' (vi/7).

vi/93 Departés vous, Malebouche et Envie. Probably by Ockeghem, to whom it is also ascribed; only one stanza of text. Pope *Montecassino*, no. 21.

vi/79 Dieu gard la bone sans reprise. Late.

vi/70 Donnés l'assault a la fortresse. ?Late; exists in versions for 3vv and 4vv.

vi/82 Du tout m'estoie abandonné. Late; only one stanza of text.

vi/66 Entre les plus plaines d'anoy. Late; only one stanza of text.

vi/26 Entre vous, gentils amoureux. Canonic.

vi/72 En triumphant de Cruel Dueil. Late, perhaps 1460–61 at the death of Binchois; in complete edition with corrupt text 'Je triomphe'. Fallows *Songs*, no. 1.

vi/58 Estrinés moy, je vous estrineray.

vi/74 Franc cuer gentil, sur toutes gracieuse. Acrostic: FRANCHOISE.

vi/49 Hé, compaignons, resvelons nous, 4vv.

vi/35 Helas, et quant vous veray? Only one stanza of text.

vi/45 Helas, ma dame, par amours. Only one stanza of text.

vi/42 J'atendray tant qu'il vous playra.

vi/65 J'ay grant dolour. ?Late; no more text.

vi/52 Je donne a tous les amoureux.

vi/51 Je n'ai doubté fors que des envieux. ?Late; only one stanza of text.

vi/29 Je ne puis plus ce que j'ai peu/Unde veniet auxilium mihi? Only one stanza of text; over repeating but diminishing tenor.

vi/36 Je ne suy plus tel que souloye.

vi/91 Je ne vis onques la pareille. Late; also ascribed to Binchois; sung at *Banquet du voeu*, 1454.

vi/57 Je prens congié de vous, Amours. One line of text missing.

vi/32 Je requier a tous amoureux.

Je triomphe. See 'En triumphant'.

vi/37 Je veuil chanter de cuer joyeux. Acrostic: JEHAN DE DINANT; perhaps composed in Savoy.

vi/80 La plus mignonne de mon cueur. Late; in complete edition with corrupt text 'Ma plus mignonne'.

Las, comment feraye. See 'Las, que feray'.

vi/69 Las, que feray? ne que je devenray?

vi/84 Les douleurs, dont me sens tel somme, 4vv. Late; text by Anthoine de Cuise; two upper voices in mensural canon, overlooked in complete edition, see above Ex. 36. Full edition in Hamm Review, pp. 252ff.

vi/92 Le serviteur hault guerdonné. Late; authorship questioned by Besseler but supported by most other writers.

vi/31 Ma belle dame, je vous pri.

vi/44 Ma belle dame souveraine, 4vv.

Ma plus mignonne. See 'La plus mignonne'.

vi/63 Mille bonjours je vous presente. ?Late; only one stanza of text.

vi/71 Mon bien m'amour et ma maistresse. ?Late; text by Charles d'Albret. Fallows *Songs*, no. 2.

vi/54 Mon cuer me fait tous dis penser, 4vv. Acrostic: MARIA ANDREASQ.

vi/90 Mon seul plaisir, ma doulce joye. Also ascribed to Bedyngham and probably by him; text by Charles of Orleans, see Fallows 'Words'.

vi/34 Navré je sui d'un dart penetratif.

vi/77 Ne je ne dors ne je ne veille. Late.

vi/60 Or pleust a Dieu qu'a son plaisir.

vi/43 Par droit je puis bien complaindre et gemir, 4vv or 3vv. Canonic.

vi/73 Par le regard de vos beaux yeux. Late. Herein p. 163.

vi/33 Pouray je avoir vostre mercy?

vi/41 Pour ce que veoir je ne puis.

vi/48 Pour l'amour de ma doulce amye. Triplum in complete edition is an alternative for the contratenor; this piece is not 4vv.

vi/64 Puisque celle qui me tient en prison. ? Late; no more text.

vi/81 Puisque vous estez campieur. Late; canonic.

vi/67 Qu'est devenue leaulté? Late; only two lines of text.

vi/94 Resistera, 4vv. Probably not by Dufay; no more text.

vi/28 Resvelons nous, resvelons amoureux/Alons ent bien tos au may. Only one stanza of text; lower voices canonic.

vi/53 Se ma dame je puis veir.

vi/62 Trop lonc temps ai esté en desplaisir. Almost certainly not by Dufay since the sole ascription is carefully erased; only one stanza of text.

vi/68 Va t'en, mon cuer, jour et nuitie. Late.

vi/55 Vo regard et doulce maniere.

vi/83 Vostre bruit et vostre grant fame. Late.

vi/56 [No surviving French text]. In only source with Latin text 'Hic iocundus sumit mundus'.

vi/89 [No surviving French text]. Probably not by Dufay; in only source with Latin text 'O flos florum virginum'.

### (D) French works of unusual form

i/20 Je sui povere de leesse. Basse danse setting; appears in one source with 'Du pist mein hort' to contratenor and in another texted 'Qui latuit in virgine'; authorship doubted by most writers but supported above, p.130. Van *Dufay* i, no. 7.

vi/25 Je vous pri, mon tresdoulx ami/Ma tres douce amie/Tant que mon argent dura, 4vv. Late; combinative chanson. Pope *Montecassino*, no. 109.

vi/12 La belle se siet au piet de la tour. ABA' form over cantus firmus tenor.

vi/10 O tres piteulx de tout espoir fontaine/Omnes amici eius, 4vv.

Through-composed lament after the manner of a motet; late, perhaps 1455, certainly after May 1453; headed in one source 'Lamentatio sancte matris ecclesie constantinopolitane'. Three others are lost, see p.71.

vi/85 Seigneur Leon, vous soyés bienvenus/ [Benedictus qui venit], 4vv. Through-composed; anon., attributed to Dufay in Plamenac 'Unknown Composition'. Perhaps 1442.

## (E) Italian songs

vi/8 Dona gentile, bella come l'oro. Late; in form of a French rondeau.

vi/6 Dona i ardenti rai. Form unclear.

vi/2 Invidia nimica, 4vv. Ballata (though text is wrongly distributed in the complete edition). Hamm *Chronology*, 8, suggests that only the fourth voice is by Dufay.

vi/4 La dolce vista del tuo viso pio. Text incomplete, but perhaps a ballata; authorship open to doubt, since the sole source is unreliable.

vi/1 L'alta belleza tua, virtute, valore. Text incomplete, but probably a ballata.

vi/3 Passato è il tempo omai di quei pensieri. Ballata.

vi/7 Quel fronte signorille in paradiso. Form unclear; curtailed contrafactum of French rondeau 'Craindre vous vueil' (vi/61); annotated in only source 'Rome composuit'.

vi/5 Vergene bella, che di sol vestita. Canzone (one stanza only); text by Petrarch.

## (F) Latin secular song

vi/9 Juvenis qui puellam. Incomplete; perhaps composed in 1438.

## (G) Contrafact texts for songs

Ave tota casta virgo. Ballade: Or me veult (vi/88).

Bone Pastor, panis vere. Rondeau: Craindre vous vueil (vi/61).

Du pist mein hort. Je sui povere, see section (D) above (i/20).

Hic iocundus sumit mundus. Rondeau without known French text (vi/56).

Imperatrix celestis militie. Rondeau: Mille bonjours (vi/63).

Jesu, judex veritatis. Rondeau: Bon jour, bon mois (vi/59).

O flos florum virginum. Rondeau without known French text and probably spurious (vi/89).

O Maria maris stella. Rondeau: Je donne a tous les amoureux (vi/52).

O pulcherrima. Bergerette: S'il est plaisir (vi/21).

O virgo pia. Rondeau: Pour l'amour (vi/48).

Portugaler. Ballade: Or me veult (vi/88).

Quam pulchri. Bergerette: S'il est plaisir (vi/21).

Qui Deus natus de virgine. Rondeau: Franc cuer gentil (vi/74).

Qui latuit in virgine. Je sui povere, see section (D) above (i/20).

Regina celi letare. Rondeau: Craindre vous vueil (vi/61).

Resone unice eterni Regis. Rondeau: Par le regard (vi/73).
Superno nunc emittitur. Rondeau: Le serviteur (vi/92).
Trag frischen muth. Rondeau: Dieu gard la bone (vi/79).

*(H) Anonymous songs attributed to Dufay*

These tentative attributions, based largely on style and manuscript context, are discussed in the preface to Reaney *Early Fifteenth-century Music* iv; page references are to editions in that volume.

Adieu, mon gracieux amy (rondeau), 37. Only one stanza of text.
Cuer triste et mas sans solas et sans joye (ballade), 58f. Only one stanza of text.
Donés confort a vostre amy (rondeau), 30f.
Je vous vieng voir, ma dame amye (rondeau), 43. Only one stanza of text.
Pleysir, soulas, desduit et joy (rondeau), 29f.

# 5 Added voices ascribed or attributed to Dufay

v/52 Exultet celum laudibus (hymn), 4vv. Appears in only source with fourth voice marked 'contratenor secundus Duffay'.
iv/30 Gloria, 4vv. In both sources the contratenor is ascribed 'du fay'.
vi/2 Invidia nimica (Italian ballata), 4vv. Hamm *Chronology*, 8, points out that the very early 3vv source is anon., and suggests that only contratenor II is Dufay's work.
vi/86 J'ayme bien celui qui s'en va (rondeau). Anon. 'contratenor trompette' replacing the original contratenor of Fontaine's rondeau. Besseler *Bourdon*, 50/49, proposes that the sheer mastery of this voice argues for Dufay's authorship; others have felt more cautious.

# 6 Theoretical writings

*Musica*. Lost, but cited in marginal annotations on the late fifteenth-century paper manuscript Parma, Biblioteca palatina, 1158, f.26v-27 and f.56. Relevant passages edited in Gallo 'Citazioni'. All of them concern mensural notation.

*Tractatus de musica mensurata et de proportionibus*. Lost, but reported by Fétis as being in a sixteenth-century quarto manuscript of some forty parchment leaves sold by auction (presumably in Paris) to an English bookseller in 1824 and not identified since. Fétis saw the phrase 'secundum doctrinam Wilhelmi Dufais Cimacensis [surely 'Cameracensis'] Hann.', which suggests it included quotations from the same source. See: Fétis 'Mémoire' (1829), 13; Borren *Dufay*, 22ff; Gallo 'Citazioni', 149.

# Appendix C

# Personalia

**Ailly,** Pierre d' (1350–9 Aug. 1420), French scholar, astrologer and ecclesiastic. He was chancellor of the University of Paris (1389–95), resigning under a cloud; Bishop of Le Puy (1395); Bishop of Cambrai (June 1397), resigning when he was nominated cardinal (6 June 1411). He was a leading figure at the Councils of Pisa and Constance. Buried in Cambrai Cathedral, 6 Aug. 1422.[1]

**Albret,** Charles 'le cadet' d' (d. 7 April 1473), French nobleman and poet, author of *Mon bien m'amour*, set by Dufay (vi/71), perhaps after 1450. He is associated with the circle of Charles of Orleans on the basis of two poems appearing in the duke's collection;[2] three more poems are ascribed to him in Paris, n.a.fr.15771, among them *Mon bien m'amour*.[3] His mother was Anne d'Armagnac, sister of Charles of Orleans' second wife Bonne. On 17 November 1456 he became Seigneur de Sainte-Bazeilh and was later executed for holding the town of Lectoure against Louis XI.[4]

**Aleman,** Louis (c. 1390–16 Sept. 1450), French cardinal. Bishop of Maguelonne (1418); Archbishop of Arles (1423); cardinal (24 May 1426). He succeeded Gabriele Condulmer as Papal Legate at Bologna on 25 May 1424, and wrote from there twice on Dufay's behalf requesting waivers of residence from Cambrai (1427, 1428). Chased from Bologna on 23 August 1428, he was at the papal curia of Martin V by December. Shortly after the accession of Eugenius IV in 1431 he left Rome, having refused to sign the papal bull dissolving the Council of Basle. He returned to Arles and in May 1434 himself joined the Council of Basle, becoming its president from 14 Feb. 1438 until its dissolution in 1449. He personally proclaimed the deposition of Eugenius IV and placed the papal tiara on the head of antipope Felix V. Eugenius removed him from the rank of cardinal in 1440, but he was reinstated by Nicholas V in 1449. In 1527 he was beatified by Pope Clement VII.[5]

**Amadeus VIII** (4 Sept. 1383–7 Jan. 1451), Count of Savoy (1391), Duke of Savoy (1916), retiring in Nov. 1434 though he formally abdicated the duchy only in Jan. 1440 to become antipope Felix V. He eventually resigned from the papacy on 7 April 1449 and was made a cardinal by Pope Nicholas V.

**Amerval,** Eloi d' (fl. 1450–80), French composer, singer and poet. A singer in the Savoy court chapel (1 May 1455–31 Aug. 1457) under Dufay; later

master of the choirboys at Ste-Croix, Orleans, 1483; perhaps he is the
'Eligio' who was cantor at the court of Milan in 1474–5. He composed the
five-voice Mass *Dixerunt discipuli*. His long poem, *Le livre de la deablerie*
(published 1508), includes a description of the main composers of his time
(headed by Dunstable and Dufay) as well as a list of musical instruments.

**Arpin**, Gile. *See* Crepin.

**Auclou**, Robert (*c*. 1400–August 1452),[6] churchman and diplomat whose
name appears as an acrostic in Dufay's motet *Rite majorem* (i/11). Curate
of St-Jacques-de-la-Boucherie (31 Aug. 1420) in Paris, but relatively early
in the 1420s he was at Rome in the curia of Pope Martin V who provided a
safe-keeping for the transferral of his books to Bologna in July 1426.[7] In
Bologna he was secretary to Cardinal Aleman until 1428 when he presumably fled to Rome with Aleman. Like Dufay he was at the papal curia
in Rome, 1429–33, though as a representative of the Burgundian court.
Canon of Besançon, of Notre-Dame de Paris and of Cambrai Cathedral
(received 28 July 1433). In 1433 he became Philip the Good's representative at the Council of Basle; when Philip withdrew his representatives in
Sept. 1438 he allowed Auclou and one other to return to Basle as independent delegates, which Auclou did as representative of Cambrai Cathedral
(appointed the same day as Dufay, 7 April 1438). His canonry of St-
Donatien, Bruges, was received on 24 Jan. 1438, only three months before
Dufay's.[8] He was back in Cambrai from Basle by April 1439 when he was
involved in the election of Jean de Bourgogne as bishop.[9] At Cambrai he
was Archdeacon of Brabant from 1437 until his death and was *écolâtre*
from 1446.[10] Two manuscripts owned by him survive: Paris, Bibl.
mazarine, Ms. 994 (dated 21 July 1923) and Cambrai, Bibl. municipale,
Ms. 1045.

**Bedyngham**, John (?1422–59/60), English composer. Biographical material
is scanty but seems to suggest that he never left England. His rondeau *Mon
seul plaisir* (vi/90) is also ascribed, with far less probability, to Dufay; its
text is by Charles of Orleans. His works are widely distributed in continental sources.

**Binchois**, Gilles de Bins, called (*c*.1400–20 Sept. 1460), Franco-Flemish
composer. Born at Mons, he received his first musical training there and
worked as an organist at Ste-Waudru before leaving for Lille in 1423. He
seems to have had some contact with the English regents of France in the
1420s but was by 1430 a member of the Burgundian court chapel choir,
where he stayed until his retirement in 1453. He probably met Dufay at
the Savoy wedding in 1434. Later he was a proctor for Dufay's canonry at
Ste-Waudru, Mons, in 1446 and attended a chapter meeting there with
Dufay in March 1449. Dufay's rondeau *En triumphant de Cruel Dueil*
(vi/72) seems to have been written at his death, as was Ockeghem's
ballade *Mort tu as navré de ton dart*. Binchois is mentioned in one breath
with Dufay by many writers of the time (and indeed since), among them

Martin le Franc, Simon Greban, Guillaume Cretin, Jean Molinet and Eloi d'Amerval.

**Boidin,** Nicolle (*d.* 1469), musician and churchman. He was a singer at the Burgundian court chapel from at least 1431; on his retirement in 1453[11] he moved to Cambrai where he was a canon. He took part in the 1461 inventory of Cathedral property with Dufay. His inventory *post mortem* records that he owned '1 livre en papier d'aucunes vieses chanteries de musique'.[12]

**Bouillart,** Alexandre (*d.* 20 Aug. 1474), Dufay's chaplain. His gravestone[13] describes him as a priest, native of Beauvais, a chaplain of Cambrai Cathedral and of Guillaume Dufay. Dufay, in his will, names him as his servant and appoints him an executor; but in the event he died three months before the composer.

**Bourgogne,** Jean de (*d.* 27 April 1480), Bishop of Cambrai (1439). Illegitimate son of Duke John the Fearless of Burgundy, he was appointed bishop while still a student at the University of Louvain and still below the statutory age of 25. He was largely an absentee bishop, preferring the life at court to that in Cambrai. But, contrary to the assertions of his early biographers, he was never married and he did visit Cambrai at least three times after his official entry in 1442.[14]

**Brassart,** Johannes (*c.* 1405–after 1445), singer and composer from Liège. He joined the papal choir early in 1431, leaving again before the end of Nov. His motet *Magne decus potencie* is for the coronation of Eugenius IV (11 March 1431), therefore being from the same year, and for the same choir, as Dufay's motets *Ecclesie militantis* (i/12) and *Balsamus et munda cera* (i/13). Brassart then went to work for King (later Emperor) Sigismund and his successors.

**Brunelleschi,** Filippo (1377–1446), Florentine architect. In 1419 he finally received the contract to build the cupola for Florence Cathedral. The cathedral was dedicated on 25 March 1436 with the music of Dufay's motet *Nuper rosarum flores* (i/16) which matches the dome in several important respects.

**Carlier,** Gilles (*d.* 1472), dean of Cambrai Cathedral (1431–72).[15] He is also the author of writings on music[16] and was a celebrated theologian.

**Castel,** Petrus du (*fl.* 1442–7), musician, master of the choirboys at Cambrai, 1442–7; his name appears as an acrostic in Dufay's motet *Fulgens iubar* (i/18). He is not to be confused with brother Petro de Castro Novo who was organist at the court of Savoy in 1446.[17]

**Cateline.** Unidentified. Dufay's rondeau *Craindre vous vueil* (vi/61) has the acrostic CATELINE DUFAI.

**Charles VI** (1368–1422), King of France from 1380. By 1400 he was known to be subject to frequent fits of madness, so his rule became increasingly weak. Under his rule much of France, including Paris, fell into English hands.

**Charles VII** (1403–61), King of France, theoretically from his father's death in 1422, though he had actually been disinherited by the treaty of Troyes in 1420. Largely as a result of the efforts of Joan of Arc, he was crowned at Rheims in 1429. Some time in the late 1440s he began to assert his true position as king; Dufay's single known encounter with the royal court (1455) came at a time when the king was extremely powerful again, though already physically weak.

**Charles of Orleans** (1394–1465), French poet and statesman, father of King Louis XII. Imprisoned for twenty-five years after the battle of Agincourt (1415), he spent his last years mostly at his court in Blois where he gathered an impressive literary circle. The single setting of one of his poems ascribed to Dufay (*Mon seul plaisir*, vi/90) is probably by Bedyngham; two other poems of his have musical settings. Poets apparently of his circle whose work was set by Dufay are Charles d'Albret, Le Rousselet and Anthoine de Cuise.

**Charles the Bold** (1433–5 Jan. 1477), Duke of Burgundy from June 1467. His rash and warlike behaviour as duke effectively led to the end of the Burgundy duchy as such; after his death his lands were divided between Louis XI of France and the Holy Roman Emperor Maximilian. His skill and interest in music are attested by many writers of the time, and two songs survive that may well be his work.[18] He visited Cambrai when Dufay was there in 1460, 1462 and 1468, on the first occasion hearing the choir sing a motet of his own composition. The inventory of Dufay's property refers to six music books (itemized as seven) which he had given to Charles but of which he had retained possession during his lifetime.

**Chemin,** Jennin du, 'cousin' of Dufay, living at Bruges when the composer died, who had for eighteen or twenty years sent him annual presents of 'confistures, roisins, fighes et aultres viandes', as mentioned in the executors' account but not the will itself.

**Ciconia,** Johannes (?*c*.1373–1412), composer born in Liège. Some authorities maintain that he was born around 1335; but there is no clear evidence of compositions earlier than about 1395, from which date begins a remarkable series of motets commemorating events in the history of Padua and the Veneto. As the earliest northern composer known to have made a career in Italy, Ciconia is a crucial figure in the 'International Gothic' of music and is considered the most important continental composer between the time of Machaut (*d*. 1377) and Dufay.

**Colonna,** Oddo. *See* Martin V.

**Colonna,** Vittoria, daughter of Lorenzo, Count of Alba (from 1419; *d*. 1423), an elder brother of Pope Martin V. Her wedding to Carlo

Malatesta da Pesaro in 1423 gave rise to Dufay's ballade *Resvelliés vous* (vi/11). Clementini reports seeing her tomb in S Apostolo at Rome with an inscription stating that she lived fifty-seven years.

**Compere**, Loyset (*c.* 1445–1518), French composer. His motet *Omnium bonorum plena* names many musicians, giving place of honour to Dufay. The motet must have been composed before July 1474 when Compere is first recorded in Milan; but it may date from 1468.

**Condulmer**, Gabriele. *See* Eugenius IV.

**Courtois**, Martin (*d.* 1481), canon of Cambrai Cathedral from 18 Nov. 1463. Perhaps born in Cambrai, he sang in the French royal chapel from at least 1451 to 1470, having previously been a *clerc* at Notre-Dame de Paris, at least 1442–5.[19] In his will Dufay left him a 'figura' of King Louis XI and a picture which he himself had brought Dufay from Tours.

**Crepin** (Crispini), Gile (*fl.*1461–81), singer at the court of Savoy (1461–4), *petit vicaire* at Cambrai (1465 and perhaps 1468), and soprano singer at San Pietro in Vaticano (1471–81).[20] In 1468–9 he visited the court of Savoy at Avigliana on his way from Picardy to Rome and brought with him from Dufay 'aucunes messes faittes en l'art de musique nouvellement'. (His name is given incorrectly by Cordero di Pamparato and all subsequent writers as 'Arpin'.)

**Cuise**, Anthoine de, author of *Les douleurs,* set by Dufay (vi/84) perhaps in 1455. He is associated with the circle of Charles of Orleans on the basis of three poems in the duke's collection.[21] Raynaud identified him with Anthoine de Guise on the basis of a misspelling of his name in two other manuscripts;[22] but Champion and Angremy reject this possibility as being too early.[23] Over a dozen poems by him survive.

**Dinant**, Jehan de. Unidentified. His name appears as an acrostic in Dufay's rondeau *Je veuil chanter* (vi/37), probably written at Savoy in 1434–5. A minstrel of that name in the Burgundian court, 1374–1409, is surely far too early to be associated with Dufay's song.[24] Conversely much too late is Joannes de Lotinis Dinantinus, praised by Tinctoris in his *De inventione de usu musice* (*c.*1487) as being a distinguished soprano singer; this man was also the dedicatee of Tinctoris's *Expositio manus* (after 1477) in which he is described as an adolescent.

**Donatello** [Donato di Bardi] (*c.* 1383–1466), Florentine sculptor, perhaps the greatest sculptor of his century. He was closely associated with Brunelleschi from about 1401, was at Rome in 1433, and was in Florence when Dufay was there in 1435–6. His high altar for the basilica of Sant' Antonio in Padua was dedicated on 13 June 1450, perhaps with music by Dufay.

**Dufay**, Cateline. *See* Cateline.

**Dufay**, Marie (*d.* 23 April 1444), mother of the composer. When she died she was living in Cambrai apparently with her son (who took new lodgings soon afterwards); and she was buried beneath the porch of St-Gengulphe in the cathedral by special permission. In 1424 she was named in the will of Johannes Huberti, canon of Cambrai Cathedral and provost of St-Géry, who described her as his 'cousine et servante'.

**Dunstable**, John (*c*. 1390–1453), English composer. He was described by Martin le Franc, Hothby and Tinctoris as the most influential composer of the generation before Dufay and as having had a direct influence on Dufay and Binchois who took on the *contenance angloise* thereby significantly changing the course of music on the continent. Exactly how Dunstable influenced Dufay is unclear if only because there is still considerable doubt as to when Dufay would first have encountered his work. On his tombstone Dunstable is described as having been musician to the Duke of Bedford: Bedford was the English regent in Paris from 1422 to 1435, so it is quite possible that Dunstable was in France during those years; yet this is hypothesis, and in any case it is not entirely clear where Dufay was before 1427. On the other hand, the rich representation of Dunstable in Italian manuscripts of the 1430s means that Dufay could easily have come to know the music without meeting Dunstable in person.

**Este**, Leonello d' (1407–1 Oct. 1450), Marquis of Ferrara from 1441, eldest son of Niccolò III. He was a celebrated patron of the arts and particularly of music. Dufay received twenty ducats from him in 1443 and perhaps wrote his *Seigneur Leon* (vi/85) for him in 1442.

**Este**, Niccolò III d' (1393–26 Dec. 1441), Marquis of Ferrara from 1393, the illegitimate but only son of Alberto d'Este. Dufay's ballade *C'est bien raison* (vi/16) praises his qualities as a peacemaker.

**Eugenius IV** [Gabriele Condulmer] (*c*. 1383–23 February 1447), pope from 3 March 1431. His uncle Pope Gregory XII made him Bishop of Siena before he had reached the minimum statutory age of 25 (1407) and made him a cardinal (9 May 1408); so he perhaps had more difficulty than he might otherwise have had in curbing the power of the Malatesta and Colonna families who had benefited so much under his predecessor Martin V. Whatever the difficulties of his papacy, he was a fine patron of the arts: he commissioned his papal tiara from Ghiberti, paintings for the chapel of the Holy Sacrament from Fra Angelico, his portrait from Jean Foucquet; he invited Donatello to Rome and ordered the restoration of the Pantheon. Six of Dufay's finest works are motets for occasions on which Eugenius seems to have been the direct patron.

**Felix V.** *See* Amadeus VIII.

**Flannel**, Gilles (*d*. 1466), called 'L'enfant'. Singer in the papal chapel (7 Jan. 1418–1441)[25] and canon of Cambrai Cathedral; for some years he was master of the papal chapel. Dufay was an executor of his will.[26] It was apparently Flannel who in 1425 was sent to seek choirboys for the papal chapel and returned with Nicolas Grenon and four boys from Cambrai.

**Fontenay,** Johannes de (*fl.* 1447–75), singer. He was a *petit vicaire* at Cambrai in 1447–8,[27] a singer at the chapel of Savoy from 1 May 1449 to 1 May 1457,[28] and at the royal chapel of Louis XI, 1461–75.[27] He is mentioned in Dufay's will as having sent him a 'figura' of Louis XI.

**Franc.** *See* Le Franc.

**Gobert.** *See* Le Mannier.

**Grenon,** Nicolas (*c.* 1380–17 Oct. 1456), French composer. First recorded in Paris (1399–1401), then as master of the choristers at Laon Cathedral (1403–8). In 1408–9 he taught grammar to the choirboys of Cambrai Cathedral where he was also a *petit vicaire*, leaving after Dufay's arrival but before Dufay was formally admitted as a choirboy. Master of the choirboys for the Burgundian court (1412–19). He then returned to Cambrai as master (1421–4), spending 1425–7 as master of the choirboys for Pope Martin V, having brought the choirboys from Cambrai. During that time he was received as a canon of Cambrai Cathedral, 7 Feb. 1426. In May 1428 he was Dufay's proctor to a benefice at St-Géry, Cambrai, and again in 1436 to Dufay's canonry at Cambrai Cathedral. From 1437 to 1442 he was master of the *petits vicaires* at Cambrai (to be succeeded by Dufay); from 1445 Dufay lived in the house next door to Grenon's.

**Grosseteste,** Pierre (*d.* 1463), member of the papal choir 1436–50 (or perhaps later), after which he retired to a canonry at St-Etienne, Besançon, in 1455. As a former colleague of Dufay in the papal choir he welcomed the composer at Besançon in September 1458.

**Hardi,** Antonius, Dufay's godson to whom he bequeathed two books. He is the first person mentioned by name in Dufay's will.

**Hardi,** Jacobus, husband of Dufay's *commère*, possibly father of Antonius. His wife was bequeathed an *Agnus Dei* of pure gold by Dufay's will.

**Hemart,** Jean, master of the choirboys at Cambrai, 1469–84. One song by him survives in the Florence chansonnier, Banco rari 229, f.226v–227.

**Hesdin,** Jean de (documented 1401–11), priest of the diocese of Noyon, *grand vicaire* of Cambrai Cathedral and treasurer of Ste-Croix, Cambrai. He is recorded in Cambrai from 1401, being paid for regular Masses from 1404–10.[29] On 26 Sept. 1410 he was accused of simony by the cathedral chapter who charged that he had purchased his positions at the cathedral and at Ste-Croix; on 6 Oct. the case was passed on to the metropolitan church at Rheims; and on 8 Oct. the chapter sent an enquiry to Rheims to find the result. On 19 June 1411 the *magnus vicariatus* left vacant by his resignation was transferred to the *cappellanus* Hellino Bourel.[30] In 1409 he was paid 77 *sous* by the chapter 'pro gubernacione cuiusdam Willelmi' [Dufay] for eleven weeks prior to Dufay's admission as a choirboy.

**Josquin Desprez** (*c.* 1440–1521), the outstanding composer of the generation around 1500. Like Dufay he spent much of his active career in Italy, returning in later life to a canonry at the church where he had probably received his first musical training, at Condé. He could easily have met Dufay who was a canon of Condé from before 1447 until 1466; Condé is only 40 km. from Cambrai.

**La Croix**, Jehan de (*d.* 1479), called 'Monami'. Canon of Cambrai. He was a singer in the papal chapel from 1431 to 1438 and was for a short time (1433) first chaplain. Like Dufay he had benefices at St-Pierre, Tournai (1431), and St-Géry, Cambrai (1431), before becoming a canon of Cambrai Cathedral. From 1450 to 1459 he replaced Dufay as master of the office of *petits vicaires*.[31] His will and executors' account survive.[32]

**Lantins**, Arnold de (*fl. c.* 1430), composer, probably born in Liège. He was a member of the papal chapel for six months (Nov. 1431 to June 1432) while Dufay was there. It is just possible that his ballade *Puisque je suy cypriarés*[33] is concerned with the marriage celebrations of Anne de Lusignan, sister of the King of Cyprus, in February 1434, the occasion for which Dufay became chapelmaster at Savoy. Music by Arnold and Hugo de Lantins appears, on the whole, in the same sources and has many features that suggest they were brothers.

**Lantins**, Hugo de (*fl. c.* 1420–30), composer, probably born in Liège. No specific documentation for him exists, though a surprising number of details seem to connect him with Dufay in the 1420s. His song *Tra quante regione* for Cleofe Malatesta seems to celebrate the same occasion as Dufay's motet *Vasilissa ergo gaude* (i/7); his song *Mirar non posso*[34] contains the words 'del fedel servo to ferma Collona' which might connect it with the Malatesta–Colonna wedding of 1423 for which Dufay wrote his *Resvelliés vous* (vi/11); his motet *Celsa sublimatur*[35] celebrates St Nicholas of Bari, as does Dufay's motet *O gemma, lux* (i/9); and his Gloria paired with a Credo by Dufay (iv/3) strongly suggests direct collaboration or competition.

**Lebertoul**, Franchois, Cambrai choirman and composer. Documented at Cambrai only for the year 1409–10 when he was paid a gratuity 'pro infirmitate sua' for having served in the choir. Five works by him survive.

**Le Franc**, Martin (*c.* 1410–8 Nov. 1461), churchman and poet. Born in Aumale, Normandy, he studied at Paris before entering the service of Duke Amadeus VIII in 1431. Canon (May 1443) and provost (Sept. 1443) of Lausanne Cathedral – positions received from Amadeus, now antipope Felix V, perhaps in recognition of services as his secretary at the Council of Basle. He was also an apostolic protonotary and a canon of Turin and Geneva. When Felix V abdicated, Pope Nicholas V retained Le Franc as a protonotary; and in 1450 he went to the household of Duke Louis I of Savoy, being one of the witnesses of the treaties of Le Cleppé and St-Pourçain between Louis and Charles VII of France. His poem *Le champ-*

*ion des dames*[36] (24000 lines), which praises the achievements of Dufay and Binchois, was probably written in 1440–2 and was dedicated to Philip the Good, Duke of Burgundy. In 1447 Felix V sent him to the Burgundian court as a legate *a latere* with considerable powers in an effort to win Philip's support.[37] His other extended poem, *L'estrif de Fortune et de Vertu*, survives in many sources (including two in the British Library). Dufay at his death owned a small paper manuscript containing 'eglogas magistri Martini le Franc'; only one lyric poem of his now survives, the rondeau *Le jour m'est nuit*.[38]

**Le Mannier,** Gobert, singer at Cambrai. Master of the choirboys, 1447–8; a *petit vicaire* at least from 1458. Dufay bequeathed him a 'figura mortis'.

**Lens** [Lench, Gavre, Leedtekirche], Jean de (*d*. 31 March 1439), Bishop of Cambrai from 5 July 1412 (solemn entry 1 Oct. 1413).

**Leonard of Chios** (*c*. 1400–1482), Genoa-born Archbishop of Mitylene (Lesbos) from 1 July 1444 until the Turks captured the island in 1462. He is famous for his lucid eye-witness account of the Fall of Constantinople. It has been suggested that Dufay's *Seigneur Leon* (vi/83) might have been composed for his installation as archbishop.

**Le Rousselet,** poet, author of *Malheureulx cueur*, set by Dufay (vi/24), probably in the 1450s. Another bergerette by him, *Quant jamais aultre bien*, is set to music in the Pavia Ms. 361, but stylistically this cannot be by Dufay. These and five other poems ascribed simply 'Le Rousselet' appear as a group in Paris, Bibl. nationale, f.fr.9223, f.59v–62v.[39] Raynaud[40] mentions several documents that could be significant: the man who was provost of Laon Cathedral in 1433 and was hanged by the French troops in Oct. of that year would perhaps be too old to have written poems collected in so late a manuscript, though Dufay might well have known him at Laon; one cited in connection with the *Etats provinciaux* of 1445 might be more to the point; so might 'J. Rousselet', an *homme d'armes* of Louis of Orleans (later King Louis XII) in 1485. In addition 'J. Rousselet' appears as an *avocat* of the *cour du trésor* at Paris in 1477.[41]

**Loqueville,** Richard (*d*. 1418), musician and composer, often considered Dufay's first composition teacher. At the Duke of Bar's chapel in 1410, he came to Cambrai as master of the choristers in 1413 and stayed until his death. He was married and was an accomplished harp player as well as composer.

**Louis XI** (1423–83), King of France from 1461. A strange and aloof character, dubbed unforgettably by his chronicler Philippe de Commynes as 'the universal spider', he is credited with being the first king to unite France as a political entity. Banished to Dauphiné by King Charles VII in 1447, he had over the next years many dealings with Louis, Duke of Savoy, whose daughter Charlotte he married in 1451. He visited Cambrai while Dufay was there in Oct. 1468.

**Louis I** (24 Feb. 1402–29 Jan. 1465), Duke of Savoy from 6 Jan. 1440. The fourth child of Amadeus VIII and Marie de Bourgogne, he became Prince of Piedmont and Lieutenant-General of Savoy when his father retired to Ripaille in 1434. He and his wife Anne de Lusignan were to be among Dufay's most important patrons.

**Lusignan**, Anne de (24 Sept. 1418–11 Nov. 1462), Duchess of Savoy. Her marriage to Louis I actually took place by procuration at Cyprus on 4 Oct. 1433; later that month she sailed to Nice where she arrived in Jan. 1434. Travelling slowly from there – and stopping at Arles, where her host was Cardinal Aleman – she arrived at Chambéry on 7 Feb. for the confirmation of the marriage followed by elaborate wedding celebrations at which Dufay was present. Her family, originating from Poitou, had been the royal family of Cyprus since 1186, though it was eventually to be deposed in 1489. Her great-grandfather, Pierre I de Lusignan, had been an important patron of the composer Guillaume de Machaut. There is some feeling that the famous 'French-Cypriot' manuscript of fourteenth-century polyphony now in Turin came with Anne from Cyprus in 1434. She was described by Olivier de la Marche as 'la plus belle princesse du monde' and by Litta as 'Greca di rara bellezza'; but she was also described as vain, imperious, deceitful and vindictive. She had at least sixteen children by Louis; and it was for her that Louis obtained the famous Turin Shroud.

**Malatesta da Pesaro**, Carlo (*d.* 14 Nov. 1438), son of Malatesta di Pandolfo (1368–1429), the father of the Pesaro line of the family who had been granted the city of Pesaro by Pope Boniface IX on 2 Jan. 1391.[42] Dufay's ballade *Resvelliés vous* (vi/11) celebrates his wedding to Vittoria Colonna in July 1423.

**Malatesta da Pesaro**, Cleofe (*c.* 1388–1433), second child of Malatesta di Pandolfo and wife of Theodore II Palaiologos, Despot of the Morea.[43] Martin V gave permission (6 April 1418) to the Byzantine delegation at the Council of Constance for the sons of Emperor Manuel II Palaiologos (1391–1425) to marry Italian princesses. By a Chrysobull of 29 March (or possibly 29 May) 1419 it was undertaken that Cleofe's religious beliefs should be respected by her Orthodox husband. On 16 July 1420 the Venetian senate authorized the passage of a galley containing Cleofe from Fano to Chioggia; on 30 Aug. they authorized *two* ladies to go on the galley (Cleofe and Sofia de Montefeltro who was to marry the eldest son, John Palaiologos). They seem to have arrived at Constantinople by Nov. The weddings both took place on 19 Jan. 1421, probably at Constantinople. Shortly after that Cleofe did in fact adopt the Orthodox faith. There is some discussion as to whether her conversion was forced on her. Two factors argue strongly that it was not. First, other brothers of Theodore were later granted permission to wed Italian princesses. Second, when the court philosopher George Gemistos Plethon died, Sigismondo Pandolfo Malatesta brought his body from Mistra and buried it in the Tempio Malatestiano at Rimini. The famous letter to Pope Martin V in which one of Cleofe's ladies in waiting stated that the Orthodox faith had been forced on Cleofe therefore probably misrepresents the true state of affairs. When Cleofe died Plethon, Cardinal Bessarion and three other Greek poets wrote poems in memory of her. Two surviving musical works celebrate her union with Theodore: Hugo de Lantins' *Tra quante regione* and Dufay's motet *Vasilissa ergo gaude* (i/7).

**Malatesta da Pesaro**, Pandolfo (1390–21 April 1441), Bishop of Brescia (1416), Bishop of Coutances (7 Oct. 1418), and Archbishop of Patras (10 May 1424); son of Malatesta di Pandolfo. Dufay's motet *Apostolo glorioso* (i/10) seems to have been composed for the rededication of a church of St Andrew at Patras in 1426. Pandolfo may have met Dufay while he was at the Council of Constance in 1415–17.

**Malatesta da Rimini**, Carlo (5 June 1368–14 Sept. 1429). senior member of the Rimini branch from the death of his father Galeotto Malatesta in 1385. Poggio Bracciolini described him as 'one of the most lettered men and the most ingenious general of our time'; and he had correspondence with Coluccio Salutati. He played important roles at the Councils of Pisa and Constance as Pope Gregory XII's representative.

**Malatesta da Rimini**, Pandolfo (2 Jan. 1370–3 Oct. 1427), second son of Galeotto Malatesta. Famous as a *condottiere* and crusader, he was Lord of Bergamo and Brescia for eighteen years, Captain-general of the Church (Spring 1422), and at his death he was Archdeacon of Bologna and titular head of the University of Bologna. A prominent patron of the humanists, he was three times married (and he had three illegitimate sons). He was probably the dedicatee of the anonymous motet *Ore Pandulphum* (*c.* 1400); Dufay's ballade *Mon chier amy* (vi/15) may have been composed at his death.

**Manetti**, Giannozzo (1396–1459), humanist from one of the richest Florentine families. Studied at Ambrogio Traversari's platonic academy at Santa Maria degli Angeli (where he would have met Cosimo de' Medici and Agnolo Acciaiuoli among others) and at the humanistic academy at S Spirito. His description of the dedication of Florence Cathedral is his earliest surviving work; his many later speeches were to mark him as the leading Italian orator of his generation.

**Martin V** [Oddo Colonna] (*d.* 20 Feb. 1430), pope from 11 Nov. 1417. His election by the Council of Constance temporarily ended the Schism; and his entry into Rome (30 Sept. 1420) marked the end of a long exile of the papacy. As pope he is famous for having favoured the Malatesta family at Rimini and his own family, Colonna. This may well have benefited Dufay who wrote works for both families before becoming a member of the papal choir in 1428; but it laid the foundation for the extreme instability of the reign of Pope Eugenius IV who followed him.

**Medici**, Cosimo de' (1389–1464), known as 'pater patriae', succeeded in being absolute ruler of Florence without ever holding an official title. He attended the Council of Constance with Pope John XXIII. Exiled from Florence, October 1433 to September 1434. A fine patron of the visual arts, of letters and of philosophy. In 1438 Cosimo established a permanent choir of four singers at the Baptistery, though its organization was in the hands of his son Piero.

**Medici,** Giovanni de' (1421–63), second son of Cosimo de' Medici. A letter to him from Antonio Squarcialupi[44] suggests that he had an active and detailed interest in music and in organ building; and he was reputed to play the lute. Dufay's letter to him and Piero (1456) confirms such an interest. According to Litta he died 'per intemperenza'.

**Medici,** Lorenzo de' (1449–92), known as 'il magnifico', son of Piero de' Medici. He wrote much poetry, including the ballata which in 1467 he asked Dufay (through Antonio Squarcialupi) to set. Later some of his poems were set by Isaac. His early interest in music is attested by a letter (Nov. 1460) from the theorist John Hothby. He also had a reputation as a singer; and at the age of eight he already owned a collection of seventeen instruments and three books of music.[45] Those to benefit from his artistic patronage include Botticelli, Poliziano, Pico della Mirandola, Pulci and Michelangelo as well as the musicians Alexander Agricola, Heinrich Isaac and Johannes Ghiselin. His second son Giovanni (1475–1521) became, as Pope Leo X, one of the finest music patrons of the next century and is himself credited with some musical compositions (albeit slender ones).

**Medici,** Piero de' (1416–69), known as 'il gottoso' – the gouty – eldest son of Cosimo de' Medici and father of Lorenzo. He owned the chansonnier that is now Vatican, Urb. lat. 1411 (c. 1440) and includes songs by Dufay; and it was he who purchased the most magnificent of the thirteenth-century Notre-Dame manuscripts, now in the Biblioteca laurenziana. As early as 1448 it was Piero who was responsible for the appointment and payment of the Baptistery singers; and he seems to have kept close personal contact with the chapel throughout his life. Squarcialupi's letter of 1467 to Dufay is largely concerned with relating Piero's pleasure at the singers Dufay had trained. And it is therefore to be expected that in 1456 Dufay should have turned to Piero and his brother Giovanni rather than to Cosimo when he was in search of patronage.

**Mellet** (Mielet), Simon (d. Sept. 1481),[46] music copyist whose work under Dufay's direction is extensively detailed in the payment records of Cambrai from 1446 to 1476. He was a *petit vicaire* (from at least 1446) and *grand vicaire* (from at least 1473) of Cambrai Cathedral. None of the music copied by him has been identified.

**Monami,** *See* La Croix.

**Mortier,** Raoul (d. 1480), canon of Cambrai and an executor of Dufay's will. His own will and executors' account survive.[47]

**Ockeghem**, Johannes (*d*. 6 Feb. 1497), Flemish composer. His birthdate is a matter of dispute, being put variously between 1410 and 1430. Listed as a singer at Antwerp Cathedral (1443–4) and the court of Bourbon (1446–8), he became a singer for King Charles VII in 1452 or 1453; and by 1454 he is described as *premier chappelain*, a position he was to retain under Louis XI and Charles VIII. He visited Cambrai in 1462 and 1464 (when he stayed in Dufay's house), but probably also when Louis XI visited Cambrai in 1468. That Ockeghem composed a Mass *L'homme armé* and a Mass *Ecce ancilla Domini* suggests further associations with Dufay, though his chanson in memory of Binchois suggests that the latter could have been his teacher.

**Orleans**, Charles of. *See* Charles of Orleans.

**Palaiologos**, Theodore II (*c*. 1395–June 1448), Despot of the Morea (1407–43), son of the Byzantine Emperor Manuel II Palaiologos (1391–1425). Manuel II sent ambassadors to the Council of Constance proposing, among other things, the reunion of Eastern and Western Churches: this came to nothing, but as a result Pope Martin V made two gestures towards Manuel. The first was to promise indulgences for anybody contributing towards the cost of the Hexamilion wall to defend the Morea from the mainland (at the straits of Corinth) – a wall which was being built on the initiative of Theodore II. The other was to grant permission for the Emperor's sons to marry Catholic princesses. Immediate beneficiaries were Theodore II, again, and his elder brother John (whose marriage turned out to be a disaster). Theodore's marriage to Cleofe Malatesta gave rise to Dufay's motet *Vasilissa ergo gaude* (i/7). Many writers take a poor view of Theodore as a ruler, but it was Theodore who inherited his father's intellectual proclivities, and he ran a cultured court in the hilltop castle at Mistra, particularly encouraging the idiosyncratic but fascinating philosopher Plethon.[48]

**Perinet**. Unidentified. Apparently the poet of *Ce moys de may* (vi/39), to judge from its last line. 'Perrinet l'organiste' was at Charles of Orleans' court in 1455–6;[49] and Peroneto des Ayes was a minstrel at the Savoy court in the years around 1433.[50] But neither is likely to be the poet.

**Petrarch** [Francesco Petrarca] (1304–74), perhaps the greatest of all Italian lyric poets. His *Canzoniere* concludes with the poem *Vergene bella*, set by Dufay (vi/5), but early settings of his poetry are rare. Not until the sixteenth century did he become the most favoured poet for composers.

**Philip**, Count of Geneva (*d*. 1444), youngest son of Amadeus VIII and Marie de Bourgogne. He was made Count of Geneva in 1434 when his brother Louis was made Prince of Piedmont. Their enmity might be explained by their difference of character. Philip was apparently the image of his father and was widely loved, whereas Louis was somewhat weak-willed.[51] Dufay's motet *Magnanime gentis* (i/17) celebrates a peace between the two signed in 1438 at Berne and Fribourg.

**Philip the Good** (1396–1467), Duke of Burgundy from Sept. 1419, one of the most powerful political leaders of his day. As a patron of the arts he was perhaps not quite so impressive as his court chroniclers suggest, but there is some circumstantial evidence that he was a patron of Dufay in the 1440s.

**Picard**, André (*d*. 29 Sept. 1455), called 'Druet', singer at the court of Savoy (1449–55).[52] Dufay was an executor of his will.

**Pius II** [Aeneas Silvius Piccolomini] (1405–64), pope from 19 Aug. 1458. He was renowned in his day as an orator and statesman; and his *Commentaries* rank as perhaps the most incisive and readable eye-witness histories of fifteenth-century politics. In the 1440s he acted as secretary to antipope Felix V (Amadeus VIII).

**Poree**, Guillaume. Benedictine monk who was a 'tenor' at the Savoy chapel from 1442 to 1459.[53] According to Dufay's will he had given the composer a book.

**Power**, Lionel (*c*. 1380–5 June 1445), English composer, the most important of his time apart from Dunstable. As a member of the Duke of Clarence's chapel (documented 1418–21) he was probably in France from October 1419 and would have been in Troyes for the wedding of Henry V and Catherine of Valois in June 1420. Much of his music appears in continental sources and was undoubtedly known to Dufay.

**Priers**, Jacobus de. 'Dominus' (or, in French, 'Sire'), described in Dufay's will as 'my relative in Tournai whom I nourished for about eighteen months'. (His name is given incorrectly by Houdoy and all subsequent writers as 'Riers'.)

**Ranchicourt**, Pierre de (*d*. 26 Aug. 1499), canon of Cambrai (9 Feb. 1446)[54] and Bishop of Arras (1463) who dedicated Cambrai Cathedral in 1472. He often visited Dufay's house at Cambrai[55] which Dufay's probate described as having a 'room of Monseigneur d'Arras'. Dufay left him a knife given to him by the King of Sicily (René of Anjou).

**Regis**, Johannes [Jean Leroy] (*c*. 1430–after 1482), composer and choirmaster. There is no apparent evidence for the commonly found statement that he was in Cambrai as Dufay's secretary, though he was the *clerc* for Dufay's benefice at Watiebraine, near Soignies where Regis was a canon. He was master of the choristers at Soignies as early as 1451,[56] so he was already experienced when invited in 1460 to become master of the choristers at Cambrai. He never accepted this position, but several of his works were copied into the cathedral choirbooks, and his connections with Cambrai evidently remained close.

**Regnault de Lyons** (*d*. before 1480),[57] executor of Dufay's will. Canon of Cambrai by the time Dufay returned in 1439. He took part, with Dufay, in inventorizing the Cambrai Cathedral property in 1461.

**René of Anjou** (1409–80), King of Sicily, brother-in-law of Charles VII; Duke of Bar (1430), Duke of Lorraine (1431, at which point he was deposed and imprisoned by Philip the Good). After a disastrous political career with more imprisonments, he somewhat retired from political life in the 1450s, devoting himself to the arts and particularly to the writing of poetry. He is also credited with some paintings. Dufay, in his will, mentions a knife sent to him by the King of Sicily, and the two could well have met in the 1450s.

**Riers,** Jacobus de. *See* Priers.

**Rosut,** Johannes de (*d.* 19 July 1491), canon of Cambrai and an executor of Dufay's will. His own will and executors' account survive.[58]

**Rousselet,** Le. *See* Le Rousselet.

**Sachet,** Franchois. *See* Sassetti, Francesco.

**St Anthony Abbot** [St-Anthoine-de-Viennois] (251 – 356), Egyptian hermit and saint, feast day 17 Jan. Considered the first Christian monk and the founder of monasticism. His remains were taken to La Motte St-Didier in the Viennois in about 1070. Here an abbey was built to house them and gave rise to the Benedictine hospital order of friars who specialized in curing a particularly painful form of gangrene ('Le feu St-Antoine'); they became a separate 'Antonine' order in 1297. Much of the present abbey was built in the fifteenth century; and the abbey had close links with the house of Savoy. In his will Dufay mentions a Mass for St Anthony Abbot which seems not to survive.

**St Anthony of Padua** (1195–1231), canonized in 1232, feast day 13 June. Born at Lisbon, he became a Franciscan missionary and the first famous Franciscan friar, going to Morocco in 1220; after an illness he came to Forlì to recover. Here he discovered his gift as a preacher, and was extremely successful as such during the last nine years of his short life. He died at Padua, and the basilica there is still an important place of pilgrimage. Dufay's Mass for St Anthony of Padua (ii/3) was hitherto thought to be that for St Anthony Abbot.

**Sassetti,** Francesco (1421–90), Florentine banker and bibliophile, manager of the Medici bank in Geneva, 1448–59.[59] In his letter to the Medici brothers (1454 or 1456), Dufay praised Sassetti for helping him when he 'needed something at the court of Rome'. Two portraits of Sassetti survive, both by Domenico Ghirlandaio, one of them in the Sassetti chapel at the church of Santissima Trinità, Florence.

**Sigismund** (1368–1437), King of Hungary (1387), King of the Romans (1410), titular King of Bohemia (1419), crowned Emperor of the Romans by Eugenius IV at Rome on 31 May 1433. Dufay's motet *Supremum est mortalibus bonum* (i/14) celebrated his entry into Rome (21 May) for that event. It was Sigismund who provided the initiative for summoning the

Council of Constance, and he was one of the most important political figures in the history of the conciliar movement.

**Simon le Breton** (*d*. 12 Nov. 1473), singer and composer. At the Burgundian court chapel by 1431, canon of Cambrai (1435); he retired to Cambrai in 1464 and was apparently a close friend of Dufay. Dufay's will mentions several items given to him by Simon; and the two were buried in the same chapel at Cambrai Cathedral.

**Spataro**, Giovanni (*c*. 1458–1541), Italian composer and theorist. His *Tractato* (1531) and his still unpublished correspondence with Pietro Aaron (1532) quote in detail from several of Dufay's works, particularly the Mass for St Anthony of Padua. He seems to have lived in Bologna most of his life.

**Squarcialupi**, Antonio [Antonio di Bartolomeo] (27 March 1416–buried 6 July 1480), Italian organist and composer. Organist of Florence Cathedral from the age of sixteen, he must have been involved together with Dufay in its dedication in 1436. Dufay's letter to the Medici brothers (1456) and Squarcialupi's letter to Dufay (1467) both suggest that the two were close friends. He owned the famous manuscript of fourteenth-century polyphony which now bears his name; yet another manuscript of his was reported by Negri[60] as being in the Pitti Palace and containing his own compositions. Lorenzo de' Medici described him as one of the finest musicians in the world; and he seems to have been almost the only Italian musician of his century to earn an international reputation.

**Tinctoris**, Johannes (*c*. 1435–*c*. 1511), theorist and composer. Though living in Naples at the time when he wrote his famous and influential series of theory treatises, he was apparently a *petit vicaire* at Cambrai for three months in 1460.

**Velut**, Gilet (documented 1409–11), composer who arrived in Cambrai as a *petit vicaire* only four months after Dufay's arrival as a choirboy. The inventive range of his surviving works may well have influenced Dufay inasmuch as Dufay's early works have this quality which is somewhat lacking in the music of other composers he would have met in the early years. Velut has been identified with Gilles Flannel, though without supporting evidence.[61]

**Werchin**, Jaquet, servant to Dufay from 1469 to 1474, as recorded in the executors' account of Dufay's will.

**Wez**, Pierre de (*d*. 1483), tenor in Cambrai Cathedral choir from 14 May 1443,[62] an executor of Dufay's will. He looked after Dufay's house for the seven years when he was 'in Savoy' during the 1450s. He also took part, with Dufay, in making the inventory of Cambrai Cathedral property in 1461. His will and executors' account survive.[63]

# Appendix D

## Bibliography

*(A) References up to 1836*

This chronological listing aims to include all early discussions or mentions of Dufay apart from biographical documents.

Martin le Franc, *Le champion des dames* (*c*. 1440–42). Relevant passages ed. Borren *Dufay*, 53f; ed. above, pp.20 and 41; trans. Reese *Renaissance*, 12f and 51.

Simon Greban, *Complainte sur la mort de Jacques Milet* (1466). Relevant passage ed. Marix *Histoire*, 182f.

Loyset Compere, motet *Omnium bonorum plena* (?1468). Ed. L. Finscher, CMM, XV/iv (1961), 32–8; relevant passage trans. Reese *Renaissance*, 227.

Bartolomeo Ramos de Pareia, *Musica practica* (*c*. 1472; pub. Bologna, 1482), Bk 3 ch. 2. Ed. Johannes Wolf (Leipzig, 1901), 84.

Johannes Tinctoris, *Complexus effectuum musices* (*c*. 1472–5), ch. 19. Ed. A. Seay, CSM, XXII/ii (1975), 163–77, on p. 176.

Johannes Tinctoris, *Proportionale musices* (1473), Prologue, Bk 1 ch. 3, Bk 3 ch. 2, Bk 3 ch. 3, Bk 3 ch. 6. Ed. A. Seay, CSM, XXII/iia (1978), 10, 14f, 47f, 49f, 57f.

Johannes Tinctoris, *Liber de arte contrapuncti* (11 Oct. 1477), Prologue and Bk 3 ch. 8. Ed. A. Seay, CSM, XXII/ii (1975), 11–157, on pp.12 and 156.

John Hothby, *Dialogus . . . in arte musica* (*c*. 1480). Ed. A. Seay, CSM, X (1964), 61–76, on p. 65.

anon., *Ars cantus mensurabilis et inmensurabilis* (1482), in manuscript Escorial, C III 23, f.3. Relevant passage ed. Bukofzer in *Acta musicologica*, viii (1936), 103ff.

Adam von Fulda, *Musica* (5 Nov. 1490), Bk 1 ch. 7, Bk 2 ch. 1, Bk 2 ch. 8. Ed. Gerbert (1784, see below), iii, 341f and 350. (Original manuscript at Strasbourg burned in 1870.)

Franchino Gafori, *Practica musice* (Milan, 1496 and later editions), Bk 3 ch. 4, Bk 4 ch. 5.

Guillaume Cretin, *Deploration sur la mort d'Ockeghem* (1497; pub. Paris, 1527). Ed. Ernest Thoinan [=Antoine Rocquet] (Paris, 1864), 33; relevant passage in Borren *Dufay*, 75, and Besseler *Bourdon*, 179/157.

Jean Molinet, *Le naufrage de la pucelle* (pub. Paris, 1531). Relevant passage ed. Marix *Histoire*, 185.

259

Eloi d'Amerval, *Le livre de la deablerie* (pub. Paris, 1508). Ed. C.F. Ward (Iowa City, 1923), 225f. Relevant passage ed. Borren *Dufay*, 76f, Marix *Histoire*, 185, and *The New Grove*, s.v. 'Eloy'.

Pierre Moulu, motet *Mater floreat* (? 12 May 1517). Ed. E. Lowinsky, *Monuments of Renaissance Music*, iii–v (Chicago, 1968), no. 17.

Pietro Aaron, *Thoscanello de la musica* (Venice, 1523 and later editions), Bk 1 ch. 38.

Giovanni Spataro, *Tractato di musica* (Venice, 1531), chs 15–16, ch. 24 and ch. 31.

Giovanni Spataro, letter to Pietro Aaron (replying to one dated 22 November 1532), Paris, Bibliothèque nationale, f.it.1110, f.66–66v.

Giovanni Spataro, letter to Pietro Aaron (replying to one dated 23 August 1533), loc. cit., f.73.

Sebald Heyden, *De arte canendi* (Nuremberg, 1540), Preface.

Adrian Petit Coclico, *Compendium musices* (Nuremberg, 1552), f.B4.

Hermann Finck, *Practica musica* (Wittenberg, 1556), f.A2.

Petrus Gregorius, *Syntacheon artis mirabilis* (Lyons, 1576 and many later editions), Bk 12 ch. 11.

Johannes Nucius, *Musices poeticae sive de compositione cantus* (Neisse, 1613), ch. 1.

Jean le Carpentier, *Histoire généalogique des païs-bas, ou Histoire de Cambray et du Cambrésis* (Leiden, 1664), ii, 475.

Johannes Moller, *Orationes duae inaugurales* (Frankfurt an der Oder, 1681), reference in speech 'De musica eiusque excellentia' (3 Jan. 1667). Relevant passage ed. Borren *Dufay*, 84.

François-Jean Foppens, *Compendium chronologicum episcoporum brugensium* (Bruges, 1731), 176.

Johann Gottfried Walther, *Musicalisches Lexicon* (Leipzig, 1732), 219.

Martin Gerbert, *Scriptores ecclesiastici de musica* (St Blasien, 1784), iii (edition of Adam von Fulda, *Musica*, 1490).

Johann Nicolaus Forkel, *Allgemeine Geschichte der Musik*, ii (Leipzig, 1801), pt 2 chs 32–7 (pp. 473–520), esp. p. 515.

Alexandre Choron and François Fayolle, *Dictionnaire historique des musiciens* (Paris, 1810–11), i, 194.

Ernst Ludwig Gerber, *Neues historisch-biographisches Lexikon der Tonkünstler* (Leipzig, 1812–14), i, 946.

André Le Glay, *Recherches sur l'église métropolitaine de Cambrai* (Paris, 1825), 199f.

[John Sainsbury], *Dictionary of Musicians* (London, 1825), i, 239.

Giuseppe Baini, *Memorie storico-critiche della vita e delle opere di Giovanni Pierluigi da Palestrina* (Rome, 1828), i, 102f, 139f, 358; ii, 400ff.

François-Joseph Fétis, 'Mémoire sur cette question: Quels ont été les mérites des Néerlandais dans la musique?' (1829), 12ff; printed in: Koninklijk-Nederlandsche Institut, *Verhandelingen over de vraag: Welke verdiensten hebben zich de nederlanders ... in het vak der toonkunst verworven* (Amsterdam, 1829).

Raphael Georg Kiesewetter, 'Die Verdienste der Niederländer um die Tonkunst' (1829), 16f, 19, 21, 180ff; printed in: Koninklijk-Nederlandsche Institut, op. cit.

Raphael Georg Kiesewetter, *Geschichte der europaeischen-abendlaendischen oder unsrer heutigen Musik* (Leipzig, 1834), 42–9 and music examples. English trans. by Robert Müller (London, 1848).

François-Joseph Fétis, *Biographie universelle des musiciens*, i (Paris, 1835): 'Résumé philosophique de l'histoire de la musique', cxcix-cci.

François-Joseph Fétis, *Biographie universelle des musiciens*, iii (Paris, 1836): 'Dufay', 349–51.


*(B) Publications since 1836*

This alphabetical listing aims to include all significant materials concerned with Dufay or his music.


Ambros, August Wilhelm, *Geschichte der Musik*, ii (Leipzig, 3/1891); iii (Leipzig, 3/1893)

Apfel, Ernst, 'H. Besseler, Bourdon und Fauxbourdon und die Tonalität', in *Aufsätze und Vorträge zur Musikgeschichte und historischen Musiktheorie* (Saarbrücken, 1977), 111–22

——, *Grundlagen einer Geschichte der Satztechnik vom 13. bis zum 16. Jahrhundert*, i (Saarbrücken, 1974)

——, 'Über den vierstimmigen Satz im 14. und 15. Jahrhundert', *Archiv für Musikwissenschaft*, xviii (1961), 34–51

Arnold, Robert, *Repertorium germanicum: Regesten aus den päpstlichen Archiven zur Geschichte des deutschen Reichs und seiner Territorien im XIV. und XV. Jahrhundert: Pontificat Eugen IV.*, i (Berlin, 1897)

Atlas, Allan W. (ed.), *Papers Read at the Dufay Quincentenary Conference, Brooklyn College, December 6–7, 1974* (Brooklyn, 1976)

Baix, François, 'La carrière "bénéficiale" de Guillaume Dufay (vers 1398–1474): notes et documents', *Bulletin de l'Institut historique belge de Rome*, viii (1928), 265–72

Bank, Joannes Antonius, *Tactus, Tempo and Notation in Mensural Music from the 13th to the 17th Century* (Amsterdam, 1972)

Bashour, Frederick Joseph, *A Model for the Analysis of Structural Levels and Tonal Movement in Compositions of the Fifteenth Century* (diss., Yale University, 1975)

Becherini, Bianca, 'Due canzoni di Dufay del codice fiorentino 2794', *La bibliofilia*, xliii (1941), 124–35

——, 'Relazioni di musici fiamminghi con la corte dei Medici: nuovi documenti', *La rinascita*, iv (1941), 84–112

Bent, Margaret, 'The Songs of Dufay: Some Questions of Form and Authenticity', *Early Music*, viii (1980), 454–9

Benthem, Jaap van, 'Ein verstecktes Quodlibet des 15. Jahrhunderts in *Fragmenter 17¹* der Kongelige Bibliotek zu Kopenhagen', *Tijdschrift*

*Dufay*

*van de Vereniging voor Nederlandse muziekgeschiedenis*, xxiii (1973), 1–11

Berlière, Ursmer, *Inventaire analytique des Diversa Cameralia des archives vaticanes (1389–1500) au point de vue des anciens diocèses de Cambrai, Liége, Thérouanne et Tournai* (Rome, 1906)

Besseler, Heinrich, *Bourdon und Fauxbourdon: Studien zum Ursprung der niederländischen Musik* (Leipzig, 1951; rev. 2nd edition by Peter Gülke, Leipzig, 1974) [citations include page references for both editions]

—— (ed.), *Guillelmi* [vols. ii & iii: *Guglielmi*] *Dufay: opera omnia*, 6 vols. (Rome, 1951–66), comprising: i: *Motetti* (1966); ii: *Missarum pars prior 1–6* (1960); iii: *Missarum pars altera 7–10* (1951); iii [a]: *Missarum pars altera: apparatus criticus* (1962); iv: *Fragmenta missarum* (1962); v: *Compositiones liturgicae minores* (1966); vi: *Cantiones* (1964) = CMM, I

——, 'Dufay', *Die Musik in Geschichte und Gegenwart*, iii (1954), cols. 889–912; text reprinted in Besseler, *Aufsätze zur Musikästhetik und Musikgeschichte*, ed. Peter Gülke (Leipzig, 1978), 276–95

——, 'Dufay in Rom', *Archiv für Musikwissenschaft*, xv (1958), 1–19; also, with added introduction, in *Miscelánea en homenaje a monseñor Higinio Anglés* (Barcelona, 1958–61), 111–34

——, 'Erläuterungen zu einer Vorführung ausgewählter Denkmäler der Musik des späten Mittelalters', in Wilibald Gurlitt (ed.), *Bericht über die Freiburger Tagung für deutsche Orgelkunst von 27. bis 30. Juli 1926* (Augsburg, 1926), 141–54

——, 'Falsche Autornamen in den Handschriften Strassburg (Vitry) und Montecassino (Dufay)', *Acta musicologica*, xl (1968), 201–3

——, 'Grundsätzliches zur Übertragung von Mensuralmusik', *Studien zur Musikwissenschaft*, xxv (1962), 31–8

——, *Die Musik des Mittelalters und der Renaissance* (Potsdam, 1931–4) = Handbuch der Musikwissenschaft, II

——, 'Neue Dokumente zum Leben und Schaffen Dufays', *Archiv für Musikwissenschaft*, ix (1952), 159–76

——, 'Von Dufay bis Josquin: ein Literaturbericht', *Zeitschrift für Musikwissenschaft*, xi (1928–9), 1–22

Bockholdt, Rudolf, 'Dufay', in Marc Honegger (ed.), *Dictionnaire de la musique*, i (Paris, 1970), 290–92; revised in *Sohlmans musiklexikon*, ii (Stockholm, 1975), 352–3; again revised in Marc Honegger and Günther Massenkeil (eds.), *Das grosse Lexikon der Musik*, ii (Freiburg, 1979), 372–5

——, 'Englische und franko-flämische Kirchenmusik in der ersten Hälfte des 15. Jahrhunderts', in Karl Gustav Fellerer (ed.), *Geschichte der katholischen Kirchenmusik*, i (Kassel, 1972), 418–37

——, 'Französische und niederländische Musik des 14. und 15. Jahrhunderts', in Thrasybulos G. Georgiades (ed.), *Musikalische Edition im Wandel des historischen Bewusstseins* (Kassel, 1971), 149–73

——, *Die frühen Messenkompositionen von Guillaume Dufay*, 2 vols. (Tutzing, 1960) = Münchner Veröffentlichungen zur Musikgeschichte, V

——, 'Die Hymnen in der Handschrift Cambrai 6: zwei unbekannte Vertonungen von Dufay?', *Tijdschrift van de Vereniging voor Nederlandse muziekgeschiedenis*, xxix/2 (1979), 75–91

——, 'Notizen zur Handschrift Trient '93' und zu Dufays frühen Messensätzen', *Acta musicologica*, xxxiii (1961), 40–47

——, Review of Hamm *Chronology* in *Die Musikforschung*, xx (1967), 221–2

Boorman, Stanley, 'The Early Renaissance and Dufay', *The Musical Times*, cxv, no. 1577 (July 1974), 560–65

Borghezio, Gino, 'La fondazione del collegio nuovo "Puerorum Innocentium" del Duomo di Torino', *Note d'archivio*, i (1924), 200–66

Borren, Charles van den, 'Dufay and his School', in Anselm Hughes and Gerald Abraham (eds.), *Ars Nova and the Renaissance: 1300–1540* (London, 1960), 214–38 = New Oxford History of Music, III

——, 'Guillaume Dufay (*c.* 1400–1474)', *The Score*, ii (1950), 26–36

——, 'Guillaume Dufay, centre de rayonnement de la polyphonie européenne à la fin du moyen âge', *Bulletin de l'Institut historique belge de Rome*, xx (1939), 171–85; also in *Revue belge de musicologie*, xxi (1967), 56–67

——, *Guillaume Dufay: son importance dans l'évolution de la musique au XVe siècle* (Brussels, 1926) = Académie royale de Belgique: Classe des beaux-arts, Mémoires, collection in 8vo, T. II, fasc. ii

——, *Etudes sur le quinzième siècle musical* (Antwerp, 1941)

——, 'A Light of the Fifteenth Century: Guillaume Dufay', *The Musical Quarterly*, xxi (1935), 279–97

—— (ed.), *Pièces polyphoniques profanes de provenance liégeoise (XVe siècle)* (Brussels, 1950) = Flores musicales belgicae, I

—— (ed.), *Polyphonia sacra: a Continental Miscellany of the Fifteenth Century* (Burnham, 1932, rev. 1962)

——, 'Du rôle international de la Belgique dans l'histoire musicale', *Société internationale de musicologie: premier congrès: Liége, 1930* (Burnham, s.d.), 17–31

Bouquet, Marie-Thérèse, 'La cappella musicale dei duchi di Savoia dal 1450 al 1500', *Rivista italiana di musicologia*, iii (1968), 233–85

Brenet, Michel [= Marie Bobillier], 'Guillaume Du Fay d'après de nouveaux documents', *Le ménestrel*, lii (1885–6), no. 37 [15 Aug 1886], 296–7; no. 38 [22 Aug], 304–5; no. 39 [29 Aug], 312–3; no. 40 [5 Sept], 319–20; no. 41 [12 Sept], 327–8; no. 43 [26 Sept], 344–5

Bridgman, Nanie, 'Dufay', in Guido M. Gatti and Alberto Basso (eds.), *La musica*, ii (Turin, 1966), 284–94

——, 'France and Burgundy: 1300–1500', in F.W. Sternfeld (ed.), *Music from the Middle Ages to the Renaissance* (London, 1973), 145–73 = A History of Western Music, I

——, *La vie musicale au quattrocento et jusqu'à la naissance du madrigal*

*(1400–1530)* (Paris, 1964)

Brown, Howard Mayer, *Music in the Renaissance* (Englewood Cliffs, 1976), 27–51 [revised version of 'Guillaume Dufay and the Early Renaissance', *Early Music*, ii (1974), 219–33]

Brown, Samuel Emmons, Jr., 'New Evidence of Isomelic Design in Dufay's Isorhythmic Motets', *JAMS*, x (1957), 7–13

——, *The Motets of Ciconia, Dunstable, and Dufay* (diss., Indiana University, 1962)

Bukofzer, Manfred Fritz, '*Caput redivivum:* a New Source for Dufay's *Missa Caput*', *JAMS*, iv (1951), 97–110

——, Review of Feininger *Propria* in *The Musical Quarterly*, xxxv (1949), 334–40

——, *Studies in Medieval & Renaissance Music* (New York, 1950)

Caraci, Maria, 'Fortuna del tenor "L'homme armé" nel primo rinascimento', *Nuova rivista musicale italiana*, ix (1975), 171–204

Carpenter, Patricia, 'Tonal Coherence in a Motet of Dufay', *Journal of Music Theory*, xvii (1973), 2–65

Castan, Auguste (with introduction by Gustave Bertrand), *Le compositeur musical Guillaume du Fay à l'église de Saint-Etienne de Besançon en 1458* (Besançon, 1881); also in *Mémoires de la Société d'émulation du Doubs* [Besançon], 5th ser., iii: 1878 (1879), 322–9; also as 'Une consultation musicale donnée à Besançon, en 1458, par le compositeur Guillaume du Fay', *Revue des sociétés savantes des départements*, 6th ser., vii (1878), 463–8

——, 'De l'éducation musicale du compositeur Guillaume du Fay', *Mémoires de la Société d'émulation du Doubs* [Besançon], 5th ser., iv: 1879 (1880), 217–20

Chew, Geoffrey, 'The Early Cyclic Mass as an Expression of Royal and Papal Supremacy', *Music & Letters*, liii (1972), 254–69

Clarke, Henry Leland, 'Musicians of the Northern Renaissance', in Jan LaRue (ed.), *Aspects of Medieval and Renaissance Music: a Birthday Offering to Gustave Reese* (New York, 1966), 67–81

Clercx, Suzanne, 'Aux origines du faux-bourdon', *Revue de musicologie*, xl (1957), 151–65

——, 'Dufay', *Riemann Musiklexikon* (12/1959–75), i, 427–9, and iv, 297

Cohen, Judith, 'Munus ab ignoto', *Studia musicologica*, xxii (1980), 187–204

Cordero di Pamparato, Stanislao, 'Guglielmo Dufay alla corte di Savoia', *Santa Cecilia – Torino*, xxvii/2, no. 272 (1925), 19–21; xxvii/3, no. 273 (1925), 34–6

Croll, Gerhard, 'Dufays Festmusik zur Florentiner Domweihe', *Österreichische Musikzeitung*, xxiii/10 (Oct. 1968), 538–47

——, *Festmusiken der Renaissance* (Salzburg, 1969)

Curtis, Gareth Richard Kenneth, 'Brussels, Bibliothèque royale MS. 5557, and the Texting of Dufay's "Ecce ancilla Domini" and "Ave regina celorum" Masses', *Acta musicologica*, li (1979), 73–86

——, *The English Masses of Brussels, Bibliothèque Royale, MS. 5557* (diss., University of Manchester, 1979)

D'Accone, Frank A., 'Antonio Squarcialupi alla luce di documenti inediti', *Chigiana*, xxiii [= New ser., iii] (1966), 3–24

——, 'The Singers of San Giovanni in Florence during the 15th Century', *JAMS*, xiv (1961), 307–58

Dahlhaus, Carl, *Untersuchungen über die Entstehung der harmonischen Tonalität* (Kassel, 1968) = Saarbrücker Studien zur Musikwissenschaft, II

Dammann, Rolf, 'Die Florentiner Domweihmotette Dufays', in Wolfgang Braunfels, *Der Dom von Florenz* (Olten, Lausanne and Freiburg im Breisgau, 1964), 73–85 = Architektur und Musik, I

Dangel-Hofmann, Frohmut, *Der mehrstimmige Introitus in Quellen des 15. Jahrhunderts* (Tutzing, 1975) = Würzburger musikhistorische Beiträge, III

Dannemann, Erna, 'Dufay', *Grove's Dictionary* (5/1954), ii, 793–5

——, *Die spätgotische Musiktradition in Frankreich und Burgund vor dem Auftreten Guillaume Dufays* (Strasburg, 1936) = Collection d'études musicologiques, XXII

Dartus, Edmond, *Un grand musicien cambrésien, Guillaume Du Fay* (Cambrai, 1974); also in *Mémoires de la Société d'émulation de Cambrai*, xciv (1974), 423–71

Davis, Shelley, 'The Solus Tenor in the 14th and 15th Centuries', *Acta musicologica*, xxxix (1967), 44–64, and xl (1968), 176–8

Delcroix, Fernand, 'La maîtrise de Cambrai', *Mémoires de la Société d'émulation de Cambrai*, lxviii (1921), 71–115

Demeuldre, Amé, *Les obituaires de la collégiale de Saint-Vincent à Soignies* (Soignies, 1904); also in *Cercle archéologique du canton de Soignies: annales*, ii/2 (1904), 101–350

Devillers, Léopold, *Chartes du chapitre de Sainte-Waudru de Mons*, iii (Brussels, 1908)

——, *Mémoire historique et descriptif sur l'église de Sainte-Waudru à Mons* (Mons, 1857)

Dewitte, Alfons, 'De geestelijkheid van de brugse Lieve-Vrouwkerk in de 16e eeuw', *Handelingen van . . . Société d'émulation te Brugge*, cvii (1970), 100–135

Dèzes, Karl, 'Das Dufay zugeschriebene *Salve regina* eine deutsche Komposition: stilkritische Studie', *Zeitschrift für Musikwissenschaft*, x (1927–8), 327–62

——, 'Van den Borrens "Dufay" ', *Zeitschrift für Musikwissenschaft*, x (1927–8), 294–307

Dubrulle, Henry, *Les bénéficiers des diocèses d'Arras, Cambrai, Thérouanne, Tournai sous le pontificat d'Eugène IV* (Louvain, 1908); also in *Analectes pour servir à l'histoire ecclésiastique de la Belgique*, 3rd ser., iv (1908)

Elders, Willem, 'Humanism and Early-Renaissance Music: a Study of the

Ceremonial Music by Ciconia and Dufay', *Tijdschrift van de Vereniging voor Nederlandse muziekgeschiedenis*, xxvii (1977), 65–101

——, Review of Nitschke *Dufay* in *Tijdschrift van de Vereniging voor Nederlandse muziekgeschiedenis*, xxi/3 (1970), 192–5

——, *Studien zur Symbolik in der Musik der alten Niederländer* (Bilthoven, 1968) = Utrechtse bijdragen tot de muziekwetenschap, IV

——, 'Zur Aufführungspraxis der altniederländischen Musik', in Jozef Robijns (ed.), *Renaissance-muziek 1400–1600: donum natalicium René Bernard Lenaerts* (Louvain, 1969), 89–104 = Musicologica lovaniensa, I

Fallows, David, 'Dufay and Nouvion-le-Vineux: Some Details and a Thought', *Acta musicologica*, xlviii (1976), 44–50

—— (ed.), *Guillaume Dufay: Two Songs* (London, 1975) = Early Music Series, XXIII

——, 'Robertus de Anglia and the Oporto Song Collection', in Ian D. Bent (ed.), *Source Materials and the Interpretation of Music: a Memorial Volume to Thurston Dart* (London, 1982), 99–128

——, 'Two more Dufay Songs Reconstructed', *Early Music*, iii (1975), 358–60, and iv (1976), 99

——, 'Words and Music in Two English Songs of the Mid-15th Century: Charles d'Orléans and John Lydgate', *Early Music*, v (1977), 38–43

Feininger, Laurence K.J. (ed.), *Missae auctore Gulielmo Dufay cum missis anonimis*, 4 fascicles (Rome, 1951–63) = Monumenta polyphoniae liturgicae sanctae ecclesiae romanae, 1st ser., II

—— (ed.), *Missae super L'homme armé*, 10 fascicles (Rome, 1948) = Monumenta polyphoniae liturgicae sanctae ecclesiae romanae, 1st ser., I

—— (ed.), *Auctorum anonymorum missarum propria XVI quorum XI Gulielmo Dufay auctori adscribenda sunt* (Rome, 1947) = Monumenta polyphoniae liturgicae sanctae ecclesiae romanae, 2nd ser., I

Ficker, Rudolf von, 'Die frühen Messenkompositionen der Trienter Codices', *Studien zur Musikwissenschaft*, xi (1924), 3–58

——, 'Zur Schöpfungsgeschichte des Fauxbourdon', *Acta musicologica*, xxiii (1951), 93–123

Fischer, Kurt von, 'Ecole franco-flamande du XVe siècle: centres artistiques; compositeurs; formes musicales', in Jacques Porte (ed.), *Encyclopédie des musiques sacrées*, ii (Paris, 1969), 280–97

——, 'Neue Quellen zur Musik des 13., 14. und 15. Jahrhunderts', *Acta musicologica*, xxxvi (1964), 79–97

Fortuna, Alberto Maria, with Cristiana Lunghetti (eds.), *Autografi dell'Archivio mediceo avanti il principato* (Florence, 1977) = Scriptorium florentinum, I

Gallo, F. Alberto, 'Citazioni da un trattato di Dufay', *Collectanea historiae musicae*, iv (1966), 149–52

Gerber, Rudolf (ed.), *Guillaume Dufay: sämtliche Hymnen* (Wolfenbüttel, 1937) = Das Chorwerk, XLIX

——, 'Römische Hymnenzyklen des späten 15. Jahrhunderts', *Archiv für Musikwissenschaft*, xii (1955), 40–73

Göllner, Theodor, 'Notationsfragmente aus einer Organistenwerkstatt des 15. Jahrhunderts', *Archiv für Musikwissenschaft*, xxiv (1967), 170–7

Gossett, Philip, 'Techniques of Unification in Early Cyclic Masses and Mass Pairs', *JAMS*, xix (1966), 205–31

Grunzweig, Armand, 'Notes sur la musique des Pays-Bas au XVe siècle', *Bulletin de l'Institut historique belge de Rome*, xviii (1937), 73–88

Gülke, Peter, 'Das Volkslied in der burgundischen Polyphonie des 15. Jahrhunderts', in *Festschrift Heinrich Besseler zum sechzigsten Geburtstag* (Leipzig, 1961), 179–202

Gurlitt, Wilibald, 'Burgundische Chanson- und deutsche Liedkunst des 15. Jahrhunderts', in Wolfgang Merian (ed.), *Bericht über den musikwissenschaftlichen Kongress in Basel . . . 1924* (Leipzig, 1925), 153–76

Haberl, Franz Xaver, *Bausteine für Musikgeschichte*, 3 vols. (Leipzig, 1885–8), comprising: i: 'Wilhelm du Fay: monographische Studie über dessen Leben und Werke', also in *Vierteljahrsschrift für Musikwissenschaft*, i (1885), 397–530; ii: 'Bibliographischer und thematischer Musikkatalog des päpstlichen Kapellarchives im Vatikan zu Rom', also in *Monatshefte für Musik-Geschichte*, xix–xx (1887–8), Beilage; iii: 'Die römische "schola cantorum" und die päpstlichen Kapellsänger bis zur Mitte des 16. Jahrhunderts', also in *Vierteljahrsschrift für Musikwissenschaft*, iii (1887), 189–296

Hamm, Charles E., *A Chronology of the Works of Guillaume Dufay Based on a Study of Mensural Practice* (Princeton, 1964) = Princeton Studies in Music, I

——, 'Dating a Group of Dufay Works', *JAMS*, xv (1962), 65–71

——, 'Dufay', *The New Grove*

——, 'Manuscript Structure in the Dufay Era', *Acta musicologica*, xxxiv (1962), 166–84

——, Review of Besseler *Dufay* vi in *The Musical Quarterly*, lii (1966), 244–54

——, 'The Manuscript San Pietro B 80', *Revue belge de musicologie*, xiv (1960), 40–55

——, 'The Reson Mass', *JAMS*, xviii (1965), 5–21

Handschin, Jacques, 'Les Etudes sur le XVe siècle musical de Ch. van den Borren', *Revue belge de musicologie*, i (1946–7), 93–9

Haydon, Glen, '*Ave maris stella* from Apt to Avignon', in Martin Ruhnke (ed.), *Festschrift Bruno Stäblein zum 70. Geburtstag* (Kassel, 1967), 79–91

Höfler, Janez, 'Der "Trompette de menestrels" und sein Instrument', *Tijdschrift van de Vereniging voor Nederlandse muziekgeschiedenis*, xxix/2 (1979), 92–132

Houdoy, Jules, *Histoire artistique de la cathédrale de Cambrai, ancienne église métropolitaine Notre-Dame* (Paris, 1880); also as Mémoires de la

*Dufay*

Société des sciences, de l'agriculture et des arts de Lille, 4th ser., VII (Lille, 1880)

Jonen, Alfons, 'Dufays Hymnenkompositionen und Fragen der Aufführungspraxis', *Musica sacra: Cäcilien-Verbands-Organ für die deutschen Diözesen im Dienste des kirchenmusikalischen Apostolats* [Bonn], lxxxiv (1964), 325–30

José, Marie, *Amédée VIII: le duc qui devint pape*, 2 vols. (Paris, 1962) = La maison de Savoie, II–III

——, 'Un musicien célèbre du XVe siècle à la cour de Savoie: Guillaume Dufay', *Revue de Savoie*, xi (1958), 249–58

Kade, Otto, 'Biographisches zu Antonio Squarcialupi dem Florentiner Organist im XV. Jahrhundert', *Monatshefte für Musik-Geschichte*, xvii (1885), 1–7 and 13–19

Kanazawa, Masakata, *Polyphonic Music for Vespers in the Fifteenth Century* (diss., Harvard University, 1966)

Kennedy, Josepha, 'Dufay and Don Pedro the Cruel', *The Musical Quarterly*, lxi (1975), 58–64

Keyser, Raphael de, *Het St. Donaaskapittel te Brugge (1350–1450): Bijdrage tot de studie van hogere geestelijkheed tijdens de late middeleeuwen* (diss., University of Louvain, 1972)

Kirsch, Winfried, *Die Quellen der mehrstimmigen Magnificat- und Te Deum-Vertonungen bis zur Mitte des 16. Jahrhunderts* (Tutzing, 1966)

Korte, Werner, *Die Harmonik des frühen 15. Jahrhunderts in ihrem Zusammenhang mit der Formtechnik* (Münster, 1929)

Kovarik, Edward, *Mid Fifteenth-century Polyphonic Elaborations of the Plainchant Ordinarium Missae* (diss., Harvard University, 1973)

——, 'The Performance of Dufay's Paraphrase Kyries', *JAMS*, xxviii (1975), 230–44

Kühner, Hans, 'Ein unbekannter Brief von Guillaume Dufay', *Acta musicologica*, xi (1939), 114–15

Lange, Augusta, 'Une lettre du duc Louis de Savoie au duc de Bourgogne à propos de Guillaume Du Fay', *Publication du Centre européen d'études burgondo-médianes*, ix (1967), 103–5

Lefebvre, Charles-Aimé [= Jean-Paul Faber], 'Biographie cambrésienne: 15e siècle: Guillaume Dufay', *Mémoires de la Société d'émulation de Cambrai*, xxvi (1858), 381–5

Lerner, Edward, R. 'The Polyphonic Magnificat in 15th-century Italy', *The Musical Quarterly*, l (1964), 44–58

Lockwood, Lewis, 'Aspects of the "L'homme armé" Tradition', *Proceedings of the Royal Musical Association*, c (1973–4), 97–122

——, 'Dufay and Ferrara', in Atlas *Dufay* (1976), 1–25

Lovegnée, Albert, *Le lieu de naissance de Guillaume du Fay compositeur wallon du XVe siècle: Soignies vers 1398 – Cambrai 1474* (Liège, 1974)

Lowinsky, Edward Elias, 'Laurence Feininger (1909–1976): Life, Work, Legacy', *The Musical Quarterly*, lxiii (1977), 327–66

Maas, Christianus Joannes, *Geschiedenis van het meerstemmig Magnificat tot omstreeks 1525* (Groningen, 1967)

MacClintock, Lander, 'Once More on the Pronunciation of Dufay', *Acta musicologica*, xxxvii (1965), 75–8

Mahrt, William Peter, 'Guillaume Dufay's Chansons in the Phrygian Mode', *Studies in Music from the University of Western Ontario*, v (1980), 81–98

Marggraf, Wolfgang, 'Tonalität und Harmonik in der französischen Chanson zwischen Machaut und Dufay', *Archiv für Musikwissenschaft*, xxiii (1966), 11–31

Marix, Jeanne, *Histoire de la musique et des musiciens de la cour de Bourgogne sous le règne de Philippe le Bon (1420–1467)* (Strasbourg, 1939) = Collection d'études musicologiques, XXVIII

——, (ed.), *Les musiciens de la cour de Bourgogne au XVe siècle . . .: Messes, motets, chansons* (Paris, 1937)

Mila, Massimo, *Guillaume Dufay*, 2 vols. (Turin, 1972–3)

——, 'Guillaume Dufay, musicista franco-borgognone', *Belfagor: rassegna di varia umanità*, xxxv (1980), 157–73

Monson, Craig, 'Stylistic Inconsistencies in a Kyrie Attributed to Dufay', *JAMS*, xxviii (1975), 245–67

Moroney, Davitt, 'Guillaume Dufay', *Music and Musicians*, xxiii/3, no. 267 (Nov. 1974), 20–23

Morse, Margaret Beverly, *A Quantitative Stylistic Analysis of the Agnus Dei Movements of Guillaume Dufay Supporting the Doubtful Authenticity of the Missa Caput* (M. Mus. diss., Hartt College of Music, 1974)

Nitschke, Wolfgang, *Studien zu den Cantus-firmus-Messen Guillaume Dufays* (Berlin, 1968) = Berliner Studien zur Musikwissenschaft, XIII

Obniska, Ewa, 'Dufay twórca nowej muzyki', *Ruch muzyczny*, xviii, no. 26 (22 Dec. 1974) 3–4

Orel, Alfred, *Die Hauptstimme in den 'Salve regina' der Trienter Codices* (diss., University of Vienna, 1919; repr. Tutzing, 1977, as Wiener Veröffentlichungen zur Musikwissenschaft, 2nd ser., IV)

——, *Über rhythmische Qualität in mehrstimmigen Tonsätzen des 15. Jahrhunderts* (Habilitationsschrift, University of Vienna, 1922; partially reprinted in *Zeitschrift für Musikwissenschaft*, vi (1923–4), 559–607)

Otterbach, Friedmann, *Kadenzierung und Tonalität im Kantilenensatz Dufays* (Munich and Salzburg, 1975) = Freiburger Schriften zur Musikwissenschaft, VII

Perkins, Leeman L., 'Toward a Rational Approach to Text Placement in the Secular Music of Dufay's time', in Atlas *Dufay* (1976), 102–14

——, with Howard Garey (eds.), *The Mellon Chansonnier*, 2 vols. (New Haven, 1979)

Pinchart, Alexandre, *Archives des arts, sciences et lettres*, 1st ser., iii (Ghent, 1881)

Pirro, André, *Histoire de la musique de la fin du XIVe siècle à la fin du XVIe* (Paris, 1940)

——, Review of Borren *Dufay* in *Revue musicale*, vii/3 (June 1926), 321–4

Pirrotta, Nino, 'Music and Cultural Tendencies in 15th-century Italy', *JAMS*, xix (1966), 127–61

——, 'On Text Forms from Ciconia to Dufay', in Jan LaRue (ed.), *Aspects of Medieval and Renaissance Music: a Birthday Offering to Gustave Reese* (New York, 1966), 673–82

Plamenac, Dragan, 'An Unknown Composition by Dufay?', *The Musical Quarterly*, xl (1954), 190–200; also as 'Une composition inconnue de Dufay?', *Revue belge de musicologie*, viii (1954), 75–83

Planchart, Alejandro Enrique, 'Guillaume Dufay's Masses: a View of the Manuscript Traditions', in Atlas *Dufay* (1976), 26–60

——, 'Guillaume Dufay's Masses: Notes and Revisions', *The Musical Quarterly*, lviii (1972), 1–23

Platelle, H., 'Cambrai et le Cambrésis au XVe siècle', *Revue du Nord*, lviii, no. 230 (July–Sept. 1976), 349–81

Polk, Keith, 'Ensemble Performance in Dufay's Time', in Atlas *Dufay* (1976), 61–75

Pope, Isabel, with Masakata Kanazawa (eds.), *The Musical Manuscript Montecassino 871* (Oxford, 1978)

Powell, Newman W., 'Fibonacci and the Gold Mean: Rabbits, Rumbas, and Rondeaux', *Journal of Music Theory*, xxiii (1979), 227–273

Randel, Don Michael, 'Emerging Triadic Tonality in the Fifteenth Century', *The Musical Quarterly*, lvii (1971), 73–86

Reaney, Gilbert (ed.), *Early Fifteenth-century Music*, 6 vols. to date (American Institute of Musicology, 1955–77) = CMM, XI

Reese, Gustave, *Music in the Renaissance* (New York, 1954, rev.2/1959)

Reeser, Eduard, 'Guillaume Dufay: "Nuper rosarum flores" 1436–1936', *Tijdschrift der Vereeniging voor Nederl. muziekgeschiedenis*, xv/3 (1938), 137–46

Reichert, Georg, 'Kirchentonart als Formfaktor in der mehrstimmigen Musik des 15. und 16. Jahrhunderts', *Die Musikforschung*, iv (1951), 35–48

Reynolds, Robert Davis, Jr., *Evolution of Notational Practices in Manuscripts between 1400–1450* (diss., Ohio State University, 1974)

Sandresky, Margaret Vardell, 'The Continuing Concept of the Platonic-Pythagorean System and its Application to the Analysis of Fifteenth-century Music', *Music Theory Spectrum*, i (1979), 107–120

Saraceno, Filippo, 'Giunta ai Giullari e menestrelli, viaggi, imprese guerresche dei principi d'Acaia (1390–1438)', *Curiosità e ricerche di storia subalpina* [Turin], iv (1880), 205–49 [apparently reprinted in Domenico Carutti (ed.), *Studi storici del conte Filippo Saraceno* (Pinerolo, 1894)]

Schering, Arnold, *Studien zur Musikgeschichte der Frührenaissance* (Leipzig, 1914)

Schneider, Norbert J., 'Die verminderte Quarte als Melodieintervall: eine musikalische Konstante von Dufay bis Schönberg', *Schweizerische Musikzeitung*, cxx/4 (July–Aug. 1980), 205–12

# Bibliography

Schoop, Hans, *Entstehung und Verwendung der Handschrift Oxford Bodleian Library, Canonici misc. 213* (Berne and Stuttgart, 1971) = Publikationen der Schweizerischen musikforschenden Gesellschaft, 2nd ser., XXIV

Schröder, Aukje Engelina, 'Les origines des lamentations polyphoniques au XVe siècle dans les Pays-Bas', in A. Smijers (ed.), *Société Internationale de Musicologie: 5ème congrès: Utrecht 1952* (Amsterdam, 1953), 352–9

Schuler, Manfred, 'Die Musik in Konstanz während des Konzils 1414–1418', *Acta musicologica*, xxxviii (1966), 150–68

——, 'Zur Geschichte der Kapelle Papst Eugens IV.', *Acta musicologica*, xl (1968), 220–7

——, 'Zur Geschichte der Kapelle Papst Martins V.', *Archiv für Musikwissenschaft*, xxv (1968), 30–45

Scott, Ann Besser, 'English Music in Modena, Biblioteca Estense, α.X. 1, 11 and Other Italian Manuscripts', *Musica disciplina*, xxvi (1972), 145–60

Sparks, Edgar H., *Cantus Firmus in Mass and Motet, 1420–1520* (Berkeley and Los Angeles, 1963)

Stainer, John, 'A Fifteenth Century MS. Book of Vocal Music in the Bodleian Library, Oxford', *Proceedings of the Musical Association*, xxii (1895–6), 1–22

Stainer, J.F.R., and C. (eds.), *Dufay and His Contemporaries* (London, 1898)

Stenzl, Jürg, *Repertorium der liturgischen Musikhandschriften der Diözesen Sitten, Lausanne und Genf*, i: *Diözese Sitten* (Freiburg, 1972)

——, 'Un fragment de Dufay au Grand-Saint-Bernard', *Revue musicale de Suisse Romande*, xxiv/1 (March 1971), 5–7

Stephan, Wolfgang, *Die burgundisch—niederländische Motette zur Zeit Ockeghems* (Kassel, 1937) = Heidelberger Studien zur Musikwissenschaft, VI

Strohm, Reinhard, 'Ein unbekanntes Chorbuch des 15. Jahrhunderts', *Die Musikforschung*, xxi (1968), 40–2

Tegen, Martin, 'Baselkonciliet och kyrkomusiken omkr. 1440', *Svensk tidskrift för musikforskning*, xxxix (1957), 126–31

Thibault, Geneviève, 'Quelques chansons de Dufay', *Revue de musicologie*, 2nd ser., xi (August 1924), 97–102

Toussaint, Joseph, *Les relations diplomatiques de Philippe le Bon avec le Concile de Bâle (1431–1449)* (Louvain, 1942) = Université de Louvain: Recueil de travaux d'histoire et de philologie, 3rd ser., IX

Trafiński, Adolf, 'Polski epizod z życia Dufeuille'a', *Ruch muzyczny*, xx/7 (28 March 1976), 9–10 [this article is a spoof, but is included here as a warning: several scholars already have wasted time trying to follow up its references and hypotheses]

Treitler, Leo, 'Dufay the Progressive', in Atlas *Dufay* (1976), 115–27

271

——, 'Tone System in the Secular Works of Guillaume Dufay', *JAMS*, xviii (1965), 131–69

Trowell, Brian, 'Proportion in the Music of Dunstable', *Proceedings of the Royal Musical Association*, cv (1978–9), 100–41

Trumble, Ernest, *Fauxbourdon: an Historical Survey*, i (Brooklyn, 1959) = Musicological Studies, III

——, 'An Interpretation of Dufay's *Juvenis qui puellam*', *Abstracts of Papers Read at the Forty-Fourth Annual Meeting of the American Musicological Society* (Minneapolis, 1978), 35–6

Ursprung, Otto, 'Der vokale Grundcharakter des diskantbetonten figurierten Stils', in Wolfgang Merian (ed.), *Bericht über den musikwissenschaftlichen Kongress in Basel . . . 1924* (Leipzig, 1925), 364–74

Van, Guillaume de (ed.), *Guglielmi Dufay: opera omnia*, 4 fascicles [of 20 planned] (Rome, 1947–9), comprising: i: *Motetti qui et cantiones vocantur* (1947); ii: *Motetti isorithmici dicti* (1948); iii: *Missa sine nomine* (1949); iv: *Missa Sancti Jacobi* (1949) = CMM, I

Vander Linden, Albert, 'A propos de Guillaume Dufay', *Revue belge de musicologie*, iii (1949), 44–6

——, 'Comment faut-il prononcer "Dufay"?', *Revue belge de musicologie*, xix (1965), 112–17

——, 'Guillaume Dufay fut-il chanoine de Soignies?', *Revue belge de musicologie*, xviii (1964), 28–31

——, 'Natus est ipse Fay', *Revue belge de musicologie*, iii (1949), 215

Vander Straeten, Edmond, *La musique aux Pays-Bas avant le XIXe siècle*, 8 vols. (Brussels, 1867–88)

Villard, Leon Jacques, *Text Underlay in the Mass Ordinary of Dufay and Some of his Contemporaries* (diss., Northwestern University, 1960)

Walker, Thomas, 'A Severed Head: Notes on a Lost English *Caput* Mass', *Abstracts of Papers Read at the Thirty-Fifth Annual Meeting of the American Musicological Society* (Saint Louis, 1969), 14–15

Ward, Tom R., 'The Polyphonic Office Hymn and the Liturgy of Fifteenth Century Italy', *Musica disciplina*, xxvi (1972), 161–88

——, *The Polyphonic Office Hymn 1400–1520: a Descriptive Catalogue* (American Institute of Musicology, 1980) = Renaissance Manuscript Studies, III

Warren, Charles W., 'Brunelleschi's Dome and Dufay's Motet', *The Musical Quarterly*, xliv (1973), 92–105

——, 'Punctus Organi and Cantus Coronatus in the Music of Dufay', in Atlas *Dufay* (1976), 128–43

Weis, J.E., *Julian von Speier (+1285): Forschungen zur Franziskus- und Antoniuskritik, zur Geschichte der Reimoffizien und des Chorals* (Munich, 1900) = Veröffentlichungen aus dem Kirchenhistorischen Seminar München, 1st ser., III

—— (ed.), *Die Choräle Julian's von Speier zu den Reimoffizien des Franziskus- und Antoniusfestes* (Munich, 1901) = Veröffentlichungen aus dem Kirchenhistorischen Seminar München, 1st ser., VI

Wolf, Johannes, 'Dufay und seine Zeit', *Sammelbände der Internationalen Musik-Gesellschaft*, i (1899–1900), 150–63 and 330

Wolff, Hellmuth Christian, *Die Musik der alten Niederländer* (Leipzig, 1956)

——, 'Dufay', in Claudio Sartori (ed.), *Enciclopedia della musica* [Ricordi], ii (Milan, 1964), 99–100

Wouters, Jos, *Harmonische verschijningsvormen in de muziek van de XIIIe tot de XVIe eeuw* (diss., University of Amsterdam, 1954)

Wright, Craig, 'Dufay at Cambrai: Discoveries and Revisions', *JAMS*, xxviii (1975), 175–229

——, *Music at the Court of Burgundy 1364–1419: a Documentary History* (Henryville, Ottawa and Binningen, 1979) = Musicological Studies, XXVIII

——, 'Musiciens à la cathédrale de Cambrai 1475–1550', *Revue de musicologie*, lxii (1976), 204–28

——, 'Performance Practices at the Cathedral of Cambrai 1475–1550', *The Musical Quarterly*, lxiv (1978), 295–328

Zenck, Hermann, Review of Van *Dufay* i–ii, in *Die Musikforschung*, iii (1950), 88–94

# Notes

## 1: Music in fifteenth-century society

1   For discussion see Vander Linden 'A propos de Guillaume Dufay', MacClintock 'Once More on the Pronunciation of Dufay', Vander Linden 'Comment faut-il prononcer "Dufay"?', and the summary in Fallows 'Nouvion-le-Vineux', 49 n22

## 2: First years: c. 1400–1414

1   References to original documents directly concerning Dufay's life appear in the notes to Appendix A.
2   Wright 'Dufay', 175.
3   Demeuldre *Obituaires*, 292.
4   Lovegnée *Soignies*.
5   'Item: messire Jehan Regis, chanoine de Songnies, qui fu clerc audict deffunct, avoit receu du personage de Watiebraine £16 13s 4d, et se li ont donné desdicts executeurs une chainture toute d'argent qui fu prisié £13; moiennant lesquelles parties s'est comprins et oblegié de fonder en ledicte eglise, comme il a fait, ung obit perpetuel pour ledict deffunct: sont £29 13s 4d' (Lille, Archives du Nord, 4G 1313, p. 35.)
6   Fétis 'Mémoire' (1829), 13f. See also Borren *Dufay*, 22ff. The treatise was sold to an English dealer in 1824 and has not been identified since; see also Gallo 'Citazioni'.
7   *Salve flos Tusce gentis* (i/15).
8   Vander Linden 'Natus'; see also Vander Linden 'Comment', 116. This emendation was taken over in the Besseler edition of Dufay's works.
9   Brenet 'Guillaume Du Fay', 304, names thirteen such places; Borren *Dufay*, 24f, names several more; see also Clarke 'Musicians', 73f, and Clarke's 'Communication' in *JAMS*, xxix (1976), 327.
10  Wright *Burgundy*, 97.
11  Fallows 'Nouvion-le-Vineux' implies this conclusion. In view of information subsequently provided by Chanoine Dartus on Jean de Hesdin (see n35 and Appendix C) and on Marie Dufay, I withdraw the argument presented in the last four paragraphs of that article; yet Dufay's established connections with Laon and that area must still eventually be explained.
12  Dartus *Du Fay*, 12f.

13  Wright 'Dufay', 176.

14  Le Glay *Recherches* (1825), 200.

15  Suggested to me by Planchart and by Dartus, who has some circumstantial evidence in its support.

16  Pirro *Histoire*, 54; Dartus *Du Fay*, 13; Wright 'Dufay', 176 n8.

17  Lille, Archives du Nord, 4G 1372, p. 64; payment to her by the executors is recorded on p. 17 of the same document.

18  Both of these documents were drawn to my attention by Chanoine Dartus when this book was at an advanced stage of preparation. Their implications go well beyond what is mentioned here, and they open the way to research that could entirely resolve the question of Dufay's birthplace and family. Huberti was also a canon of Ste-Waudru, Mons, and chaplain to Duke Albert of Bavaria at Mons. In that context he knew Jean de Binche, father of the composer Binchois; moreover the story involves Jean Vivien and Pierre Beye, both of whom so far have only a small place in Dufay's life-story. Yet the sparsity of relations mentioned in Dufay's will and its execution account makes the story seem perplexing.

19  Wright 'Performance', passim but especially p. 306.

20  Wright 'Musiciens', 205; it should be mentioned as a qualification of this comment that the bishop used it as part of his plea for more money to add to the glory of the cathedral, see Platelle 'Cambrai', 373f.

21  Houdoy *Cambrai*, 58f.

22  Ed. in Reaney *Early Fifteenth-century Music* iii, 1–24.

23  See Schoop *Entstehung*, 50f.

24  Ed. in Borren *Polyphonia*, no. 16; for attribution see Schoop *Entstehung*, 48f. The list of other continental 'cursiva' settings is short: a Gloria by Grenon, mentioned below, a Credo by Zacar (Reaney *Early Fifteenth-century Music* vi, 85–91) and two Gloria settings that are the complete surviving works of Bosquet (Reaney *Early Fifteenth-century Music* ii, 4–12). One fourteenth-century example is a Credo by Garinus, printed in CMM, XXIX, no.40. Several more do, however, appear in English manuscripts from the years around 1400, and the use of that technique might conceivably be construed as showing English influence among the composers mentioned. Further on the style, see Dannemann *Spätgotische Musiktradition*, 85, and Oliver Strunk's observations in *JAMS*, ii (1949), 107.

25  Ficker 'Schöpfungsgeschichte', 96; Hamm *Chronology*, 3.

26  Pirro *Histoire*, 75, suggests that the structure of the Credo of Dufay's Mass *Sancti Jacobi* (ii/2) shows Loqueville's influence, particularly in its duo/full alternation.

27  Trent 92, f. 121v (no. 1477). For Grenon's works see list in *The New Grove*, s.v. Some are published, but a complete edition is being prepared for a future volume of Reaney *Early Fifteenth-century Music*. The fullest discussion of his music is in Pirro *Histoire*, 63f.

28  Lille, Archives du Nord, 4G 6789: 1409–10, f. 4v–5.

29  ibid., 4G 6788, f.6 and f.6v.

30  Ed. in Reaney *Early Fifteenth-century Music* ii, 118–48.

31  Ed. in Reaney *Early Fifteenth-century Music* ii, 41–8; against possible influence of Lebertoul on Dufay, see Besseler *Bourdon*, 38ff/39f.

32  Ed. in Reaney *Early Fifteenth-century Music* ii, 14–18.

33  Houdoy *Cambrai*, 259; Vander Straeten *Pays-Bas* vii, 93, points out that one of the vielles had the inscription 'en bien le fay' and suggests that someone called Dufay could have made the instrument.

34  Pirro Review, 322; Pirro *Histoire*, 55f; the document is printed in *JAMS*, xxxiv (1981), 551–2.

35  Although he was a priest of Noyon, this offers no evidence of Dufay's origin since Jean de Hesdin had been fully resident at Cambrai Cathedral since at least 1401. I am grateful to Chanoine Dartus for this information.

36  Schuler 'Konstanz', 167; Wright 'Dufay', 177.

37  Max Lens, quoted in Louis Salembier, *Le cardinal Pierre d'Ailly* (Tourcoing, 1932), 53.

38  Salembier, op. cit., 92; on the duties of a *chantre*, see Wright *Burgundy*, 13 n14.

39  The complete poem is edited in Palémon Glorieux (ed.), *Jean Gerson: Oeuvres complètes*, vii/1 (Paris, 1966), 144–54; on its authorship, see Pierre-Yves Badel, 'Pierre d'Ailly auteur du *Jardin amoureux*', *Romania*, xcvii (1976), 369–81.

40  Wright 'Dufay', 178, misreads this as a single cushion.

### 3: Constance, Rimini, Laon and Bologna: 1414–1428

1  J. H. Mundy in Louise Ropes Loomis, *The Council of Constance: the Unification of the Church* (New York, 1961), 3.

2  The only composers that can be documented there are Oswald von Wolkenstein and Hugo von Montfort, see Schuler 'Konstanz', 167.

3  Pirrotta 'Text Forms', 676ff; Lockwood 'Dufay and Ferrara', 2.

4  Wright 'Dufay', 177.

5  Schuler 'Konstanz', 150.

6  Schuler 'Konstanz', 163.

7  Schuler 'Konstanz', 158.

8  Schuler 'Konstanz', 159. One manuscript of the chronicle omits any mention of the *prosunen*, but the chronicle itself was originally written in Latin: this version is now lost, and the version cited here is normally thought to be the most reliable, see Höfler 'Trompette de menestrels', 131 n143.

9  Schuler 'Konstanz', 165.

10  In addition Wright *Burgundy*, 52 n205, gives evidence for instruments other than the organ used for Mass at Paris in 1412.

11  This idea is offered in Frank Ll. Harrison, *Music in Medieval Britain* (London, 1958), 245. Wright *Burgundy*, 159f, presents information

suggesting that the Burgundian court had a carefully planned musical embassy at the Council of Constance.

12  The whole passage appears in Borren *Dufay*, 53f.

13  Their complete surviving works are edited in Reaney *Early Fifteenth-century Music* i.

14  As a qualification to several important studies of fifteenth-century style it should be pointed out that Martin le Franc nowhere says or even implies that Dufay and Binchois began composing in the continental style and then changed when they heard English music. This is a misconception based originally on a mistranscription in Fétis, see Borren *Dufay*, 54 n2.

15  Wright 'Dufay', 177; Louis Salembier, *Le cardinal Pierre d'Ailly* (Tourcoing, 1932), 248ff.

16  See Donald M. Nicol, *The Last Centuries of Byzantium* (London, 1972), 345f, and John W. Barker, *Manuel II Palaeologus (1391–1425): a Study of Late Byzantine Statesmanship* (New Brunswick, 1969), 348. The wedding took place in January; authorities differ as to whether it was in Constantinople (where John, the elder son and future emperor, married Sofia de Montefeltro on the same day) or at Mistra, the capital of the Morea; see Steven Runciman, *Mistra* (London, 1980), 69.

17  The dates, first established by Besseler ('Neue Dokumente', 160ff), have been questioned, particularly on the grounds that Cleofe is claimed in the text to be fluent in both languages (i.e. Italian and Greek) – 'utraque lingua facunda'. Besseler's suggestion that she had started learning Greek at the time of the engagement seems dangerous. See also Pirrotta 'Text Forms', 678. In addition, Hugo's *Tra quante regione* includes the line, addressed to Cleofe, 'Tu fosti albergo de Elena regina'. This might just imply that the Empress Helena had stayed in Pesaro or Rimini; but it seems to mean that Cleofe had already lived in Byzantine lands for some time. Yet while these questions are pending probability seems to favour Besseler's arguments.

18  Ed. in Borren *Pièces*, no. 32.

19  Ed. in Borren *Polyphonia*, no. 27.

20  Again the documentation is due to Besseler's brilliant researches. All political histories, to this day, erroneously follow Clementini in putting the wedding seven years too early. The papal dispensation, which may have been easily achieved since Vittoria was the pope's niece, is dated 30 May 1423, see Besseler 'Neue Dokumente', 162f. Until Besseler established this date studies of Dufay often suggested a much earlier birthdate for the composer to take account of so masterly a piece written apparently in 1416.

21  More complexity in purely mensural terms appears in Hugo de Lantins' brief rondeau *Je suy extent,* ed. Borren *Pièces*, no. 25; and comparison suggests that the two works could represent some kind of rivalry (particularly in view of both composers' having written works for

Cleofe's departure in 1420). But Dufay's is musically by far the more complex work.

22  See Antoine Bon, *La Morée franque* (Paris, 1969), i, 290ff.

23  Again, the evidence and the arguments for this are brilliantly laid out in Besseler 'Neue Dokumente', 163ff.

24  Practically all trace of these is gone, but for a reference to 'several churches here dedicated to [St Andrew]' and a description of two of them see George Wheler [= Wheeler], with Dr [Jacob] Spon of Lyons, *A Journey into Greece* (London, 1682), 294f.

25  In any case the formerly amicable relations between the Rimini and Pesaro branches of the family changed for the worse some time between 1423 and 1425, see Philip J. Jones, *The Malatesta of Rimini and the Papal State* (Cambridge, 1974), 166f.

26  Most fully described and discussed in Pirro Review, 322; a curtailed version of the story is in Pirro *Histoire*, 61.

27  Wright 'Dufay', 178 n18. Pirro *Histoire*, 61, and José 'Un musicien', 250, suggest improbably that this experience may have led to the composition of *Je me complains* (vi/14).

28  Oxford, Bodleian Library, Can. misc. 213; see particularly Schoop *Entstehung*, 118f; see also below p.285 n13.

29  Schoop *Entstehung*, 43.

30  Earlier writers suggested that it was for a plague in Milan (Haberl *Bausteine* i, 83; Pirro *Histoire*, 72), but this presumably derives from a misreading of the line 'Tu mediolanus civis' which is simply an address to St Sebastian as having supposedly been Milanese. Besseler 'Dufay in Rom', 4f, suggested association with a plague at Rome in 1429 but evidently reconsidered this, for in his edition of the motets (1966) he made no reference to the suggestion and placed the work much earlier. During the years 1419–23 there was plague in many parts of Lombardy, see Walter Brandmüller, *Das Konzil von Pavia–Siena 1423–24*, i (Münster, 1968), 97.

31  Commentary to i/8.

32  Commentary to i/9.

33  Haberl *Bausteine* i, 102, notes that the papal letters patent of 24 April 1431 fail to describe Dufay as a priest. I cannot resolve this discrepancy except to say that the Cambrai document of 1428 unambiguously describes him as 'presbiter'.

34  Earlier writers suggested that Auclou was in Paris until 1428. This was first questioned in Clercx 'Aux origines', 160ff; and Planchart 'View', 27, has demonstrated that it goes back to a misreading of documents at Besançon.

35  Suggested in Planchart 'View', 29.

36  Planchart 'View', 33, suggested that it was for the Augustinian council at San Giacomo Maggiore in 1425, but there is no evidence of Dufay's presence in Bologna so early.

37  Planchart 'View', 28f. Note, however, that although Planchart success-

fully demolishes the case for the Mass having been composed for St-Jacques-de-la-Boucherie in Paris, he brings no direct evidence to associate it with the church in Bologna.

38  His death was received 'cum grandissimi pianti de citadini, perché era molto dilecto da tutto el populo', see Jones, op. cit. (n25 above), 165.

39  Wright 'Dufay', 178; Gabriel Pérouse, *Le cardinal Louis Aleman* (Paris, 1904), 82–5.

40  Wright 'Dufay', 187, and José 'Un musicien', 251.

41  The information that it was a *prebenda libera jurista* comes only from an eighteenth-century manuscript at Cambrai, Ms. 1046, f. 86; but it is endorsed by Dufay's funeral monument which credits him with the degree.

42  Pirro *Histoire*, 63, quotes Pérouse, op. cit. (n39 above), 73, who cites, for a whole series of statements, Bologna, Archivio di stato, Campioni III, ff. 329, 330, 338v etc.

## 4: The papal chapel and Savoy: 1428–1439

1  Schuler 'Konstanz', 155; in 1409 Pope Alexander V had a chapel of twelve singers and two clerics, see Schuler 'Martin V', 31 n6.

2  Haberl *Bausteine* i, 65.

3  Schuler 'Martin V', 33 and passim.

4  Marix *Histoire*, 165.

5  Full list in Haberl *Bausteine* i, 60.

6  Schuler 'Martin V', 32f.

7  Trent 87, f.51v–52 (no.30).

8  Ed. Reaney *Early Fifteenth-century Music* ii, 90–93.

9  Baix 'Carrière bénéficiale', 267.

10  Schuler 'Eugen IV', 220.

11  Dewitte 'Geestelijkheid', 111f, confuses the issue by describing Dufay as cantor and chaplain at St-Donatien from 1431. In fact the document concerned (Bruges, Archief van het bisdom, Reeks A 50, f. 201) is a chapter act of 3 September 1431 ratifying letters from Pope Eugenius IV – dated 24 April, received 12 June – requesting an expectative for Guillelmus du Fay 'cantor et capellanus papae'.

12  Ed. in CMM, XXXV/ii, no. 10.

13  Haberl *Bausteine* i, 66.

14  This date has been much disputed. Hamm *Chronology*, 67–70, following Haberl *Bausteine* i, 88, and adding new evidence, suggests a date nearer 1436. Since the work is so different from anything else of Dufay's it is difficult to reach a firm decision. Reynolds *Evolution*, 384ff, answers some of Hamm's queries.

15  For text sources and discussion see Van *Dufay* ii, XI–XIII.

16  For a full account, see Joseph Aschbach, *Geschichte Kaiser Sigmund's*, iv (Hamburg, 1845), 107–14. The wrong dating of the motet has a curious and disturbing history. It seems to have originated as one of

Rudolf von Ficker's characteristically wild ideas, and was incorporated into his edition, DTO, LXXVI, Jg. xl (Vienna, 1933), 100. It was followed in Van *Dufay* ii, XVII, where the information is based on Edmond Martène and Ursin Durand (eds.), *Veterum scriptorum . . . amplissima collectio*, viii (Paris, 1733), cols. 579–82 – a collection of documents which de Van misunderstood by not referring to more recent historical studies. Unfortunately he also had a misprint in his commentary, citing vol. 5 instead of vol. 8. Evidently Besseler, when he came to re-edit the motets, looked up the reference in vol. 5 and, finding no relevant information, simply turned to a more obvious source, Ferdinand Gregorovius, *Geschichte der Stadt Rom im Mittelalter*, vii (Stuttgart, 1870), 38f; see Besseler *Dufay* i, XVIII. But he failed to note that Gregorovius not only makes no mention of a treaty of Viterbo but presents the correct story, though in a much more compact form than in Aschbach. Pirro *Histoire*, 70, identified the occasion correctly but has apparently been ignored by all subsequent writers. The Poggio quote is from his *Historiae de varietate fortunae* (Paris, 1723), 92f. On the iconography of Filarete's relief (which has sometimes been differently construed), see Carroll William Westfall, *In This Most Perfect Paradise: Alberti, Nicholas V, and the Invention of Conscious Urban Planning in Rome, 1447–55* (University Park, Pennsylvania, 1974), 8–15.

17  Bent 'Songs', 457f.
18  See in particular Besseler 'Dufay in Rom'.
19  Hamm 'Dating a Group'; Ward 'Hymn and Liturgy', 181–6.
20  See also Haberl *Bausteine* i, 102. Hamm *Chronology*, 37–74, places very few works in this timespan. Apart from those already mentioned he offers only *O sancte Sebastiane* (i/8, placed considerably earlier by Besseler, see above p.28), *C'est bien raison* (vi/16, for which he accepts Besseler's date of 1433, but see below), *Vergene bella* (vi/5, which, to judge from its position in the manuscript BL, must be considerably earlier), *O beate Sebastiane* (i/4), and two songs, *Belle, veulliés moy retenir* (vi/30) and *Belle, veuilliés vostre mercy* (vi/47). Beyond that he places (p. 35) a group of sixteen works in the long timespan 1423–33: two are spurious, at least two more are almost certainly from the Savoy years, and one (*Adieu ces bons vins* vi/27) is dated 1426. To some extent these dates are restricted by the assumption that Dufay had by 1429 discarded major prolation as the main mensuration for a work; but at least they give a striking picture of how few works are now associated with the Roman years.
21  He would have studied at the Studium of the Roman Curia which remained active (particularly in canon law) while the city university was in considerable financial difficulties. See: D. S. Chambers, 'Studium urbis and *gabella studii*', in Cecil H. Clough (ed.), *Cultural Aspects of the Italian Renaissance: Essays in Honour of Paul Oskar Kristeller* (Manchester, 1974), 68–110; Raymond Creytens, 'Le "Studium romanae curiae" et le maître du sacré palais', *Archivum*

*fratrum praedicatorum*, xii (1942), 5–83; Hastings Rashdall (ed. F. M. Powicke and A. B. Emden), *The Universities of Europe in the Middle Ages* (Oxford, 1936), ii, 28–31, which includes the observation that the pope could permit degrees after a curtailed course or even no course at all.

22 See Joseph Gill, *Eugenius IV: Pope of Christian Union* (London, 1961), passim, for the material in this paragraph.

23 Haberl *Bausteine* i, 66f.

24 On the iconography of this picture see José *Amédée VIII* i, 424f, and Clément Gardet, *Le livre d'heures du duc Louis de Savoie* (Annecy, 1960). It is generally thought to represent Louis and his father Amadeus VIII (surmounted by a tiara) crowning Anne de Lusignan. Strictly speaking the figures in the picture are God the Father and the Son crowning the Virgin, but the figures of Louis and Amadeus are unmistakable. Anne is not known from any firmly identified portrait of the time – despite her famed beauty – but the young lady represented here appears several more times in this manuscript, and identification with Anne seems more than likely. This conflation of sacred and secular themes is particularly characteristic of fifteenth-century art (another prominent example being ills. 9–10); it also occurs in Dufay's music.

25 For fuller information on the occasion see Samuel Guichenon, *Histoire généalogique de la royale maison de Savoye* (Lyons, 1660), ii, 476 and 521.

26 See Besseler *Bourdon*, 51ff/50ff, and Höfler 'Trompette de menestrels', 94f.

27 All this information from Saraceno 'Giunta', 235, and Borghezio 'Fondazione', 207ff and 217–33.

28 Ed. in Reaney *Early Fifteenth-century Music* ii, 1–4; the editor records three possible identifications for Adam, but none seems so convincing as the one offered here. See also Cordero 'Dufay', 20f.

29 See Besseler's commentary to vi/16, and Lockwood 'Dufay and Ferrara', 2f.

30 Borghezio 'Fondazione', 209, points out that Adamo Grand is recorded as 'maestro dei putti', as opposed to 'maestro di canto', on 24 December 1433. This might imply that Dufay had arrived by then.

31 François Morand (ed.), *Chronique de Jean le Févre*, ii (Paris, 1881), 287–97, from which all the information in the previous paragraph comes.

32 Marix *Histoire*, 242, gives the earliest surviving chapel list, from 1436.

33 His comments have been taken as referring to the Savoy chapel, but Wright 'Dufay', 179, showed that this is to misread the chronicle.

34 Marix *Histoire*, 117. A tradition going back to Pinchart *Archives* iii, 152, erroneously gives January 1435 as the date of their arrival, thus encouraging the idea that the occasion described was the Peace of Arras in August to December 1435, at which Dufay cannot have been present since he was in the papal choir at the time. For arguments that it was at

the Chambéry wedding see Wright 'Dufay', 180, and Fallows 'Two More Dufay Songs', 360 n4.

35 Marix *Histoire*, 30 n1.

36 Pirro *Histoire*, 75. Besseler, in his commentary to iv/23, here as elsewhere was evidently not aware of Pirro's work and assigned the Gloria to Quadragesima, the first Sunday in Lent, whereas the title in the only manuscript clearly refers to 'Caresme' – Shrovetide. Elders 'Aufführungspraxis', 91–5, attempts to associate the work with Holy Saturday on the basis of its sevenfold tenor repetition.

37 See below, pp. 88 and 173f.

38 These documents could refer to the same payment.

39 This parish had a special place in Amadeus's affections, see José *Amédée VIII* ii, 192f.

40 Cf. Hamm 'Dating a Group'. It might be suggested that Dufay would be expected to return to Savoy in time for the birth of the first child of the marriage, the future Duke Amadeus IX, born at Thonon on 1 February 1435.

41 Ward 'Hymn and Liturgy', 181–6.

42 See especially Hamm 'Dating a Group'.

43 Ludwig Pastor, *Geschichte der Päpste*, i (Freiburg im Breisgau, 1886), 229 n1, reports that Eugenius was the twenty-sixth pope to flee from Rome.

44 Giannozzo Manetti, 'Oratio de secularibus et pontificalibus pompis in consecratione basilicae florentinae' (1436); complete modern edition in appendix to Eugenio Battisti's article 'Il mondo visuale delle fiabe', *Archivio di filosofia, 1960, ii/iii: Umanesimo e esoterismo* (Padua, 1960), 291–320, on pp. 310–20. The sections that mention music are printed in Haberl *Bausteine* iii, 34, and Van *Dufay* ii, XXVII. For a list of the seven surviving manuscripts see Heinz Willi Wittschier, *Giannozzo Manetti: das Corpus der Orationes* (Cologne and Graz, 1968), 52–8, where there is a sensitive description of the treatise, its rhetorical techniques and its position as Manetti's first surviving work.

45 Haberl *Bausteine* i, 68. Dammann 'Domweihmotette', 85, states without further documentation that the cathedral musicians in March 1436 included a *joueur de bombarde* and four German minstrels.

46 Fully described in Warren 'Brunelleschi's Dome and Dufay's Motet', though Warren's figures on the proportions of the building seem open to discussion.

47 Hamm *Chronology*, 89; Besseler 'Dufay in Rom', 6f, places it in his Roman years.

48 See below, pp. 179ff.

49 See Elders 'Humanism', 77.

50 Lockwood 'Dufay and Ferrara', 3, mentions one such visit in June 1436.

51 As did Besseler 'Neue Dokumente', 166f, and commentary to vi/16.

52 As did Lockwood 'Dufay and Ferrara', 3.

53 Haberl *Bausteine* i, 67, and Brenet 'Guillaume Du Fay', 312, imply that he left because he had secured his Cambrai canonry and therefore no longer needed papal patronage.

54 Pastor, op. cit. (n43), 235. For fuller details see Joachim W. Stieber, *Pope Eugenius IV, the Council of Basel, and the Secular and Ecclesiastical Authorities in the Empire* (Leiden, 1978), 19–44.

55 Pastor, op. cit., 236.

56 Earlier writers suggested that he stayed there for seven years, but this is impossible in view of the information in Grunzweig 'Notes', 76ff, and especially Pirro *Histoire*, 87; see also Wright 'Dufay', 181–7.

57 This suggestion derives from a related suggestion put forward in Trumble 'Interpretation'. The text of the work is translated in Elders 'Humanism', 101.

58 As noted in Warren 'Brunelleschi's Dome and Dufay's Motet', 97.

59 All the documentation is cited in Besseler 'Neue Dokumente', 167–70, where there is a brilliant reconstruction of the opening line of the motet and an object-lesson in documentary research. Two years later, Count Philip was apparently to supply no fewer than eight hundred musicians of his own for the entry of Amadeus VIII into Basle as Pope Felix V, see José *Amédée VIII* ii, 197f.

60 Cordero 'Dufay', 34.

61 See José *Amédée VIII* ii, 184f, for a map of Europe showing which powers supported Felix V as pope.

62 In April–May 1439 Philip the Good, using all his diplomatic and political powers, managed to secure the appointment of Jean de Bourgogne – his illegitimate half-brother – as Bishop of Cambrai.

## 5: Interim assessment: 1440

1 See Roger Bowers, 'Some Observations on the Life and Career of Lionel Power', *Proceedings of the Royal Musical Association*, cii (1975–6), 103–27.

2 See above, p.28.

3 Noted in Pirro *Histoire*, 81f.

4 See the entry in Appendix C.

5 The minstrel Peroneto des Ayes was at the court of Savoy during Dufay's first visit there (see p.40), but the name is relatively common and the wording of the song seems to imply that Perinet is the poet.

6 I shall tentatively suggest on musical grounds (p.178) that this song was for the court of Savoy.

7 If Pope Eugenius had any control of this it seems unlikely that any such music would have been allowed in his choir, for he was highly ascetic in his habits.

8 Anthony Pryer has privately communicated to me ideas that suggest an affirmative answer to this question.

9 I have attempted to characterize his work from this point of view in *The*

*New Grove*, s.v. 'Binchois', §.8.

10   See below, pp. 71 and 75.

11   No attempt is made here to discuss the manuscripts in detail or to itemize the extensive bibliography concerning them. For details see: the commentaries to the volumes of the complete edition; *The New Grove*, s.v. 'Sources, MS'; and Charles Hamm and Herbert Kellman (eds.), *Census-Catalogue of Manuscript Sources of Polyphonic Music 1400–1550* (American Institute of Musicology, 1979–) = Renaissance Manuscript Studies, I.

12   Bockholdt 'Hymnen' suggests that they could be later, but his evidence seems forced, see below p.288 n10.

13   For evidence that they are dates of composition, not of copying, see Fallows 'Nouvion-le-Vineux', 46, and literature cited there; but note that the one apparently anomalous date mentioned there has now been shown to be correct by Hans Schoop, see *The New Grove*, s.v. 'Antonius de Civitate Austrie'. Material there and in Schoop *Entstehung* surely closes the matter. Over the years scholarly caution has repeatedly resisted the view that they are composition dates; but it now seems to be a caution based on incomplete assessment of the manuscript and of the literature concerning it.

14   See above p.35.

15   Lockwood 'Dufay and Ferrara', 8ff, but note that the watermark evidence is interpreted rather more narrowly then it was intended, that the main evidence is based on a payment for binding 'a large music book' in 1448, and that some of the argument seems too eager to associate payment records that happen to survive with manuscripts that happen to survive.

16   Feininger *Propria*.

## 6: Cambrai and the south: 1439–1458

1   See Wright 'Dufay', 182.

2   List taken from the chapter acts for 1442 (Lille, Archives du Nord, 4G 1090); information on papal singers from Haberl *Bausteine*, Schuler 'Martin V' and Schuler 'Eugen IV'.

3   Translation after Wright 'Dufay', 191f.

4   For a street-map of the area including Dufay's house and Grenon's see Wright 'Dufay', 211; an eighteenth-century floorplan of the house itself is on op. cit., 213.

5   Lille, Archives du Nord, 4G 7762:1441–2, f.9. For other documents on Petrus see Wright 'Dufay', 222 – firmly eliminating speculations in Kennedy 'Dufay and Don Pedro the Cruel'.

6   Lille, Archives du Nord, 4G 7762:1447–8, f.11v.

7   Loc. cit., f.12v.

8   As first noted in Clarke 'Musicians', 70.

9   Toussaint *Relations*, 175; see also Houdoy *Cambrai*, 375f.

10   Dupont, *Histoire ecclésiastique et civile de la ville de Cambrai et du Cambrésis* (Cambrai, [*c*. 1759–67, issued in seven parts]), ii (part 4), iv–xv, on p.xii.

11   Dupont, op. cit., xiii–xiv, and Houdoy *Cambrai*, 402.

12   Plamenac 'Unknown Composition'.

13   Scott 'English Music', 157–60, suggests the arrival of Lionel Power at the Council of Ferrara; but Dufay was certainly not at Ferrara since he was aligned with the competing Council of Basle, and there is no evidence that Power was at either. Kennedy 'Dufay and Don Pedro the Cruel', 62ff, associates the work with the translation to Madrid of the remains of Don Pedro (King of Castile, 1350–69) in 1447 – extrapolating from the demonstrably false hypothesis that *Fulgens iubar* was associated with that king.

14   A document on music copying printed in Lefebvre 'Biographie', 385 (and Borren *Dufay*, 17), is incorrectly dated May 1445 for May 1446.

15   For copying payments see Houdoy *Cambrai*, 188–201, and Wright 'Dufay', docs. 16–20. Many more such payments appear in the accounts used there, those of the *Office de la fabrique*. One item from 1442–3 shows that the recopying of the chant books was being planned at that date: 'Item: instituti sunt magistro Nicolao Grenon pro exemplo cuiusdam scriptoris de Duaco ad videndum si sufficiet eius scriptura ad faciendum antiphonaria pro ecclesia: 3s 4d' (Lille, Archives du Nord, 4G 4649, f.26). Perhaps the scribe who was being examined was the one who was eventually employed, Girard Sohier of Douai.

16   *The New Grove*, s.v. 'Binchois'.

17   Bruges, Archief van het bisdom, Reeks A 51, f. 142v–143 (chapter acts for May 1445).

18   Discussed in Devillers *Mémoire*, 6f.

19   Wright 'Dufay', 185.

20   Dupont, op. cit. (n10), ii (part 4), xvi–xxi, on p.xxi.

21   Bruges, Archief van het bisdom, Reeks A 51, f.38v (30 June 1440).

22   Loc. cit., f.15 (15 June 1439).

23   Wright 'Dufay', 185.

24   Wright 'Dufay', 203f.

25   Horst Woldemar Janson, *The Sculpture of Donatello* (Princeton, 1957), ii, 170 and 184.

26   Janson, op. cit., ii, 110.

27   Janson, op. cit., ii, 232–5.

28   F. Alberto Gallo, 'Marchetus in Padua und die "franco-venetische" Musik des frühen Trecento', *Archiv für Musikwissenschaft*, xxxi (1974), 42–56; see also *The New Grove*, s.v. 'Marchetto da Padova'.

29   The basilica had no cappella until 1487, though there was a large organ with fifty-six pipes begun in 1436 and organists are recorded from early in the fourteenth century. See *The New Grove*, s.v. 'Padua', and Erice Rigoni, 'Organari italiani e tedeschi a Padova nel quattrocento', *Note d'archivio*, xiii (1936), 7–21.

30 Planchart 'View', 38ff. The suggestion was originally based on a date for the wedding contract as 14 February 1450 instead of the correct date, 1451, only three weeks before the precipitate wedding itself; during that time Dufay was in Cambrai. Professor Planchart generously informs me that he accordingly rejects his earlier proposal.

31 Bouquet 'Cappella', passim.

32 Borghezio 'Fondazione', 210.

33 Samuel Guichenon, *Histoire généalogique de la royale maison de Savoye* (Lyons, 1660), i, 557. This was suggested to me by Alejandro Planchart who discusses it in an article to be published in *Studi musicali*.

34 Gaston du Fresne de Beaucourt, *Histoire de Charles VII*, vi (Paris, 1891), 72–5; Bouquet 'Cappella', 245.

35 Pierre Champion, *Vie de Charles d'Orléans* (Paris, 1911), 682.

36 Fallows 'Two More Dufay Songs', 359f.

37 The letter has sometimes been dated 1454, but for the dating 1456 see Grunzweig 'Notes', 73ff, and, more briefly, Wright 'Dufay', 190.

38 Three related chronicles record the complete text of a lament for Constantinople performed at the *Banquet du voeu* in Lille on 17 February 1454, see the collated edition in Gaston du Fresne de Beaucourt (ed.), *Chronique de Mathieu d'Escouchy* (Paris, 1863–4), ii, 154–9. But this is hardly likely to be the text for one of Dufay's lost laments: Dufay had been away from the north for two years at the time of the banquet; the poem specifically addresses the Duke of Burgundy, which is unlikely for a text written in Naples (as we know Dufay's to have been); there is no hint in any of the narratives that the lament was sung (whereas they are otherwise quite specific about singing at the feast) and the poem is in any case abnormally long for a polyphonic song, having 107 lines; moreover, if the date of the letter is correct Dufay's laments were composed in 1455. See also Schröder 'Lamentations'.

39 Champion, op. cit. (n35), 471.

40 Castan 'Education'.

41 The word 'est' in the antiphon title is missing from the transcription in Castan 'Compositeur' and from all subsequent publications of the document, though this and one other small error are tacitly corrected in the library catalogue: Auguste Castan, *Catalogue des manuscrits des bibliothèques publiques de France: Départements: tome XXXII: Besançon*, i (1897), 438. The antiphon is a rhymed Office Magnificat responsory for the feast of Saints Victor and Ursus (30 September or 11 February). Its full text is printed (from Paris, f. lat. 1318, f. 15) in *Analecta hymnica*, v, 243. I have not been able to locate the melody.

42 Gallo 'Citazioni'; see above p. 242. Further on the intellectual tendencies in Dufay's music, see Bockholdt *Dufay* i, 203.

### 7: Last years and aftermath

1 Wright 'Dufay', 192 n103, also suggests increasingly unsteady financial affairs at Savoy as a reason for his return.

2 Wright 'Dufay', docs. 11–12, and pp. 194f.

3 Excerpts in Houdoy *Cambrai*, 350–60, see p. 352.

4 Wright 'Dufay', 197 and 205f.

5 'Charle conte de Charoloys, filx de Phelippe duc de Bourgogne etc, fist ung mottet et tout le chant, lequel fu chanté en se presence apres messe dicte en le venerable eglise de Cambray par le maistre et les enfans. En l'an 1460, le 23e jour d'octobre qui fu le jour de Saint Severin.' (Cambrai, Bibliothèque de la ville, Ms. 38, f. 72v.)

6 See David Fallows, *Robert Morton's Songs* (diss., University of California at Berkeley, 1978), 309–24.

7 Wright 'Dufay', doc. 30.

8 Wright 'Dufay', 208.

9 For the copying accounts see p. 286 n15. Note that the dates given by Houdoy are misleading: the accounting year ended in the summer, and an account described by Houdoy as, for instance, 1459 is in fact for 1459–60; it is impossible to tell when in the year a particular payment was made since each book represents a single accounting operation (unlike the chapter acts which were written up after each chapter meeting).

10 Hamm 'San Pietro', 44f, offers an identification for the Magnificat which he subsequently withdrew, see Besseler *Dufay* v, III. I cannot accept the suggestion in Bockholdt 'Hymnen' that an unascribed setting of the hymn O *quam glorifica* in Cambrai Ms. 6 is the one mentioned in the copying accounts for 1463–4. Certainly its style could suggest Dufay's authorship (as could that of *Iam ter quaternis* in the same manuscript and which Bockholdt also attributes to Dufay), but it must be much earlier; and to suggest a date so late for this particular manuscript seems frivolous, since most of its contents are demonstrably pre-1440. In fact if a documentary date for Ms. 6 is to be sought, it might be 1442–3 when Grenon added the musical notation to a volume containing 'pluribus Patrem, Et in terra, ac aliis carminibus musice', see Wright 'Dufay', doc. 20.

11 See Fallows 'Two More Dufay Songs'.

12 All earlier writers follow Cordero di Pamparato in giving the wrong name (Arpin) and the wrong date (1467).

13 D'Accone 'Antonio Squarcialupi', 8ff.

14 Not necessarily *several* letters, as some writers have suggested. The Latin word, 'litteras', can imply a single letter.

15 D'Accone 'Singers', 321f, where there is a translation of the first half of the letter.

16 Ed. Emilio Bigi, *Scritti scelti di Lorenzo de' Medici* (Turin, 1955), 211.

17 D'Accone 'Singers', 322ff.

18 Hamm 'San Pietro', 48f.

19 A necessary qualification since a slightly earlier anonymous English Mass setting has the cantus firmus *Requiem eternam*.

20 Proposed in Planchart 'Notes', 20–23. Firm evidence is lacking. Moreover since this Mass was among the 'six' books of music (actually seven, see p. 82) given to Charles the Bold during Dufay's lifetime it might be possible to argue that the Mass was composed by the time of Charles's last visit to Cambrai in October 1468.

21 Itemized in Wright 'Dufay', 212 n207.

22 Houdoy *Cambrai*, 199f.

23 Le Glay *Recherches* (1825), 13f.

24 Wright 'Dufay', 219, notes the opinion of Professor George Rosen that this could be 'some cardiovascular disorder that resulted in dropsy'.

25 I am less convinced by the speculation in Wright 'Dufay', 219, that the death of another Cambrai canon earlier the same day prevented the singing. Incidentally, the executors' account of Dufay's will mentions a legacy received from that canon, Jaques Michael.

26 Mons, Archives de l'état, Chapitre de Soignies, no. provisoire 500. This is also unpublished but is described in Manfred Schuler, 'Neues zur Biographie von Gilles Binchois', *Archiv für Musikwissenschaft*, xxxiii (1976), 68–78.

27 Given in Houdoy *Cambrai*, 414, and all subsequent publications, as 'Riers'. This is one of the few transcription errors in his edition of the will. The only other important error is on p.410, 3 lines from the end of the second paragraph, which should read: 'ad discretionem meorum executorum. Item lego cuilibet dominorum meorum presentium in'.

28 'Item: a Messire Pierre de Wez pour son salaire de avoir gardé l'ostel dudict deffunct l'espasse de 7 ans qu'il fut demourant en Savoye, receu les biens et revenues qu'on li devoit chacun an et en rendu compte, et pour pluisieurs autres services qu'il avoit fais audict deffunct sans ce qu'il en ait esté recompensé, ont esté donnes pour lesdictes causes et autres ad ce monnans lesdicts executeurs: £30.' (Lille, Archives du Nord, 4G 1313, p. 25.)

29 The dukes of Savoy always had close ties with the father-house of the Carthusians; and Amadeus VIII had even directed that all members of his Order of the Garter should bequeath one hundred florins to them, see Raoul Naz, 'La vie merveilleuse du Comte Vert', *Vieux Chambéry*, vi (1974), 38–52, on p. 45. Further on this see Borren *Dufay*, 52.

30 Wright 'Dufay', 217.

31 This cannot be considered any part of the manuscript Brussels, Bibliothèque royale, 5557, see Curtis 'Brussels', esp. p. 85.

32 Houdoy *Cambrai*, 201.

33 All items listed in this and following paragraphs are more fully described in Appendix D. Important summaries of early writings on Dufay appear in Haberl *Bausteine* i, 6–42, and Borren *Dufay*, 72–84.

34 Wright 'Dufay', doc. 35, trans. p. 220.

35 Wright 'Performance', 303.

### 8: The early songs

1   Stainer *Dufay* (1898).

2   Besseler prints eighty-four songs with an appendix containing another ten. Of the two put in the appendix as 'attribuenda', I accept *Seigneur Leon* (vi/85), so convincingly attributed in Plamenac 'Unknown Composition', but reject *J'ayme bien celui* (vi/86) for which there seems no compelling evidence. Among Besseler's 'opera dubia' I wish to reinstate *Le serviteur* (vi/92), p.159 and p.296 n10. From the main body of the volume I reject four works. Hamm *Chronology*, 8, convincingly suggests that only the (rather poor) second contratenor of *Invidia nimica* (vi/2) is likely to be by Dufay. Bent 'Songs', 458f, gives considerable reasons for rejecting *Je languis en piteux martire* (vi/17). *Trop lonc temps* (vi/62) is a casualty of the microfilm age: all photographs show Dufay's name on its unique source, but examination of the manuscript itself shows that the ascription has been very carefully erased. (It is an extremely flimsy piece, and nobody is likely to be sorry to lose it from the Dufay canon.) In addition *S'il est plaisir* (vi/21) shows considerable clumsinesses of part-writing and has very little to recommend it; its sole ascription is in a peripheral and generally unreliable source. For further studies of the songs,  not otherwise mentioned here,  see Bashour *Model*, Dannemann *Spätgotische Musiktradition,* Marggraf 'Tonalität', Mahrt 'Phrygian Mode', Otterbach *Kadenzierung*, and Treitler 'Tone System'.

3   Further discussed in Pirro *Histoire*, 61f; Besseler *Bourdon*, 97f/90ff; Mila *Dufay* i, 76ff. An earlier anonymous ballade on a similar subject, *Cheulx qui voelent retourner/en Lanoys*, is in many ways surprisingly similar to this one, particularly in its melodic structure; see edition by W. Apel, CMM, LIII/iii (1972), no. 285.

4   See Lloyd Hibberd, 'On "Instrumental Style" in Early Melody', *The Musical Quarterly*, xxxii (1946), 107–30.

5   See above, p. 42. For a detailed discussion see Bockholdt *Dufay* i, 18–47; see also Nitschke *Dufay* 126ff. On the possible origins of the tenor see Nitschke *Dufay*, 439 n210, and Gülke 'Volkslied', 183f.

6   Further discussed in Borren *Dufay*, 272f, and Mila *Dufay* i, 100f.

7   For a general discussion see especially Richard L. Crocker, 'Discant, Counterpoint, and Harmony', *JAMS*, xv (1962), 1–21; a more detailed study is Klaus-Jürgen Sachs, *Der Contrapunctus im 14. und 15. Jahrhundert* (Wiesbaden, 1974); see also *The New Grove*, s.v. 'Counterpoint'.

8   Extensively discussed earlier in this century, but see Borren *Dufay*, 261f, and Mila *Dufay* i, 80–83.

9   As noted in Besseler *Bourdon*, 74/229 n41. Later in the century the theorist Guilielmus Monachus described the manner of composing for three equal high voices, ed. A. Seay, CSM, XI (1965), 30.

10  See Besseler *Bourdon*, 73f/70ff and passim; Apfel 'Über den vierstim-

migen Satz', 45f, disagrees with Besseler's view of this song.

11   See, for example, Bockholdt *Dufay* ii, and the editions by Feininger.

12   Further discussed in Borren *Dufay*, 233–6, and Reichert 'Kirchen-tonart'.

13   Besseler *Bourdon*, 43f/42ff.

14   Further discussed in Borren *Dufay*, 256f, and Mila *Dufay* i, 78ff.

15   Borren *Dufay*, 245f, hints at this point and finds it one of Dufay's most original songs. Apfel 'Über den vierstimmigen Satz', 46, finds the contrapuntal treatment weak; see also Apfel *Grundlagen*, 194.

## 9: The isorhythmic motets

1   The fullest general survey of the subject is Ernest H. Sanders, 'The Medieval Motet', in Wulf Arlt et al. (eds), *Gattungen der Musik in Einzeldarstellungen: Gedenkschrift Leo Schrade*, i (Berne, 1973), 497–573; see also his shorter contributions to *The New Grove*, s.v. 'Motet' and 'Isorhythm'. But these say little of the fifteenth-century motet which is studied more comprehensively in Brown *Motets*; a good explanation of the style is in Margaret Bent, *Dunstaple* (London, 1981), 52–71. See also Dannemann *Spätgotische Musiktradition*, 56–78.

2   It should be noted that there are two entirely different editions of Dufay's motets, both called CMM, I: that by Guillaume de Van (1948) has a far fuller commentary and therefore remains indispensable; Besseler's (1966) is easier to use and corrects many of the errors in the earlier edition.

3   This chapter concerns only the thirteen isorhythmic motets. Both editors were surely right to reject *O gloriose tiro* (i/22) as being quite unlike Dufay's work, though Besseler seems to have changed his mind on the matter several times, see Besseler *Bourdon*, 174f/152ff; Apfel 'Über den vierstimmigen Satz', 39f, suggests English origin for the work and Van *Dufay* ii, XXXII, even proposes Dunstable as the composer. Hamm *Chronology*, 70ff, makes a convincing case for attributing the anonymous motet *Elizabet Zacharie* to Dufay, but it is not discussed here since its inclusion, if incorrect, could disturb the historical picture; it seems to me quite likely to have a contrafacted text. Among the later motets, *Salve flos Tusce gentis* (i/15) presents a complex historical problem: its form and structure set it apart from the others, and its harmonic style puts it alongside the lament for Constantinople (vi/10) of 1455: until the work can be firmly dated it is perhaps better not discussed too fully. The non-isorhythmic motets and other works containing hints of isorhythmic technique are discussed in chapter 10.

4   Further discussed in Borren *Dufay*, 166–71, and Brown *Renaissance*, 37ff.

5   The collation of all medieval chant manuscripts with a view to identifying the precise versions set in medieval polyphony would have useful

results but at present the labour entailed seems out of proportion to its probable value. Where we do have Dufay's model, as in the hymns and sequence settings, he seems to follow it carefully.

6   The terms are used in this sense first in the writings of Johannes de Muris in the fourteenth century. The term 'isorhythm' was coined in 1904 by Friedrich Ludwig to describe their use.

7   Full details are in the critical notes to Van *Dufay* ii; a simpler and clearer tabulation appears in Brown *Motets*, 277.

8   On imitation in the motet see also Dannemann *Spätgotische Musiktradition*, 75f.

9   See Apfel 'Über den vierstimmigen Satz', passim.

10  A similar opening duo appears in the anonymous motet *Clarus ortus* (ed. Borren *Polyphonia*, no. 23) which has several stylistic features in common with Dufay's *Vasilissa ergo gaude*; it seems to be for the coronation of Pope Martin V three years earlier. Another is in the anonymous motet *Elizabet Zacharie*, mentioned above (n3).

11  Besseler 'Erläuterungen'; Reese *Renaissance*, 79f. The first person to see this seems to have been Ficker 'Messenkompositionen', 34f.

12  For fuller details see Brown 'Isomelic', but note that his suggested emendation (p. 12) to the triplum at bars 112–3 is withdrawn in the less easily available but later Brown *Motets*, 291. For the most extensive discussion of this relatively neglected subject see Brown *Motets*, 38–50, 181–8, 280–93.

13  See Davis 'Solus Tenor'; see also Besseler *Bourdon*, 93ff/87f.

14  Noted in Van *Dufay* ii, XXI.

15  Pirrotta 'Text Forms', 677; see also Mila *Dufay* i, 142–5, where the motet is more fully discussed.

16  Listed in Van *Dufay* ii, XIV–XVI.

17  This is difficult to explain and may well be an error in the manuscript.

18  Sanders, op. cit. (n1 above), 567; its form is intriguingly discussed in Powell 'Fibonacci', 258–67.

19  Brown 'Isomelic', 10

20  Wolff *Niederländer*, 98, sees this motet as a reversion to the style of Machaut.

21  *Fauxbourdon* is further described later p. 141.

22  See further: Brown *Renaissance*, 40; Elders 'Humanism', 79f; and Mila *Dufay* i, 148–53.

23  All of Ciconia's motets seem to have original tenors of the same kind; but that is otherwise rare in the motet repertory.

24  See especially: Besseler 'Erläuterungen'; Boorman 'Early Renaissance'; Borren *Dufay*, 171–8; Borren *Etudes*, 74ff; Brown *Renaissance*, 40ff; Carpenter 'Tonal Coherence'; Croll 'Dufays Festmusik'; Croll *Festmusiken*, 25–31; Dammann 'Domweihmotette'; Mila *Dufay* i, 153–60; Reese *Renaissance*, 79f; Reeser 'Nuper rosarum flores'; Warren 'Brunelleschi's Dome and Dufay's Motet'; Wolff *Niederländer*, 100f.

25  A similar opening duo appears in the anonymous motet *O sacrum manna* (ed. DTO, LXXVI, Jg. xl (Vienna, 1933), 29ff).

26  Also noted in Besseler *Bourdon*, 167/246 n42, and Mila *Dufay* i, 166.

27  Briefly, the ø mensuration for the final section is ambiguous: it might imply a true doubling of speed (as happens in the upper voices of *Rite majorem* and *Balsamus et munda cera*) with exact 3:2:1 proportions but an immense tempo-difference between the first and last sections; or it might imply a smaller increase of tempo ('diminution' rather than 'semidity') with a resulting proportion of 6:3:4, corresponding more closely to the scheme of *Nuper rosarum flores* and *Magnanime gentis* and making for more comfortable performance. Some of this is discussed at length in Hamm *Chronology*, 37–40 and 57–65.

28  Trowell 'Proportion', 101–4; Margaret Bent, *Dunstaple* (London, 1981), 7ff.

29  A statistical diagram of the cadences appears in Brown *Motets*, 320; further on this motet see Mila *Dufay* i, 161–7.

30  Based partly on Brown 'Isomelic', 9.

31  Johannes Wolf, 'Ein Beitrag zur Diskantlehre des 14. Jahrhunderts', *Sammelbände der Internationalen Musikgesellschaft*, xv (1913–14), 504–34.

## 10: Cantilenas and related works

1  Ed. Borren *Polyphonia*, nos. 38 and 40; see also Besseler *Bourdon*, 136/122.

2  See also Mila *Dufay* i, 145–8, and Besseler *Bourdon*, 136/122.

3  Besseler *Dufay* i, II, attributes the difference to the work's being based on a *Harmonieträger* contratenor (see also Besseler *Bourdon*, chapters II–IV); further discussed in Borren 'Guillaume Dufay'.

4  See also Borren *Dufay*, 190ff, and Sparks *Cantus Firmus*, 440 n31.

5  See also Bockholdt *Dufay* i, 196ff, and *The New Grove*, s.v. 'Binchois'.

6  Note that this work is printed as being in four voices. The top voice appears in only one source – that peripheral – and is clearly an alternative to the contratenor. For the present purposes the song should be considered as comprising only the three lower voices in the edition. It is further discussed in Borren *Dufay*, 236f, and Mila *Dufay* i, 111–114.

7  See Brown *Motets*, 274.

8  The two sources of v/48 in fact have different rhythmicizations for this passage: in the commentary to v/48 the version in Trent – which is in equal *breves* – is misplaced and appears on p. XI.

9  Warren 'Punctus Organi'.

10  See also Mila *Dufay* ii, 26–9.

11  See also Borren *Dufay*, 192ff, and Borren *Etudes*, 76ff.

12  Compare also *Celsa sublimatur* by Hugo de Lantins (ed. Borren *Polyphonia*, no. 32) which is, however, isorhythmic.

13  Discussed widely but see in particular: Borren *Dufay*, 303–14; Mila

*Dufay* i, 63–72; Reese *Renaissance*, 52f; Wolff *Niederländer*, 103f.

14 Discussed in Borren *Dufay*, 178–82, noting similarities in the Magnificat 'sexti toni' (v/33); see also Besseler 'Neue Dokumente', 170–73.

15 See also Borren *Dufay*, 283, and Bent 'Songs', 455f.

16 See also Mila *Dufay* i, 123–134.

17 Hamm *Chronology*, 32f, suggests that only the second of these voices is by Dufay and that the main body of the piece is therefore by an earlier composer. Bashour *Model*, 77f, apparently supports this by showing that the piece's tonal prolongation is unlike that of any other Dufay song; but then the piece as a whole fits uncomfortably with the rest of Dufay's secular work. I am inclined to accept all three voices as Dufay's. Further on the piece, see: Borren *Dufay*, 268–72; Mila *Dufay* i, 83–6; Stainer *Dufay*, 8–11.

18 They are edited in Frederick Crane, *Materials for the Study of the Fifteenth Century Basse Danse* (Brooklyn, 1968), 62f and 65f. The three tenors were first identified by Bukofzer (*The Musical Quarterly*, xliv, 1958, 16f); see also Charles Hamm, 'A Group of Anonymous English Pieces in Trent 87', *Music & Letters*, xli (1960), 211–215, and the ensuing comments, *Music & Letters*, xlii (1961), 96f.

19 See also: Bent 'Songs', 457; Borren *Dufay*, 247ff; Mila *Dufay* i, 107–110.

20 As established by Geneviève Thibault in Jacques Chailley (ed.), *Précis de musicologie* (Paris, 1958), 158, and independently in Hamm Review (1966).

21 On all three songs see also Bent 'Songs', 456f.

22 See Besseler *Bourdon*, 129ff/116ff.

23 Often discussed, but see especially: Bank *Tactus*, 155f; Borren *Dufay*, 199–208; Borren *Etudes*, 78–81; Dèzes 'Salve regina'; Mila *Dufay* i, 171–84; Planchart *View*, 45; Stephan *Motette*, 14ff; see also below, pp. 211f.

## 11: Hymns and other chant settings

1 On the hymn settings in general see: Gerber *Hymnen*, Introduction; Gerber 'Hymnenzyklen'; Kanazawa *Vespers*, 42–61; Mila *Dufay* ii, 5–23; Ward 'Hymn and Liturgy'. For recently discovered sources see: Fischer 'Neue Quellen', 92ff (Merseburg); Stenzl 'Un fragment' and Stenzl *Repertorium*, no. 67 (Grand St-Bernard); Ward *Polyphonic Office Hymn*, 54 (Cividale).

2 Gerber 'Hymnenzyklen', 41f, Haydon 'Ave maris stella', Kanazawa *Vespers*, 16–24, *The New Grove*, s.v. 'Hymn'.

3 Bockholt 'Kirchenmusik', 423 and 429.

4 More fully discussed in Sparks *Cantus Firmus*, 42–82.

5 No apology is needed for referring to bars, barlines and first beats: see above p. 98.

6 This often happens in Dufay's works, but an astonishingly clear and

similarly structured example is in the discantus of his Magnificat antiphon *Salve, sancte pater* (v/43).

7   Further discussed in Mila *Dufay* ii, 7–11.

8   Further discussed in Mila *Dufay* ii, 20–23; Kanazawa *Vespers*, 47, says that Dufay's opening 'loosens the tension of the original melodic line'.

9   Bockholdt 'Kirchenmusik', 436, compares the two melodies rather more to Dufay's favour; see also Haydon 'Ave', 82ff.

10  See *The New Grove*, s.v. 'Fauxbourdon' and 'Faburden'.

11  As noted in Ficker 'Schöpfungsgeschichte', 114.

12  Further discussed in Mila *Dufay* ii, 17–20.

13  See above pp. 75 and 288 n10.

14  Hamm 'Dating a Group', 70f, and Hamm *Chronology*, 78; Hamm also implies that the sequences of Johannes Roullet may be part of the same cycle. They are further discussed in Besseler 'Dufay in Rom', 8f.

15  Hamm 'Dating a Group', 68f, and Hamm *Chronology*, 79f.

16  The papal bull providing for a choirschool at Santa Maria del Fiore is dated 25 March 1436, the day the church was dedicated, see Albert Seay, 'The 15th-century Cappella at Santa Maria del Fiore in Florence', *JAMS*, xi (1958), 45–55.

17  Discussed in: Borren *Dufay*, 161–6; Kanazawa *Vespers*, 249–71; Kirsch *Vertonungen*, 314ff and 538f; Maas *Magnificat*, 42–52; Mila *Dufay* ii, 31–40.

18  See Maas *Magnificat*, 46–52, and Pope *Montecassino*, 602f.

19  Discussed in Kanazawa *Vespers*, 390ff, and Planchart 'View', 33–7; some are put into a possible context herein pp. 190f.

## 12: The late songs

1   The text is applied wrongly to the music in the complete edition. The correct form (using Besseler's lettering of the music sections and numbering of the text sections) is: A1 BC2 [A1] BC3 [A1] B4C5 [A1]. Pirro *Histoire*, 69, attempts to connect the song with Parisina Malatesta's decapitation for adultery in 1425.

2   See above p. 290 n 2.

3   Further discussed in Borren *Dufay*, 273–7, and Mahrt 'Phrygian Mode', 90–4.

4   This is precisely how the theorist Pierre Fabri described it later in the century, see Alexandre Héron (ed.), *Le grand et vrai art de pleine rhétorique de Pierre Fabri*, ii (Rouen, 1890), 71f.

5   Noted in Schneider 'Verminderte Quarte', 206, which puts the work in a wider historical context and makes the point that this opening outlines the G tonality which is not fully established until the concluding cadence at bar 20. Schneider also mentions a diminished fourth outline in *Helas, ma dame* (v/45), at bars 25–7, but in his efforts to present a 'semantic' history of the interval overlooks its appearance at bars 8–10,

19–20 and 26–8 of the same song: it is in fact a structural building-block in this case.

6 For this and several other features, see the interesting analysis in Felix Salzer, *Structural Hearing* (New York, 1952), ii, fig. 536. The song is further discussed in Besseler *Bourdon*, 159f/140f, Mahrt 'Phrygian Mode', 86f, and Wolff *Niederländer*, 178.

7 Fallows 'Robertus'.

8 Further discussed in Fallows 'Robertus', 103f.

9 See Fallows 'Two More Dufay Songs'.

10 Besseler 'Falsche Autornamen'. Arguments for Dufay's authorship appear in: Allan Atlas, *The Cappella Giulia Chansonnier*, i (Brooklyn, 1975), 178ff; Fallows 'Robertus', 114f; Peter Reidemeister, *Die Chanson-Handschrift 78 C 28 des Berliner Kupferstichkabinetts* (Munich, 1973), 62ff.

11 Further discussed in Borren *Dufay*, 279–83, and Mila *Dufay* i, 91ff.

12 Tonality and tonal sense are subjects difficult to treat within the scope of this book. Among the more important discussions are: Besseler *Bourdon*; Dahlhaus *Entstehung*; Randel 'Emerging Triadic Tonality'; Reichert 'Kirchentonart'; Treitler 'Tone System'.

13 Wright 'Dufay'.

14 See above p. 65; for the other, see Marix *Histoire*, 207, and Reese *Renaissance*, 99.

15 See for instance the article in *MGG*, Besseler 'Dufay'.

16 See above n7.

17 Further discussed in Bent 'Songs', 456f.

18 Further discussed in Gülke 'Volkslied', 181.

19 Since then it has served as an example in Perkins 'Text Placement', 109ff, and been discussed in Reidemeister, op. cit. (n10 above), 34f and 63; see also Perkins *Mellon* ii, 399–404, Benthem 'Quodlibet', and Besseler 'Grundsätzliches', 38.

20 This is not the place for a critical commentary on the edition – though in all the musical examples deviations from Besseler's readings are based on a careful reconsideration of the sources. Here the text for the closing line is taken from the Colombina chansonnier because it retains the caesura after the fourth syllable, a detail which seems important to the bipartite structure of each musical line.

## 13: The early Mass music

1 On all these movements, particularly their dissonance treatment and texting, see Bockholdt *Dufay*; see also Villard *Text Underlay*.

2 Anthony Pryer reached the same conclusion independently; I am grateful to him for generously sharing his thoughts with me. Mila *Dufay* ii, 68–77, gives a blow-by-blow description of the cycle (and in fact mentions the ballade *Resvelliés vous*, p. 73, in conjunction with the fermata chords in the Gloria, though these seem more characteristic of the style in general and not specifically reminiscent of the ballade).

3 Hamm 'Reson Mass', 12; Hamm 'Manuscript Structure', 180f; the idea was first hinted at in Dèzes 'Borren', 300. Their arguments derive partly from the appearance of the cycle in one source (Venice, IX 145) with a different Credo; but that movement has far less in common with the others, with lower ranges, extensive movement in semiminims (which appear nowhere else in the cycle), and entirely different contrapuntal structure. The correct Credo appears later in the same manuscript.

4 Gossett 'Techniques of Unification', passim.

5 The following discussion is based on the more detailed remarks in Planchart 'View', 30ff; see also Apfel *Grundlagen*, 269f, and Besseler *Bourdon*, 150/134.

6 In the complete edition the Credo also has an alternative, shorter ending; but this is in only one source, Trent 92, and is merely an adaptation to new words of two sections from the Gloria. It can safely be ignored as a copyist's effort to replace a passage that was perhaps missing from his exemplar: the two lower voices of the last section are in fact missing from the version in the closely related manuscript Trent 87.

7 Even within the second layer the differences in style are significant. Whereas there is a tradition at the time of pairing Sanctus and Agnus movements, there is little trace of that here. The Sanctus chant is from Mass II in the *Liber usualis*, whereas the Agnus is on that of Mass XI; and the mensural treatment is severely dissimilar; see Bockholdt *Dufay* i, 72–5.

8 The three-voice sections of the Offertory surprisingly have their chant in the second discantus. It seems likely that the chant in the two-voice section of the Alleluia is in the same voice.

9 Besseler *Bourdon*, 13–19/18–23.

10 See Planchart 'Notes', 14.

11 Further discussed in Dangel-Hofmann *Introitus*, 19–31.

12 Mila *Dufay* ii, 61, invoking Besseler without precise source but presumably going from Besseler 'Dufay', col. 910: 'das man wohl als die erste niederländische Messe des 15. Jahrhunderts ansprechen darf'; see also Besseler *Bourdon*, 152f/136f.

13 Ed. in Reaney *Early Fifteenth-century Music* vi, 31–41.

14 Bockholdt *Dufay* i, 76–82, tentatively argues the same conclusion in much greater detail.

15 Schoop *Entstehung*, 48f. The movement is discussed in Ficker 'Messenkompositionen', 30f.

16 Ed. in Borren *Polyphonia*, no.16; see Schoop *Entstehung*, 48f and 51.

17 Besseler *Bourdon*, 210–14/182–5; Bockholdt *Dufay* i, 155f; Nitschke *Dufay*, 102–8; Pirro *Histoire*, 73f.

18 Further discussed in Nitschke *Dufay*, 109–120; Apfel 'Über den vierstimmigen Satz', 44, seems to be suggesting that the work began life in three voices.

19   Bockholdt *Dufay* i, 121ff and 148ff; further discussed in Ficker 'Mes-
     senkompositionen', 31.

20   On the Kyrie settings see Kovarik 'Paraphrase Kyries'; on all of these
     see Bockholdt *Dufay* i, passim. Hamm *Chronology*, 76, points out that
     the alternatim Gloria settings v/25 and v/26 between them set the entire
     Gloria text but that they cannot belong together since they both include
     absolutely clear chant paraphrase in the discantus and they are based
     on different Gloria chants.

21   Monson 'Stylistic Inconsistencies'; on this work see also Mila *Dufay* ii,
     53ff.

22   An extended discussion is in Borren *Dufay*, 142–52, with full historical
     context; see also Mila *Dufay* ii, 43–6.

23   Further discussed in: Bockholdt *Dufay* i, 98–102; Nitschke *Dufay*, 35ff
     and 429 n68; Sparks *Cantus Firmus*, 88f.

24   Further discussed in Borren *Dufay*, 152–9, and Mila *Dufay* ii, 55–60.

25   Wright 'Performance', 305ff.

26   Ed. in DTO, LXXVI, Jg. xl (Vienna, 1933), 90f.

27   Ed. in DTO, LXI, Jg. xxxi (Vienna, 1924), 55ff.

### 14: The St Anthony Masses and other doubtful Mass music

1    Houdoy *Cambrai*, 411ff.

2    Bk 3 ch. 2–3 (ed. CSM, XXII/iia, 47ff), quoting Gloria bars 184–9; Bk 1
     ch. 3 and Bk 3 ch. 6 (ed. CSM, XXII/iia, 14f and 57), quoting Credo bars
     202–210.

3    Bk 4 ch. 5.

4    Besseler *Dufay* iii, I; Besseler 'Neue Dokumente', 173f.

5    Van *Dufay* iii, I; in more detail Hamm *Chronology*, 103–113 (but see
     Planchart 'Notes', 15 n23); on this cycle see also Bockholdt 'Notizen',
     46f.

6    For a discussion of this, and the considerations it entails, see Planchart
     'Notes', 15f.

7    He quotes from bars 16–21, 85–9 and 102–5 (bar numbers from the
     edition in CMM, XLI (1967), 1–18). His other quotation from this
     movement is from the 'contrabasso' which was presumably a fourth
     voice, now lost. His citations appear in Paris, Bibliothèque nationale, f.
     it. 1110, f. 66v.

8    In particular Gloria, bars 152ff. Several other curiosities in Besseler's
     edition are easily rectified copying or transcription errors, many of
     them corrected in the edition in Bockholdt *Dufay* ii, 68–86. Hamm
     *Chronology*, 110ff, shows that this manuscript is often demonstrably
     corrupt.

9    Ch. 31. It is mentioned in Haberl *Bausteine* i, 11, and Borren *Dufay*, 67.

10   Many of the most complex in fact baffled Besseler, see Gloria, bars 31ff,
     160–64, 194–203, Credo, bars 177–80, 218f, 263f, Sanctus, bars
     27–33 – all of which are corrected in Bockholdt, loc. cit.

11 See for example the striking passages in the Credo, bars 248f and 253–8. Bank *Tactus*, 142–7, discusses the proportional notation in detail and concludes (p. 143) that 'one would be inclined to think that this work was not written by Dufay, and one would prefer to suggest 1460 rather than 1440 for its date'.

12 Wright 'Dufay', 228 doc. 30, and Houdoy *Cambrai*, 267.

13 Ed. in Feininger *Propria*, 135–8. The cycles are described in Robert E. Gerken, *Polyphonic Cycles of the Proper of the Mass* (diss., University of Indiana, 1969), 36–102, see esp. pp.75ff on the cycle for St Anthony of Padua; Gerken is opposed to Feininger's attributions which are further discussed in Bank *Tactus*, 152ff, Bukofzer Review, 335ff, and Hamm *Chronology*, 131–6.

14 Planchart 'Notes', 14–19; they are edited in Feininger *Propria*, 10ff and 151ff.

15 Wright 'Dufay', 198f, quoted with approval in Lowinsky 'Feininger', 335; it is edited in Feininger *Propria*, 90–3.

16 Most cogently argued in Planchart 'Notes', 17f.

17 Dangel-Hofmann *Introitus*, 115f; they are edited in CMM, XXXV/i (1965), 1–15, see also op. cit., p.XI, for a discussion of their authorship and a brief reference to Dufay's cycles.

18 Hamm *Chronology*, 132f.

19 Dangel-Hofmann *Introitus*, 118f, shows further reasons why comparison with Dufay's other chant movements is irrelevant and concludes that the best comparison would be with his Magnificat 'sexti toni' (v/33), but that even this gives no significant further insight. Note, incidentally, that her inconclusive comparison is based on the Introit *Os iusti* which Planchart has now shown to be an authentic Dufay work according to Spataro.

20 Firmly as a footnote, this information also suggests that it might be time to reconsider the authorship of the *Salve regina* setting so firmly dismissed from the canon of Dufay's works in Dèzes 'Salve regina' (1927). Compelling though they may seem, his arguments are limited by the relatively small quantity of Dufay's later music that was available in print at the time. If the Trent Proper cycles are by Dufay, many (though not all) of Dèzes's arguments evaporate. See also Besseler 'Von Dufay bis Josquin', 15.

21 Information drawn to my attention by Professor Lowinsky as appearing in a forthcoming article by his wife, Bonnie J. Blackburn.

22 Ficker suggested that Dufay was referring to another motet *O sidus Yspanie* which survives in one source immediately followed by Dufay's i/6. On this proposal, its history and its rejection, see Planchart 'View', 34f; see also Besseler *Bourdon*, 169/149.

23 First noted in this context in Planchart 'View', 34ff. Planchart expands his argument into a further area of hypothesis different from mine, but his views are best read in his own words. On Julian see Weis *Julian* and Weis *Choräle*.

24 Wright 'Dufay', 228 doc.30.

25 Discussed briefly in Dangel-Hofmann *Introitus*, 126f and 161, with the possibly relevant observation that no other early plenary cycle is known apart from that of R. Libert and Dufay's Mass *Sancti Jacobi*. A transcription of the cycle is in Louis E. Gottlieb, *The Cyclic Masses of Trent Codex 89* (diss., University of California at Berkeley, 1958), ii, 301–32. The ascription 'Piret' there and in the published inventory of the Trent manuscripts appears only on the second opening of the Gloria and is therefore probably not an ascription at all (though I must confess myself baffled as to what it might be); no composer of that name has been identified.

26 Important discussions appear in: Borren *Dufay*, 129–38; Bukofzer *Studies*, 217–310; Mila *Dufay* ii, 78–98; Nitschke *Dufay*, 11–84. But there is an enormous additional literature on this cycle.

27 Bukofzer *Studies*, 242–9 and 257ff; Bukofzer 'Caput redivivum', 102ff.

28 Walker 'A Severed Head'; Planchart 'Notes', 1–13.

29 Planchart, loc. cit.; Curtis *English Masses* i, 93ff and 132. It should be said that the complete argument for dismissing the *Caput* Mass has yet to be mounted.

30 Feininger *Dufay* iii, 'Praefatio'; Nitschke *Dufay*, 292–374; see also Hamm *Chronology*, 147.

31 Feininger *Dufay* i.

32 Sparks *Cantus Firmus*, 134f; Walker 'A Severed Head'; see for fuller details the commentary to Margaret Bent (ed.), *Four Anonymous Masses* (London, 1979) = Early English Church Music, XXII; see also Hamm *Chronology*, 147f.

33 Feininger *Dufay* ii.

34 Feininger *Dufay* iv.

35 Hamm *Chronology*, 146f; see also Sparks *Cantus Firmus*, 136.

36 Hamm *Chronology*, 137. His proposal is now made all the more attractive by the discovery that the man who was travelling from Picardy to Rome and brought 'various Masses' by Dufay to the court of Savoy in the later 1460s was not Gile Arpin but Gile Crepin (see p. 247). In his forthcoming dissertation (Princeton University) Christopher Reynolds shows that Crepin was directly involved in the production of musical manuscripts for the chapel of San Pietro in Vaticano during the years when the manuscript San Pietro B 80 was being prepared for its use. This manuscript would therefore be almost the first place to look for more works by Dufay.

### 15: The cantus firmus Masses

1 Further discussed in: Borren *Dufay*, 104–129; Borren *Etudes*, 115–9; Brown *Renaissance*, 45–51; Dèzes 'Salve regina'; Korte *Harmonik*, 87ff; Mila *Dufay* ii, 98–116; Nitschke *Dufay*, 85–160; Reese *Renais-*

*sance*, 69–72; Sandresky 'System', 112ff; Trowell 'Proportion', 136ff; Wolff *Niederländer*, 29–32.

2 Further discussed in Borren *Dufay*, 105ff and 262–8; Mila *Dufay* i, 86–91.

3 Planchart 'View', 37–43, but see above pp. 68 and 287 n 30.

4 That of the Mass *Se la face ay pale* appears as 'Tenor' (Rome CS 14) and 'Tenor bassus' (Trent 88); of the Mass *L'homme armé* as 'Contra' (Rome CS 14), 'Contra bassus' (Rome CS 49) and 'Tenor' or 'Tenor secundus' (Lucca; in the Edinburgh manuscript it is not labelled at all); of the Mass *Ecce ancilla* as 'Contra' (Rome CS 14) and 'Tenor secundus' (Brussels 5557); of the Mass *Ave regina celorum* as 'Bassis' (Brussels 5557), 'Bassus' (Modena) and 'Contrabassus' or 'Bassus' (Rome San Pietro B 80).

5 See also Sparks *Cantus Firmus*, 121f.

6 Further discussed in: Cohen 'Munus ab ignoto', 194f; Mila *Dufay* ii, 117–39; Nitschke *Dufay* 201–43 and plate VI; Sandresky 'System', 115–19; Sparks *Cantus Firmus*, 122–5; Treitler 'Dufay the Progressive'.

7 Planchart 'View', 41f.

8 Nitschke *Dufay*, 202f, 385–9, 415ff and 455 n399; Hamm *Chronology*, 144f (though his criterion for including works in this group is merely the presence of *fusae*); see also Reese *Renaissance*, 72.

9 Particularly the counting of the relative frequency of different note-values in sections that are comparable in point of mensuration and texture.

10 On this much-discussed melody see, most recently, Caraci 'Fortuna', Chew 'Early Cyclic Mass', 265ff, Cohen 'Munus ab ignoto', and Lockwood 'Aspects of the L'homme armé Tradition' (with extensive further bibliography).

11 David Fallows, *Robert Morton's Songs* (diss., University of California at Berkeley, 1978), 203–44.

12 On this and much else in the work's motivic treatment, see Treitler 'Dufay the Progressive'; for the later history of this particular figure, see Lockwood 'Aspects of the L'homme armé Tradition', 116ff.

13 This passage is discussed in Bank *Tactus*, 153.

14 Implied for the Mass *Se la face ay pale* in Trowell 'Proportion', 137f.

15 See in particular John Shearman, *Raphael's Cartoons* (London, 1972), ch. 2.

16 Further discussed in: Borren *Etudes*, 146–57; Bukofzer *Studies*, 307ff; Nitschke *Dufay*, 161–200; Sandresky 'System', 114–17; see also Ambros *Geschichte* ii, 292–8.

17 See Planchart 'View', 44, and Wright 'Dufay', 221; the Ockeghem cycle contrasts with Dufay's in having highly irregular motto treatment.

18 Strictly speaking, one source (Rome CS 14) directs that the first 'Agnus Dei' be repeated for the third, and the other (Brussels 5557) offers the alternative of repeating the first 'Agnus Dei' or using the 'Osanna'. In

terms of cantus firmus usage only the latter makes sense and it seems likely that the scribes suggested the former merely because it was the more common practice at the time. See also Nitschke *Dufay*, 193f.

19   For a comparison see Nitschke *Dufay*, 164–79 and plates IV–V. Sparks *Cantus Firmus*, 450 n16, points out that although the two chants now appear in different services they were in many rites both appropriate for the Annunciation (25 March), see also Nitschke *Dufay*, 164f. Nobody seems to have located a chant source for *Ecce ancilla Domini* which includes the first note set by Dufay, which is to say that the rising fourth at the beginning seems at present to be unique to Dufay's setting and that by his close associate Johannes Regis.

20   Further discussed in: Borren *Etudes*, 157–65; Mila *Dufay* ii, 140–151; Nitschke *Dufay*, 244–91 and plates VII–IX; Planchart 'View', 44–9; Reese *Renaissance*, 76; Sparks *Cantus Firmus*, 125–33; Sandresky 'System', 118ff.

21   Borren 'Light', 290f, sees this passage as evolving from the rondeau *Donnés l'assault* (vi/70) – another detail of Dufay's self-borrowing or rewriting of material.

22   See Nitschke *Dufay*, 448f n342; see also Curtis *English Masses* i, 278, and ii, 163–205 (edition).

23   See Curtis 'Brussels', extrapolating from Planchart 'View', 47ff; see also Nitschke *Dufay*, 274.

### Appendix A

*Introduction*

A study of Dufay – or of practically any other figure of his time – necessarily entails much guesswork and imaginative reconstruction from the available information. So it is particularly important to attempt to assemble in one place references to the documentation on which it is based. Practically all the archival material cited here has been checked at first hand (the main exception being that I have felt able to take on trust many references in Wright 'Dufay'); several references are different from those in earlier publications, often because libraries and classifications have changed.

This list, keyed to the facts presented in the column 'Life' of Appendix A, identifies the main documents on Dufay's life. Many more exist but are less important: many of those at Cambrai and Lille are noted in Wright 'Dufay'; some at Rome appear in Haberl *Bausteine*. In the bibliographical references a simple citation implies a description or a partial transcription; 'ed.' implies a full publication; items listed in parentheses are taken directly from the preceding publication, usually without consultation of the original document.

Archive abbreviations:
C    Cambrai, Bibliothèque municipale

L   Lille, Archives départementales du Nord
R   Rome, Archivio di stato, Fondo Camerale I
T   Turin, Archivio di stato, Conti dei tesorieri generali di Savoia (inv. 16)
V   Vatican City, Archivio segreto pontificio

1   L 4G 7758:1409–10, f.8: Pirro *Histoire*, 54.
2   L 4G 6789:1409–10, f.3v–4: Wright 'Dufay', 177; Wright *Burgundy*, 94.
3   L 4G 7758:1411–12, f.9v: Pirro *Histoire*, 54.
4   L 4G 7759:1413–14, f.9: Pirro *Histoire*, 55; Wright 'Dufay', 177.
5   Paris, Archives nationales, KK 38, f.20v–21: Pirro Review, 322; Pirro *Histoire*, 61; Wright 'Dufay', 178 n18. See also above p. 26.
6   L 7G 573, f.107v: Pirro *Histoire*, 63; Wright 'Dufay', 178.
7   L 7G 573, f.108: Pirro *Histoire*, 63; Wright 'Dufay', 178.
8   V Introitus et exitus 387, f.83v (olim f. 114v): ed. Haberl *Bausteine* i, 60 (Baix 'Carrière', no.1). Document duplicate in R 1752, f.114v.
9   V Diversa cameralia 11, f.257v–258 (olim f.243v–4): Berlière *Diversa*, no.253 (Baix 'Carrière', no.2).
10  V Introitus et exitus 389, f.95 (olim f.96): Haberl *Bausteine* i, 60f.
11  V Diversa cameralia 13, f.61–61v (olim f.54–54v): ed. Haberl *Bausteine* i, 61f; Berlière *Diversa*, no.262 (Baix 'Carrière', no.3).
12  Vatican City, Biblioteca apostolica vaticana, Cappella sistina 703.1: ed. Haberl *Bausteine* i, 115–19 (Baix 'Carrière', no.4).
13  V Registri laterani 303, f.19v–20v (dated 6 Oct. 1431): Baix 'Carrière', no.5; Arnold *Repertorium*, no.1500 (citing further relevant documents).
14  R 827, f.160: Haberl *Bausteine* i, 66.
15  T 79, f.464 (payment dated 21 March 1434); ed. Cordero 'Dufay', 20; ed. Borghezio 'Fondazione', 231 (ed. Borren *Dufay*, 42).
16  T 79, f.391–391v & f.448v: ed. Borghezio 'Fondazione', 229f (ed. Borren *Dufay*, 41).
17  L 4G 7434, f.7. See also above p. 42.
18  T 80, f.161v: Cordero 'Dufay', 34.
19  R 828, f.41v (June), f.51v (Aug.), f.59 (Oct.): Haberl *Bausteine* i, 68.
20  V Annate VII, f.20 (28 Sept. 1436); Schuler 'Martin V', 33; Dubrulle *Bénéficiers*, no.98. Also V Registri laterani 343, f.76–77v, and V Registri laterani 338, f.245v–246: Baix 'Carrière', nos. 7–8.
21  C 1057, f.39: Wright 'Dufay', 181.
22  V Diversa cameralia 19, f.256 (olim f.251): Berlière *Diversa*, no.333 (Baix 'Carrière', no.10); ed. Haberl *Bausteine* i, 63.
23  Modena, Archivio di stato, Camera marchionale estense 4986/99, f.158v: ed. Besseler 'Neue Dokumente', 166.
24  R 828, f.120v & 122: Haberl *Bausteine* i, 69.
25  Lausanne, Archives cantonales vaudoises, Dg 7/1, f.48v: Schuler 'Eugen IV', 223.

26  T 83, f.165v: Cordero 'Dufay', 34.

27  C 1057, f.66v: Pirro *Histoire*, 74; Wright 'Dufay', 181 and 90.

28  Bruges, Archief van het bisdom, Reeks A 50, f.253.

29  T 84, f.353–354: Cordero 'Dufay', 34 (Borren *Dufay*, 361).

30  L 4G 5074, f.16: ed. Wright 'Dufay', doc. 1, see also p. 182.

31  L 4G 7439–41, etc (on last page of each): Wright 'Dufay', 182–5.

32  V Annate VIII, f.288v (olim f.307v) (dated 26 Feb. 1442): Dubrulle *Bénéficiers*, no.397 (Baix 'Carrière', no.12).

33  Aosta, Archivio regionale (formerly Châtillon), Archives Challant, lettres, vol. 259, doc. 4: ed. Lange 'Une lettre' 103f; trans. Wright 'Dufay', 191f.

34  Turin, Archivio di stato, Archivio di corte, Bollario di Felice V, IV, f.259v–160 & f.260v–261v: José 'Un musicien', 253ff.

35  L 4G 7762:1442–3, f.9: Wright 'Dufay', 202.

36  L 4G 1090, f.122: ed. Lockwood 'Dufay and Ferrara', 13.

37  Inscription on tombstone (lost): ed. Le Glay *Recherches* (1825), 200 (ed. Haberl *Bausteine* i, 36; ed. Vander Straeten *Pays-Bas* vi, 313; ed. Dartus *Du Fay*, 14); see also L 4G 1090, f.143v & f.147: Wright 'Dufay', 183.

38  C 1058, f.14v: Wright 'Dufay', 183.

39  C 1058, f.34v: Wright 'Dufay', 197. See also above p. 286 n14.

40  L 4G 1086, doc.375: ed. Wright 'Dufay', doc.24.

41  C 1058, f.80: ed. Wright 'Dufay', doc.4.

42  Original document burned in 1940: described Devillers *Chartes* iii, 231 (no.1249).

43  C 1058, f.129v: Wright 'Dufay', 184.

44  C 1058, f.184v and L 4G 5082, f.15: ed. Wright 'Dufay', docs.5a–b.

45  C 1058, f.155 & f.158v: ed Wright 'Dufay', doc.6, see also p.186.

46  Original document burned in 1940: ed. Pinchart *Archives* iii, 47f (ed. Vander Straeten *Pays-Bas* vi, 315).

47  C 1058, f.256–256v: Wright 'Dufay', 185.

48  T 98, f.270–270v: ed. Cordero 'Dufay', 35; Borren *Dufay*, 361.

49  C 1058, f.245, 246v, 256, 259, 261, etc: Wright 'Dufay', 188.

50  Turin, Archivio di stato, Protocolli ducali 76, f.303: ed. Borghezio 'Fondazione', 246 (ed. Borren *Dufay*, 50f; ed. Bouquet 'Cappella', 238); José 'Un musicien', 256.

51  C 1059, f.21v: ed. Wright 'Dufay', doc.8 (trans. p.189), see also doc.9.

52  T 104, f.281: Cordero 'Dufay', 35.

53  Chambéry, Archives générales de la Savoie, SA 3605; ed. Bouquet 'Cappella', 239f.

54  idem, SA 3605, separate sheet: ed. Bouquet 'Cappella', 239; facs. herein, ill.19.

55  idem, SA 3605, f.10v (payment for choir clothing): ed. Bouquet 'Cappella', 245.

56  Florence, Archivio di stato, Mediceo avante il principato, VI, 765: facs. and ed. Fortuna *Autografi*, 38f; facs. herein, ill.18; ed. Kühner 'Brief',

114f; ed. Grunzweig 'Notes', 86; ed. Becherini 'Relazioni', 87f; trans. D'Accone 'Singers', 318f.

57 Besançon, Bibliothèque municipale, Ms. 712, f.226: ed. and trans. Castan 'Compositeur', 6f (ed. Houdoy *Cambrai*, 88f; ed. Vander Straeten *Pays-Bas* vi, 560; ed. Haberl *Bausteine* i, 47), but see herein p. 287 n41.

58 C 1060, f.29v, 30v, 49v, etc: Wright 'Dufay', 190 and 194.

59 L 4G 6789:1459–60, f.1: Wright 'Dufay', 194.

60 L 4G 4667, f.25v: ed. Houdoy *Cambrai*, 192.

61 C 1060, f.97v–98: Wright 'Dufay', 197 and doc.15.

62 L 4G 4554: partial ed. Houdoy *Cambrai*, 350–60.

63 L 4G 4670, f.26v: ed. Houdoy *Cambrai*, 194.

64 L 4G 4671, f.24–24v: ed. Houdoy *Cambrai*, 194.

65 L 4G 7462, f.5: ed. Wright 'Dufay', doc.26b; also L 4G 5098, f.13: ed. Wright 'Dufay', doc.26c.

66 L 4G 4672, f.23v–24: ed. Wright 'Dufay', doc.18, trans. p. 198; ed. (incomplete) Houdoy *Cambrai*, 195.

67 L 4G 6789:1465–6, f.1: Wright 'Dufay', 196.

68 C 1060, f.243: ed. Wright 'Dufay', doc.13, see also p. 195.

69 Florence, Archivio di stato, Mediceo avante il principato, XXII, 118: facs. and ed. Fortuna *Autografi*, 104f; ed. Kade 'Squarcialupi', 13f; trans. (in part) D'Accone 'Singers', 322, remainder herein p. 76.

70 T 114, f.261 (in register for March 1468–March 1469): ed. Cordero 'Dufay', 35f (Borren *Dufay*, 361).

71 L 4G 4678, f.22v: ed. Houdoy *Cambrai*, 198.

72 L 4G 4681, f.24v: ed. Wright 'Dufay', doc.19, trans. p.198; ed. (incomplete) Houdoy *Cambrai*, 200.

73 L 4G 1313, p.69–76: ed. Houdoy *Cambrai*, 409–14 (ed. Haberl *Bausteine* i, 119–23). Corrections noted above p. 289 n 28.

74 L 4G 5106, f.12v: ed. Wright 'Dufay', doc.34. Executors' inventory of property, L 4G 1313, p.39–66, and distribution account of will, L 4G 1313, p.1–36: partial ed. Houdoy *Cambrai*, 267ff; partial ed. Wright 'Dufay', doc.30 (trans. p.215ff), docs.7 and 31–3. Dufay's funeral monument, Lille, Musée des Beaux-Arts, Inv. 1912 LAP 10: reproduced many times since 1859 and herein, ills.1–2.

## Appendix B

1 Besseler's edition had been planned to begin as early as 1930 in the *Publikationen älterer Musik*, see Besseler 'Von Dufay bis Josquin', 2, and Van *Dufay* i, If; but other projects intervened.

2 Readers are warned that many recent publications confuse the two editions called CMM, I.

3 The numbering is Besseler's. The Mass cycles in vols. ii and iii are numbered together.

4 In the absence of any comprehensive survey or edition of fifteenth-

century chant, chant numbers are taken from the *Liber usualis*. Often the melodic details are slightly different, and in any case liturgical implications should be treated with some caution.

5 Besseler classed these as Mass music; but the *Benedicamus* appears in the Mass only during seasons when the Gloria is omitted whereas it always appears in the Office ceremonies.

## Appendix C

1 Louis Salembier, *Le cardinal Pierre d'Ailly* (Tourcoing, 1932); John P. McGowan, *Pierre d'Ailly and the Council of Constance* (Washington DC, 1936); Houdoy *Cambrai*, 48 and 53–6.

2 Pierre Champion (ed.), *Charles d'Orléans: Poésies* (Paris, 1923–7), 370 and 431.

3 Annie Angremy, 'Un nouveau recueil de poésies françaises', *Romania*, xcv (1974), 1–53.

4 See also B. de Mandrot, 'Louis XI, Jean V d'Armagnac et le drame de Lectoure', *Revue historique*, xxxviii (1888), 241–304; Charles Samaran, *La maison d'Armagnac au XVe siècle* (Paris, 1907), passim; Pierre Champion, *Vie de Charles d'Orléans* (Paris, 1911), 627f; Fallows 'Two More Dufay Songs'.

5 Gabriel Pérouse, *Le cardinal Louis Aleman* (Paris, 1904); Edith Pásztor, 'Louis Aleman', *Dizionario biografico degli italiani*, ii (1960), 145ff.

6 Keyser *Donaaskapittel* iii, 162f.

7 Berlière *Diversa*, 200f.

8 Bruges, Archief van het bisdom, Reeks A 50, f.250 and f. 262v.

9 Houdoy *Cambrai*, 373.

10 See also Martin Marrier, *Monasterii regalis S. Martini* (Paris, 1636), 444–8; Etienne-François Villain, *Essai d'une histoire de la paroisse de Saint Jacques de la Boucherie* (Paris, 1758), 225f; Jacques Meurgey, *Histoire de la paroisse Saint-Jacques-de-la-Boucherie* (Paris, 1926), 85ff; Le Carpentier *Histoire de Cambray* (1664), ii, 443f; Toussaint *Relations*, 25f, 262f and passim; François Baix, *La chambre apostolique et les 'libri annatorum' de Martin V* (Brussels, 1942–60), 279; Le Glay *Recherches* (1825), 113; Van *Dufay* ii, XXI; Wright 'Dufay', doc.10b; Planchart 'View', 27.

11 Marix *Histoire*, 175 and 192f.

12 Lille, Archives du Nord, 4G 1217, see Houdoy *Cambrai*, 265; further details in Keyser *Donaaskapittel* iii, 283f.

13 Printed in Le Glay *Recherches* (1825), 199; see also Haberl *Bausteine* i, 36, and Vander Straeten *Pays-Bas* vi, 313.

14 C. Thelliez, 'A propos d'un testament (Jean de Bourgogne)', *Mémoires de la Société d'émulation de Cambrai*, xciii (1970), 7–69.

15 Le Glay *Recherches* (1825), 116; see also Fétis, *Biographie universelle*, s.v., and Dupont, *Histoire . . . de Cambrai* (cited above, p. 286 n10),

vol.ii (part 4), 92f.

16 Albert Seay (ed.), *Egidius Carlerius: Duo tractatuli de musica* (Colorado Springs, 1977).

17 Auguste Dufour and François Rabut, *Les musiciens, la musique et les instruments de musique en Savoie* (Chambéry, 1878), 41f.

18 David Fallows, *Robert Morton's Songs* (diss., Berkeley, 1978), 299–324.

19 Wright 'Dufay', 207 n182; Pirro *Histoire*, 101f.

20 Bouquet 'Cappella' 283; Lille, Archives du Nord, 4G 6789:1465–6, and 4G 6789:1468–9; Haberl *Bausteine* iii, 49f.

21 op. cit. (n2 above), 530ff.

22 Gaston Raynaud (ed.), *Rondeaux et autres poésies du XVe siècle* (Paris, 1889), XVIII.

23 opp. cit. (n2 and n3 above).

24 Wright *Burgundy*, 24 n16.

25 Haberl *Bausteine* i, 69 and passim; Schuler 'Martin V', 39; Schuler 'Eugen IV', 221.

26 Lille, Archives du Nord, 4G 1337, see Houdoy *Cambrai*, 264.

27 Wright 'Dufay', 207 n181.

28 Bouquet 'Cappella', 283.

29 Lille, Archives du Nord, 4G 4608, f.6; 4G 4609, f.6v; 4G 4610, f.7; etc.

30 Cambrai, Bibliothèque municipale, 1055, f.235v, 237v, 238, 250v. All information on Hesdin was kindly provided by Chanoine Edmond Dartus.

31 Haberl *Bausteine* i, passim; Wright 'Dufay', 188.

32 Lille, Archives du Nord, 4G 1413, see Houdoy *Cambrai*, 269.

33 Ed. Borren *Pièces*, no.8.

34 Ed. Borren *Pièces*, no.30.

35 Ed. Borren *Polyphonia*, no.32.

36 Ed. (in progress) Arthur Piaget and Eugénie Droz (Lausanne, 1968–); editio princeps Lyons, *c*.1485.

37 Toussaint *Relations*, 286–90.

38 Ed. Raynaud, op. cit. (n22), 52. See also: Gaston Paris, 'Un poème inédit de Martin le Franc', *Romania*, xvi (1887), 383–437; Arthur Piaget, *Martin le Franc, prévôt de Lausanne* (Lausanne, 1888); Augusta Lange, 'Martin le Franc, recteur de St-Gervais à Genève, et les fresques de cette église', *Publication du Centre européen d'études burgondo-médianes*, ix (1967), 98–102.

39 Ed. Raynaud, op. cit. (n22), 98–103.

40 Raynaud, op. cit., XXIIIf.

41 Gustave Dupont-Ferrier, *Les origines et le premier siècle de la cour du trésor* (Paris, 1936), 222 = Bibliothèque de l'Ecole des hautes études, CCLXVI.

42 Much of this information on Carlo and other members of the Malatesta family comes from: Cesare Clementini, *Raccolto istorico della fondatione di Rimino* (Rimini, 1617); L.A. Muratori, *Rerum italicarum*

*scriptores*, xv/2 (rev. ed. Bologna, 1922–4); Philip J. Jones, *The Malatesta of Rimini* (Cambridge, 1974).

43 See also: Sp. P. Lampros, *Palaiologeia kai Peloponnesiaka*, iv (Athens, 1930), 143–76; Van *Dufay* ii, X; Georg Hofmann, 'Kirchengeschichtliches zur Ehe des Herrschers Theodor II Palaiologos (1407–1443)', *Ostkirchliche Studien*, iv (1955), 129–37; John W. Barker, *Manuel II Palaeologus* (New Brunswick, 1969), 348; Gudrun Schmalzbauer, 'Eine bisher unedierte Monodie auf Kleope Palaiologina von Demetrios Pepagomenos', *Jahrbuch der österreichischen Byzantinistik*, xx (1971), 223–40.

44 Ed. Kade 'Squarcialupi', 5f.

45 Luigi Parigi, *Laurentiana: Lorenzo dei Medici cultore della musica* (Florence, 1954), 33 and passim.

46 Wright 'Performance', 298.

47 Lille, Archives du Nord, 4G 1467, see Houdoy *Cambrai*, 270f.

48 See items in n43 above; also Steven Runciman, *The Fall of Constantinople 1453* (Cambridge, 1965), 48.

49 Wright 'Burgundy', 109.

50 Saraceno 'Giunta', 235.

51 José *Amédée VIII* i, 65.

52 Bouquet 'Cappella', 239f and 284.

53 Bouquet 'Cappella', 284; Borren *Dufay*, 356; Borghezio 'Fondazione', 235.

54 Le Glay *Recherches* (1825), 146.

55 Wright 'Dufay', 212.

56 Mons, Archives de l'état, Chapitre de Soignies, no. prov. 28.

57 Houdoy *Cambrai*, 270.

58 Lille, Archives du Nord, 4G 1324, see Houdoy *Cambrai*, 271.

59 Albinia de la Mare, 'The Library of Francesco Sassetti', in Cecil H. Clough (ed.), *Cultural Aspects of the Italian Renaissance: Essays in Honour of Paul Oskar Kristeller* (Manchester, 1976), 160–201. One of the books in his collection (op. cit., p. 179) had earlier belonged to Martin le Franc. See also Jean-François Bergier, *Genève et l'économie européenne de la renaissance* (Paris, 1963), 304.

60 Giulio Negri, *Istoria degli scrittori fiorentini* (Ferrara, 1722), 69.

61 Reaney *Early Fifteenth-century Music* ii, I.

62 Wright 'Dufay', 187 and 189.

63 Lille, Archives du Nord, 4G 1705.

# Index

Page numbers in **bold type** denote a definition or an otherwise important reference.